Oppression and Scarcity

Oppression and Scarcity

The History and Institutional Structure of the Marxist-Leninist Government of East Germany and Some Perspectives on Life in a Socialist System

PETER W. SPERLICH

PRAEGER

Westport, Connecticut
London

Library of Congress Cataloging-in-Publication Data

Sperlich, Peter W., 1934–
Oppression and scarcity : the history and institutional structure of the Marxist-Leninist government of East Germany and some perspectives on life in a socialist system / Peter W. Sperlich.
p. cm.
Includes bibliographical references and index.
ISBN 0–275–97565–7 (alk. paper)
1. Germany (East)—Politics and government. 2. Germany (East)—Social conditions. 3. Germany (East)—Economic conditions. 4. Socialism—Germany (East)—History. 5. Communism—Germany (East)—History. 6. Communist state. I. Title.
DD286.4.S67 2006
943'.1087—dc22 2005025502

British Library Cataloguing in Publication Data is available.

Library of Congress Catalog Card Number: 2005025502
ISBN: 0–275–97565–7

First published in 2006

Praeger Publishers, 88 Post Road West, Westport, CT 06881
An imprint of Greenwood Publishing Group, Inc.
www.praeger.com

Printed in the United States of America

The paper used in this book complies with the Permanent Paper Standard issued by the National Information Standards Organization (Z39.48–1984).

10 9 8 7 6 5 4 3 2 1

This book is dedicated to the memory of my friends in Minnesota, Michigan, and California for whose help, kindness, and affection I will always be grateful:

Janesville, Minnesota

August Kuester, Al Hirscher, John Koehler,
and the Elmer and Mabela Schultz family

Mankato, Minnesota

Eddice Barber, Winston W. Benson,
C. L. Crawford, Mrs. Eby of Searing Hall,
Vilhelmine Kaufmanis, D. Paul Miller,
Robert R. Roberts, G. R. Schwartz,
and Les and Opal Manecke

Ann Arbor, Michigan

Ralph Bisco, Clyde and Lolagene Coombs,
Frank Grace, James H. Meisel,
Ernst F. Mueller, James K. Pollock,
and Donald G. Stokes

Berkeley, California

Victor Jones, Carl G. Rosberg, Paul Seabury,
and Aaron Wildavsky

Contents

Acronyms and Abbreviations

ANTIFA	Antifascist Bloc
BRD	Bundesrepublik Deutschland (Federal Republic of Germany)
CDU	Christlich Demokratische Union (Christian Democratic Union)
CIA	Central Intelligence Agency
CMEA	Council for Mutual Economic Assistance
COMECON	Council for Mutual Economic Assistance
CPK	Communist Party of Korea
CPSU	Communist Party of the Soviet Union
CSU	Christlich Soziale Union (Christian Social Union)
CSCE	Conference on Security and Cooperation in Europe
DBD	Demokratische Bauernpartei Deutschlands (Democratic Peasants Party of Germany)
DDR	Deutsche Demokratische Republik (see GDR)
DEFA	Deutsche Film Aktiengesellschaft; later: Deutsche Filmgesellschaft (German Film Company)
DFD	Women's Democratic League of Germany
DM	Deutsche mark
DP	Deutsche Partei (German Party)
DSF	German-Soviet Friendship Society
EAC	European Advisory Commission
EC	European Community

EEC	European Economic Community
EG	Europäische Gemeinschaft (European Community)
ESS	Economic System of Socialism
FDGB	Freier Deutscher Gewerkschaftsbund (Free German Trade Union Federation)
FDJ	*Freie Deutsche Jugend* (Free German Youth)
FDP	Freie Demokratische Partei (Free Democratic Party)
FRG	Federal Republic of Germany
GDR	German Democratic Republic (see DDR)
GNP	Gross National Product
GO	Grundorganization (Basic Unit of the SED)
GST	Society for Sports and Technology
HJ	Hitler Jugend (Hitler Youth)
IOC	International Olympic Committee
JW	Jugendweihe (Youth Consecration)
KB	Cultural Federation for Democratic Renewal
KGB	(NKGB) People's Commissariat of State Security
KPD	Kommunistische Partei Deutschlands (Communist Party of Germany)
KVP	Barracked People's Police
LDPD	Liberal Demokratische Partei Deutschlands (Liberal Democratic Party of Germany)
MfS	Ministerium für Staatssicherheit (Ministry for State Security)
NATO	North Atlantic Treaty Organization
NES	New Economic System (of Socialism)
NF	National Front
NKFD	National Committee for a Free Germany
NKVD	People's Commissariat of Internal Affairs
NDPD	National Democratische Partei Deutschlands (National Democratic Party of Germany)
NSDAP	Nationalsozialistische Deutsche Arbeiterpartei (National-Socialist German Workers Party)
NVA	National People's Army
PDS	Partei des Demokratischen Sozialimus (Party of Democratic Socialism)

PRC	People's Republic of China
SAG	Sovietische Aktien Gesellschaft
SBZ	Soviet Zone of Occupation
SED	Sozialistische Einheitspartei Deutschlands (Socialist Unity Party of Germany)
SMAD	Soviet Military Administration in Germany
SPD	Sozialdemokratische Partei Deutschlands (Social Democratic Party of Germany)
SPK	State Planning Commission
STASI	Staatssicherheitsdienst (State Security Service)
SZ	Soviet Zone
UK	United Kingdom (Great Britain)
USSR	Union of Soviet Socialist Republics
VAT	Value-Added Tax
VDGB	Vereinigung für gegenseitige Bauernhilfe (Peasants Mutual Aid Association)
VEB	Volkseigener Betrieb (People-Owned Enterprise)
VP	Volkspolizei (People's Police)
ZK	Zentral Komitee (Central Committee of the SED)

Chapter 1

Introduction

This book is the second volume in a series of three treatments of several aspects of the former German Democratic Republic (GDR), aka. East Germany. The GDR was the first socialist (Marxist-Leninist) state on German soil. It came to an inglorious end in November 1989. The citizens who had endured the quasi-totalitarian dictatorship of the Socialist Unity Party (SED), the Communist Party in the GDR, for forty years, rose up in revolt. It was a remarkably peaceful revolution. There was practically no bloodshed, and what blood was shed was all spilled by the security forces of the state. However, the GDR did not see a "Chinese solution" (Tiananmen Square). Things had gone so badly in the last years of the GDR, particularly economically, and the will of the people was so obvious and so strong, that the regime could not bring itself to order an all-out assault on the peaceful demonstrators, marching in the country's major cities. When Gorbachev decided that the Soviet troops stationed in the GDR would stay in their barracks and would not save the regime from its own people (as they had in 1953), it was all over. The GDR, thus, no longer exists, but there are important lessons to be learned from its existence—most of them negative but a few quite positive.

The **first** volume examined the ideological foundation of the GDR and its SED regime. The title of the book states the basic conclusion: *Rotten Foundations: The Conceptual Basis of the Marxist-Leninist Regimes of East Germany and Other Countries of the Soviet Bloc.* As the title also indicates, the book is not solely focused on the GDR; its discussions are applicable to the other socialist regimes. This was feasible because, however different the countries might be in other respects, they share the same ideological underpinnings.[1] If these are "rotten," they are so everywhere. The book starts with an examination of the ideas of the precursors of Marx (especially Hegel), reviews the conceptions of Marx and Engels, and surveys the ideas of those who came after (especially Lenin and Stalin). Next, the book moves to an investigation of some of the key issues of socialist theory. Is Marxism-Leninism truly a science (or even the only science)? Is Marxism-Leninism a utopian construct, even with a strong religious flavoring (a matter, of course, strongly denied by socialist theorists)? Is there really a unity of theory and practice in the socialist realms, as so proudly claimed by these regimes? Finally, the book examines the issue of totalitarianism regarding socialist states in general and the GDR specifically.

The conclusions are devastating to the pretenses of Marxism-Leninism. It is not a science; to the contrary, it is a thoroughly antiscientific construct. Where it is dominant, true science withers, and pseudoscientific blather holds sway. Marxism-Leninism also has a strong utopian flavor and is much closer to a conventional religion (in beliefs as well as in action) than to a secular scientific construct. The much glorified unity of theory and practice turns out to be just another one of Marxism-Leninism's many unity conceits. Only with the mumbo jumbo of the dialectic is it possible to issue such declarations as the unity of means and ends, of morality and utility, and of the interests of all classes in society. While not a popular conclusion (not even in the West and particularly not among the academic Left), the characterization of the GDR as a totalitarian system is unavoidable. Over the years, the system became less brutal, but it never relinquished its claims to the complete control of practically all of the citizen's life. The overall conclusion of this book was that the SED regime of the GDR imposed on an unwilling population a flawed and unpalatable doctrine. It could not possibly hope to gain the support and loyalty of the people (with the exception of those who were the beneficiaries of the system). When the Soviet troops would not come out to save it, it simply crumbled and collapsed.

While the first book concentrated on the theoretical aspects of Marxism-Leninism and the GDR,[2] the present volume, the **second** in the series, deals with the practical sides of life in the GDR. Chapter 2 begins the inquiry by examining the partition of Germany after World War II, the Allied policies toward defeated Germany, and the founding of the two separate German states: the Federal Republic of Germany, FRG (West) and the German Democratic Republic, GDR (East). Chapter 3 deals with the early politics and governmental institutions of the GDR, in particular the imposition of communism, the Stalinist transformations of Party and state, and the regime's lack of historical legitimacy. Chapter 4 continues the discussion of GDR politics. It gives attention to the nature of the rule of the communist party, the Socialist Unity Party of Germany, SED. It reviews the nature of citizen participation in the politics of the GDR, which was extensive but without real influence. It also considers the nature of the GDR state and why this state did not wither away. Finally, the chapter regards the role of the security apparatus, particularly the "secret police" (Stasi), which, however, will receive a more extensive treatment in the third volume.

Chapter 5 deals with the economic system of the GDR. It examines the early economic policies and the several efforts at reform. It reviews the nature of the planned economy, particularly its effects on productivity, modernization, and work ethic. The picture is one of unrelieved breakdown and failure. It was aid from the West, particularly the massive West German subsidies, that kept the GDR's economy afloat, not the system's own efforts.

Chapter 6 takes up some issues relating to civic culture. It examines the state of public opinion (and of opinion research) in the GDR. The emerging picture is one of control and manipulation, and of censorious and dishonest communications. The chapter next examines the case of letters to the editor and what insight can be derived from these letters. Such letters were an extensively used means of communication, but their value is limited by the fact that many letters were ordered to be written by the authorities, and yet other letters were plainly bogus. Finally, the chapter deals with the socialist personality cults, which in the GDR attached importantly to the persons of Walter Ulbricht and Erich Honecker. It raises the questions of how genuine the adoration was and why it was such an important feature of socialist regimes, whose basic theory was tied to the "iron laws of history" and not to a "great man" concept.

Chapter 7 continues the examination of GDR culture and raises the question: What was it like to live in the GDR? The chapter begins with a series of basic questions that need attention in the East German context. First, there is the problem of what was understood to be the "truth" in the GDR and how one could tell it. Second, there is the old issue of freedom and security, particularly the interaction (trade-off) between these two values. In the second and third part of the chapter, vignettes are presented that offer some views of the daily life of GDR citizens—they range from education, to youth organizations, to quasi-religious rituals, to sports, and to consumer experiences. The chapter concludes with some observations on the mentality and psychology of GDR citizens, noting that, for the most part, they certainly were not "the new socialist personalities" that the regime had hoped to create.

Chapter 8 deals with the persistent exodus from East Germany. It describes the situation before and after the building of the Berlin Wall, and the ways of fleeing the GDR before and after the Wall. Then the chapter considers the revolution of 1989, the "bloodless revolution," when peaceful demonstrators and vastly growing numbers of refugees brought down an oppressive and brutal regime—which no one had thought possible beforehand. Next, the chapter provides a brief account of the events that led to the dissolution of the SED regime and, ultimately, to the reunification of Germany. The chapter ends with a short comment on the aftermath of reunification, which did not turn out quite as expected.

Many of these chapters and topics are important and weighty enough to deserve books of their own. In the present space, most could be given no more than a summary treatment. However, for the reader who wishes for more information and a more thorough treatment of some of the themes, I have included fairly extensive bibliographical references. At times, these hamper the free flow of the text, but it seemed a price that could be justified in the interest of furnishing a more satisfactory information resource. I should also note that some general conclusions are not supported directly by specific citations. These are inferences that are the result of an immersion in the political culture of the GDR over many years and of discussions with GDR citizens from all walks of life. They cannot be attributed to a single, specific source.

To anticipate, the **third** volume of this series will examine the laws, the legal system, and the law enforcement practices of the GDR: *Popular Justice in a Marxist-Leninist Society: The East German Social Courts and Other Aspects of GDR Law*. Some of the third volume will once again[3] have to deal with the most unpleasant side of GDR policy and procedure. The Stasi (*Staatssicherheitsdienst* = state security service) occupied a similar place as that of the Gestapo and the GPU in other totalitarian regimes. The third volume will differ importantly from the first two in that we will finally get to a *positive* aspect of the GDR: its system of *social courts*. These courts were hybrid institutions of state and society in the system of "advanced socialism." They enacted a significant transfer of functions from the state to society. On the one hand, these courts were entirely *lay* organs, conducting their adjudicative functions without state judges or even official prosecutors and defense attorneys. On the other hand, these courts were considered to be part of the state court system, and their decisions could be reviewed by the regular courts.

The social courts performed several consequential services. Most importantly, they adjudicated very large numbers of civil and criminal cases, which, otherwise, would have required the attention of the regular courts. In addition, the social courts had these functions: crime prevention, legal advice, arbitration and mediation, and the rehabilitation of offenders. Most indications are that they functioned quite well. At a time when the U.S. courts are greatly overburdened—thus giving rise to much dissatisfaction—the detailed review of an alternative system seems beneficial. This will be the core of the third volume.

The third volume will also include a discussion of GDR statistics, or rather the lack of it. The GDR was notorious for not making statistical data available and often falsifying them when made available. Further, the volume will take note of the GDR officials' attitude toward GDR research (mostly negative) and cooperation with Western scholars (largely nonexistent). Here it will suffice to say that GDR research was one of the most frustrating forms of inquiry. The chief characteristics of the GDR regime were paranoia, suspiciousness, and bureaucratic inflexibility. Whereas in the West, aid commonly is provided to scholars unless there are good and specific reasons not to do so, in the East, aid was routinely denied unless there was a good and specific reason to provide it. However, there existed only one kind of good reason in the GDR to provide any sort of assistance: the end product would be helpful to the regime in general and/or to the decision maker in particular.

While my empirical work on the GDR, especially on the "social courts," fully intended to be fair, GDR officials assumed that it was not very likely to glorify East German socialism and its leaders: ergo, assistance denied.[4] Other scholars had similar experiences. Since "socialist scholarship" (to employ what is rather an oxymoron) had the absolute duty and obligation to support and glorify socialism,[5] socialists always had great difficulty comprehending the possibility that a "bourgeoise scholar" could be anything other than a propagandist for capitalism and a devoted "class enemy." Socialist dogma, then, included its own punishment.

• • •

I want to thank my colleagues Steven L. Coombs and A. James Gregor for their many helpful comments on the first draft of this book. I am indebted to my students Jordan Bornstein, who labored beyond the call of duty to find many of the writings I needed in the preparation of this volume, and Karim Moussally, who saw to it that my computer would cooperate. I am grateful to my brother, Werner Sperlich, who secured for me many important books out of various East German libraries, as these were abandoned in the aftermath of the collapse of the GDR. Finally, I want to thank my sister, Christa Schumann, for all her efforts to keep my files and papers organized and orderly.

NOTES

1. This remains true for this book. Therefore, there are occasional references to other socialist countries.

2. I should note that the first book is foundational for the second; accordingly, there will be a fair number of cross-references. Important topics, already treated at length in the first book, thus will not need to repeated.

3. A brief discussion of the Stasi can be found in the present volume (Chapter 4).

4. Deeply suspicious of anyone and anything from the West, GDR officials did not permit themselves to be swayed even by the fair and rather appreciative tone of two relevant convention papers (Sperlich, 1982, 1985), of which they were aware. There was no element of "red-baiting" in my reports. But, for all I know, the officials may have thought that these papers were mere bait and that wild denunciations would flow from my pen as soon as they had provided me with the access that I sought.

5. The matter of socialist partisan scholarship has been discussed in my *Rotten Foundations*, Chapters 3 and 5.

Chapter 2

The Partitioning of Germany and Allied Policies

THE DIVISION AND DISMEMBERMENT OF GERMANY

Allied Plans for Postwar Germany

The London (September and November 1944), Yalta (February 1945), and Potsdam (July–August 1945) Agreements established the regional structure for the Allied occupation and administration of defeated Germany. Within the boundaries of 1937, the German territories were divided into *eleven* parts[1]:

four occupation zones (Central and Western Germany),

four occupation sectors (Berlin),

two administrative regions (Eastern provinces), and

one special status region (Saar).

The *occupation zones* and the *occupation sectors* were assigned to the United States, Great Britain, the Soviet Union, and France. France, it should be noted, was not initially included among the occupying powers to be. The agreement that there should be a French Zone and French Sector (Berlin), to be carved out of the occupation territories of the United States and Great Britain (but not of the Soviet Union), was reached at the Yalta Conference in February 1945.

The *administrative regions* were placed under the control of the Soviet Union and Poland, the latter country obtaining by far the greater share of this German territory. The *special status region* of the Saar did not come into being until 1946. France separated the Saar from the rest of the French Zone of Occupation to make it an integral part of France (Mellor, 1978, 134). The annexation effort—the most recent manifestation of traditional French imperialism (its own "*Drang nach dem Osten*") in bloom at least since Francis I (1515–1547)—did not succeed because of the resistance of the Saar's wholly German population. On the basis of a 1955 popular referendum, the Saar finally was returned to Germany and became a state (*Land*) of the Federal Republic of Germany on January 1, 1957 (Grosser, 1960, 32). It should also be noted that France demanded (but did not get) all German territories to the left of the Rhine and some territories even to the right of that river. Finally, France also called (again without success) for the internationalization of the Ruhr industrial region.

In addition to the noted elevenfold partition of Germany, Belgium, Luxembourg, and the Netherlands advanced claims for the annexation of German territories. These claims were supported only by France and, except for some minor "border corrections," did not succeed (Thilenius, 1957, 99–102). Czechoslovakia, however, again was able (as in 1919 and contrary to the Munich Agreement of 1938) to extend its control over the Sudetenland—a thoroughly German area of settlement—by expelling all German ethnics (about 3 million), many of whom, together with the Slovac, Polish, and Hungarian minorities of post–World War I Czechoslovakia, had resisted Czech political domination and cultural hegemony. A theory of "collective guilt" was invented to justify the expulsion (Duffy, 1991, 271; Skilling, 1979, 11).

There had been numerous suggestions (the first apparently made by Stalin in December 1941) and discussions (e.g., during Eden's March 1943 visit to Washington) regarding a postwar dismemberment of Germany. At the August 1943 Eden-Hull conference in Quebec the United States and Great Britain opposed compulsory fragmentation but favored a voluntary partition of Germany—counting apparently on indigenous separatist tendencies. However, by October 1943, the American position had changed, supporting the involuntary division of Germany into three or more entities (Sutterlin & Klein, 1989, 3, 46). At Teheran (November–December 1943), the United States even proposed a division of Germany into five separate nations and two trust territories (Ruhr and Saar). Although Great Britain and the Soviet Union preferred somewhat different segmentation plans, there was agreement in principle: Germany would be partitioned. A division of Germany into three zones of occupation was first proposed by the British at the Quebec Conference in August 1943. The Moscow Conference (November 1943) assigned the task of working out the specifics to the European Advisory Commission (EAC) in London. The Commission's work was completed by September 1944, and its proposals influenced the decisions made at the Yalta Conference (February 1945) (Hubatsch, 1967, 18–19). The EAC proposals, however, were not followed regarding the Eastern Provinces of Germany. The EAC had assigned them to the Soviet Zone of Occupation, clearly not intending to separate them from the rest of Germany (Hancock, 1989, 222–

23; Spencer, 1984, 6–9). In fact, of course, they were simply annexed by the USSR and Poland. In 1989, the FRG was forced to relinquish all claims to the Eastern territories to Poland and the USSR as the price of these countries' consent to the reunification of Germany.

Great Britain was the least enthusiastic among the victors about partitioning and expressed certain reservations at the March 1944 meeting of the EAC.[2] The Soviet Union in the meantime appeared to have had second thoughts about the Teheran Accords and followed the British lead. Indeed, Stalin declared in his radio address the day after Germany's capitulation that it was not Soviet policy to dismember or destroy the German nation. The reasons for this change appear to have been the expectation of more sizable reparations from a united Germany and the planned use of the Soviet Zone and the Soviet Sector as beachheads for the communist domination of all of Germany. The United States continued to support partition but did not prevail. France was not a member of the EAC and could not assist U.S. efforts. Contrary, then, to earlier plans, the capitulation documents and memoranda, as well as the Potsdam Agreements, did not incorporate provisions for the permanent partitioning of Germany or the loss of any of its 1937 provinces, nor did they create two German nations or draw the postwar boundaries of Germany.

Joint Military Government and Its Failure

As the Allied armies began to occupy German territories, military governmental units were established on an ad hoc basis. The Potsdam Conference (July–August 1945) formalized the structure of military government, establishing separate (for the different zones and sectors) as well as joint military authorities. While occupied separately, the four *zones* of Germany were to be governed jointly by commanders in chief of the occupation forces of the United States of America, USSR, UK, and France within the framework of the *Allied Control Council.* The commanders in chief also were to function as the heads of government in their respective zones. The four *sectors* of Berlin were to be governed jointly by the four Allied military commanders of the city within the framework of the *Allied Kommandantura.* Joint governance of zones and sectors was to continue until the establishment of an all-German government. The zones and sectors were not designed to be forerunners or prototypes of multiple Germanys. They were divided from each other only by freely crossable "demarcation lines," not by borders. In 1946, however, the Soviets began to transform the demarcation lines into what ultimately would become one of the most heavily fortified and deadly borders in the world. For a time, the French also transformed the demarcation line of their zone into a border. As late as 1946, even U.S. personnel had difficulty in gaining access to the French Zone (Hartmann & Kuensting, 1990, 78).

Joint governance was short-lived. It became obvious that each of the Allies had a different agenda for postwar Germany (Bacque, 2002). France and the Soviet Union were the main impediments to central administration and uniform policies. The greatest initial obstacle was France, vetoing the establishment of any central (all-German) administrative departments (Hancock, 1989, 24; Hiscocks, 1957, 39). Having designs for the annexation of the Rhineland (an old French dream) as well as the Saar, France even blocked the issuance of common postage stamps (Goldman, 1974, 41–42). Later, the Soviet Union played the key role in preventing central governance. Contrary to the provisions of various Allied agreements, the Soviet Union restricted interzonal travel, unilaterally imposed reparation obligations, and embarked on policies of industrial and agricultural expropriations.

The Allied Control Council soon proved to be an unworkable instrument. Burdened not only by the increasing mutual distrust of its members but also by the requirement to decide unanimously, the Council quickly stalemated and soon disintegrated. It made its last actual decision in March 1946. It stopped functioning altogether when the Soviets walked out on March 20, 1948. The rapid development of discord among the Allies was not particularly surprising. The alliance, after all, was based not on shared principles but on a common danger that had disappeared. Furthermore, the Soviet Union and the Western powers had been suspicious of each other even before the war and while the war was still in progress.

Both sides had their reasons: the Soviets remembered the Western intervention in opposition to the Bolshevik takeover in 1918–1920 (Kennan, 1960, 19–30), the delay in establishing the Second Front, and the refusal of the United States of America to provide funds for the postwar reconstruction of the USSR, for which a $6 billion loan had been requested. The West remembered the Hitler-Stalin Pact of 1939, the Soviet attack on Finland in 1939, the participation of the Soviet Union in the defeat and partition of Poland in 1939 (Read & Fisher, 1988), the Soviet murder of the Polish officers at Katyn[3] (Kadell, 1991; Mackiewicz, 1951; United States Congress, 1952), and the failure to assist the Warsaw uprising in 1944 (Davies, 1984, 76–78; Halecki, 1978, 322–323).

Matters were made worse when, only a few months after the end of the war, Soviet leaders began to articulate the doctrine that the roots of fascism had not been extirpated and that capitalist encirclement had not disappeared with the defeat of Germany (McLellan, 1966, 5). As increasingly severe disagreements arose between the Western Powers and the USSR, the zones and sectors of occupied Germany inevitably were drawn into opposing camps on each side of the Iron Curtain. The chief results were the forty-year division of Germany into two separate states and the de facto annexation of Germany's Eastern provinces by the Soviet Union and Poland.

The Western Allies, in effect, permitted the Soviet Union to seize half of prewar Germany—and much of the rest of Europe. This, of course, was not a matter of deliberate policy, at least not on the part of the United States. There is considerable support for the point of view that Stalin was the only one among the Allied leaders who had taken the trouble to develop long-term goals and a long-term strategy. The thesis that the advance of the USSR into Eastern and Central Europe was a mere reaction to the German attack is of dubious validity. There exists substantial evidence that Soviet expansion plans existed before 1941 and that the USSR–Germany (August 23, 1939) and the USSR–Japan (April 13, 1941) Non-Aggression Pacts were part of a long-range strategy for Soviet expansion. These pacts fitted well with Lenin's conception (1920) to weaken the noncommunist camp by using Germany and Japan as tools against the "Western Imperialist" (Bechtoldt, 1988, 137; Hillgruber, 1983, 59; Topitsch, 1985, 12, 26–27, 145–155).

The lack of a Western (especially, American) postwar preparedness seems mostly to have been due to the limitations of a purely military (rather than political) approach to the war (Ziemke, 1968, 6), a lack of long-range planning and proper preparation for the impending postwar negotiations, an unwillingness to assume major postwar responsibilities, an overeagerness to accommodate Stalin—whom American leaders insisted on viewing as a "good and reasonable partner" (Feis, 1957, 275; Gatzke, 1980, 149, 163)—unfounded optimism about postwar Soviet goals and conduct, and the customary American lack of knowledge of European politics, history, and geography, which already had caused such havoc at Versailles (Butz, 1954, 11–17, 26–29; Freund, 1961, 7; Pounds, 1962, 2; Richert, 1966, 9).

The American weakness for "politics of sentiment" also played a part, managing to transform a murderous dictator into the lovable "Uncle Joe" (Wagner, 1959, 65, 81). "Roosevelt . . . spent World War II in pursuit of Josef Stalin, convinced that he, FDR, could smooth out the wrinkles in Uncle Joe, spruce him up, and make a New York Democrat out of him" (Nisbet, 1988, 30). Roosevelt, of course, "badly miscalculated" regarding Stalin and the Soviet Union (Herzstein, 1989, 408).

ALLIED POLICIES IN THE ZONES OF OCCUPATION

Interaction with Germans

The Allied governance of Germany proceeded without central administrative agencies and uniform policies. There were but few efforts at voluntary coordination, even within the Western Bloc. Each of the four Occupying Powers confronted similar problems, and the initial programs and procedures were alike in many respects. Official Soviet policies, however, were more conciliatory toward the Germans than those of the United States of America and the other Western nations. While the Americans viewed national-socialism as a unique evil arising out of German culture and psyche, the Soviets adopted an institutional explanation. "In the Communist view . . . fascism was but another expression, albeit a virulent one, of the moribund economic system of monopoly capitalism" (Sandford, 1983, ix). While the Americans bombarded the Germans with unrelenting messages about their unique and *collective* guilt,[4] the Soviets made a clear distinction between national-socialists and other Germans, emphasizing individual responsibility for specific crimes.[5] Thus, Soviet officials and soldiers were able to interact quite freely with ordinary Germans. By contrast, the U.S. Directive JCS 1067 took a very hard line and prohibited all "fraternization." Americans were not permitted to shake hands with *any* German.[6] For example, U.S. colonel Keegan, in search of acceptable German leadership, found that Fritz Schaeffer had a thoroughly democratic and antifascist background and was the right man to be appointed the first minister-president (prime minister) of postwar Bavaria. At the appointment proceedings, however, Keegan would not shake Schaeffer's hand (Engelmann, 1982, 40). The French took the most extreme view: French soldiers were told that "any German of any age and either sex is an enemy [and that] the child, the woman, the old man who implore your pity are . . . Nazi agents . . . [which is] why every contact with the German is forbidden to you" (Malzahn, 1991, 72). Unfortunately for the Soviets, the goodwill they gained with their differentiated treatment of the Germans, they lost again by installing a communist dictatorship in their zone of occupation.

Political Parties

The zonal governments drew on surviving and returning antifascists to fill vacant positions in the public and private sectors, and issued licenses to "democratic forces" to publish newspapers and to organize political parties. The Communist Party (KPD), Social Democratic Party (SPD), Christian Democratic Union (CDU),[7] and the Liberal Party (LDPD, FDP)[8] were soon licensed in all zones and sectors. The Soviets, however, were the first to permit the organization of political parties (June–July 1945), which brought them considerable public relations advantages. The United States of America and Great Britain began to license political parties in September, and France in December 1945 (Behr, 1985a, 22). KPD and SPD were recognized as active anti-Nazi forces, CDU/CSU and LDPD/FDP as representing the democratic middle-class constituencies of the Weimar Republic.

In the Western Zones, a wide variety of other parties received permission to organize at later dates. In the Soviet Zone of Occupation (SZ), organizing additional political parties was prohibited. When other parties tried to register in Berlin in 1945, the KPD deputy lord major, Karl Maron, declared that no new parties would be permitted because this would interfere with "the urgent task of reconstruction" (Krisch, 1974, 57). The policy persisted. Until the end of the regime, there came into being no additional *and* freely-organized political parties. The two additional GDR parties, founded in 1948, were communist-organized and communist-controlled. They were the

National Democratic Party of Germany (NDPD) and the Democratic Peasants Party of Germany (DBD). The former was to recruit German nationalists to the communist cause; the latter to recruit the rural population (Reichelt, 1997).

Territorial Organization

Within each zone, the Occupation Powers redesigned the subordinate administrative territories. Since the zonal demarcation lines generally did not correspond to previous provincial or state borders, new geographical units had to be created. Only Bavaria and the city-states of Hamburg and Bremen retained their prewar boundaries. Prussia was abolished altogether, under the rather witless notion that Prussia was the origin of all that was bad in Germany. (For more balanced views on Prussia, see Fernau, 1997; Schoeps, 1951, 1967.) The United States and France encouraged the development of a federal system with strong states; Great Britain and the USSR proposed a more centralized governmental structure. While Britain ultimately joined the United States of America and France in setting up the federally-structured FRG, the USSR prescribed a unitary governmental structure with weak states for its zone. This policy was taken to its final conclusion in 1952, when the GDR abolished the traditional states altogether, replacing them with a fully centralized system of fifteen subordinate regions (including East Berlin), with merely administrative functions. German reunification, however, brought a restoration of the states within the federal structure of the FRG.

Denazification and the Judiciary

Substantial differences emerged in the denazification programs adopted by the Occupying Powers (Henke, 1996, 21ff; Henke & Woller, 1991, 7ff). The French and British concentrated on the higher echelons of the national-socialist hierarchy, while the Americans sought to review the case of every member of the National Socialist Party (NSDAP) and affiliated organizations, and in some respects were stricter than any of the other three powers (Macrakis & Hoffmann, 1999, 195). The Soviets had their own views and purposes:[9]

> For the Communists, denazification was part of the class struggle. Their purpose was not, like that of the Western powers, to eliminate a specific obnoxious political phenomenon, but rather to transform the entire reactionary power structure, replacing bourgeois-aristocratic hegemony with their own. (Sandford, 1983, 31–32)

In the end, the denazification process probably was not significantly less thorough in the West than in the SZ. There are some estimates that, per capita, there were more denazification trials in the GDR than in the FRG[10] (Steele,

1977, 43). Exact statistics about SZ denazification are lacking, however. For a fairly detailed analysis of denazification in two states of the Soviet Zone, see Welsh, 1989, 1991. For a similar analysis in one state (Brandenburg), see Vogt, 2000.

The clearest difference regarding denazification emerged in respect to the *judiciary*. Many of the judges active during the Nazi period were retained in office (or reinstated after a short time) in the Western Zones, but nearly all were dismissed in the Soviet Zone (Amos, 1996). (Similar policies were followed in respect to the members of the police and the teaching profession.) The cause does not appear to have been a greater commitment to antifascism on the part of the Soviets. There were, for example, major efforts to persuade former national-socialists to support the new regime, including several amnesties and the founding of (practically) their own political party, the NDPD. Rather, the cause was a different legal philosophy, namely, the Soviet view of the judiciary as an instrument of the Party for the construction of socialism versus the Western tradition of an independent judiciary.

The Western criticism of the Third Reich judiciary was that many of its members had let themselves be used for *political* ends. The Soviet criticism was that they had let themselves be used for the *wrong* political ends. The Western Allies thought that most judges could be brought back to judicial neutrality. The Soviets were less sure that they could be converted to instruments of Communist Party policies.[11]

To fill the resulting void, Soviet officials relied on two sources: on Left-oriented jurists who had retired before 1933 and, most importantly, on the development of an entirely new contingent of judicial personnel, the "*peoples' judges*." In later years, *lay adjudicators*, including the social court judges, came to fill a large number of the GDR's judicial positions.[12] In any case, "the new rulers were perfectly willing to accept economic losses, governmental mismanagement and a lowering of educational standards through expelling the people they distrusted before they were able to replace them with experts of their own choice" (Wassmund, 1981, 339). Accelerated training of members of the working class was provided by the specially founded Worker-and-Farmer-Academies (*Arbeiter-und-Bauern-Fakultäten*) (Schneider, 1998).

ALLIED POLICIES IN BERLIN

The Failure of Allied Joint Governance and the Blockade

Berlin had become an enclave about 100 miles inside the GDR. As the capital city of Germany, it was singled out for special treatment by the Allies' European Advisory Committee. It was not included in any of the zones of occupation. Though geographically located inside the Soviet Zone, it was treated as a separate territory.[13] It was partitioned into four sectors but was to be governed jointly by the Allied city military commanders within the framework of the *Allied Kommandantura* (created on July 7, 1945). As with the Allied Control Council, the decisions of the *Allied Kommandantura* were to be made unanimously. In spite of the joint-occupation and joint-governance agreements, the Soviets hindered the Western military presence and the exercise of political power in all of Berlin from the very beginning. The Western Allies, on the other hand, were prompt in withdrawing their troops from those regions of the Soviet Zone that they had captured initially—thereby giving away, as Churchill had warned, "the only card the West had held for inducing the Soviets to honor their agreements" (Gelb, 1986, 25).

The Kommandantura became inoperative on June 16, 1948, when the Soviet representatives walked out. Four-Power cooperation came to an end altogether on July 1, 1948, when the Soviets declared that they would no longer participate in the Kommandantura. Eight days later the USSR began the blockade of West Berlin,[14] which was to last for almost a year, until May 12, 1949 (Clay, 1950, 358–392; Davison, 1958). The Soviet blockade effectively ended what few sympathies existed in the Western Zones for the USSR and communism, and the determined Allied response of supplying Berlin by air was a major factor in bringing West Germany firmly into the Western camp (Davison, 1958, xi; Kiep, 1974, 111). Allied resolve also made General Clay into a German folk hero. The end of the blockade did not, however, restore the status quo ante of Four Power responsibility for all of Berlin.

The End of Joint Governance and the Status of the Two Berlins

Because of persistent Soviet interference in the work of the duly elected noncommunist[15] city officials and because of SED-organized council-chamber riots, the (all-Berlin) city administration (*Magistrat*) moved from the City Hall, located in East Berlin, to the Town Hall of the District of Schoeneberg in West Berlin at the end of 1948. The *Magistrat* had been elected by he voters of all four sectors. Its duty was to administer the *entire* city—the successful discharge of which was not conditional on the specific location of the *Magistrat*'s offices. The Soviets, however, used the change in locale as a pretext for setting up a separate governing body for East Berlin (Wightman, 1971, 181). Thus, German as well as Allied joint governance of Berlin was lost by the end of 1948.

In the negotiations that led to the establishment of the FRG (see later), the Western Allies did not permit full incorporation of West Berlin into the FRG. While the ties between the FRG and West Berlin became closer over the years, the city remained subject to the special provisions of the Occupation Statute of 1949 and the Allied Declaration of 1955 (Mahnke, 1972, 140–148, 364–387). The Western Allies retained various rights and obligations as well as a limited criminal and civil adjudicatory competence. This competence was broad enough to permit convening American courts with American judges and American-style juries to try cases in West Berlin—in effect, applying American law to offenses committed in Berlin and (even) Eastern Europe.[16]

The GDR was willing at first to acknowledge that East Berlin was not a part of the SZ or (later) of the GDR.[17] The Electoral Law of August 9, 1950, for example, provided that there would be representatives from East Berlin to the People's Chamber (GDR legislature), but only as nonvoting observers—which also was (and remained) the arrangement for the West Berlin representatives to the West German parliament. The annual statistical reports (*Statistische Jahrbücher*) of the GDR also evidenced the changing interpretations. Until 1971, they displayed separately the data for the GDR and East Berlin members of the People's Chamber. The differentiation was abandoned with the volume for 1972. The GDR Constitution of 1949 (Art. 2.2) had identified Berlin as the capital of the "Republic" (presumably of a unified German Republic), while the GDR Constitution of 1968 (Art. 1), by contrast, designated Berlin as the capital of the GDR—in both cases the reference was to all of Berlin.[18] The 1968 Constitution of the GDR reflected shifts in the Soviet position. The USSR had begun to support GDR Berlin claims in 1958. All branches of GDR government, except for the Ministry of Defense, resided in East Berlin. The equivalent FRG bodies were located in Bonn and a number of other West German cities, with only some branch offices and agencies in West Berlin.

Not encumbered by a commitment to quid pro quo or fair play, however, East Germany continued to the very end to protest the presence of West German governmental branch offices in West Berlin. The GDR, of course, was aware of the flaws in its position. East German status insecurities were reflected in the disapproval of the term "East Berlin" and in the practically mandatory use of the phrase "Berlin, Capital of the GDR," rather than simply "Berlin" in all GDR statements and publications. In any case, by 1967 Walter Ulbricht had obtained the easy-to-get USSR backing for the claim that West Berlin was a borough of Berlin and that Berlin was the capital of the GDR (Mahnke, 1979, 111–127). The USSR supported this position to the end. Mikhail Gorbachev, for example, on his visit to Berlin to attend the XIth Party Congress of the SED (1986), declared that the Four-Power status applied only to West Berlin (whereas East Berlin was fully integrated in the GDR and was its capital) and that the border between the Soviet sector and the other sectors was an international frontier (*German Tribune*, June 15, 1986, p. 5; Marbach, 1986).

There were various attempts to force the Western Allies out of (West) Berlin. Most notable, in addition to the blockade of 1948, was the Berlin Crisis of 1958, caused by Khrushchev's ultimatum that the Western Powers were to withdraw from the city within six months, leaving West Berlin with the status of a "free city." These developments reached their culmination with the building of the Berlin Wall in 1961—a fortification unique in history:

"built to keep people in, rather than to keep invaders out" (Possony, 1963, 21). The communist regime had the remarkable nerve to call it the "antifascist protective wall" (*antifaschistischer Schutzwall*). The building of the Wall entailed cutting the direct transport and telecommunication links between the two halves of the city, and limiting Western Allies' access to East Berlin. This was followed shortly by an attempt to deny to the Western Allies *all* access to East Berlin (October 1961).

The Four-Power Agreement of 1971 reaffirmed joint responsibility of the Western Allies and the USSR for all of Berlin. It also safeguarded the road, rail, and water traffic between West Germany and West Berlin. The prior lack of a formal agreement safeguarding Western access had made it easier for the Soviets to undertake the Berlin blockade. It is instructive to note that the failure to secure unquestioned access to Berlin across the GDR resulted from the U.S. belief that there was no need to be concerned about access to Berlin and that to raise the issue "would arouse Soviet suspicion and make mutual understanding more difficult to attain" (Clay, 1950, 15).

FROM FOUR ZONES TO TWO STATES

The Founding of the FRG

Limited Consolidation

The United States and Great Britain combined the economies of their zones by way of the Bizonal Fusion Agreement (December 1946) and, with German participation, set up bizonal administrative agencies in Frankfurt/Main. The next step was the creation of German instruments of government, the first of which (June 1947) was the *Bizonal Economic Council* (*Wirtschaftsrat*). Its members were selected by the (German) state legislatures. The Bizonal Economic Council had legislative authority, subject to Anglo-American approval. Next (February 1948) came the *Bizonal Council of States* (*Länderrat*). Its members were representatives of the executive branches of the (German) state governments, usually cabinet members. Its functions also were legislative. In fact, the Economic Council developed into the lower house and the Council of States into the upper house of a bicameral, bizonal German legislature.

The *Bizonal Executive Council* (*Verwaltungsrat*), established in May 1947 but substantially modified early in the following year, was the first German governmental structure with executive authority. It consisted of the directors of the five existing German interzonal departments, plus a chairman. The six members were responsible to the two legislative houses (see earlier) and could be removed from office (by these houses) via a vote of nonconfidence. The task of the Executive Council was the implementation of legislation. The actual enforcement of laws, however, remained the responsibility of the separate states. The authority of the Executive Council as well as of the legislative bodies was restricted to economic matters.

To round out the structure of bizonal government, the United States and Great Britain established the *German High Court* (*Deutsches Obergericht*) in February 1948. The justices were appointed by the military governors. The court had original and appellate jurisdiction. The three branches of government, thus formed, received increasing responsibilities and powers in the period from 1946 to 1947. Their activities established important patterns and precedents, and significantly affected the development of the governmental branches and agencies of the FRG.

In the meantime (September 6, 1946), U.S. secretary of state Byrnes had asserted in a major speech that it was not the policy of the United States to deny the Germans the right to manage their internal affairs, as long as they did it in a democratic manner. He also called for the early establishment of a provisional all-German government and outlined specific procedures for reaching this goal (Byrnes, 1947, 188–191). No progress was made, however, at various meetings of the quadripartite Council of Foreign Ministers and the Allied Control Council.

Partly in response to the lack of progress through the established channels toward all-German government agencies, a conference of the Western foreign ministers was convened. This was the London Six-Power Conference (February 23 to March 6, 1948). It included additional representatives of Belgium, Luxembourg, and the Netherlands. Representatives of Czechoslovakia, Poland, and Yugoslavia attended at the beginning but left the conference on Soviet orders even before the first session had ended. The governments of the United States and Great Britain accepted a limited merger of their zones of occupation with that of France—no longer being willing to wait for the Soviet Union's acceptance of a central government for all four zones. Agreement was reached at the London Conference on the nature of the merger of the three Western zones, on the basic structure of the prospective German government, and on the procedures for the drafting and ratification of a German Constitution.

While the London Conference was in session, the Soviets, as noted earlier, walked out of the Allied Control Council (March 20, 1948). Three months later (June 16, 1948), the Soviets also walked out of the *Allied Kommandantura* for Berlin. Joint four-power governance, thus, had ended. Two days later (June 18), the Western Allies announced the long-needed reform of the German currency for their territories. Eight days later the Soviets began the blockade of West Berlin (June 24, 1948 to May 12, 1949).

It may be argued that the Western Powers proceeded on their own since, as seen, the USSR had prevented a common undertaking.[19] Currency reform, in any case, was badly needed if there was to be any kind of economic reconstruction. The value of the old reichsmark had entirely collapsed, and the "black market" dominated the economy. The reform of the currency was the first step toward economic recovery and carried with it the commitment to a "free market" system. Currency reform and free market politics are closely linked to Ludwig Erhard, the first minister of economics of the FRG. The chief American architect of currency reform was Edward A. Tenenbaum, of General Clay's staff. The Marshall Plan (announced June 1947) supplied much of the capital for West German reconstruction.

The Constitution and Government of the FRG

On July 1, 1948, the three Western military governors met with the chief executives of the eleven West German states and empowered them to convene a constitutional assembly to draft a democratic and federal constitution. German concerns that such action might intensify the growing division of the country led to the request for a number of changes, which were agreed to by the Allies: that the body to be convened would be a "Parliamentary Council" rather than a constitutional convention, that the document would be known as "Basic Law" rather than as Constitution, and that the Basic Law would clearly be designated as provisional. The state chief executives commissioned a group of experts to produce a draft of the Basic Law.

The state legislatures elected the members of the (Basic Law drafting) Parliamentary Council, which convened on September 1, 1948, in Bonn, electing Konrad Adenauer (CDU) as its president. After various revisions of the draft, in part on the request of the military governors, the Basic Law was approved by the Parliamentary Council (May 8, 1948) by a majority of fifty-three to twelve. The chief opposition came from Bavaria, which preferred a confederation to the proposed federal system. The Allies approved the document (with certain reservations) on May 12, 1948. Between May 18 and May 21 the state legislatures ratified the Basic Law by ten states to one (Bavaria) (Conradt, 1978, 16–17; Goldman, 1974, 46–48; Kitzinger, 1960, 4–5).

The first general (trizonal) elections took place on August 14, 1949. The lower legislative chamber (*Bundestag*) had a total of 402 members. The following parties gained representation, with the number of seats won in parentheses: CDU-CSU (139), SPD (131), FDP (52), DP (17), KPD (15), and various minor parties (48) (Pollock et al., 1955, 182). The upper legislative chamber (*Bundesrat*) was not popularly elected but consisted of state delegations—an arrangement still in effect. The Federal Parliament convened for the first time on September 7, 1948, in Bonn. It elected Theodor Heuss (FDP) to be president of the Federal Republic on September 12 and Konrad Adenauer (CDU) to be chancellor on September 15. The first FRG *Bundestag*, as noted, had 402 members. The chancellor was to be elected by a simple majority, that is, by at least 202 votes. Adenauer received exactly 202 votes. He had been elected, thus, by virtue of his own vote—a matter of much jesting but readily and without embarrassment acknowledged by Adenauer, who clearly thought himself to be the right man for the job (Behr, 1961, 17–18). On September 21, 1949, the Allied high commissioners received the chancellor for an exchange of statements. With this ceremony the Federal Republic of Germany formally came into existence.

The Basic Law of the FRG provided for a federal system with a clear division of federal and state jurisdictions, three branches of government with various checks and balances, and an independent judicial branch that could review the constitutionality of executive and legislative acts. All governmental authority was said to be derived from the people. More than the Weimar Constitution, the prototype for the Basic Law was the Constitution of the United States. Paying close attention to the defects of the Constitution of the Weimar Republic, the Basic Law provided for a less centralized and more stable form of government, with considerable safeguards against minority party mischief and executive misuse of power, such as made possible by Article 48 of the Weimar Constitution (Merkl, 1965, 9–10). Article 48 permitted emergency rule (when "public safety and order were seriously disturbed") by presidential decree, as well as the suspension of certain civil rights. In principle, such decrees had to be endorsed by the *Reichstag*, but this check was largely voided by the fact that the president could dissolve the *Reichstag* and rule without a parliament for the required sixty days between dissolution and a new election. Article 48 was one of the fatal flaws of the Weimar Constitution. Its frequent use contributed greatly to the fall of the Weimar Republic (Reinhardt, 1989, II/649). The new Basic Law contributed significantly to the development of a stable and democratic polity in West Germany. With the reunification of Germany, the Basic Law became the Constitution for all of (what now remains of) Germany.

The Founding of the GDR

Early Soviet Expectations and Policies

The Soviets, it seems, were confident that large parts of the German population would embrace communism and that the Communist Party would be a strong force in all regions of Germany, which was also the expectation of the German communists in the USSR. With this in mind, the Soviets went to considerable lengths to present themselves as the true friends of Germany, eager to assist in postwar reconstruction. Actual conduct, of course, was significantly at variance with the stream of friendship declarations, for example, the dismantling of German industry, the heavy requisitions imposed on the remaining enterprises, conversion of German firms into Soviet-owned companies, the seizing of cultural objects, and the widespread and long-lasting raping and looting on the part of members of the Red Army[20] (Benz, 1984, 13; Davison, 1958, 27–29, 171; Greve, 1999, 44–65; Minnerup, 1982, 34–35). Most Germans, however, saw the newly reconstituted Communist Party (KPD) as Moscow's agent and helper, which severely delimited its popular acceptance. Soviet military and economic conduct also greatly reduced the attractiveness of the Russian "role model." The East Germans "never tried to become Russians . . . in quite the same way that West Germans went for what they saw as American culture and American lifestyle" (Malzahn, 1991, 12). After an initial period of greater hostility (see pp. 11–12 *supra*), the American approach "was less offensive, and much more cooperative. There simply was no parallel to the Stalinist pattern of domination and exploitation" (Brzezinski, 1965, 8).

The original policy of the USSR had not been to transform its zone and sector into a separate communist German state. Except for the radical restructuring of the courts and schools, and the expropriation of large agricultural estates and industrial enterprises, the first Soviet policies tended to resemble those of the Western Allies. There was, for example, no general abolition of the private ownership of the means of production. The expropriations that took place were justified as antifascist rather than anticapitalist measures. Nor were there (open) demands to establish a one-party regime. The first public declaration of the KPD of the Soviet Zone (June 11, 1945) called for the establishment of a parliamentary democratic republic with full civil rights and civil liberties for its citizens. Significantly, the declaration stated that it would be wrong to insist on the immediate establishment of socialism or to force Germany to adopt a Soviet-style system of government (Ulbricht, 1961, 28).

The Soviet Military Administration (SMAD) licensed several political parties. SMAD Order No. 2, however, "did not simply create political parties; it gave the Soviets the opportunity to monitor, check, and control all political activities in their zone of occupation" (Naimark, 1995, 272). In any case, the newly licensed parties did not encounter a level playing field. Various forms of important SMAD assistance to the new political parties were available only to the Communist Party. For example, newsprint, crucial for reaching the voters, was scarce. Its distribution was entirely in the hands of SMAD. To carry on the campaign for the local elections of September 1946, the Communist Party received 800 tons of newsprint, the two middle class parties 9 tons together (Schneider, 1978, 21). The KPD of the SZ had been founded by Moscow-directed functionaries, such as Walter Ulbricht. Not surprisingly, it acted as SMAD's German implementation agency.

Soviet policies changed when the Allied Control Council ceased to be a functioning body, when no agreement could be reached among the Allies regarding reunification, and when the expectations of "natural" communist strength turned out to be false. It became the new Soviet goal to establish a separate East German state under communist control.[21] The process of reaching this goal was relatively slow, in marked contrast to the rather speedy transformation of the other East European countries into "people's democracies" and Soviet satellites. On the other hand, Soviet control was stricter and more extensive in East Germany than in the other Soviet satellites. It also was stricter than Allied control in West Germany. The GDR always had considerably less autonomy than the FRG. What independence the GDR did enjoy at any given time was determined less by formal treaties than by shifts in Soviet policies (Pucher, 1984, 13).

Soviet Control of East German Parties and Politics

The Communist Party (KPD) was licensed first (June 1945), the Social Democratic Party (SPD) and the Christian Democratic Union (CDU) shortly thereafter. The Liberal Democratic Party (LDPD) was licensed somewhat later. The LDPD was organized on SMAD initiative and with SMAD help. In some localities of the Soviet Zone, SMAD even commissioned KPD functionaries to establish SPD organizations—which then were boycotted by the real SPD members (Bouvier & Schulz, 1991, 35; Huebsch, 2002; Wettig, 2002).

The licensing of the LDPD had its humorous aspects. Only after KPD, SPD, and CDU had been recognized did it occur to SMAD that this disposition would divide the votes of the workers between KPD and SPD, whereas the CDU would receive the votes of the rest of the population. This caused considerable alarm in Soviet circles. Thus, "Soviet Communist political liaison officers were sent scurrying around to help organize another 'bourgeois' party, the Liberal Democrats" (Bolling, 1950, 390).

SPD and CDU initially functioned as independent parties, but not for long. The SPD was simply incorporated into the KPD (see Chapter 3). The CDU remained formally a separate entity but, in effect, became a subsidiary of the KPD/SED. The initial group of (independent-minded) CDU leaders escaped to the West, retired, went to prison, or were executed (Richter, 1990, 208–259). Those who remained in office gave in sooner or later. They were

> worn down by pressure, blackmail, and the lures of privilege. They made their peace with Ulbricht who rewarded them for playing his game. They have become members of the East German elite, serve in the Volkskammer, and have second-rate government posts. They are non-communist only in name. (Dornberg, 1974, 114)

To weaken what little influence the bourgeois parties did have in the first years after the war, two communist-initiated and communist-controlled parties were added to the roster in 1948: the National Democratic Party (NDPD) and the Democratic Peasants' Party (DBD). Most of the leaders of these new parties appear to have had actual Communist Party affiliations. The others were known to have strong communist sympathies. The founder and first chairman of the DBD (Ernst Goldenbaum) had been a member of the Communist Party since 1923. The founder and first chairman of the NDPD was Lothar Bolz, who had been a prisoner of war in the USSR and a key member of the communist-controlled German war-prisoners organization, the National Committee "Free Germany" (NKFD). The parties' tasks were to compete with the CDU and the LDPD and to guide the nonsocialist voters—including former members of the NSDAP—toward the acceptance of SED policies.

The initial and continuing suitability of Party leaders was determined by Soviet control officers. Soviet removal of German Party officials was common. The first leaders of the CDU of East Germany, Andreas Hermens and Walther Schreiber, were removed as early as December 1945 because of their opposition to the expropriation of large landholdings. They were succeeded by Jacob Kaiser and Ernst Lemmer. Kaiser and Lemmer came to differ with SMAD on a number of policy issues, and in December 1947 they, in turn, were replaced with Georg Dertinger and Otto Nuschke. In Dertinger and Nuschke, SMAD finally had found individuals who accepted Soviet policies without question. They remained in SMAD's good graces throughout their active careers.

The LDPD leadership, not surprisingly, was more willing to follow the Soviet line from the beginning. The (supposedly) *free enterprise* party of East Germany supported the early agricultural expropriations (1945), the conversion to public ownership of all large enterprises and natural resources (1948), the introduction of central economic planning (1951), the policy of building socialism in the GDR (1952), and the absolute leadership claim of the Communist Party (1957). Nevertheless, some of its leaders also experienced difficulties with SMAD, even including charges of sabotage (Childs, 1969, 114–117).

The official GDR story always was that the several parties drew up their party programs freely and independently. However, these separate and independent party programs

> had a remarkably similar ring. Communists didn't say anything about communism and Liberal Democrats didn't say much about free enterprise. They all came out against nazism, war criminals and profiteers, and for democracy, social reform, and a lasting peace. (Bolling, 1950, 391)

In later years, all pretense of independence was dropped. The minor parties submitted their prospective platform planks and policy proposals to the SED for prior approval.

On its (re-) founding, the KPD advertised itself as having a strong and sincere willingness to cooperate with all (nonfascist) political parties. Its founding proclamation (June 11, 1945) made no mention of Marx and Engels, much less of Lenin and Stalin. Nothing was said about a "dictatorship of the proletariat."[22] The KPD's proclamation quite clearly took its lesson from the Bolshevik Peace Decree of 1917: "The talk was of democracy, not Bolshevism or the dictatorship of the proletariat. Specifically Bolshevik principles were not mentioned at all: the terms 'socialism,' 'world revolution,' 'civil war against imperialism,' etc. were nowhere to be found" (Geyer, 1987, 127).

Purely tactical considerations prevailed. There was much talk about German national interests and a "German road to socialism" (Wassmund, 1981, 327). Anton Ackermann (KPD) was the chief proponent of this position. Ulbricht and Pieck publicly supported it—at least for the time being. The KPD's bondage to Moscow and its Stalinist orientation were carefully (if not always successfully) disguised. As Walter Ulbricht said in May 1945: "It must look democratic, but we must have everything in our hands" (Leonhard, 1981, 358). It was only at the very end of its existence, when opposing Gorbachev's reforms, that the communist regime of the GDR rediscovered national self-determination, declaring that the "old thesis of the . . . convergence of socialist systems was false . . . [and that in addition to the path of the USSR] there was also a German path to socialism. This, unfortunately for Honecker, was precisely when the East German citizens started to believe the old slogan that 'to learn from the Soviet Union is to learn victory'" (Bryson & Melzer, 1991, 19–20).

In the summer of 1945, SMAD also began to license "mass organizations" on the Soviet model. The first to be authorized were the Free German Trade Union Federation (FDGB), June 1945, the Cultural Federation for the Democratic Renewal of Germany (KB), July 1945, and the Free German Youth (FDJ), March 1946. Important additions were the Peasants' Mutual Aid Association (VDGB), early 1946, the Women's Democratic League of Germany (DFD), March 1947, the German-Soviet Friendship Society (DSF), June 1947, and the Society for Sports and Technology (GST) in 1952, a paramilitary organization (Autorenkollektiv, 1980; Panorama-DDR, 1976, 65–68). Each mass organization represented, presumably, the interest of a specific group, for example, youth, women, labor. In its sphere, each mass organization had a monopoly. Each functioned as an organ of communist mobilization and control (transmission belt). By way of the "unity list" of the National Front (see Chapter 3), several of the mass organizations came to have seats in the legislative bodies of the GDR—where, of course, they fully and invariably supported communist policies.[23]

People's Congresses and the First GDR Constitution

Soviet work toward a postwar German Constitution had begun when the USSR still envisioned a unified and communist-dominated Germany. Acting through the SED, the Soviet Military Administration convened a *People's Congress* (*Volkskongress*) in East Berlin, which met December 6–7, 1947. It was designed to be an all-German, all-party representative assembly. Its most important responsibilities were to be charting the organization of a new central government, securing a peace treaty, and drafting a constitution. The delegates to the Congress were to come from all zones and sectors. By customary Soviet formula, however, the delegates would be appointed by the political parties and mass organizations, rather than being chosen in free and popular elections.

It was obvious that this Congress would be dominated by the SED and its subsidiaries. The LDPD was willing to cooperate. Its chairman (Wilhelm Kuelz) thought it "unrealistic" not to do so, hoping to have some influence on the ultimate products. The CDU declined to participate, whereupon its leaders (Kaiser and Lemmer) were charged by the SMAD with espionage and sabotage for the West and were forced to relinquish their offices. The new CDU chairman (Otto Nuschke) agreed to Soviet wishes. The rewards for Kuelz and Nuschke were cochairmanships of the People's Congress, together with Pieck (SED). Real influence, of course, was not part of the rewards. Not wishing to legitimate what would obviously be a communist-and USSR-controlled happening, most political organizations and leaders in the Western zones declined to participate. The actual composition of the People's Congress turned out to be about 1,100 members from the Soviet Zone, 450 from Berlin, and 500 from the Western zones (mostly members of the KPD). The communist control of the Congress could not be doubted.

A *Second* People's Congress was convened on March 18, 1948. However, there had been no new delegate elections or appointments. The March 1948 gathering was, in fact, the second meeting of the First People's Congress and is sometimes referred to as such. This Congress elected a 400-member *People's Council* (*Volksrat*), assigning to it certain administrative and advisory functions. The composition of the People's Council was 300 members from the SBZ and 100 from the West (again mostly KPD). The People's Council, in turn, delegated the task of drawing up a new Constitution to a *drafting committee* selected from among the Council's members, chaired by Grotewohl (SED by way of SPD).

The drafting committee, to no one's surprise, was wholly under communist control. The SBZ contingent consisted of sixteen SED and nine (SED-allied) middle-class members. The Western representation was nine KPD members and two officially unaffiliated persons, who, however, appeared to be communist sympathizers. This arrangement gave the SED-KPD at least twenty-five of thirty-six seats, or better than a two-thirds majority (69.4%), even without the votes of the SED-dominated other members. The drafting committee did not have to look far for a suitable blueprint. Already in 1946, the SED had produced a preliminary draft for a German Constitution. It had been widely discussed in the East German press and in meetings of the parties and mass organizations. This document (plus several amendments) served as the basis for the committee's deliberations, and the committee's final product closely resembled it.

The People's Council accepted the committee's formal draft in August 1948 and submitted it to public discussion. The communist propaganda machine was fully activated in support of the draft, producing endless laudatory commentaries in the broadcast and print media. More than 9,000 meetings were held to explain the draft and to solicit citizens' suggestions. When the revised draft was submitted to the People's Council (March 1949), more than one-third of the text was reported to have been amended in conformity with the wishes of the people. Responding to "the wishes of the people" is a standard communist tactic: all show and no substance. While some suggestions for changes in minor details and unimportant technicalities were accepted, the gist and spirit of the draft remained untouched.[24] On March 19, 1949, the People's Council unanimously approved the revised document and forwarded it to the People's Congress for ratification.

The constitution-making process in the Soviet Zone had come under criticism from the West for lacking the input and authorization of popularly elected representatives. To counter this challenge to the democratic legitimacy of the proposed constitution, SED and Soviet authorities employed the (risk-free) technique of bloc elections. On May 15–16, 1949, the citizens of the Soviet Zone were given the opportunity to elect the members of the *Third* People's Congress. As with all bloc election schemes, who would be elected to the Congress and how many seats each party and mass organization would receive were determined well in advance. The role of the voters was to endorse the bloc list, not to choose among competing parties or candidates. The language of the ballot *did not* ask the electorate to vote for or against the constitution but to cast their votes for "German unity and just peace." The ballot provided no marking-space or any other way by which to cast a negative vote. Nevertheless, the not yet fully intimidated and controlled electorate cast 34% *no* and 5% invalid votes. Even the meager 61% of *yes* votes could be reached only with the help of fraud. When the first counts showed that the *yes* votes would not reach 50%, a substantial number of ballots were reclassified from invalid to *yes*, by order of the SED election officials (Fricke, 1974, 948).

The Third People's Congress convened at the end of May. Not surprisingly, the SED was again in full control. The Congress quickly approved the Constitution. Only parliamentary implementation remained to be arranged. For this purpose and undeterred by legal niceties, the Third People's Congress reconstituted itself on October 7, 1949, as the (provisional) East German parliament, the *People's Chamber* (*Volkskammer*).[25] The First People's Chamber, thus, came into existence without the benefit of democratic elections—not even in the form of bloc elections, by which all subsequent People's Chambers were then fashioned. Johannes Dieckmann (LDPD) was elected president of the body. The First People's Chamber completed the task of constitution-making by unanimously approving the required Articles of Implementation.

The first GDR Constitution can be characterized as a "middle path" between Weimar and Moscow. The *Weimar* contributions (mostly civil liberties provisions) remained on the books until 1968, when the second GDR Constitution was adopted. However, they were never implemented. The wording of the Constitution was largely compatible with genuine democracy. In practice, however, its provisions were used to support a communist dictatorship. The SED controlled the state organs in two ways: first through overlapping memberships (practically all government officials were members of the SED or an affiliated party and, thus, subject to party directives), and second through a Party committee structure that paralleled government organizational units. The Party committees had the right to issue directives to their respective governmental units. Party directives had the force of law, notwithstanding Article 5.3 of the GDR Constitution, which stated: "At no time and under no circumstances can organs other than those provided by the Constitution exercise state power." The organs provided for were, of course, the legislature, the executive, and the judiciary, *not* the SED.

The most important *Soviet* contributions to the GDR Constitution were the specification of the economic system of the GDR, for example, the planned economy (Art. 21), public ownership of all natural resources (Art. 25) and of certain citizen rights (e.g., the right to work [Art. 15.2]), the right to rest and recreation (Art. 16.1), and the right to an education (Art. 35.1). The Constitution of the GDR, just as the Basic Law of the FRG, claimed applicability to all of Germany. Both documents also provided for a single German citizenship, covering GDR and FRG residents. As a practical consequence this meant that citizens of one country moving to the other one automatically were citizens of the second country. The vast majority of such cases, of course, regarded GDR citizens escaping to the FRG. One fundamental difference: the GDR Constitution was designed to be a permanent construct, whereas the Basic Law of the FRG was meant as a temporary device (Krieg, 1993).

The Organization of Government

The formal structure of GDR government, created by the first Constitution, was that of a bicameral parliamentary system, a dual executive, and a separate judiciary—the typical pattern of European governments. By constitutional provision (Art. 50.1), the lower house (People's Chamber) was the repository and source of all power. The People's Chamber had 500 members, elected for a period of five years. The number of candidates seeking election tended to correspond very closely to the number of deputies to be elected. In the 1981 elections, for example, there were exactly 500 candidates. All of them were elected, of course. The number of seats for each party and mass organization always was determined beforehand, by way of a single electoral list—the National Front—that included all political parties as well as the major mass organizations. (The National Front is discussed in Chapter 3.)

On paper, the People's Chamber's primary task was legislation: it was to be the fountainhead of all law. In addition, it elected the two chief executives of the GDR: the president of the republic (the head of state with largely ceremonial functions) and the prime minister (the head of government, the actual chief executive)—later it elected the collective head of state: the Council of State. Furthermore, it had to approve appointments to the cabinet. The People's Chamber also could remove the president and the prime minister, being able to dismiss the prime minister and his administration by a vote of nonconfidence.

In theory, the People's Chamber determined public policy. The work of the ministries was to be guided by the policy principles adopted by the People's Chamber, and all legislative acts were to be faithfully implemented. In practice, the People's Chamber was merely an acclamation organ for the policies decided on by the Politbureau and other Party agencies. (More about this later and in Chapter 3.)

Upon nomination by the government, the People's Chamber elected the judges of the Supreme Court (*Oberstes Gericht*). These judges were responsible to the People's Chamber and could be removed by it. The People's Chamber also appointed the attorney general (*Generalstaatsanwalt*) and the members of the National Defense Council (*Nationaler Verteidigungsrat*). In fact, of course, all these functionaries were responsible to the Party and were appointed by the Party and removed by the Party. The task of the People's Chamber merely was to applaud the Party's decisions.

This, however, did not prevent the regime from proclaiming that legislative supremacy was the keystone of the GDR's political structure. In accordance with Marxist-Leninist principles, the GDR's power structure had to be *unitary*. Any notion of a separation of powers was explicitly rejected on the grounds that (1) the popular will is singular, and (2) there could not be any opposition to it—a matter closely related, of course, to the doctrine of the dialectical unity of opposites (for a discussion of which see my *Rotten Foundations*, Chapter 5).

The formal constitutional arrangements, of course, were of little consequence. In practice, the People's Chamber was not only not supreme but wholly devoid of any real power. In Fried's (1966, 43) terms, it was a "captive assembly." Christopher (1985, 21), very properly, called it an "organ of acclamation" (*Akklamationsorgan*), that is, a body merely assenting to decisions made elsewhere. Almost no legislation originated in the Chamber. The Chamber did not subject to any real analysis or discussion the bills originating in the executive branch, in effect, that is, in the SED Politbureau. Indeed, the Chamber "was not even permitted to question or criticize . . . the executive branch" (Plischke, 1961, 192).

The "legislators" had only these functions: to deliver speeches of praise and approval for the wise policies of Party and government, and to cast unanimous votes for SED bills. The approval of bills was not, by the way, a major activity. Since at least 1954, GDR lawmaking most often took the form of issuing executive decrees and administrative ordinances. The People's Chamber voted on few laws—as few as ten per year; indeed, it hardly ever met. In the five-year period from 1976 to 1981, for example, there were only thirteen plenary sessions (in which, according to Art. 48 of the constitution, the "basic questions of state policy" were to be decided), each lasting only a day or two. Some of the standing committees met more frequently, but not to make basic decisions. Meeting with constituents (a propaganda function) ranked higher in importance among the deputies' tasks than any legislative sessions. The real tasks of GDR legislators were to popularize SED policies and to provide a link between leadership and grass roots. The legislators, in effect, were not lawmakers but "auxiliary organs for the executive" (Heidenheimer, 1961, 188).

The second Chamber of the GDR legislature was the *States' Chamber* (*Laenderkammer*). On October 10, 1949, the several state legislatures chose the members of the States' Chamber. The States' Chamber always was subordinate to the People's Chamber, though this was of little practical consequence since both chambers were fully controlled by the SED. The States' Chamber lost its political base with the abolition of the traditional states in 1952 and was itself abolished in 1958.

As noted, the first GDR Constitution provided for a dual executive, with a president as head of state and a prime minister (or more correctly, "Chairman of the Council of Ministers") as head of government. On October 11, 1949, the two legislative chambers met jointly and elected Wilhelm Pieck (SED by way of KPD) president of the German Democratic Republic. The office did not last. Wilhelm Pieck, still in office, died on September 7, 1960. Five days later, the People's Chamber (unanimously and without debate) abolished the single-person presidency and replaced it with a collective presidential body, the twenty-four-member *Council of State* (*Staatsrat*). The People's Chamber also enlarged the functions of the office, allowing it to interpret laws and to enact resolutions having the force of law. The Council of State, in effect, combined the executive, legislative, and judicial functions. Walter Ulbricht (SED by way of KPD) was elected chairman of the new Council of State. Subsequently, the chairmanship was held by Willi Stoph (SED by way of KPD) and Erich Honecker (SED by way of KPD). On October 12, 1949, the People's Chamber elected Otto Grotewohl (SED by way of SPD) prime minister (*Ministerpraesident*). It also elected the members of the cabinet, the Council of Ministers (*Ministerrat*). Subsequently, the position of prime minister was held by Horst Sindermann (SED by way of KPD) and Willi Stoph.

In whatever form and with whatever occupants, the structure of governmental agencies camouflaged to some degree the Party's unlimited control of all aspects of GDR life (Neugebauer, 1978, 11). The real (German) power in the GDR always was the SED, and the real power in the SED always was the first secretary/general secretary of the central committee/politbureau. Walter Ulbricht was the first GDR leader to combine the highest offices of Party and state: first secretary/general secretary of the SED from 1950 to 1971 and head of state (chairman of the Council of State) from 1960 to 1973.[26] Ulbricht's successor, Erich Honecker (SED by way of KPD), also combined the top positions of Party and state, holding these since 1971 and 1976, respectively. Egon Krenz, finally, held both positions from October to December 1989, after the SED Politbureau removed Erich Honecker in a desperate (and futile) attempt to salvage the regime and an independent GDR.

The GDR judiciary, as all other state organs, was not independent and autonomous. Judges, as all other state employees, were subject to Party directives. Even constitutional guarantees could not withstand Party policy. Not surprisingly, there was no procedure in the GDR for filing a constitutional complaint. There was no court adjudicating issues of constitutional law. Inquiries and complaints about the constitutional conformance of a law were to be directed to the People's Chamber—the very body that had issued the law in the first instance. As one would expect, there were no complaints from ordinary citizens and very few from other sources. Church officials, for example, raised some constitutional questions regarding military instruction in the schools—to no effect, of course.

Also, practically to the very end of the regime, there were no administrative courts in the GDR. Citizens could not sue the government or any of its agencies to obtain relief from invasions of their rights. The only procedure available for the redress of grievances was to complain to the relevant office or agency (*Eingabe*)—which (as in the case of the People's Chamber) was responsible for the infraction in the first place (Behr, 1985b, 323–329; Mueller-Roemer, 1974, 45; Schulz, 1968, 73, 79). Not surprisingly, there seem to have been few such complaints. In the first instance, they had almost no chance of success, and in the second instance, it would have identified the petitioner as a troublemaker and (possibly) an agent of the class enemy.

Finally, there was no provision for an independent and politically neutral civil service in the GDR. Civil servants were state employees, without a tenure system to protect them from political pressures. The lack of a tenured civil service was no oversight. Civil servants were expected to be advocates and partisans of the regime—failing that, easily removable. They were expected to follow Party directives in all aspects of their work. To reach the higher career levels, of course, civil servants had to be members of the SED or one of the satellite parties. To the rulers of the GDR (Soviet and German), administrative inexperience and inefficiency seemed a small price to pay for Party loyalty.

Formal Sovereignty

In March 1954, the Soviet Union declared the GDR a sovereign state. The Treaty of September 1955 replaced the Soviet High Commission with an embassy. In actuality, of course, the country remained under extensive and intensive Soviet control—far exceeding that of the Western Allies in the FRG. The second Constitution of the GDR (1968) even incorporated a declaration of friendship and cooperation with the USSR (Art. 6.2), and the 1974 revision (Art. 6.2) proclaimed that the GDR "is forever and irrevocably allied with the USSR." This is one of the more intriguing GDR innovations: foreign policy making by constitutional codification.

It was, of course, in the foreign policy area that the GDR most lacked independence. It was not uncommon for GDR foreign policy statements to consist almost entirely of quotations from Soviet prototypes. Contrary to other socialist countries (e.g., Poland, Bulgaria, Romania), the GDR generally played down the national theme. It was the strongest advocate among the countries of the Council for Mutual Economic Assistance (COMECON) of close and multiple ties with the USSR. Until Gorbachev's era of *glasnost* and *perestroika*, the GDR was the USSR's most loyal ally. Not all of this was unvarnished devotion to international proletarian solidarity. The leadership of the GDR knew perfectly well that it would not survive without Soviet troops. The official East German version of the Soviet role in the GDR's emphasized voluntarism, of course:

> The liberation of a number of European and Asian countries by Soviet armed forces provided favorable opportunities for democratic developments. The Soviet Union furnished manifold and effective assistance to the people of these countries to enable them to exercise their right to national and social self-determination. (Buske et al., 1981, 22–23)

Some Western commentators took such assertions at face value. Szajkowski (1981, 76), for example, adopted the position that the Soviet military presence was an important, but not decisive, factor in creating a communist regime in East Germany, and that this regime was not simply imposed on the East Germans by the Soviet Union and its agents but reflected popular preferences.

Constitutional Revisions

The GDR adopted a *second* constitution in 1968. Substantial changes were made in that document in 1974—amounting to the framing of a *third* constitution. Whereas, prior to its adoption, the 1968 Constitution had been the object of extensive publicity and a public referendum,[27] the 1974 version was developed in almost total secrecy. It was not submitted to the public for approval but was adopted by the People's Chamber in that body's customary way—unanimously and without discussion. The reason for the secrecy appears to have been the SED's concern about the public's response to the deletion of any and all commitments to the German nation and to reunification,[28] to the codified bonding of the GDR to the USSR, and to the elevation of Marxism-Leninism to constitutional rank.

Since the formal organization of government always had been of little consequence in the GDR, there is no need to discuss the various changes in detail. Some of them, in fact, had been made earlier and were only now given a legal basis via incorporation into the new Constitution. For example, a 1955 amendment to the Constitution of 1949 provided the legal basis for the establishment of East German armed forces (NVA). However, the first units of the NVA were organized in October 1952, then called "barracked people's police" (KVP). The actual establishment of the armed forces, thus, preceded constitutional authorization *by nearly four years*. Indeed, the lag was *nine years*, if one begins the count at the 1946 creation of some clandestine East German military units (Bundesministerium für innerdeutsche Beziehungen, 1985, 710).

As noted earlier, the States' Chamber (upper house) ceased to function in 1952 and finally was abolished by constitutional amendment in 1958. The GDR Constitution authoritative in 1952 required a working States' Chamber. But here, too, the regime paid no attention to authoritative constitutional provisions. For six years governmental practice clearly did not conform to constitutional requirements. In this, as in other things, the GDR learned from the Soviet Union, where constitutional mandates were routinely disregarded (e.g., Wolfe, 1961, 143–152).

In other constitutional changes, the single president of the republic was replaced by a collective head of state, the Council of State (*Staatsrat*) in 1960. The Council of State had representational as well as administrative duties, for example, receiving ambassadors and supervising the ministerial apparatus. However, under Honecker the Council of State lost many of its supervisory functions to the Council of Ministers (*Ministerrat*). In the last decades of the GDR, the Council of State had twenty-six members, with one chairman (Honecker) and nine deputy chairmen, including members of the SED and other political parties, as well as members of the mass organizations. The members of the Council of State were elected by the People's Chamber. The term of office was five years.

The Council of Ministers (its members also elected by the People's Chamber for five-year terms) was the actual government of the GDR. It directed the execution of policies, verified fulfillment of economic plans, and guided the activities of the central ministries as well as of the regional executive organs. The Council of Ministers consisted of forty-two members, drawn from all five political parties. It also included a number of ex-officio members, such as the mayor of East Berlin, the chairman of the State Planning Commission, and the president of the State Bank. The large size of the Council resulted from the GDR practice of establishing separate ministries to deal with particular economic problems. Thus, there was at the end a set of eleven separate "industrial ministries," each responsible for a specific sector of the GDR industry.

The Council of Ministers was headed by a chairman, who, together with two first-deputy chairmen and nine deputy chairmen, formed the body's "presidency" (*Praesidium*). Council membership was exceedingly stable, with lengthy terms of office, particularly for the key members. For example, for the entire duration of the GDR, the council had only three chairmen: Otto Grotewohl, 1949–1964; Willi Stoph, 1964–1973 and 1976–1989; Horst Sindermann, 1973–1976—not counting the short postcollapse chairmanships of Hans Modrow (SED) (November 1989–March 1990) and Lothar de Maiziere (CDU) (April–October 1990).

There were other fundamental changes. For example, the original five states[29] (*Laender*) of the GDR were abolished in 1952 in favor of fifteen administrative regions (*Bezirke*).[30] Including the area of East Berlin, there were fifteen regions (*Bezirke*), each centered on a major urban industrial core. Within each region there were a number of administrative districts (*Kreise*), altogether about 200 in number. The districts, in turn, were divided into communes (*Gemeinden*) and city boroughs (*Stadtbezirke*), about 9,000 in all.

Military service was introduced in 1955 and made compulsory in 1962. Significant changes also were made in regard to the concept of a German nation. The Constitution of 1949 had proclaimed that Germany was an "indivisible democratic republic" (Art. 1.1) and that there was "only one German citizenship" (Art. 1.4). The Constitution of 1968 dropped these statements and declared, instead, that the GDR was "a socialist state of German nation" [*sic*] (Art. 1). With the 1974 Constitution, all references to Germany or the German nation disappeared.[31] The equivalent article now read that the GDR was "a socialist state of workers and peasants" (Art. 1). The new text also elevated to a constitutional principle "the leading role of the working class and its Marxist-Leninist Party" (Art. 1). At about the time of the 1974 Constitution, the GDR also removed the word "German" from the names of most of its institutes and organizations. Furthermore, since 1972, the national anthem of the GDR was no longer to be sung but to be performed only as an instrumental piece (Gotschlich, 1999, 108). This avoided public expression of the text's commitment to German unity, especially the line *Deutschland, einig Vaterland* (Germany, united fatherland). For the full text of the anthem, see Dittmar, 1984, 1136.

The initial goal of a united Germany was replaced by that of the indefinite preservation of a communist state on German soil. The three constitutions can be viewed as the stages from the goal of a united democratic Germany to that of a communist dictatorship in one part of Germany, or, as Mampel (1974, 1152–1153) has remarked, they may be seen as marking the major steps on the GDR's road from Weimar to Moscow.

NOTES

1. Twelve parts if the boundaries of 1938 are used as a basis. The additional part would be the Sudetenland (see p. 8).

2. Great Britain, however, was not very strongly opposed to partition, seeing that partitioning could serve the old British goal of containing Germany as a commercial competitor and military power, as well as that of stopping the westward spread of communism and Soviet domination (Deighton, 1990, 225–230).

3. Here is an excellent example of the West German Left's need to propagate socialism as the better system, even in its Stalinist form. In 1988, when the facts of Katyn had long become clear, the Left-leaning paper *Die Zeit* wrote as heading to a

picture of the mass graves: Polish officers *probably* killed by the Red Army (emphasis added) (as reported in Berg, 1988, 21).

4. Messages, one might note, that still have not yet come to an end and of which Goldhagen's absurd book (1996) is but a recent manifestation. (Compare my *Rotten Foundations*, Chapter 2.)

5. Soviet perspectives on national-socialism/fascism and the individual nature of guilt remained the same throughout the postwar period (e.g., see Gorbachev, 1987, 201).

6. This included even a strict prohibition to associate with children (Berg, 1988, 20).

7. The Bavarian equivalent is the Christian Social Union (CSU). It is a separate party but closely affiliated with the CDU.

8. In the Soviet Zone, the liberal party took the name Liberal Democratic Party of Germany (LDPD); in the West, it took the name Free Democratic Party (FDP).

9. The GDR regime persistently claimed that former national-socialists achieved high postwar positions *only* in the FRG (Kappelt, 1981, 15). This was far from the truth. A substantial number of high-ranking national-socialists came to occupy important positions in the upper echelons of state and society in the GDR (Investigating Committee of Free Jurists; Kappelt, 1981; Muhlen, 1951, 9–10; Schwarze, 1973, 25; Stadtmueller, 1963, 230–231; Wiesenthal, 1968; Zank, 1987, 55). Some additional materials on denazification will be found in Chapter 4.

10. There is much reason to doubt, however, that, from an overall perspective, denazification was more successful in the Soviet Zone than in the Western Zones (e.g., Vogt, 2000, 232–234, 244).

11. While some judicial retentions (reappointments) in the FRG were scandalous, in general, the confidence in being able to restore judicial neutrality does not seem to have been misplaced. Any remaining national-socialist judges in the GDR did not have to discover judicial neutrality, of course. They were to act as before, only on the basis of a different text.

12. The details will be found in my forthcoming book *Popular Justice in a Marxist-Leninist Society: The East German Social Courts and Other Aspects of GDR Law.*

13. However, the Soviets and the GDR frequently advanced the claim that all of Berlin was part of the Soviet Zone. See Mahnke, 1969.

14. The first steps toward the blockade of Berlin were taken already on April 1, 1948, when significant obstructions to Allied transit were put into place (Sutterlin & Klein, 1989, 27).

15. The Soviets, occupying all of Berlin entirely by themselves for two months, had placed a large number of German communists and collaborators into the local offices and administrative positions in the Western Sectors of the city (Langguth, 1987, 11; see also Hanauske, 1995).

16. A well-known case—reported by Judge Herbert J. Stern (1988), who presided over it—was the trial of the hijackers of a Polish airliner, which had been forced to land in West Berlin.

17. The Soviets began to refer informally to *all* of Berlin as being part of the Soviet Zone in late 1947—a Berlin in which the Western Powers were present "only as guests." The first formal statement that all of Berlin was part of the Soviet Zone came on July 14, 1948 (Sutterlin & Klein, 1989, 32–35).

18. In 1957 the West German parliament declared Berlin to be the capital of the FRG. The seat of the FRG government, however, remained in West Germany, prin-

cipally Bonn. West Berlin, however, was not nearly as integrated into the FRG as East Berlin was into the GDR. For example, the citizens of East Berlin were subject to the GDR's military draft, whereas the citizens of West Berlin were not subject to the military draft of the FRG.

19. This is not how the GDR saw it. Willy Stoph (1949, 27), member of the Politbureau, chairman of the Concil of Ministers, and chairman of the Council of State, declared that the division of Germany was due to the "big imperialist powers"—and he did not mean to include the USSR in that category.

20. Raping, looting, and various mistreatments of the civilian population and of prisoners of war also were a part of the comportment of Western military occupation, but these acts did not last quite as long as in the East (Arndt Verlag, 1997; Bacque, 1999; Barnouw, 1996; Naimark, 1995; Nolywaika, 1994, 1998; Sudholt, 1998).

21. But see Loth, 1994.

22. It appears that this phrase was not used officially in SZ and GDR until May 5, 1953. The June 17, 1953, revolt, however, led to a new period of nonuse (Prauss, 1960, 100–101).

23. It is interesting to compare the parallel postwar developments of divided Germany and Korea. The Communist Party of North Korea (CPK) also began with declarations of respect for other points of view, but National Front (United Front) tactics soon produced a one-party dictatorship. The CPK, initially open to persons of all backgrounds, was purified. The other parties became CPK puppets. The CPK appropriated key national symbols in its quest for legitimacy. Mass organizations were created and assigned the task of transmission belts (Scalapino, 1992, 41; Scalapino & Lee, 1972, 691–711).

24. This also became the *modus operandi* for the frequent citizen consultations in the GDR that followed and formed one basis for the country's claims to be a true democracy.

25. On the role of elected representatives in the GDR, see Patzelt and Schirmer, 2002 and Richert, 1958.

26. Prior to becoming chairman of the Council of State, Ulbricht held other governmental offices, such as deputy prime minister. Ulbricht was preceded as first secretary by Pieck (KPD, 1945–1946) and Pieck and Grotewohl (SPD/SED) jointly (1946–1950). However, Ulbricht had been the real leader of the KPD/SED since 1945.

27. See Chapter 3 on the manipulation of the voting rules in this referendum and in other elections.

28. The second constitution (1968) already had abandoned the principle of a single German citizenship, following the proclamation of a separate GDR citizenship in 1967.

29. They were Brandenburg, Mecklenburg, Thuringia, Saxony, and Saxony-Anhalt.

30. Local and regional governmental agencies, although strengthened somewhat in 1973, remained without truly independent powers. Their chief political function was to enlist the citizenry in the performance of public tasks and to add to the veneer of "participatory legitimacy."

31. The GDR was quite willing, of course, to be part of the German nation when economic benefits were at stake, such as taking advantage of the FRG's European Economic Community (EEC) membership (Schweitzer et al., 1984, 377–378). See Chapter 5 for the details.

Chapter 3

Beginnings and Governmental Structure

THE IMPOSITION OF COMMUNIST RULE

The Socialist Unity Party

The Three Communist Organizing Groups

Most of the postwar leaders of the Communist Party of the Soviet Zone had survived the Third Reich in the USSR.[1] They returned with the Red Army as members of three *Initiativgruppen* (initiative groups): Group Ulbricht in Berlin, Group Ackermann in Saxony, and Group Sobottka in the northern part of the Soviet Zone. The Soviet Military Administration (SMAD) quickly placed them into positions of key influence. As Ulbricht later would admit, the aim was to place the communist stamp rapidly "on the basic institutions of government while the situation was still fluid, before the communists' adversaries could regroup and reassert their influence"[2] (Sandford, 1983, 24). Most important among the three primary *Initiativgruppen* was the one in Berlin, led by Walter Ulbricht. Ulbricht was Stalin's German deputy and the effective ruler of the SZ/GDR from 1945 to 1971 (Stern, 1965, v).

The initiative groups were wholly dependent on Soviet support and were used by SMAD to carry out its policies. The groups also imposed order and uniformity on the communist cells that had been formed independently (i.e., without Soviet direction) by local activists in the first postwar days. Pre-1933 KPD leaders, for example, had established an autonomous (non-Moscow) KPD organization in Leipzig. Hermann Matern, "true to KPD and SMAD policies effected its dissolution in the summer of 1945 by arresting two of its more prominent members" (Krisch, 1974, 73). Antifascist committees that had been established quite spontaneously (not controlled by communists) had to be dissolved (Leonhard, 1990, 151). Antifascists who had survived the Third Reich in Germany (often in concentration camps) or in Western exile were quickly removed from positions of influence, leaving the Stalinist core in full control—first of the party, then of the state. The regions of the SZ initially occupied by the American army received special attention in this respect.

The Weimar Record

During the years of the Third Reich, there developed considerable sentiment among the members of the Social Democratic Party and the Communist Party to form a single proletarian political party. Indeed, the promerger sentiment initially was stronger in the SPD than the KPD. This was true at least for the SPD in the East. There were two centers of social democratic activity in postwar Germany: East Berlin (for all of Berlin and the Soviet Zone) and Hannover (for the Western Zones). Merger inclinations were fairly strong in Berlin[3] but weak in Hannover. Kurt Schumacher, the leader of the Western SPD, played a key role in preventing a merger with the KPD in the Western Zones and Sectors. Schumacher regarded the communists as nothing but "German-speaking members of the Russian state party" and the "mouthpieces of their Soviet masters" (Edinger, 1965, 157–158). In any case, the first Party Program of the KPD called for coalition politics (bloc politics), whereas the first Party Program of the SPD (of the Soviet Zone) called for "the organizational unity of the working class" (Bouvier & Schulz, 1991, 30–31).

Both SPD and KPD parties assigned much of the blame for the national-socialist takeover in Germany to the warfare between SPD and KPD during the Weimar period—differing sharply, however, about who was to blame for that warfare (see later). It is clear, however, that if the KPD had supported the traditional Weimar coalition (SPD and Center Party) instead of combating it, Hitler would not have become chancellor. In the last free elections of the Weimar Republic (November 1932), the NSDAP received 11.7 million votes, and the two working-class parties together, 13.2 million (SPD: 7.3; KPD: 5.9). In addition, the Center Party obtained 4.2 million and the German National Party, 3 million votes.

Claiming to be the only party representing the interests of the proletariat, the Communist Party regarded any other workers' party as fraudulent. In the eyes of the KPD, the Weimar SPD was the "traitor party," and its members were "social fascists, lackeys of monopoly-capitalism, and the twins of the national socialists." The last several years of the Weimar Republic saw particularly bitter conflicts between the SPD and the KPD. From about 1929 to Hitler's chancellorship (January 30, 1933) and even to 1935, the KPD was guided by Stalin's remarkably absurd theory of "social fascism."[4] It considered the fascism of the NSDAP and "social fascism" of the SPD as the two sides of the same antirevolutionary coin (Peukert, 1994, 40) and, incredibly, insisted that the *main enemy* was the SPD rather than the NSDAP.[5] As late as the (so-called) Brussels Conference of the KPD (October 1935), KPD leader Wilhelm Pieck (1947, 7), while acknowledging some KPD errors, spoke of the social democrats as the "enemies" and declared that they had to assume "the historical responsibility for the victory of fascism in Germany" (Weber, 1982b, 8–10; Wachtler, 1983, 183). The official SED history of the German labor movement repeated this account, merely adding "right-wing union leaders" to "right-wing SPD leaders" as the principal culprits. The foremost culprits, according to the KPD, were the SPD leaders Otto Wels and Rudolf Breitscheid. The former, for example, had stated at the 1931 party conference that "bolshevism and fascism are brothers," and the latter had added at the same meeting that "Moscow and Rome are identical in character" (Autorenkollektiv, 1985b, 63). Wels and Breitscheid were eminently correct, of course. (See my *Rotten Foundations*, Chapters 4, 6.) As one would expect, the official SED history affirmed that KPD policies had been correct and always in the best interest of the nation (Weber, 1964, 71; Kuehnrich, 1983, 14–16). The allocation of blame for Hitler remained an important issue with the East German communists to the very end. As late as the mid-1980s, even GDR *travel guides* were enlisted to proclaim the thesis of unique blameworthiness of the SPD (e.g., *Reisebuch DDR*, 1986, 34).

Aiming at the overthrow of the (SPD-supported) Weimar Republic, communist (Comintern) strategy sought the destruction of constitutional democracy and the establishment of a communist dictatorship in Germany. Until the very end, the KPD, in effect, worked with the NSDAP against Weimar (Hoyles, 1991, 59–60, 67ff; Mann, 1961, 83, 99; Merkl, 1965, 297–298; Stuermer, 1986, 241). A (presumably intermediate) period of fascist dictatorship was more acceptable to the KPD than the continuation of democratic government.[6] The postwar KPD/SED assessment, however, always was that the SPD had to bear the blame for Hitler's chancellorship; the KPD merely made some (minor) "tactical errors."

Soviet Merger Policies: From Opposition to Command

For most of 1945 SMAD (i.e., Moscow) opposed the formation of a single working-class party. The KPD followed the Moscow line and rebuffed the SPD, most bluntly on June 25, 1945, in Ulbricht's speech at the first postwar conference of KPD functionaries in Berlin (Ulbricht, 1961, 30–31). There appear to have been two reasons for this opposition. First, a delay of the merger would allow the KPD to build up its own cadres and, thus, be in a better position to monopolize the leading positions in a future "unity party," should there ever be one. Second, the Soviets appear to have assumed that the Communist Party could win parliamentary majorities on its own. It did not take long to demonstrate to the Soviets that the second postulate was mistaken.

In spite of major SMAD assistance, the KPD's membership lagged behind that of the SPD even in the Soviet Zone and East Berlin. Just before the merger, the SPD had about 681,000 members and the KPD 600,000 in the SZ and East Berlin (Weber, 1985a, 131). In the West, support for the KPD was extremely low. As measured by the votes of the 1949 FRG election, the KPD had only about one-fifth the strength of the SPD. The 1949 FRG election results were: SPD: 29.2%; KPD 5.7%; CDU/CSU: 31.0%. The KPD underwent a further decline and received only 2.2% of the popular vote in the next FRG election (1953) (Pollock et al., 1955, 181). The appeals of communism also turned out to be quite limited in the postwar election results in other countries. In the November 1945 elections, for example, the communists received less than 18% of the popular vote in Hungary and less than 6% in Austria (Guestrow, 1983, 284).

Clearly, the Communist Party was not likely to triumph in free and fair elections, not even in areas under Soviet control. Not surprisingly, Soviet policy now changed in favor of the merger of KPD and SPD—at which point the merger became mandatory. As late as July 19, 1945, KPD chairman Pieck had declared that "the time to create this united party has not yet come because there must first be a great spiritual revolution in the working class in order to create a firm foundation for this united party" (Schneider, 1978, 15). Before the year was out, "the great spiritual revolution" had taken place, and "the firm foundation" had been established. The prospect of electoral defeats, it seems, can powerfully accelerate historical developments.

In the latter part of 1945, SMAD began to promote the fusion of KPD and SPD, preferably for all of Germany. The KPD leaders Ulbricht and Pieck invited the SPD leadership to a conference in December 1945 and proposed a merger of the two parties "from the bottom up." The Central Committee of the SPD disagreed with this procedure, arguing that the development of separate, nationwide parties should come first and that any fusion decisions should be made by the national (all-German) conferences of each party. The joint statement issued after the December meeting was silent on procedure and spoke only of a "common will" to develop unity.

Deception was an important part of the merger process. The leaders of the Communist Party went to great lengths to persuade the social democrats that they had a genuine commitment to democracy, liberty, and constitutionality. Anton Ackermann (member of the Ulbricht group and chief ideologue of the KPD) declared:

> Our demand for the creation of an antifascist, democratic republic, which will grant to the people full rights and freedom, is no tricky tactic, no diplomatic maneuver, no camouflage. (Krisch, 1974, 84)

In 1946, Walter Ulbricht solemnly assured the SPD of equal rights and the adoption of non-Soviet ideological positions. By 1948, when Ulbricht could afford to be frank, he wrote that fusion had never been intended to hew to a "middle line" and that the ideological foundation of the new (unified) party was never planned to be anything else than the teachings of "Marx, Engels, Lenin, and Stalin" (Riedel, 1973, 17). The last two names, of course, provide the key to the nature of the merger and the hoax that was being perpetrated on those SPD members who trusted KPD assurances.

SPD Merger Policies: From Advocacy to Resistance

In the meantime, the first local elections in the American Zone of Germany (January 1946) had taken place: the Communist Party received only 3.5% of the popular vote. This confirmed the other indications of communist weakness and added urgency to the SMAD/KPD campaign for a unity party. State elections were scheduled to take place in the Soviet Zone in the latter part of 1946. Something clearly needed to be done if the Communist Party was to gain control of the state apparatus via the ballot box. The methods adopted to persuade the, by now, largely reluctant SPD members ranged from social pressure to outright force, including the arrest of uncooperative SPD leaders. It has been estimated that from December 1945 to April 1946 at least 20,000 social democrats were arrested, many imprisoned (even for lengthy periods), and some even executed (Fricke, 1984, 34). The joint KPD-SPD "unity meetings" at the local level were manipulated and dominated by the KPD. At KPD caucuses before these meetings, roles were allocated and strategies worked out to control the joint gatherings, while preserving the appearance of free discussion and voluntarism. Even so, coercion often was blatant and obvious, such as when uniformed Soviet control officers took down the names of naysayers (Prauss, 1960, 24–25).

Many social democrats still resisted. On January 15, 1946, the SPD Central Committee (Berlin) once again voted to oppose the merger and instructed the regional and local units of the party not to agree to mergers at their levels. The publication of this directive was banned by SMAD. Soviet Zone SPD leaders, especially Grotewohl (who at numerous times had spoken out against the merger), were pressured and threatened at SMAD headquarters. In view of these developments, Schumacher asked for the dissolution of the SPD in the Soviet Zone so as to prevent the collective (and largely involuntary) incorporation of SPD members into the new communist-dominated party. Grotewohl refused. On February 11, 1946, the Soviet-Zone SPD Central Committee (by a bare majority) voted in favor of a merger with the KPD. Some of the SPD members who favored the merger were encouraged in this position by the numerical superiority of the SPD. They assumed that the influence of the former SPD and KPD in the SED would be a function of the size of the membership that each party brought into the new organization. They were mistaken.

Schumacher was able to block the forced merger in the Western Sectors of Berlin. Together with members of the Berlin SPD leadership, he organized a referendum on the merger. SMAD prevented the referendum from taking place in the Soviet Sector. In the Western Sectors the SPD members voted 20,000 to 3,000 against the merger. West Berlin as well as West Germany, thus, retained a separate and independent Social Democratic Party.

The Merger and Its Aftermath

In the Soviet Zone and East Berlin, the new party—the Socialist Unity Party (*Sozialistische Einheitspartei Deutschlands*: SED)—was formally founded at the "Unity Party Congress" of April 21–22, 1946. The founding of the SED was an important step in the division of postwar Germany. After April 1946, SMAD recognized the SED as the only legitimate socialist party—which, in effect, outlawed the SPD in the East. The SED, in turn, could not operate in the Western Zones, where SPD and the KPD continued as separate parties. GDR accounts, of course, denied that pressure had been used and that SMAD had anything to do with the merger, reporting: "In contrast to the Western powers, the Soviet Union respected the German people's right of self-determination and . . . denied [itself] any interference in the internal affairs of the two parties in question, or in the process of unification" (Thomas, 1966, 242).

At the time of the merger, the SED consisted about equally of former SPD and KPD members. Party positions, as promised, were assigned on the basis of parity, with the most important party offices being assigned to two persons—one from each party. In a short time, however, parity and duality—while remaining the official principles—were discarded in practice. Former KPD members were placed into the majority of positions and into nearly all of the key positions of the new party. By the second half of 1948, practically all former social democrats had been removed from leadership functions. Many of the former SPD members were expelled: An estimated 200,000 former SPD members were purged from the SED in the years 1948–50" (Bouvier, 1996; Teresiak, 1994). "More than 5,000 landed in GDR prisons or Soviet labor camps, and at least 400 died while incarcerated" (Turner, 1987, 105). Parity was formally abandoned at the First Party Conference in January 1949 (Leonhard, 1981, 473). The IIIrd SED Congress (1950) elected fifteen full members and candidate members to the Politburo. Twelve were former members of the KPD; only three had been members of the SPD.

By April 1946, the Soviet Zone had a single working-class party, with the supposed ability (supposed by SMAD and SED) to win popular majorities in fair elections. Though already having more members than all other SZ parties combined, the SED actively recruited new members to broaden its base. (At the end of the mass-party recruitment phase [June 1948], the SED had a membership of about 2 million. Reflecting changes in party policy, this figure dropped to about 1.2 million [minus 40%] in 1951. In 1953 policy changed again, and membership was permitted to rise. In the 1980s, SED membership was about 2.2 million [Bundesministerium für innerdeutsche Beziehungen, 1985, 1185]).

In preparation for the SZ *state* elections of 1946, the SED tried to gain the support of the broadest range of voters, appealing not only to the working class but also to Christians (stressing common elements in Marxism and Christianity), to refugees from the eastern provinces (emphasizing that the final status of these regions had not yet been determined),[7] and even to lower-echelon former national-socialists (promising fair treatment). The SED was by far better organized than the two middle-class parties against which it competed, and it alone enjoyed SMAD support and assistance.

> During the election campaign itself, numerous posters and broadsheets of the CDU and LDPD were outlawed by the local SMAD; approval for other posters and broadsheets was delayed so long that their effective use was destroyed. . . . as a result of the Soviet censure, the non-communist parties were unable to present their arguments effectively in the election campaign. Permission to hold a large number of proposed gatherings was either not granted or otherwise continually deferred. The SMA also blocked certain party speakers or demanded that the speech be officially approved before being delivered. Non-communist speakers were frequently harassed following election speeches. (Schneider, 1978, 21)

The two middle-class parties were not even permitted to publicly recruit new members (Kuppe, 1985b, 209).

In spite of all this, the election results of October 20, 1946, gravely disappointed communist expectations.[8] The SED received only 47.5% of the total votes, versus a combined 49.1% for the CDU and LDPD. The SED was unable to obtain a majority of the votes in even one of the five states of the SZ, its share ranging from 43.9% to 49.5% (*Statistisches Jahrbuch der DDR*, 1955, 87). Indeed, the SED could not even win popular majorities in areas of greatest working-class strength, that is, in the urban centers of Leipzig, Dresden, Halle, Erfurt, Jena, Weimar, and Zwickau. Accepting the popular will was not part of the communist repertory.[9] SMAD had interfered before the elections, and it did so again afterward. In the states of Brandenburg and Saxony, CDU and LDPD together obtained a majority of the legislative seats and, thus, were entitled by law to form the government. SMAD intervened by refusing to approve any ministers who were not communists or communist sympathizers (Wolfe, 1971, 465–466).

There was more bad electoral news for SMAD and the East German communists. Elections also had been held in all four Sectors of Berlin, where, on the insistence of the Western Powers, the SPD was permitted to compete in all parts of the city. The popular vote for *all of Berlin* was: SPD (48.7%), CDU (22.2%), SED (19.8%), LDPD (9.3%). Even in the traditional "Red" District of Wedding (where in 1932 the KPD received 60% of the votes), the SED could gain no more than 29% of the popular vote. Furthermore, the results in the *Soviet Sector* of Berlin clearly contradicted the communist claim that the great majority of SPD members had supported the KPD–SPD merger: SPD (43.6%), SED (29.8%), CDU (18.7%), and LDPD (7.9%) (Childs, 1983, 19). It was transparent now that, even after the coerced fusion of KPD and SPD, the road to a communist Germany would not be traversed via competitive parties and free elections—of which, thus, there would be no more in the Soviet Zone or (later) in the GDR.

The National Front

SMAD's *first* postelection step to secure communist dominance in the Soviet Zone was to cancel the next scheduled elections. Local elections had been planned for the fall of 1948; state and district elections for 1949. The *second* step was the creation of a single electoral list, including all political parties[10] as well as the major mass organizations. This was the *National Front* (NF). Organizationally, it developed out of the Secretariat of the German People's Council, which reconstituted itself as the Secretariat of the National Front. Politically, the National Front grew out of the "Antifascist Bloc," the preliminary instrument of communist bloc politics, founded on June 14, 1945. The Antifascist Bloc was set up on the "recommendation" of the KPD, expressed in Ulbricht's speech of June 12, 1945 (Ulbricht, 1961, 11–15). It was presented as a temporary institutional framework for the cooperation of the new political parties, until such time as elections could be held. It did not disappear, of course, after the first elections. "After state parliaments were elected and began to function in 1947, the Antifa [Antifascist Bloc] Committees took no back seat, but instead predetermined what issues the parliaments would consider and how they would vote" (Bolling, 1950, 391).

Bloc politics and single-list techniques were not a new invention. In the SZ/GDR, as elsewhere, communists eagerly took advantage of coalitions and united-front structures to camouflage who was in control. The GDR term was *Buendnispolitik* (alliance politics). The rulers of East Germany seemed to be under the impression that their citizens regarded it as an instrument of true democracy—a major failure of political intelligence. *Buendnispolitik* was advertised as having its foundation in orthodox Marxism-Leninism and, very importantly, as being a major achievement of advanced socialist democracy (Buske et al., 1981, 10–18). It was said to make indispensable contributions to the fight against imperialism and for world peace (Akademie für Gesellschaftswissenschaften beim ZK der SED, 1981, 6). It also was said to bring together all strata of the population, resting on the identity of the interests and goals of all groups in society (Wassmund, 1981, 332). Any criticism of *Buendnispolitik* was interpreted as an attempt to defame the GDR (Huemmler, 1983, 1989).

Reflecting SMAD's strategy of *Buendnispolitik*, all governmental units of the SZ/GDR—local, regional, state, national—were administered by coalitions, first by way of the Antifascist Bloc, then by way of the National Front. Communists, however, always occupied the key positions. For example, of the roughly 13,000 new mayors appointed in the SZ in 1945, about 8,000 were communists or communist sympathizers.

Organizational devices were supplemented by insistent appeals to patriotism and social harmony. From the moment that new political parties were licensed in the SZ, the KPD insisted that there be no partisan strife and demanded the creation of a bloc of antifascist parties to prevent interparty discord (Ulbricht, June 12, 1945, as quoted in Krisch, 1974, 60). The theme was repeated by Grotewohl, when he wrote in his commentary on the first GDR Constitution that there must be no "irresponsible opposition"[11] in the parliament of the new German democracy (Fricke, 1974, 950). *All* parties, the Soviets insisted, must participate in the government. Free competition among democratic political parties and a free interplay between (circulation of) government and opposition were not what SMAD and KPD/SED had in mind.

The National Front was the ultimate form of the *Buendnis*. According to official East German sources, it was a popular socialist movement that

> unites all parties and mass organizations, all popular forces—whether they are politically organized or not, whether they are affiliated with any party or not—for active cooperation in the construction of an advanced socialist society in the GDR. . . . [It] shares prominently in bringing classes and sections together on the basis of working-class ideals. . . . [It] engages in political and ideological work, encouraging a wide range of activity in the economic and cultural spheres. . . . Some 17,000 National Front committees are active on county, urban district, village and neighborhood levels. These unpaid committees are elected by the public and have more than 335,000 members. . . . The National Front committees are concerned, among other things, with drawing the greatest possible number of people into discussing, carrying out and monitoring decisions taken by administrative departments, both on a local and national level. . . . The National Front is the organizing force behind elections to parliament and local authorities. (Panorama-DDR, 1976, 68–69)

The National Front was formally founded on February 15, 1950 (Matern, 1959, 29; Timmermann, 1985, 313). The mass organizations of the GDR quickly let it be known that they were eager to join. This was no surprise, since the key offices of these mass organizations were occupied by SED members, who were subject to party directives.[12] The leaders of the other parties (then, CDU and LDPD) were not quite as eager, but they had no choice. CDU and LDPD were pressured to support not only SED organizational devices but also SED policies, such as opposition to the Marshall Plan. Leaders who resisted were deposed by SMAD and replaced with more pliable individuals. Many CDU (e.g., Jacob Kaiser and Ernst Lemmer) and LDPD leaders (e.g., Leonhard Moog and Hermann Kastner) ultimately made their way to the West, some of them building new political careers in the FRG (Fricke, 1974, 950–953). For some autobiographical accounts, see Bloch, 1986; Gradl, 1981; Lemmer, 1968. SED leaders later would boast that in 1949–1950 they transformed CDU and LDPD from semi-independent middle-class parties into organizations that "recognized the leadership of the working class and its party" (Agsten et al., 1985; Hanhardt, 1968, 47). The key offices of the National Front, of course, always were held by SED members.

The National Front had no counterpart in the West. It was a mechanism for the simultaneous enforcement and camouflage of a communist one-party dictatorship. It was designed to control all political parties and social organizations, and to mobilize all segments of the population. By way of the National Front's unity list of candidates, the SED was able to determine (before any votes had been cast) how many parliamentary seats would be obtained by each party and mass organization. Still, they hoped that the democratic veneer of the National Front would garner some legitimacy for an undemocratic, communist regime.[13]

During the last years of the GDR, the unity list included five parties and five mass organizations. The figures in parentheses are the (predetermined) number of seats assigned (prior to the election) to each party and organization in the People's Chamber (*Volkskammer*), the national parliament, for the 1986 elections.

Parties: SED (127), DBD (52) CDU (52), LDPD (52), NDPD (52).

Mass organizations: FDGB (61), FDJ (37), DFD (32), KB (21), VDGB (14).

The VDGB (Peasants Mutual Aid Association) was included in the joint list of the National Front for the first time in 1986.[14] From 1963 to 1986, however, there had been no changes in the total number of seats awarded to the parties and mass organizations. The 1986 change affected only the mass organizations. For the political parties, thus, the "election results" were exactly the same for more than twenty-five years. Not only were the GDR election results predetermined in respect to the number of seats to be "won" by the parties and mass organizations, but they also were manipulated in terms of demographic strata. Age, gender, and employment groups, for example, were represented across time and within the different legislative bodies always in very similar proportions to those of the population.

Nonsecret, Compulsory, and Collective Voting

The creation of the unity list of the National Front was not yet enough, as it turned out, to secure the desired "overwhelming support" for the regime. The first elections under National Front auspices (for the third People's Congress in May 1949) gave only 61% of the popular vote to the unity list—that in the complete absence of any ballot alternatives: a box to be marked for the United Front was the only choice that appeared on the ballots.

A *third* step became necessary for SMAD and SED. Voting procedures were changed to "open balloting." From now on, the voter would obtain the ballot and deposit it, unmarked or marked openly, into the ballot box. Unmarked ballots were treated as valid and counted as votes for the unity list. Thus, a voter who supported the unity list had no need to mark the ballot or to use a voting booth. Knowing full well that observers recorded the name of anyone who used a voting booth, the vast majority of voters did the predictable. Voting booths remained a feature in all GDR elections, but their presence at the polling places was purely symbolic. Few dared to use them; the intimidation worked. The referendum for the second GDR Constitution, for example, was conducted by these rules. It was made clear to the voters that the authorities would view the use of the voting booth as casting a *no* vote and that casting a *no* vote would be regarded as a subversive act. The results: participation was 98.1%; 99.8% of the ballots were counted as valid; and 94.5% of the valid ballots were *yes* votes (*Neues Deutschland*, April 9, 1968, p. 1).

The regime, lacking all shame, continued to proclaim stridently that the GDR elections were secret, free, and democratic. In this, as in so many other prevarications, the GDR followed Soviet examples. Commenting on Soviet elections, Wolfe (1961, 177) wrote:

> But one wonders what the authorities meant when they said that the vote was "secret." Since there was only one candidate, it was no secret if you voted for him. To vote against him, the voter had to go openly to a special booth where pencils were provided, and had to cross out the only name. He was not allowed to insert another. The only thing secret about it was how many people actually went through this brave, defiant, mortally dangerous and—so far as direct results are concerned—futile gesture.

There did, however, remain significant concerns about the participation rates. Citizens opposed to the system could try to express this opposition by not casting a ballot at all.

Thus, a *fourth* step was taken to secure (at least the appearance of) the unanimous popular support, craved by communist regimes: compulsory participation. A variety of organizational devices and social pressures were brought to bear on the citizens of the GDR, which, then, for all practical purposes, made electoral participation mandatory.[15] They included visits by neighbors and colleagues to "encourage" participation (the well-known "agitators"), keeping official records of persons' participation, and having all the employees of a firm marching together to the polls and collectively casting their (unmarked) ballots. Not casting an unmarked ballot amounted to a public declaration of opposition, the consequences of which were known only too well. Not surprisingly, participation rates and votes for the unity list became very high, generally ranging from 95% to 99%.

In addition to these manipulations, the regime resorted to outright falsifications of election results. This had frequently been suspected but could not be proven until after the demise of the GDR (Gedmin, 1992, 63; Merkl, 1993, 110–111). Erich Honecker, however, had the nerve to declare in a 1990 interview that (1) it was entirely new to him (and probably not true) that there had been manipulations and falsifications of election results in the GDR, and that (2) it was a false and foul rumor that nonvoters had to suffer any civic disadvantages (Andert & Herzberg, 1990, 83–85). Egon Krenz, Honecker's short-lived successor, who had been in charge of producing the desired results for the May 1989 elections denied, of course, that the election had been anything but the free expression of the popular will.

In an apparent recognition and remarkable admission of how meaningless East German voting data had become, the *Statistical Yearbook of the GDR* stopped reporting them after 1958. The last *Yearbook* report showed that *99.90%* of the eligible citizens participated in the People's Chamber election of November 16, 1958, *99.88%* of the votes were valid, and *99.87%* were cast for the unity list of the National Front. Subsequent election results (reported in the daily press) were equally grandiose. The figures for the People's Chamber election of July 2, 1967, for example, showed *98.82%* participation, *99.98%* valid ballots, and *99.93%* of the votes cast for the unity list. The last elections under the communist regime—the members of the county and municipal assemblies (boards of supervisors)—were held on May 7, 1989. The results of the *county* elections were as follows:

Participation	98.78%
Valid votes	99.91%
Unity List (National Front)	98.85%

These were the results of the *municipal* elections:

Participation	98.75%
Valid votes	99.92%
Unity List (National Front)	98.66%

Some counties achieved even more spectacular results: *Suhl* produced a participation rate of 99.48%, and *Rostock* gave 99.50% of its votes to the Unity List. Some of the municipalities did even better: *Erfurt* had a participation rate of 99.60%, and *Magdeburg, Neubrandenburg,* and *Suhl* voted for the Unity List at 99.97% (*Neues Deutschland*, May 10, 1989, pp. 3–4). As in all GDR elections, not yet satisfied with the overwhelming rates of participation and Unity List approvals generated by intimidation and "open balloting," the SED manipulated the outcome to further increase the percentages.

With customary brazenness and effrontery, the *Neues Deutschland* of May 8, 1989 (p. 3) commented that the election results showed that "the people of the GDR are determined to continue to stride with success on the road toward the developed socialist society and to strengthen the socialist fatherland," that the people are looking back at the forty years of the GDR's existence "with joy and pride, because in the GDR the work of the people benefits the people," and that there exists "a relationship of solid confidence and close unity between party and people." The *Neues Deutschland* also discerned that election results were "a further step toward the further perfection (*Vervollkommnung*) of our democracy." Egon Krenz,[16] who had fathered the actual election results, decided nevertheless that they were "an impressive declaration of support for the politics of peace and socialism of the Party of the Working Class and the Worker-and-Farmer-State." As chair of the Election Commission, Krenz also certified that the elections "were conducted properly and lawfully" (*Neues Deutschland*, May 10, 1989, p. 1).

The first free elections in the GDR (March 18, 1990) produced a rather different outcome:

Participation	93.38%
Valid votes	99.45%
PDS (formerly SED)	16.40%
SPD	21.88%
CDU & associated parties	48.05%
Liberals (FDP)	5.28%
Greens	1.97%
all others	6.42%

While high participation habits persisted (aided by a new interest in the now-meaningful politics), the crucial result is found in the PDS (*Partei des Demokratischen Sozialismus*) percentage. Only about one-sixth of the East German voters opted for communism in a free election. If this figure still seems high, it should be remembered that a substantial number of individuals benefited from the regime, including most of those in medium and high party and government positions—as well as those who had been the hangers-on of the leadership. In the Baltic Sea spa of Bansin, for example, the votes for the PDS were extraordinarily high (about one-third of the popular vote). I conducted some interviews with local officials, who explained to me that Bansin had been a resort heavily frequented by the GDR leadership. A substantial proportion of the population had benefited from this arrangement, for example, by having goods available to them that could not be obtained most other places. High-level tourist trade fell off after reunification. The former beneficiaries expressed their gratitude for the crumbs from the regime's table via votes for the PDS.

It is difficult to estimate the number of regime functionaries and various direct and indirect beneficiaries. It is interesting to note, however, that in 1990 the number of PDS voters (1,892,329) corresponded roughly to the number of SED members (about 2 million). In any case, the election results, like many other indicators (e.g., the difficult and risky flight of GDR citizens to the FRG), gave dramatic testimony to the chronic lack of legitimacy of the SED regime and the lack of citizen support for the GDR system.

THE STALINIST TRANSFORMATIONS

The Party of a "New Type"

By the beginning of 1948, the SED gave up on the attempt to present itself as a democratic mass party. With a broad range of control mechanisms in place and protection by the Red Army assured, the regime's Stalinist designs could now be brought out into the open. Contrary to earlier assurances, the Soviet model was to be the blueprint, after all, for East German political, social, and economic developments. The SED was not exempted. At the Second Party Congress (September 1947), Ulbricht had spoken of the SED becoming "a party of a new type." It now became clear what this meant: a party modeled on the CPSU, Leninist in organization and Stalinist in conduct.

In the period from June to September 1948, the party leadership decided on a series of transformations—without membership consultation or sanction. The SED became a disciplined and efficient ruling mechanism: operating on the principle of "democratic centralism," capable of controlling state and society, and ready to execute Moscow's orders. Unquestioning acceptance of the Leninist-Stalinist orthodoxies of the day and strict obedience to Moscow became the defining characteristics of successful East German leaders. Stalinist paranoia soon suffused all levels of state and society. As in the Soviet Union, Stalinist paranoia did not even exempt communist comrades. In 1949, for example, the Soviet Military Government decreed that those Germans, *including communists*, who, during the Hitler years, had been in exile in Western countries were to be removed from all positions of responsibility in East Germany.

Many of the Party members who had joined the SED during the "mass party" phase now were purged. Membership declined by about 40%. New members were accepted only after long periods of candidacy and upon demonstration of unquestioning loyalty.[17] In a fairly short time, the SED transformed itself from a mass party into a cadre party of the Soviet type, organized strictly from the top down. In socialist usage, a *cadre party* is an organization whose members are neither passive nor opportunistic but are dedicated political activists, fully accepting the principle of democratic centralism, faithfully executing all Party directives, maintaining strict Party discipline, striving to strengthen the tie between Party and masses, convincing the masses of the rightness of Party policy, supporting the alliance with the USSR, and never letting up in the struggle against imperialism. Party members have a high degree of political consciousness and ideological purity.

They participate faithfully in all Party activities and work unceasingly to increase labor productivity. Their private lives are an example to all citizens. They willingly accept Party control of their lives (Schultz, 1956).

The Party Congresses (meeting every four years since 1950 and every five years since 1971), Party Conferences, and all other such spectacles became mere acclamation events, serving to demonstrate the (supposedly) unanimous membership support for whatever policies had been adopted by the Secretariat and the Politburo of the Central Committee of the SED. The resolutions of the Politburo and the Secretariat invariably were accepted without any type of real debate and without any sort of criticism. To the very end, this was the guiding principle, memorialized even in a SED song: "The Party Is Always Right."

The End of the "German Road"

The changes also included the invalidation of the principle of the "German road to socialism." Once it became clear to the SED and its SMAD masters that the Western Zones were immune to the appeals of communism and that even in the Soviet Zone communism would prevail only by force, all prior USSR declarations about German unity and self-determination quickly were discarded. In September 1948, Anton Ackermann, who appears to have been genuinely supportive of the "German road," was forced to recant and engage in "self-criticism."

Ulbricht's and Pieck's support for the "German road" appears always to have been purely tactical, useful in the immediate postwar years when the close ties to Moscow were to be concealed. Contrary to previous pronouncements, the theoretical journal of the CPSU, *Bolshevik*, now proclaimed:

> The assertion that every country advances towards Socialism along its own specific path cannot be recognized as correct, as well as the contention that there are as many roads in this direction as there are countries. . . . The general laws of transition from capitalism to Socialism, discovered by Marx and Engels, and tested, put to concrete use and developed by Lenin and Stalin on the basis of the experience of the Bolshevik Party and the Soviet State, are binding upon all countries. (as quoted in Friedrich & Brzezinski, 1956, 79)

The Party System: Monopoly and Subservience

The SED claimed for itself an absolute monopoly of leadership and rule regarding all aspects of society and state. The leadership claim of the GDR's Communist Party even made its way into the second (1968) Constitution of the country. Article 1 reads (in part): "The German Democratic Republic is a socialist state of German nation [*sic*]. It is the political organization of the working people in town and countryside who are jointly implementing socialism under the leadership of the working class and its Marxist-Leninist Party" (*Verfassung der Deutschen Demokratischen Republik*, 1968). This language also became part of the 1974 version (*Verfassung der Deutschen Demokratischen Republik*, 1974, Art. 1). All other parties, organizations, and institutions (including state organs, such as the judiciary) were reduced to transmission belts of communist policy.

This particular command structure of GDR politics was not publicly acknowledged, of course. Reporting that nonsocialist parties and organizations such as the CDU, LDPD, NDPD, and DBD (German Farmers Association) had voluntarily changed their policy positions to that of the SED, a Party publication asserted that this change took place because these bodies "had convinced themselves that the working class and its Party, the SED, showed the most forceful and consistent commitment to peace and German unity" (Akademie für Gesellschaftswissenschaften beim ZK der SED, 1981, 69). Indeed, some GDR authors have been sufficiently brazen to deny the dominance of the SED altogether (Autorenkollektiv, 1985b, 153–156).

The depth of subservience of the minor parties was extraordinary. Manfred Gerlach (1984, 200–201), chairman of the LDPD, the "middle-class" party of East Germany, had this to say:

> And we can be certain that our specific contribution to social progress, our active cooperation in the National Front on the further path of socialism and communism are more than ever in demand, both materially and in spirit.

Gerlach also announced that cooperation with the SED had produced "true freedom." Gerald Goetting (1984, 322–326), chairman of the CDU, the "Christian" party of East Germany, was no less obsequious: The GDR

> is the reality that progressive and peace-loving Christians . . . longed for and strove for since time immemorial. . . . The educational and persuasive work of the CDU . . . has helped countless . . . Christians to recognize the humanistic character of the socialist system and to become engaged in society for the policy of our state. . . . We Christian Democrats are doing what we can to help with continued success to carry out the policy designated by the Ninth Party Congress of the SED.

In Heidenheimer's words (1961, 164), the GDR had become a "camouflaged one-party state."

In 1950, the SED held only 25% of the seats in the People's Chamber *directly* but, by way of the mass organizations, actually controlled 70%. The CDU and LDPD each was assigned 15% of the seats. In 1986 the distributions were similar, except that the representation of CDU and LDPD *combined* had been reduced to 20.8% (*Statistisches Jahrbuch der DDR*, 1987, 393). The actual distribution of seats, however, mattered little in a body proceeding by acclamation rather than debate and producing unanimous rather than majority votes. When the People's Chamber set about to approve legislation that had originated with the SED (and there was little else), *all* members could be counted on to cast their votes correctly.[18] It is of some interest to note that there seems to have been only one exception to unanimity in four decades of People's Chamber voting: on March 9, 1972, fourteen CDU delegates voted in opposition to a bill liberalizing abortions, and eight CDU delegates abstained. It is quite certain, however, that the casting of a few antiabortion votes had received prior SED consent. In any case, there were no dissenting votes *ever* in matters of real political significance and support for unlimited SED rule.

Leninism-Stalinism in Party and State

Not only had East Germany become a one-party state, but it had become a *Leninist-Stalinist* one-party state. All decision-making power was concentrated in the top leadership of the SED, particularly in the persons of Walter Ulbricht and (later) Erich Honecker.[19] The lower echelons of the SED had little influence on policy making, as did the other parties and the mass organizations. According to the *formal* organizational structure of the SED, the Party Congress (elected by the membership and meeting every five years) was the highest Party authority. It adopted the Party Program and statutes and elected the Central Committee. The Central Committee (meeting every six months) implemented the decisions of the Party Congress; it also elected the Party Secretariat (including the general secretary) and the Politburo. The Secretariat directed the implementation of Party policy; it also dealt with personnel matters. The Politburo gave political direction to the work of the Central Committee and Secretariat.

Democratic form, however, was not the same as democratic practice. Party elections were a mere ritual. Party leaders neither gained nor retained office by the will of the general membership. Party offices were acquired through co-optation. The leadership was, in effect, self-perpetuating. Party offices and policies were controlled entirely from above. The lower echelons could not affect the higher ones, but the decisions of the higher echelons were entirely binding on those below—the well-known principles of *Party discipline* and *democratic centralism*. Democratic centralism, of course, was only partially operational: there was plenty of *centralism*, but there was no *democracy*. As far as the regime was concerned, there could be no legitimate disagreement with SED policies, whether it might arise from within or from outside the Party.

Subordination of Party and State to Moscow

The Stalinization of the SED also entailed the full subordination of the Party to Moscow. The 1976 statutes of the SED contained this clause: "The [SED] unceasingly deepens the inviolable friendship and fraternal alliance with the Communist Party of the Soviet Union, the vanguard of the communist world movement" (McCardle & Boenau, 1984, 87). The subordination of the SED to the CPSU found its parallel in the subordination of the GDR to the USSR. The Soviets secured the domination of the GDR (and of the other satellites) not only by way of Moscow-loyal native communists but also through their own agents:

> The Russians, declining to rely solely on the doctrinal loyalty of their East-European comrades, moved swiftly to establish more reliable controls over the satellites by infiltrating Russian agents directly into their police and military organizations. With all the lines of influence at the Russians' disposal it was easy in most cases for them to shake up any satellite leadership which was too independent-minded, and assure an unquestioning response to Moscow's demands. (Daniels, 1962, liii)

No attacks on the Polish and Czechoslovakian advocates of "humanitarian socialism" and on the leaders of the Hungarian and Chinese uprisings were more vituperative than those in the official GDR press. At the same time and almost to the very end of the GDR, no country was more slavish in support of Soviet goals and policies than the GDR leadership,[20] even when such support was clearly contrary to East German interests (Croan & Friedrich, 1958, 44–46). The reasons are not difficult to discern. The rule of the SED rested on Soviet bayonets, a fact that even Ulbricht confessed: "In East Germany . . . the peaceful, democratic road was taken, but only because of the conditions of the protection of this peaceful road by Soviet troops" (Croan & Friedrich, 1958, 61). When, in 1989, Soviet tanks became unavailable to protect the regime, it collapsed.

The key phases of GDR history toward the complete subordination to Moscow can be identified as follows: *1945–1949*: an initial antifascist democratic resurgence and reforms, then the forceful establishment of Soviet-style socialism. *1950–1961*: general transition from capitalism to socialism; the final integration of GDR into the Eastern Bloc and Stalinization of the GDR; collectivization of agriculture; and emphasis on the protection of the state borders. *1963–1970*: (following VI Party Congress in 1963): the comprehensive construction of socialism; the New Economic System (NES) experiment; victory of the socialist conditions of production; and the beginnings of "developed socialism." *1971–1980s*: (following the VIII Party Congress in 1971): formation of the developed socialist society; worldwide recognition of GDR; increased rivalry with FRG and adoption of the policy of *Abgrenzung* (demarcation, delimitation); transition from Ulbricht to Honecker (at least in part because of Ulbricht's growing independence); emphasis on ideological indoctrination; and finally total subordination to the USSR in all matters (Krisch, 1985, 10–22; Page, 1985, 51–55; Wassmund, 1981, 323–324).

THE GDR'S LACK OF HISTORICAL AND POLITICAL LEGITIMACY

Neither the citizens of West Germany/FRG nor the citizens of East Germany/GDR freely chose the early postwar policies, the initial constitutional arrangements for their regions, or their first political leaders. Subsequent developments, however, diverged sharply. Genuine support for the FRG developed quickly, broadly, and uncoerced. The various FRG governments soon were freely chosen by popular majorities. Support for the GDR was coerced for most of its citizens; and no GDR citizen ever had a true choice of system, policies, or leadership. Indeed, the East German regime treated as a criminal act the mere voicing of a preference for a system other than "real socialism" and for leaders other than those supplied by the SED. Some Western observers, however, have been unable to see the difference between GDR and FRG politics—even after twenty years of massively divergent development. Jean Smith (1967, 377), for example, produced this piece of foolishness: it is true "that Ulbricht would [not] command a majority in a free election in East Germany, but then neither would any of the parties or personalities in Bonn."

The key developments in GDR history clearly were not in accordance with the wishes of the people of East Germany. Indeed, most of what occurred was transparently contrary to popular preferences. None of the following were freely chosen by the citizens of the GDR; they came about through manipulation, deceit, and coercion:

the founding of the GDR as a separate state,
the imposition of single-party rule,
the abolition of competitive elections,
the construction of a Marxist-Leninist system,
the obligatory adherence to communist ideology,
the abolition of political freedoms and civil rights,
the obsequious subservience to the USSR,
the integration into the communist bloc system,
and the abandonment of German unification.

There were no credible grounds upon which the East German regime ever could claim that it was the true choice of its citizens. Notwithstanding massive internal and external propaganda efforts to persuade its people and the rest of the world of its legitimacy, it remained obvious to all but the most naive observers that the communist regime of the GDR never managed to obtain *historical or political legitimacy*.

Being well aware of its lack of legitimacy and knowing that its continued existence remained dependent on force—ultimately on that of the Soviet Union—the GDR regime waged unrelenting mobilization efforts to persuade GDR citizens to become "active participants" in the political life of the country and thereby, presumably, becoming more loyal citizens. There is no doubt that the various forms of organized political participation, including the *social courts*, were used by the regime not only to obtain unpaid services but also to enhance (at least the appearance of) its legitimacy. The social courts—as will be seen in my forthcoming book *Popular Justice in a Marxist-Leninist Society: The East German Social Courts and Other Aspects of GDR Law*—performed a number of useful and salutary functions; increases in legitimacy and loyalty, however, were not among them.

NOTES

1. Many of the German Communists who fled to the USSR did not survive. Fleeing Hitler, they became the victims of Stalin. See my *Rotten Foundations*, Chapter 6.

2. Thus was one totalitarian dictatorship replaced by another. See Kuehnhardt, 1994.

3. There was much concern within the SPD, however, regarding the correct "ideological basis" for consolidation, that is, social-democratic (Marxist) versus communist (Leninist).

4. For a discussion of the theory of "social fascism," see Hook, 1934.

5. On the cooperation of KPD and NSDAP against the SPD, see Hoyles, 1991, 59–60, 67ff.

6. This was the communist (Stalinist) policy during the 1920s and 1930s not only in Germany but elsewhere. In Italy, it greatly facilitated the rise of Mussolini (Shub, 1958, 400–401).

7. Max Fechner (vice-chairman of the SED, later minister of justice), for example, wrote on September 14, 1946, in *Neues Deutschland*: "The SED will oppose any reduction in German territory. The eastern border is purely provisional" (Behr, 1961, 204–205). On the treatment of refugees in the SZ and the GDR, see Herms and Noack, 1997; Plato and Meinicke, 1991; Ther, 1998; Wille, 1993a, 1993b, 1996, 1999.

8. In the earlier *local* elections (September 1946), CDU and LDPD had not been able to compete in all venues. They were unable to run candidates in many of the rural areas, the bastions of their strengths. In many communities, the SED was the only party on the ballot. Still, the SED received only a bare majority of the (overall) vote even in these elections (Plischke, 1961, 207).

9. For a detailed account of the 1946 elections, see Hajna, 2000.

10. Which thereafter became known as the "block parties" (Lapp, 1988; see also Harder et al., 1986, 1988).

11. Under the principle of the "dialectical unity of opposites," *all* opposition, of course, was irresponsible, unnatural, and reprehensible. See my *Rotten Foundations*, Chapter 5.

12. The citizens of the GDR were under heavy pressure to join mass organizations, and most were members of at least one. In addition to performing (unpaid) civic tasks, the mass organizations had the typical transmission belt functions of indoctrination, mobilization, and control (Schwarze, 1969, 253–259).

13. The last multiparty elections were held in 1946. Beginning in 1950, only the single-list entry of the National Front appeared on the ballot. This was contrary to the GDR Constitution, which provided for a proportional electoral system (Leonhard, 1990, 67), but, as seen earlier, constitutional provisions always gave way when party wishes sought different procedures.

14. In earlier elections the other mass organizations had received the seats assigned to the VDGB in 1986 (Panorama-DDR, 1987, 14; VEB Bibliographisches Institut, 1984, 224).

15. Nonpartipation was risky. Loss of employment and prohibition of working in one's field were likely consequences, as was coming to the attention of the Stasi (Bielke, 1997, 140).

16. Egon Krenz was the chairman of the Election Commission. He also was a member of the Politburo and the Central Committee of the SED, as well as Honecker's deputy. A few months later he would be Honecker's successor as general secretary of the SED and chairman of the Council of State.

17. SED returned to the 2 million-member level by the mid-1970s. A substantial degree of differentiation, however, had developed since the mid-1950s between "high-level activists" and regular party members (Croan & Friedrich, 1958, 55; Scharf, 1984, 44–56).

18. This is not a GDR-specific contrivance. All socialist dictatorships make use of it; for example, in North Korea, the Assembly (parliament) "has never . . . rejected a measure submitted to it by its Presidium, which in turn is subservient to the Korean Workers Party" (Shinn et al., 1969, 208).

19. Not surprisingly, considerable personality cults became attached to these two leaders. See Chapter 6.

20. Foreign Minister Oskar Fischer, for example, wrote: "The foreign policy of the Soviet Union is an excellent example of [correct action]. From it we draw confidence and encouragement. Consequently, we orient ourselves in research and teaching toward Soviet foreign policy, Soviet diplomacy, in order to learn from it for [our] practice" (Fischer, 1984, 39). As late as 1988, discussions of East German cultural developments required the avowal that this progress would have been "completely unthinkable" except for its alliance with Soviet culture and art (Koch, 1988, 162).

Chapter 4

Politics: Party, State, and Citizen

THE STRUCTURE OF SED RULE

Soviet Dominance

As noted previously in several places, the German Democratic Republic was entirely the creation of the Soviet occupying power and its German agents (Naimark, 1995; Nettl, 1951; Peterson, 1999; Phillips, 1986). It remained under Soviet protection until almost the very end. All aspects of East German society were constructed on the Soviet model, not the least of which were total power in the hands of the Party leadership, concentration on heavy industry (versus consumer goods), and the purging of "suspicious elements" from Party and state (Croan, 1976a, 15–37; Wassmund, 1981, 328). The GDR was heavily dependent on the Soviet Union at all times and in all respects: politically, militarily, economically, educationally, ideologically, and in terms of its internal security arrangements (Childs, 1985, xii–xiii; Page, 1985, 51–55; Wassmund, 1981, 321). When, finally, in 1989, the USSR decided that it would not use its troops to defend the GDR regime against the GDR's own citizens, the SED rule collapsed quickly and ignominiously.

Of course, the leaders of the GDR had always known that they could not survive without the protective mantle of the USSR. Even when in the last few years of the GDR, the leadership sought to disassociate itself from the Gorbachevian reforms, no attempt was made to lessen the Soviet presence in the GDR[1] (Childs, 1988; MacGregor, 1989; Staadt, 1995, 13). A curious exception to that rule was the prohibition of the sale of the German edition of the Soviet magazine *Sputnik*.[2] *Sputnik* carried rather positive reports about the workings of glasnost and perestroika and, more importantly, reported about the Hitler-Stalin Pact of 1939. This was information to which a (still rather Stalinist) SED did not want to expose the East German people[3] (Rein, 1990, 121). Honecker, however, contended that *Sputnik* had to be banned because it contained "counter-revolutionary articles"[4] (Staadt, 1995, 135).

Whereas for some forty years it had been GDR dogma that to learn from the Soviet Union was to learn how to be victorious (e.g., Weichelt, 1982a), now, in the words of Honecker, there was to be in East Germany a "socialism in the colors of the GDR" or, in the words of Kurt Hager (1996, 385) (member of the Politbureau and chief ideologist of the GDR), one did not have to change one's wallpaper just because one's neighbor was doing it. What Mikhail Gorbachev thought of having his reforms compared to a change in wallpaper is not known. He was not willing, in any case, to use Soviet troops in defense of the dated and quite dowdy East German wallpaper.

Before these disagreements, however, the USSR had no partner more subservient than the GDR. According to Erich Honecker,[5] friendship with the USSR was the "decisive foundation of our state" and "a vital necessity"[6] (McCauley, 1985, 147–148). One manifestation of this special relationship was that the GDR invariably voted with the USSR in the United Nations.

The Party Is Always Right

Ideologies, secular or religious, typically present themselves as The Truth. Marxism goes this one better, proffering itself as The True Science.[7] The claim is comprehensive.[8] Marxism is the only true philosophy, the only true system of scientific explanation, and the only unfailingly successful guide to action. Naturally, the SED claimed exclusive competence to proclaim the truth in all theoretical questions, to set indisputable guidelines for all spheres of life, and to have its will executed without any constraints. The other political parties (of which there were four) existed in a subordinate position to the SED. "They have no independence and perform subsidiary functions of integrating and educating those that have difficulty in becoming direct and unconditional supporters of the communist regime" (Wassmund, 1981, 333–334). Furthermore, the will of the SED was to be executed not only because it was invariably right but also because it worked in the interest of all citizens. An East German Party song, sung seemingly without embarrassment, contained the words "The Party Is Always Right." (For the complete text see Rodden, 2002, xxix; also Faulenbach et al., 1994.) It appears that the incessant party propaganda led a substantial number of people to believe that that was indeed the case (Wroblewsky, 1990a, 195).

It is a fundamental dogma of communism that there will always be complete agreement between the policies of the Party and the interests of all citizens. The Communist[9] Party simply knows what is best (Deinert, 1983, 52; Richert, 1966, 47). There is no conceivable way to disconfirm this proposition, particularly not when any and all opposition to the Party and its policies is interpreted as machinations of counterrevolutionary or foreign elements—a line of falsification that began in reaction to the 1919 revolt of the Kronstadt sailors, continued with the revolts in East Germany (1953) and Hungary (1956), and most recently could be observed in connection with the 1989 demonstrations in China.

Stalin (1939, 39) wrote: "Without the Party as the main guiding force, a dictatorship of the proletariat to any extent durable and firm is impossible." The SED, of course, agreed:

> All the experience of our era fully confirms Marx's fundamental conclusion that the working class, more than anything else, needs a revolutionary party "to ensure the triumph of the social revolution and of its ultimate goal: the abolition of classes." Only with a party guided by scientific socialism was the working class in the Soviet Union and the other socialist countries able to tackle its world historic mission and carry it out step by step. Only a party which is equal in both theory and practice to the problems of its time, which understands how to make creative use of the universal laws of history and which is linked firmly with the masses can guarantee success in accomplishing the task posed in the period of transition from capitalism to socialism and carrying forward the homogeneous revolutionary process by building advanced socialism. (Sozialistische Einheitspartei Deutschlands, 1983, 38–39)

The masses trust the Party because it has scientifically founded policies, which are in creative conformity with the lawfulness of socialist revolution and socialist construction of society, and which can foresee developing problems and work out solutions for them (Kintzel et al., 1988, 18–19). Of course, by 1988 it had become quite clear to anyone who wanted to see that solutions were precisely what the Party did not have.

The Party is not only *needed* but it is indeed *ready* to undertake its great historical task. Leninist principles of Party organization are essential for this. The most important among them is *democratic centralism*: all Party organs are democratically elected; all those elected must regularly report to those who elected them; all resolutions of higher organs are binding on all lower ones, and there must be strict Party discipline: the minority must submit to the majority decision (Christopher, 1985, 21). Communist practice, of course, has long deleted the democratic component of "democratic centralism." The "democratic elections" were quickly replaced by a system of co-optation, and the "regular reports" became little else but ritualized shams and fervent acclamations. The centralism component, however, flourished. It was the key tool to suppress intraparty dissent and concentrate all power in the highest Party offices.

The actual working principles of SED rule (modeled, of course, on those of the CPSU) were (Wassmund, 1981, 326):

1. Marxism-Leninism is the infallible tool of social analysis and provides the scientific instrument to shape the future;

2. the ideology of Marxism-Leninism is absolutely binding on all Party members;
3. all Party members must act according to leadership directives;
4. the creativity of the Party (leadership) ensures the unity of theory and practice through a permanent process of adaptation;
5. the principle of partiality requires an unconditional siding with the interests of the working class and socialism.

There can be no doubt that, in this view, the Party leadership has an absolutely dominant role in Party, state, economy, and society. The obligation of all others is to obey Party directives without hesitation and without prevarication.[10] There was to be no legal opposition. There even was to be no legal political dissent (Fricke, 1984; Scharf, 1984, 162–167).

Such were the rules from the beginning, but there was yet an ever-increasing stress on the leading role of the SED since the VIIIth Party Congress (1971) and especially since the IXth Party Congress (1976) (Christopher, 1985, 19). In other words, Erich Honecker asserted Party dominance even more strongly than Walter Ulbricht.[11]

The Party is the vanguard of the working class and leading force in the creation of the developed socialist society. Who else but the omnicompetent and omniscient Party of the working class could determine what organization and what policies will lead society and the masses[12] toward its glorious future? As Kintzel et al. (1988, 18–19) wrote:

> The masses have confidence in the party because the party actualizes a scientifically based politics, the party creatively applies the laws of the socialist revolution and of socialist construction, and the party anticipates problems and with great foresight develops the appropriate solutions.

These are standard rationales for the leading role of the working class and its Party: (1) the working class represents numerically the largest part of the population, (2) the workers are the most productive part of the population, and (3) the working class has a historical mission and thus the right and the duty to lead the state in the period of transition to communism (Christopher, 1985, 19). The first justification is false in most cases (Russia 1917, China 1949, etc.); the second one, even if true, is of questionable logic; there is no necessary link between economic productivity and the qualities required for political leadership; and the third justification—the historical mission—has no meaning outside Marxism-Leninism and amounts to no more than blowing bubbles.

Party Organization

The SED was a rigidly hierarchical and strictly disciplined Party. All decision flowed from above. Consultation with the lower ranks was limited and generally undertaken purely for show. The function of the lower levels of the Party was to obey the directive of the general (first) secretary, the Politbureau, and the Central Committee. *Democratic centralism*,[13] the first principle of Party life, was fraudulent in respect to elections, reporting, and decision making. Concerning Party elections, in theory, the lower levels freely elected the members of the higher ones. In practice, no one could be elected to a Party office without approval from above. Most often offices were filled by co-optation. Concerning reports to the electors, there were not real accounts of past work but ritualistic exercises, such as the report of the general secretary to the Party Congress. Concerning policy decisions, in theory, minority submission to the majority position was to occur after full discussion and democratic voting. In practice, there were no genuine discussions, and vote taking was purely pro forma. There was much centralism but little democracy.

Now that the archives have been opened and some of the leading SED functionaries have told their stories, it has become obvious that other major principles of Party life also were pretense—that of *collectivity*, for example. Wassmund (1981, 325) described socialist collectivity as follows: "All leading cadres must consider and decide in the collective the problems confronting the Party, measures to be taken, and the planning of activities." In fact, not even the Politbureau followed this pattern. Typically, the general secretary proposed, and the other members assented.[14]

Only the principle of Party absolutism seems to have been honored in practice as well as in theory. Marxism-Leninism always was taken to be the infallible method of social analysis and was regarded as unequivocally binding on all Party members. All Party members were absolutely obligated to follow leadership directives. The greatest possible offense against the Party was *factionalism*, the transgression of taking a position divergent from that of the leadership.[15] Of course, any kind of real advancement depended on being a member of the Communist Party (SED) (Hiller, 1986, 69).

In 1948, on orders from Moscow, the SED was transformed from a mass to a cadre Party.[16] (At the same time, there was the abandonment of the theory of the "German road to socialism," the total bolshevization of the Party, and its complete subordination to Stalin's orders [Duhnke, 1955; Mayer, 1998; Wassmund, 1981, 328].) Nevertheless, membership remained rather sizable. In the last year of the GDR's existence, the Party had about 2.3 million members and candidates.[17] This was about 13% of the total population and about 19% of the population over the age of eighteen. Party membership tended to fluctuate—fewer members when the Party was concerned with purity and absolute loyalty,[18] more members when the Party sought to demonstrate mass support. Thus, the membership rose from 1.3 million in 1946 to 1.8 million at the end of 1947. In the 1950s and 1960s it varied between 1.4 and 1.7 million, rose again in the 1970s, and reached its highest level of 2.3 million in 1986. The SED also was a workers' Party consisting disproportionately of nonworkers, a matter of considerable embarrassment.[19]

The formal organization of the SED had a dual configuration: territorial and industrial. The basic Party units (*Grundorganizationen* = *GO* and *Abteilungsorganizationen*)[20] had various configurations. Larger ones were organized on a workplace basis. Party members who were employed at enterprises with fewer than three members (of which there were not many in the GDR) were organized at their place of residence.

Each succeeding higher level (up to the national level) of the Party organization corresponded to a geographic-administrative unit of the state. In the late 1980s there were about 59,000 GOs. In addition there were about 4,600 larger GOs, which were in turn divided into 29,000 *Abteilungsorganizationen* (departments). The GOs had many responsibilities, apart from being the basic membership team. They were to encourage higher productivity, greater civic consciousness, and greater ideological awareness.

> The official view is that these basic units secure the party's political-ideological influence . . . in all spheres of social life and for the individual members they are a political home in which the member is firmly rooted and in whose communist atmosphere he feels at home and from which he draws new strength. (Krisch, 1985, 32; quoting from the official program of the SED)

The GOs were organized successively into local, district (Kreis), regional (Bezirk), and national bodies. Especially important political or economic institutions are given territory-equivalent status; for example, the Ministry for State Security was equivalent to a district, the Wismut industrial complex to a region (Krisch, 1985, 32). At the national level could be found the Central Committee (Zentral Commitee [ZK]), the Party Secretariat, and the Politbureau. The head of the Party Secretariat was the general secretary,[21] who also functioned as the chair of the Politbureau and who was the most powerful person in the GDR.[22] In the history of East Germany there were only three general secretaries: Walter Ulbricht (1950–1971), Erich Honecker (1971–1989), and Egon Krenz[23] (October 18, 1989–December 3, 1989).

The highest *formal* authority in the Party structure was the Party Congress. Party Congresses, according to the SED statue of 1946, were to meet annually. In fact, Party Congresses took place every four years (1950–1970) and, later, every five years (1971–1986). The Congresses were rather large bodies. The Xth Congress (1981), for example, consisted of 2,573 voting delegates and 180 advisory delegates. The presidency of the Congress had no fewer than 200 members. Obviously, these are not the numbers associated with useful discussion and real decision making. The true function of the Congresses was to provide a democratic veneer for the Party leadership and to serve as organs of acclamation for the leadership's wisdom.

The Central Committee was elected by the Party Congress and was (formally, again) the highest Party authority between the Congresses. The election, of course, did not deserve the name—the ZK submitted a list of the names of persons to be elected to the ZK, which list was always accepted without discussion and by acclamation. The Central Committee did not, in fact, function as the highest authority between Party Congresses. The real power was in the hands of the Secretariat of the ZK and, even more, of the Politbureau and, especially, in the hands of the person who served as general secretary of the ZK *and* head of the Politbureau.

Over the years, the Central Committee met less and less—only twice a year by the end of the GDR. Apart from the fact that the real power was elsewhere, the Central Committee also was too large to function as a ruling body. In 1986, the ZK had 165 full members and fifty-seven candidates. As with all GDR political bodies, the membership was fairly aged. In 1986, the average age of the full members was sixty-four and of the candidates, fifty-two years (Eppelmann et al., 1996, 717–718). The Central Committee had a staff of about 2,000 persons, who worked in more than forty departments. These departments dealt with all societal and economic issues. Interestingly, in addition to the "normal" departments (including those for international relations and security matters), there was the department for the "devastation of opposition" (Eppelmann et al., 1996, 719).

In the hierarchical structure of the Party, at each geographic level there were equivalent Party committees. Each of these had a first secretary, who constituted the highest Party power at that level. There were 261 district first secretaries, who represented an important tier of policy implementation—they attended closed sessions with high Party leaders to get information and directions. Above these there were sixteen regional first secretaries (fourteen & East Berlin & the Wismut industrial complex). "These sixteen Party leaders were key figures in securing implementation of policies in their area, providing a pool of talent for higher Party positions, and forming the political basis for a given political leadership" (Krisch, 1985, 32–33). In the 1980s, all the regional first secretaries were members of the Central Committee, and two were members of the Politbureau (one full member and one candidate). The first secretaries of districts and regions were an extremely stable set of Party functionaries. Only retirement typically caused them to vacate their offices. This great stability of officeholders could also be observed for most of the time in the Central Committee and the Politbureau. Only at the time of Honecker's takeover was there a significant change in personnel.

Party and State

Party rule was supreme. The Party stood above the state and all other organizations. The state, in fact, became a subsidiary of the Party. The Party had the right and duty to direct the activities of the state and of all other organizations.[24] The will of the Party was actualized via:

1. multiple officeholding in the highest reaches of party, state, and mass organizations, that is, "those who take the decisions in the leading bodies of the party also carry them through as the top functionaries of the principal governmental institutions";
2. the right of the Party "to determine with its cadre policy which posts, at all levels, are held by whom"; and
3. doubling of the apparatus: "the party branch guides and controls the equivalent section of the state apparatus and governmental agencies in the economic, social, and cultural fields (Wassmund, 1981, 326–327).

The last point created a system of permanent consultation and exchange of information between Party and state (though the flow tended to be rather one-directional). With it went much red tape, doubling of work, friction, and tension, but with it also went the guarantee that absolutely nothing could happen without the approval of the Party. Especially important were the GOs in the government ministries offices and the armed forces. They reported to higher Party organs in the ministry, as well as to geographically higher Party organs. Since they supervised the work in the ministries and armed forces, they greatly increased the ability of the Party to maintain control of these state organs. The armed forces GOs worked according to special instructions from the Central Committee via political officers (Krisch, 1985, 31–32).

The Party's control of the state proceeded in two ways, then. First, all important state offices were held by Party members, who, of course, were subject to Party orders and Party discipline. Second, each state agency had a parallel Party branch, whose task was to supervise and direct the state agency. This system of dual control, it should be noted, applied not only to the state but also to all other agencies, political, legal, economic, and societal. The only exception to this control system was the churches, though the SED certainly also sought to bring the churches under its influence (Henkys, 1989; Hoellen, 1989). It should be noted in this context that Party resolutions had the fore of (legal) commands to all organs of state and society, including the courts (Riedel, 1973, 7). The dictatorship of the Party was as comprehensive as it was intensive.

Intra-Party Conflicts

There was no tolerance of dissent from the official line within the SED. Outright opposition was nearly impossible. There were, first of all, the matters of democratic *centralism* and the Marxist-Leninist *ban on factions*. But there also was a willingness among the top leadership to be utterly ruthless in the suppression of dissidence. Actual, but more often merely imagined, opponents of the regime were ferociously destroyed. All internal Party disputes ended brutally in 1948, when the SED was transformed into a Party of the "new type" (Saechsische Landeszentrale, 1999; Jahnke, 1993; Klein et al., 1996). Thereafter, there were periodical *Säuberungen* (cleanups, purges) of the SED. In 1950, for example, the purge included the Politbureau member Paul Merker as well as hundreds of Party members and functionaries. Particularly affected were those SED members who had survived the Hitler years in Western rather than Soviet exile (Leonhard, 1990, 69).

It did not, however, end all policy disputes, particularly when there seemed to be some support for change in the USSR. In 1953 the high-ranking Party members Wilhelm Zaisser and Rudolf Herrnstadt[25] advocated certain changes in opposition to Ulbricht; specifically, they argued in favor of more liberal and flexible Party policies (Schirdewan, 1994; see also Hoffmann, 2003). They were aligned with Beria and Malenkov in the USSR. The fall of Beria[26] and Malenkov also brought down Zaisser and Herrnstadt and strengthened Ulbricht's hold on the Party (Baras, 1975; Wassmund, 1981, 342–343; Weber, 1991, 54–55). Max Fechner, the first minister of justice of the GDR, opposed the criminal persecution of the workers who went on strike in June 1953,[27] whereupon he not only lost his office but also was sentenced to eight years of imprisonment.[28]

There also were echoes of Khruschev's anti-Stalinist campaign in the GDR. They involved such personalities as Karl Schirdewan (1998), Ernst Wollweber, Friedrich Behrens, and Arne Benary.[29] The regime was shaken by the events of 1956 in Hungary, and some voices critical of SED orthodoxy could be heard (Kieslich, 1998). The philosopher and literary critic Wolfgang Harich put forward a democratic program of German socialism that earned him ten years of imprisonment because of "conspirative, counterrevolutionary, and state-hostile" activities (Harich, 1993; also of interest: Brodersen, 1990; Dokumentation, 1990; Janka, 1994; Rodden, 2002, 344–364). Other well-known Marxist intellectuals left the country at that time (Ernst Bloch, Hans Mayer, Alfred Kantorowicz). The strict regimentation of ideas made any attempt at revisionism extremely difficult, but occasionally a brave voice was heard. There was the example of the physicist Robert Havemann.[30] His efforts to construct a more democratic socialism ("Dialectic without Dogma") brought him dismissal from his professorship, a ban from his profession (*Berufsverbot*), an expulsion from the SED, and permanent house arrest (Havemann & Widmann, 2003; Mueller & Florath, 1996; Kolakowski, 1981, 3: 470; Rottleuthner, 1999; Vollnhals, 1998).

THE PARTICIPATORY SYSTEM

Lack of Legitimacy and Regime Insecurity

Regimes, much like individuals, desire most what they do not have, in the case of the GDR: *legitimacy*. As Baylis (1972, 47) has noted:

The anomaly of a putative workers' and peasants' state rule by a narrow elite of functionaries has not been entirely lost even on the GDR leaders, and they have sought to enhance their legitimacy while preserving their own position of dominance. These goals, however, are not fully compatible, and the search for authority in the GDR since 1945 has been a persistently troubled one.

All authoritarian regimes seek popular legitimacy and support (Perlmutter, 1981, 10). In fact, they are obsessed by these concerns. Since genuine legitimacy and support are not likely to be forthcoming from an unfree population, these regimes have discovered other ways: faking it. The main methods to this end are (1) mobilization of the masses and (2) development of their own elites: Party functionaries, top managers and technocrats, the security apparatus, and the top military.[31] The first involves many people but cannot be depended upon for real regime support. The second is quite real (these are the regime beneficiaries) but includes only a small fraction of the population. The regime's task is, thus, to make the counterfeit appear real and to make minority support appear as majority support. Not many people tend to be fooled by such efforts.[32]

As I have argued in my previous book on the GDR—*Rotten Foundations*—and in earlier chapters of this volume, the GDR regime lacked legitimacy because of its origins and its conduct: the Soviet occupiers imposed and preserved communist rule[33]; they also forced the merger of the KPD and SPD. Lack of legitimacy also was the product of the effective ouster of the SPD component in the SED; the transformation of the SED into a Stalinist cadre Party[34]; the imposition of National Front bloc politics on the country; the endless election frauds; the activities of the Stasi (State Security Service); and the imprisonment of the GDR's people by way of the Berlin Wall and the Iron Curtain through the middle of Germany. The obviously false claims advanced in the defense of the official ideology, especially the claims that communism was a science,[35] was freely accepted by the masses (Hahn, 1985; Mueckenberger, 1983) and was the infallible guide to action, as well as the laughable assertion of the unity of theory and practice. There were instead the continuous performance failure of the system (material scarcity as well as political unfreedom) and, finally, the sterility and hypocrisy of GDR life. The utter bankruptcy of communism, in theory as well as in practice, has been obvious to reasonably observant persons at least since the dissolution of the Russian parliament in 1917 and the Kronstadt revolt of 1919. Post–World War II, the same signs could be read in East Germany in 1953, in Hungary in 1956, in Czechoslovakia in 1968, and, finally, in China in 1989 (Tiananmen Square). From the beginning to the end, the GDR was without a foundation in popular will.[36] The system was created and maintained by communist fiat and Soviet force.[37] When the latter became unavailable, the regime fell.

The GDR regime was well aware, of course, of its lack of popular legitimacy and lack of popular support. The revolt of 1953 had demonstrated that not even the workers were fond of the East German "workers' paradise." What kept the SED in power were not the persuasive logic and practical success of communist doctrine but force (particularly in the form of Soviet tanks) and Western aid (noted in Chapter 5). Yet, the GDR leadership felt a deep need for some manifestation of popular approval, to assure themselves and the world of solid popular support—even if it did not exist. "As far as political respectability, legitimacy of the regime, and popular support are concerned, the leadership [was] constantly prey to strong feelings of insecurity, fear, and mistrust" (Wassmund, 1981, 354). Rightly so; the GDR never did reach any democratic legitimacy in the generally accepted sense (Behr, 1985a, 29ff).

The strikes of June 17, 1953, expressed the workers' dissatisfaction with shortages in basic necessities, high work quotas, and the lack of fundamental liberties. It was the most serious challenge to the regime prior to November 1989. It traumatized the regime because it had been the *workers* who had rebelled, not some leftover class enemies. The regime took the lessons of 1953 seriously and made major efforts to quickly improve GDR standards of living—with some success, particularly since the USSR was willing to assist the GDR economically (e.g., lowering the occupation cost, extending credits, and transferring to the GDR almost all of the Soviet enterprises in East Germany) (Croan & Friedrich, 1958, 47; Heidenheimer, 1961, 49). Most importantly, the regime forever after indulged the workers, much to the detriment of economic improvement. (For details, see Chapter 5.)

Not surprisingly, the SED leadership also undertook every possible effort (except allowing the political freedoms that might endanger the SED dictatorship) to bring about regime legitimacy and citizen loyalty—or, at least, the appearance of it. The major weapon was propaganda, first regarding the superior virtues of socialism, later adding the appeals of nationalism. Propaganda and agitation were everywhere, from morning to night, from kindergarten to funeral services. Ubiquity had a predictable consequence: the message was filtered out—much in the same way that repetitive commercials are filtered out in the West, and filtering out becomes ever more prevalent to the degree that the message is known to be dishonest.

The ideology-based propaganda was standard communist fare: the rule of the SED was said to be legitimated because of the Party's correct understanding of the laws of history and of the science of social development, and because only the Party elite had the necessary revolutionary consciousness to correctly guide social, political, and economic developments in the transformation from capitalism to communism. SED governance also was said to be legitimate because the working class was entitled to rule and the Party constituted the avant-garde of the working class.[38] The working class needed this avant-garde (rather than being able to rule directly) because only the Party could effect the necessary move of proletarian consciousness from "trade unionism" to socialism. In later years, external (international) recognition also became important in the quest for internal acceptance. It is doubtful, however, that for the average GDR citizen the appearance of Erich Honecker at foreign capitals and with foreign leaders greatly compensated for their incarceration in a defective system.

More than the legitimate governments of the West, the GDR, the USSR, and the other socialist regimes felt a perpetual need for some sort of show of approval of its rule and deeds by its victims. This quest for legitimacy and at least an outward show of legality explains alike the rubber-stamp legislatures, the plebiscites in which the only possible vote was to say *yes*, the elections in which there was no choice of whom to elect,[39] and the publicly staged trials and confessions of those who were to be destroyed. Not only was there no right of opposition, of real choice, of control from below, but there was not even the right of abstention—not even the right of silence[40] (Wolfe, 1961, 174–175). Traditional autocratic rulers demanded little more than silence from their subjects. Modern totalitarian rulers, however, require endless hymns of praise (Curtis, 1969, 66–67)—which they will coerce, if they are not sung voluntarily.

Hymns of praise must be sung not only by individual citizens but also by collectives and organizations. There could be no meetings of work collectives and similar bodies without fulsome praise for the wisdom of the Party and the country's leadership or without formal offerings of thanks for their extraordinary accomplishments. As noted earlier, even the Party Congresses were mere acclamation events. The GDR's national legislative body (the People's Chamber) also proceeded by acclamation rather than debate, almost always producing unanimous votes.

The GDR, as the other socialist countries, presented the extraordinary spectacle of insisting on the greatest possible participation of all of its citizens *and* making sure that all such participation would, in effect, be meaningless (Herlemann, 1984). With very few exceptions, the results of popular participation were predetermined by the regime. This included the endless "citizen consultations" in the development of policies as well as the outcomes of the elections. As Krisch (1985, 38–39) noted:

> The political system of the GDR combines elaborate and ostensibly genuine forms of participation with centrally directed control and supervision of the resulting institutions and processes, as exemplified by the elections to, and work of, the national legislature.

These were the two key operating principles of the state organs: (1) socialist democracy—proclaimed as qualitatively new and historically the highest type of socialism—defined as opening the way to *real participation of all people* in the creation of a society corresponding to the wishes of all groups and individuals, and (2) concentration of power—as against Western separation of powers and checks and balances; since the socialist revolution has overcome all divisions and conflicts in society, these have no (further) function[41] (Wassmund, 1981, 334). In other words, all participate in the decision-making process, but there is really nothing to decide, since all are naturally in agreement. Since the Party, of course, well knows what that uniformity is, it does not really need citizen input.

In its own eyes, of course, the GDR regime was legitimate, because the country was governed by an elite that was unique in its revolutionary consciousness and in its knowledge of the science of social development, thus, the only competent group to guide social and political developments (Richert, 1963, xxxviii). Any day of the week, the East German people would be subjected to lectures that explained that in the "historically necessary transformation" from capitalism to communism, the Communist Party (SED) must have the leading role, because the Communist Party is the avantgarde of the working class, the leading class of the future. But since the proletariat cannot exercise its leading role directly, it must rely on the action of the (Marxist-Leninist) Party of the proletariat. This "party of the new type" must move proletarian consciousness from "trade unionism" to real socialism, which is the work of the socialist intelligentsia, that is, the Party elite. The difference between the proletariat as class and the Party of the proletariat is *revolutionary consciousness* (Neugebauer, 1978, 17–20). Thus, the dictatorship of the proletariat became the dictatorship (of the leader) of the Party.

GDR Nationalism

The GDR regime also discovered quite quickly nationalism as a potential fountainhead of citizen support.[42] Nationalism became a propaganda tool for at least two reasons: (1) to supplement communist appeals, which obviously were not having the desired effects with a majority of the GDR's people and (2) to disjoin the GDR more clearly from the FRG, the well-known policy of the *Abgrenzung* (delimitation/demarcation).[43] If people would not identify with communism, perhaps they could be made to identify with the GDR as a nation.[44] Some of the efforts were quite touching.[45] It became standard linguistic usage to refer to the country not simply as the GDR but always as "our GDR" ("*unsere DDR*").[46] In the 1974 revision of the 1968 Constitution, references to "German" were replaced wherever possible by "GDR."

There were major efforts to foster patriotism—never for Germany as a whole but only for the GDR as the "better Germany," the inheritor of "all that was best in German history."[47] The regime emphatically rejected the claim of a common German culture, claiming instead that the GDR had developed a new "socialist German national culture"[48] (Hexelschneider & John, 1984, 5). Already in 1960, the GDR *Institut für Philosophie* published a book with the title *Der Staat Sind Wir* (We Are the State) to demonstrate the development of a separate "GDR socialist state consciousness." The West German thesis of the "unity of German culture" was denounced as being part of the nationalist propaganda of the FRG. It was characterized as "hegemonic, big-power-chauvinistic, revanchist, peace-endangering, and revisionist" (Koch, 1988, 159, 175, 386).

The incorporation of German history into GDR mythology was a most selective and rather variable one (Dornberg, 1974, 196; Hoffmann, 1986, 246; Richert, 1966, 127; Stuermer, 1986, 237–244). GDR historiography found it not altogether easy to identify all the "progressive forces" in German history and even more so to demonstrate that they belonged—or would have belonged—to the GDR (Alter, 1992; Nothnagle, 1999; Scharf, 1984, 4–6; Zimmering, 2000). Was Martin Luther a "progressive" religious reformer, or should that title go to Thomas Muentzer (Daehn & Heise, 1996; Friedrich-Ebert-Stiftung, 1983; Herold, 1984; Siemon-Netto, 1995)? Were the Prussian generals Gneisenau and Scharnhorst progressive military reformers, or were they the instruments of reactionary militarism? What about Frederick the Great and Bismarck (Brinks, 2001)? How could they be linked to the "real existing socialism" of the GDR?[49] The superbly trained theorist of socialism managed even that, demonstrating again that no cognitive feat, however absurd, is beyond the capabilities of the dialectics (Sperlich, 2002, 61–63). However, in their ultimate purpose, to gain legitimacy for the SED regime by associating it with these historical figures,[50] it did not work. The dialectics make for splendid cognitive games; reality, however, remains unaffected.

In spite of all the efforts to create regime loyalty and GDR-patriotism, in the last years of the GDR its leadership still faced the same problem as at the beginning: "the vast majority of the population did not accept the GDR as their own, legitimate state" (Scholz, 1988, 20). Some Western visitors came away with the impression that GDR stability was based on GDR patriotism or at least an identification with the East German state (e.g., Adomeit, 1991, 533). Since the building of the Berlin Wall, some Western travelers reported on the great stability and widespread acceptance of the communist regime in the GDR. Thus, the English journalist Neal Ascherson (1967, 22) observed that "on any traveler in East Germany the conviction grows that the [communist] party has roots far more reliable and authentic here than in Poland or even in Czechoslovakia." Such impressions, most likely, came from talking to Party functionaries. Ardagh (1987, 338) surely exaggerated when he wrote that the East German people "have come to identify with the GDR."[51]

It cannot be denied that many East Germans developed a certain pride in (what they were told were) their accomplishments (Feifer, 1976, 14; Hanhardt, 1968, 104; Grunert-Bronnen, 1970, 92; Picaper, 1982, 237). This was particularly true among the younger age cohorts. However, what stabilized the GDR were, above all, these three factors: popular resignation, the Soviet military forces in the country, and the massive FRG subsidies. Compliance, at least in psychological terms, is not the same as loyalty and allegiance (Di Palma, 1990, 145; Staritz, 1986, 44). The great stability in the GDR leadership should not have been confused, as often it was, with popular regime acceptance and legitimacy (Croan, 1976a, 165–166). Forty years of existence did not reconcile people and regime—and forty years of separate existence had not been able to destroy the feeling of a common nationality (Cattani, 1993, 28; Scholz, 1988, 79).

The FRG's *Ostpolitik*, aimed to stabilize the GDR, and quite deliberately tried to create the impression that the SED regime had gained considerable acceptance and esteem among the GDR population[52] (Pucher, 1984, 232). This policy started on the Left (which never overcame the illusion that the GDR, as a socialist state, was superior to the FRG) but then captured even a substantial part of the rest of the West German political spectrum. However, *Ostpolitik* was based on delusions and mirages. In reality, great deficits in legitimacy and loyalty persisted to the last moments of the GDR and with it a political style characterized by dishonesty, distrust, fear, and paranoia. All Eastern and Western pretense about a separate GDR identity/nationality came to a full stop when the chants of the GDR demonstrators changed from "We are the people" to "We are one people."[53]

The Pretense of Citizen Influence

The leadership of the GDR never ceased to congratulate itself that it created a state in which all citizens exercised great and real influence on the making and implementation of public policy through their participation in public affairs (Maaz, 1995, 6). The slogan "Participate in work, participate in planning, participate in governing" even became part of the GDR Constitution![54] *There was much participation, but there was little genuine influence.* The GDR, in the words of Henry Krisch (1985, 38–39), combined "elaborate and ostensibly genuine forms of participation with centrally directed control and supervision of the resulting institutions and processes" from the manufacture of "letters to the editor" to the outcome of national elections. The official line presented a different picture: "Those citizens who do not hold political office are nevertheless able to discuss and inspect the activities of all state functionaries and inspect and control the policies that have been adopted (Institut für Theorie . . . , 1986, 24).

It needs to be pointed out, however, that some of the consultation of citizens was real, but it regarded only minor details. The fundamentals of the regime were never subject to critical discussion, but only to support by acclamation. "[A]ll public discussions ended either in tormented silence or boring, sickening declarations of agreement; the capacity and readiness for open exchange of opinion was completely lost" (Maaz, 1995, 24). In respect to the fundamentals, the discussions and consultations that did take place had very little impact and certainly no significant impact on the outcome, for example, on a proposed new law or whatever (Stammen, 1974, 43). A GDR social science text (Schulze, 1978, 184) listed the number of participants in the consultations, the number of suggestions made, and the number of suggestions accepted in respect to a number of new law codes under discussion. Even numbers as such are not particularly impressive. Of course, the mere numbers say nothing about the nature (importance) of the suggestions. Here are the numbers (as can be seen, fewer than 2.5% of the suggestions were accepted):

Legal Code	*N of Participants in the Consultations*	*Suggestions Made*	*Suggestions Accepted*
family law ('65)	750,000	23,737	230
youth law ('74)	5,400,000	4,821	200
civil law ('75)	260,000	4,091	360

Citizens could have real influence at the local level on *administrative/technical* matters, particularly when these did not involve issues of ideology or Party policy and when they did not require additional resources. For example, when it had been decided to build a new overpass in some locality, the view of the residents might be genuinely sought regarding its best location, but even then, the ultimate decision remained with the Party functionaries. Most of even truly local efforts remained futile (Richert, 1963, 281; Scharf, 1984, 34–35). As Unger (1974, 31) has pointed out: "The only kind of activism compatible with totalitarian government is controlled activism."

The Mobilization Regime

Why did the regime bother to put on the participatory circuses that no one (with the exception of a few Left radicals in the West) took seriously or believed to be effective? The *mobilization of the masses* is an ingrained and even instinctive feature of totalitarian systems.[55] Since the leadership believes (or pretends to believe) that it serves the masses, carries out the will of the masses, and is borne by the masses, it appears to be reassuring to have the masses parade before you on May Day, carrying the official Party slogans as if they were their own. It appears to be reassuring to have the masses come to meetings and rallies and the voting places, as ordered by the Party.

For various reasons, of course, substantial political participation is desirable. Voluntary, meaningful participation is likely to increase support of the government. Intelligent citizen input is likely to aid and improve effective policy making. These, however, require significant citizen autonomy as political actors: reasonable access to unbiased information and a penalty-free expression of points of view and policy preferences. These, of course, were lacking in the GDR. In effect, the people of East Germany were treated as serfs—not a condition that would motivate most individuals to genuine participation in public affairs. The typical GDR citizen was a most reluctant participant in the political life of the GDR. His or her preferred realm was what little private sphere the regime allowed him or her to have—and it was very little. Thus, if there was to be participation—and the regime insisted that there was to be—it had to be mobilized and, in the last analysis, coerced. The obedient participation in Party-sponsored events provided at least the illusion of popular support, craved so desperately by all totalitarian regimes, but since much of GDR citizen participation was not entirely voluntary, there was much formalistic, rather than genuine, compliance (Scharf, 1984, 131).

Types of Participation

Citizen participation in the political process serves as the key legitimizing factor in political systems that lay claim to the appellation "democratic." Its perceived validating power is rivaled in liberal democracies only by the coherence of laws with the country's constitution (written or unwritten) and in socialist democracies only by the coherence of laws with Marxist-Leninist doctrine (in the form presently accepted as authoritative). Popular elections of officeholders tend to be the primary form of citizen participation, followed by policy referenda in the West and various forms of public reporting and consultation in the East.

Elections

The GDR had a great number of elective positions. The regime obviously thought that this would be counted as evidence for democracy and provide the system with legitimacy in the eyes of its citizens and outside observers[56] (Weichelt, 1964). Unfortunately, the election lacked the key democratic element: meaningful choice. The GDR electoral system was wholly manipulative, from the selection of candidates by the National Front (SED),[57] to the candidates' meetings, to the compulsory and "open" form of voting (see Chapter 3), and to the election results announced by the election control board[58] (Kloth, 2000; Laatz, 1983, 119–120). Elections, of course, could not possibly bring about a change in government but could serve only to affirm the rule of the SED. "According to Marxist-Leninist teaching, the working class, led by their party, once having gained power must maintain a firm grip on the organization of the state and must use the state as an instrument towards their goal" (Christopher, 1985, 19). *Free* elections can bring another group or party to power. Since this is not permissible, elections cannot be permitted to be free.

As is typical in socialist countries, the GDR elections showed extremely high rates of participation and extremely high rates of support for the unity list.[59] In the 1981 election, for example, participation was 99.2%, and the unity list of the National Front received 99.86% of the vote. The electoral process (not simply the election) was an elaborate system of meetings and discussions, and served primarily as a tool of socialization and legitimation. There were almost 200,000 elected deputies at all legislative levels, from local to national bodies, of which there were nearly 8,000. There were also 268 electoral commissions (primarily nominating agencies) with over 2,800 members, and there were 24,000 electoral boards (*Wahlvorstände*) to run the elections, having more than 250,000 participants (Krisch, 1985, 39). From the official GDR perspective, this was seen as testifying to the superiority of the GDR governmental structure relative to its Western counterparts. The people have a real chance to participate in the decisions, their execution, and the control of the results. Unfortunately, GDR elections were tainted by fraud, even the very last one. Elections, like all other forms of public participation in the political process, were not about real choices or genuine influence but were tools serving legitimation and socialization.

Reporting to Voters

All elected officials had the duty to report at regular intervals to their electors, providing an accounting of their activities (*Berichterstattung*). These reports of officeholders to their constituents, however, were merely ritualistic exercises. They certainly were not meant to empower the voter with complete and accurate information.[60] The officials typically presented set pieces about the wisdom of the Party, the glories of socialism, and the unstoppable improvement of life in the GDR. The first two items were usually screened out by the listeners; they had heard them too often already. Drawing on their own experiences, the electors knew that the third item was largely false.

The electors were encouraged to ask questions, but they knew that there was a range of appropriate questions beyond which they dare not step. GDR citizens were constantly being told to discuss things, but there were neither free discussions nor discussions related to their fundamental concerns. Only in respect to minor and technical matters could criticism be expressed. It looked good (democracy!) but was risk-free and inconsequential (Dahrendorf, 1967, 403; Mueller-Roemer, 1974, 24; Richert, 1963, 281; Scharf, 1984, 34). There could be questions about the effects of the weather on the harvest; there could not be questions about the effects of Party policy on the harvest. Foreign journalists, it might be noted, worked under the same rules. Those who reported critically about East Germany were expelled. GDR journalists who reported about the alleged exploitation of the working class in the FRG were, of course, rewarded (Hanrieder, 1982, 127, 158).

Criticism could be real, and this was offered as proof of the truly democratic nature of the GDR, but once again, it could regard only minor details. There were strict boundaries regarding permissible questions and criticisms. The fundamentals of Party policy were not subject to critical analysis. New laws[61] generally were subjected to extensive public consultation before being adopted by the legislature. In respect to the basic features of the new laws, these consultations had practically no impact on the final product (see previous list). Only minor aspects and technicalities were subject to real citizen input. Richert (1961, 33) usefully distinguished between technical and policy participation, the first with occasional success, the second purely for show. The much practiced and (even more) praised consultation with the citizens must also be regarded as largely a fraud.

As noted earlier, citizens could have real influence at the local level in respect to administrative and technical matters, as long as these did not involve issues of ideology or Party policy and as long as these did not require additional expenditures but regarded only "instrumental" matters, such as a different allocation of the foreordained level of resources. This type of criticism could have useful (informative) functions for the regime and, therefore, often was welcome (Spechler, 1982, 29).

Other Forms of Participation

GDR citizens were active in various other public and quasi-public functions. These took the form of worker-farmer inspection committees, neighborhood associations, citizens' commissions associated with branches of local governmental organs, and social courts. The social courts are of particular interest. They were lay adjudicative agencies, dealing with minor criminal offenses and civil disputes. They were features (under various names) of practically all the socialist countries. As the Communist Party of the Soviet Union declared: "The Party attaches great importance to instilling in people a high sense of civic responsibility, respect for Soviet laws and the rules of socialist conduct, irreconcilability to any violations of socialist legality, and a readiness to take an active part in the maintenance of law and order" (Congress of the CPSU, 1986, 58). Socialist lay adjudication presents the most believable case of genuine citizen influence. Certainly in the GDR, the lay adjudicators had considerable authority and autonomy in dealing with small criminal and civil matters.[62]

Multiple Activities and Affiliations

It was common for GDR citizens to participate in a variety of civic activities, belong to several civic organizations, and hold several offices in such organizations. There were the various neighborhood associations (Sahr: 1987, 87; Scharf, 1984, 135), the citizens commissions related to local government units (Scharf, 1984, 135), the worker-farmer Inspection Committees (Scharf, 1984, 50), and the service as members of the social courts—to name just a few of the many participatory opportunities/obligations.[63] Multiplicities of participation were expected by the Party and were rewarded with advancement and special benefits, yet it was precisely the younger age cohorts who participated less (Buescher & Wensierski, 1984; Zschiedrich, 1985, 71). Reflecting norm conformity rather than the citizens' real interests, most participation came to be purely perfunctory. As Scharf (1984, 141) rightly pointed out, there were multiple affiliations but minimal involvement.

The Special Case of Adjudicatory Participation

In all socialist states, great importance was affixed to mass participation in law enforcement and adjudication. To a large degree, this simply was a matter of yet another control mechanism: norm incorporation through participation. "The Party attaches great importance to instilling in people a high sense of civic responsibility, respect for Soviet laws and the rules of socialist conduct, irreconcilability to any violations of socialist legality, and a readiness to take an active part in the maintenance of law and order" (Congress of the CPSU, 1986, 58).

There was, however, one area of adjudicative participation in which the citizen could have (and often did have) real influence: the area of *lay adjudication*. Nearly all countries—East and West—give ordinary citizens some role to play in the adjudicative process. In the United States, this takes the form of the jury. In most European countries it takes the form of lay assessors.[64] In both of these cases the laypersons perform their function under the direction and, to some degree, control of the professional judge. The lay courts of the GDR (and the other socialist countries), however, worked independently of any professional judge and independently of any trained jurist.

The right of the (nonjurist) citizen to participate in the adjudicative process was guaranteed by the Constitution of the GDR (Section IV, Art. 90, Part 3) and restated in all specific codes: Civil Code (ZGB),[65] Preamble and Part 1, Chapter 1, Paragraph 9; Criminal Code (StGB),[66] Preamble and Chapter 1, Article 6; Criminal Procedure Code (StPO),[67] Chapter 1, Paragraph 4; and Court Organization Law (GVG),[68] Chapter 1, Paragraph 9). In addition, there is a special Code of the Social Courts (GGG)[69] and there are decrees regarding the election and work of the members of the dispute commissions (KKO)[70] and arbitration commissions (SKO).[71] Of particular interest are the dispute commission and the arbitration commission. Collectively, they are known as the *social courts*[72] of the GDR.[73]

The social courts of the former GDR provide the most important example of a pure and autonomous *lay* adjudicative agency. There are only a few other such institutions, for example, the American justice of the peace. While all socialist countries had social courts, those of the GDR were unique (Buchholz, 1989, 72). The jurisdictional scope was unmatched elsewhere, as was the number of laypersons participating. The functions assigned to the social courts of the GDR included not only adjudication, arbitration, and mediation but also legal advice and education, crime prevention, rehabilitation of offenders, and preserving peace and order at work and in the residential areas. Altogether, in the last years of the GDR, there existed about 60,000 social courts with nearly 500,000 members.

While the social courts, as everything else, clearly had political (regime-supportive) functions, they also had genuine and significant legal tasks. They conducted about 10,000 formal deliberations per year, plus many other types of work. The social courts substantially reduced the caseload of the East German state courts, a considerable benefit to a country with persistent workforce shortages. The state also profited financially, since the lay judges performed their duties without pay *and* while continuing to work full-time at their regular places of employment.

The GDR social courts consisted of six to fifteen lay judges. They had civil and criminal jurisdiction and could impose a variety of conventional and unconventional sanctions. Their decisions were enforced through the regular law enforcement agencies; they could be appealed to the state courts. The social pressure brought to bear on the accused was intense in the social courts. Most of the sanctions, however, were not particularly harsh. The primary orientation of the social courts was educational and preventive rather than punitive.

While the GDR social courts did not work without professional supervision, and while the state provided many forms of training and instruction,[74] they were largely autonomous in their day-to-day work. In the case of the social courts, the claim of citizen influence is, indeed, credible—but it also is the *only* credible case.

Magnitude and Meaning of Participation

The magnitude of participation was very high. In a country of fewer than 17 million people there were (to present just a few figures):

450,000 participants in the committees of representative bodies at all levels,

over 300,000 lay judges and members of arbitration bodies,

over 200,000 participants in the work of the Workers' and Peasants' Inspection,

thousands of members of the trade unions engaged in discussions of economic plans,

various hundreds of thousands active in youth, women's, sports, and other social groups,

almost 2 million industrial "innovators," and

over 600,000 participants in parent-teacher groups. (Krisch, 1985, 40–41; Scharf, 1984, 33ff).

The question, of course, remains what such membership and participation figures really mean. It probably was not the approval and allegiance that the regime so desperately sought. On the other hand, it must have been some civic affirmation, given the high proportions of eligibles participating.[75] It is not inconceivable that there developed a sentiment of mutual citizen solidarity, even if this solidarity did not translate into regime approval and support.

When the Soviet composer Muradeli wrote an opera that was not to Stalin's liking, the Central Committee of the Communist Party passed a resolution harshly condemning this "formalist, anti-people, decadent" music. Muradeli saved his neck by submitting to the Party's guidance and confessing his errors.[76] Shostakovich commented sarcastically:

> As you know, the resolution drew heated interest among the toiling masses. Meetings and gatherings were held everywhere, in factories, communal farms, industrial cartels, and places of public food consumption. And the workers discussed the document with enthusiasm, since, as it turned out, the document echoed the spiritual needs of millions of people. . . . Muradeli began making appearances at various organizations. He came to the people and repented. I was a so-and-so, a formalist and cosmopolite . . . but the Party showed me the way in time. (Volkov, 1979, 144)

Apart from the degradation of the artist,[77] the example throws into stark relief the real nature of socialist meetings, discussions, and consultations of the masses. As meaningful participation, the procedure is a pure farce.[78] As camouflage for a brutal dictatorship, however, it did work at times—particularly with the Western naives.

Political participation in the GDR, as in other socialist systems, was mandatory. It simply cannot be interpreted as a voluntary showing of support on the part of the citizens for the regime. It was also mandatory to show enthusiasm. The regime was not satisfied with mere attendance. Long-lasting enthusiastic acclamations and praises were expected. Unfortunately for the regime, just as attendance can be perfunctory, so can enthusiasm be faked. If the leaders of the GDR believed that they had the support, nay love, of the enthusiastically waving masses, they were gravely mistaken—accommodation, *yes*; genuine support, *no*.

It can rightly be said that the regime's efforts to generate support via massive and multiple forms of participation were essentially unsuccessful. There was little interest in participating in what were understood to be meaningless exercises that, with few exceptions, did nothing to give citizens real political influence. Participation could not be avoided altogether. To remain a citizen in good standing, a certain minimum of pro forma activities was unavoidable, but even here citizens sought to limit their participation. The mass demonstrations of May 1 were famous for this: as soon as the marchers had passed the tribune of domestic and foreign dignitaries, they would quickly disappear (*verkruemeln*) into the side streets and return to the activities in which they really wanted to participate[79] (Braun, 1996, 25).

Frequent and (seemingly) enthusiastic participation was needed for a citizen's occupational and other advancements. This did not mean solely marching in the many parades. It was also important, for example, to be a member of certain associations (e.g., the FDJ and German-Soviet Friendship Society) and to show up at their many organized meetings and activities (Bothe, 1983,

62; Scharf, 1984, 139, 149). The people of the GDR were fully aware that the participation demanded by the regime was far removed from the exercise of real power. Accommodation and acquiescence characterized GDR citizens, not active and freely given support for the system in which they found themselves. The typical form of public participation in the GDR has rightly been called "formalistic compliance."

However, there is the intriguing possibility that the praxis of maximum citizen participation together with the claim of real influence (real effects) may have created a compelling dynamic for *real* participation (Hutzler-Spichtinger & Schoenberger, 1994; see also Lane, 1976, 90). It may have helped to prepare the grounds for citizen activism outside the approved channels and finally inspired the demonstrations that led to the downfall of the regime.[80]

THE STATE

The State That Did Not Wither Away

The state, according to socialist theory, is the executive committee of the property-owning class (*Herrschaftsausschuss der besitzenden Klasse*). According to Vyshinsky (1948) (paraphrasing Engels), the state is the product of society at a certain stage of its development, namely, when society is inextricably involved in conflict with itself, when it has split into irreconcilable contradictions and is impotent to rid itself of those contradiction. The state is the force that moderates this conflict and keeps it within bounds, but while it issues out of society, it puts itself above society, ever more alienating itself from society. Finally, the state becomes the servant of one of the conflicting classes—in capitalism this is the propertied class, which thereby becomes the ruling class.[81]

When there are no more antagonistic classes (as in the "classless society" of triumphant socialism), there is, according to Engels, no further need for the state, and the state "withers away" (*stirbt ab*). Marx thought that the state would wither away in stages. It disappears in proportion to the growth of the forces of production and to the spread of democracy to an overwhelming majority of the population. It is the process of "the actual overcoming of the dualism between the civil society and the state, the proess of the emancipation of man" (Bibic, 1970, 6). Such were the canons of orthodox Marxism. They did not survive Stalin (and even to some degree, not even Lenin).[82] With Stalin, the state in developed socialism was not to wither away but to grow and become ever stronger. In nice dialectical fashion Stalin decided (in *Question of Leninism*): "The withering away of the state will come, and not through weakening of state power, but through the maximum intensification of it." Or as Fred Oelsner (1955, 29), member of the GDR Politbureau, put it, in the transition period to communism, the class struggle does not diminish but becomes more acute. Honecker nicely fell into place. In 1977 in a speech to the Central Committee, he declared that the constant strengthening of state power was a key task of the Party (Honecker, 1978, 252). Or, according to the *Neues Deutschland*, "the socialist state is the chief instrument for executing the policies of the toiling masses under the leadership of the working class and its party. Without a strong and well-functioning socialist state there can be no socialist achievements for the people"[83] (as quoted in Krisch, 1985, 35). Indeed, it became possible in the GDR to issue lengthy books on the transition to, and the nature of, the communist society, without any discussion of the state—withering or not withering (Dlubek & Merkel, 1981).

Orthodox Marxism now became "counterrevolutionary and degenerate."[84] Those who predicted an early withering away of the state now were "enemies of the people" (Vyshinsky, 1948, 62–78). GDR authors, of course, as in all things, remained Stalin's disciples, writing: "An outstanding moment in the development of socialist state power in the GDR is the insoluble connection between the *increasing* role of the state and the development and perfection of socialism"[85] (Autorenkollektiv, 1985c, 160; emphasis added). Orthodoxy became a dangerous posture. "Jurists who thought that the state should begin to 'wither away' as socialism was achieved were denounced and removed from their positions" (Hazard, 1948, vii). In fact, *society*, not the state, withered away in the GDR (Meuschel, 1992, 10).

The new socialist ruling class needed a strong state. Orthodoxy had focused too much on *class* antagonism and not enough on other possible forms of conflict. There was the notion of "capitalist encirclement," but there also was substantial dissent within the (nearly) classless societies of the USSR and the GDR. Only a strong state could hope to deal successfully with the external and internal opponents of the socialist regimes. More, the state is necessary not only to defend socialism but also to *build* it. At its Second Party Conference in 1952, the SED declared that the power of the state was the "chief instrument" to create the foundations of socialism in the GDR[86] (Eppelmann et al., 1996, 582). This is as close as one can get to an admission that socialism was not freely chosen by the citizens of East Germany but was imposed and coerced.

The socialist state, according to the socialists, belongs to a particular historical period, the period of transition from capitalism to communism. It takes the form of the revolutionary dictatorship of the proletariat. It is a "transition state." Indeed, it is not strictly a state at all because it is in hands of the majority of toiling masses, not in hands of the exploiter minority. The proletariat still *needs* the state, in the interest not of freedom but of crushing its adversaries. "When it becomes possible to speak of freedom, then the state as such ceases to exists" (Vyshinsky, 1948, 40).

Stalin (1947, 104–105) also predicted "that since the party was 'an instrument of the dictatorship of the proletariat . . . it follows that when classes disappear and the dictatorship of the proletariat withers away, the party will also wither away'" (see also Unger, 1974, 16). The more reasonable perspective is that neither would ever have disappeared in socialist systems. The Party was needed to control the state, and the state was needed to quash dissent and opposition. It is not likely that socialist regimes would ever have been without foes, regardless of how highly developed and close to communism they were. Some people just do not like to be patronized and oppressed and to have their enthusiasm mandated. Thus, there would ever have been a need for Party and state.

There was, it should be noted, never a clear separation of Party and state. As previously discussed, the Party entirely controlled the state. The state had no independent existence and practically no independent functions. As noted, the methods of Party control were overlapping membership and a dual agency structure. "The activities of party officials in monitoring, coordinating, and intervening in the leadership structure of governmental and social institutions [were] an ever-present reality" (Scharf, 1984, 58). All Party decisions were obligatory for state organs. State decision making, in other words, took place in the Party offices. The socialist state is, above all, the Party's machinery to crush all elements hostile to the Party's rule. As the Party organ—*Neues Deutschland*—declared in 1981, "the socialist state is the chief instrument for executing the policies of the toiling masses under the leadership of the working class and its Party. Without a strong and well-functioning socialist state there can be no socialist achievements for the people" (Krisch, 1985, 35).

The State of All the People?

The GDR, having achieved, at least by its own testimony, the level of mature socialism, proclaimed itself "a state of all the people." This followed the Soviet example. Novosti Press Agency (1978, 10–11) produced the following description:

> Today, a developed socialist society, as described by Lenin in 1918, has been built in the Soviet Union. It is defined as one in which socialism has taken firm root in all spheres—political, economic, social and cultural—of the life of society.
>
> With the building of socialism, the state of the dictatorship of the proletariat gradually turns into a state of the entire people, a political organization of the whole people with the working class playing the leading role. As the exploiting classes are abolished, the function of suppressing their opposition becomes redundant, and the main functions of the socialist state, those of organizing and running the economy and promoting education and cultural progress, develop in every possible way. This is the principal difference between the state of the entire people and the dictatorship of the proletariat.[87]

One should not overlook the claim that even in the period of the dictatorship of the proletariat the state works in the interest of *all* the people, not just the proletariat[88] (Schuessler, 1979, 75). The socialist regime works tirelessly and exclusively not only for the welfare of the people but for the welfare of all the people equally. Unfortunately, some people are always "more equal" than others. While the average citizen of the GDR did not know about the extravagant privileges of the New Class, he or she did know enough to recognize the self-serving regime propaganda for what it was.[89] The payback came in November 1989.

Civil Liberties and Information Flow

Civil liberties were not regarded favorably by the GDR rulers. This can be seen quite clearly in the sequence of the three constitutions. The first Constitution (1949) was largely democratic in format, if not in application.[90] It incorporated a number elements of the Weimar Constitution, such as legislative supremacy and traditional individual liberties. However, as an indication of things to come, its Article 6 already permitted to criminalize expressions of opposition to the new political order. The 1968 Constitution still guaranteed political rights such as freedom of speech and assembly but only as long as their exercise did not question the ruling position of the Party, its policies, or its goal of a socialist society (Richert, 1968). The matter became a constitutional principle. Article 3.2 was explicit: "The political parties and mass organizations pool all forces of the people for joint action for the development of a socialist society."

The 1974 revision of the 1968 Constitution further limited civil liberties.[91] Articles 19–40 dealt with the basic rights and duties of citizens, but both rights and duties were conceived very differently from such notions in the West. In the West, a basic right is not granted by (and therefore removable by) the state but exists prior to the state as an innate human right (typically based on divine and natural law notions). Not so in the GDR. All rights are grants of the state (Party), not to be used in opposition to the state (Party) and removable at any time.[92] Rights, in other words, existed only in harmony with regime policies. This, however, did not prevent regime officials (e.g., Josef Streit, the chief state prosecutor of the GDR) to proclaim loudly that "the state protects the rights of the citizens" (Streit, 1962). In addition, the rights were tied to duties; the benefit of the former depend on the fulfillment of the latter. It should be noted that neither rights nor duties had adequate legal definitions (Luchterhandt, 1985, vi–x).

GDR writers tend to admit that the concept of basic rights is different in a socialist democracy; there "basic rights emanate from socialist social conditions." There is no continuity between socialist and bourgeois basic rights; there are no eternal, innate human rights; all rights and laws reflect the interest of the ruling class and, thus, have historical character. To this is usually added the criticism that Western rights have not been realized in practice since there are continuing suppression and exploitation. By contrast, in the GDR the exploitation of man by man has been abolished forever (Art. 2.3, Constitution of 1968). Western conceptions of human rights *as rights against the authority of the state* no longer make sense when the state is the instrument of the working class and its Party (Christopher, 1985, 23; Woywod, 1987).

GDR writers also like to point out that man is at the center of all efforts of socialist society and its state (Art. 2.1, Constitution of 1968). This, however, does not mean Western-style individualism. It means man in the context of society, in the context of, and as part of, his collectives. Having rights basically only as a member of a collective is not seen as a denial of individual rights (Eichhorn, 1985; Stiehler, 1984a, 692). It presents no difficulty to Marxist-Leninist theorists since they postulate a fundamental agreement (unity) between the interests of society and those of the individual. Socialist theory simply denies the possibility of a conflict between the politics of the dictatorship of the proletariat and personal freedom (Steininger, 1988, 202; Stiehler, 1984b; Zschiedrich, 1981, 293).

Socialist theory also denies the possibility of conflicts between the different spheres of a citizen's life, for example, public versus private, work versus leisure, and so on (Panorama-DDR, 1976, 57, 70). This is part of the socialist folly to bring together various opposites and call them unities. There is the unity of theory and practice (Autorenkollektiv, 1978a, 18), of rights and obligations (e.g., Schuessler, 1981a, 52; Seidel, 1981, 112), of discipline and democracy (Schuessler, 1980, 271), of economic and social policy (Weichelt, 1981, 338; Autorenkollektiv, 1978a, 30; Panorama-DDR, 1976, 50–51), of law, morality, and utility (Bley & Mueller, 1979, 389), of socialist law and the people (Heuckendorf, 1981, 186), of socialism and democracy (Autorenkollektiv, 1978a, 74), of individual and society, of citizen and state, of the Communist Party and the people, of trade unions and the state, and of firms and employees[93] (Autorenkollektiv, 1978a, 20, 225–227; Panaroma-DDR, 1976, 34, 57; Riemann & Schwabe, 1976, 9–11, 25–27). Such assertions, of course, help if the principles of political pluralism are to be rejected[94]—together with the separation of powers, checks and balances, and so on. Massive uniformity was the axiom of the GDR.[95]

Socialist basic rights are granted by the state for the purpose of personality development (the famous "socialist personality") (Lemke, 1980), for the person's own good, and for that of society (Art. 19, Constitution of 1968). Rights always are paired with duties, the fulfillment of which "is a high moral obligation of each citizen" (Art. 21, Constitution of 1968). Great emphasis is given to the citizen's right and duty to participate in the shaping of socialist society. Article 21 contains the endlessly repeated slogan: "participate in working, in planning, and in governing." As GDR commentators have pointed out: "It is necessary for society that the citizen recognizes and implements his rights in an inseparable unity with his responsibilities towards society and his duties as a citizen" (Christopher, 1985, 24–25).

Some 1949 rights became an embarrassment to the GDR and were dropped in 1968, for example, the right to strike (Art. 14, Constitution of 1949) and the right to emigrate (Art. 10.3, Constitution of 1949). The basic rights still remaining in the 1968–1974 Constitutions, of course, were not absolute and, worse, not enforceable.[96] While Article 30 of the 1968 Constitution declared the inviolability of the "person and liberty" of every citizen, official commentaries envisaged restrictions on this liberty, not only in cases where the action infringes on the legal order but also where "socialist morality" would be offended. Thus, freedom of speech is conditioned on its use "in accordance with the spirit and the aims of the constitution," which means that opinions cannot be expressed that would question or criticize the socialist nature of the state, the leading role of the Party, or the special ties to the USSR. As the constitutional commentaries have it, criticism has to be "constructive," and there can be no freedom for "anti-socialist propaganda" (Christopher, 1985, 25). This regards not only opinions but also peaceful assembly and the forming of associations. It is the Party that decides what is "constructive" and what is "anti-socialist" and, obviously, what offends "socialist morality."[97]

The penalties for not being constructive are severe. "The 1979 amendments to the Penal Code extended the catalogue of culpable actions in this context and raised the punishment for such crimes to a maximum of eight years imprisonment for individuals acting on their own, and ten years for those who collaborate with organizations or persons whose activities are directed against the GDR." The difficulties of political prisoners did not end at their ultimate release. First, they had to take a residence and a job as required by the police. Second, they had to report to the police at regular intervals. Third, people in the community were not left in doubt about their "state-hostile" attitudes and that decent citizens better avoid them (Kessler & Miermeister 1983, 18).

Citizens who felt that their constitutional rights had been violated could submit a petition or complaint to the elected bodies or to state and economic organs (Art. 103 of the constitution of 1968), but they had no access to an independent arbitrator, that is, a constitutional court (Lehmann & Pohl, 1986). The GDR parliament (*Volkskammer*) decided on the constitutionality of legal regulations (Art. 89 of the Constitution of 1968)—which, thus, made a Party-controlled agency the judge of Party-generated laws[98] (Christopher, 1985, 25–26). This, as much as anything, demonstrates the lack of basic legal protections of the GDR citizen (Obst, 1983, 105).

There also was no right of access to information, to inform oneself freely from generally accessible sources.[99] As Stefan Heym (1990, 253) said: The GDR media are not information organs; they are organs for the propagation of official announcements. Nor was there a right to inform others, if the content of the message is deemed to be critical of Party or state.[100] The GDR regime saw quite correctly that a free flow of information can be dangerous to the rulers. The same applied to "freedom of the press" (Raue, 1986). There was no institutional independence of the media. The purpose of the media was not to freely inform but to serve up Party propaganda[101] (Lendvai, 1981). The media had the function of ideological guidance and increasing socialist consciousness—another transmission belt (Holzweissig, 1997; Jaeger, 1995; Wichner & Wiesner, 1993; Zipser, 1995). There may have been on occasion some real debates in elite journals, but "publications with mass circulation [were] almost completely devoted to the propagation of mythology," that is, to the propagation of regime pieties (Shlapentokh, 1986, xv). Any kind of publication in the GDR required a specific official license.[102] In principle every publication was prohibited, except those specifically authorized. As in other socialist countries, the private possession of copying machines and printers was prohibited. The following experience may be of interest. Once at a visit to Humboldt University in Berlin (easily the most prestigious university in the GDR [Jordan, 1985; Klein, 1985; also Mueller & Mueller, 1953; Richert, 1967]), I needed to have a few pages of text photocopied. The process was an eye-opener. My host, a professor, had to complete an elaborate request form. The original and the request form had to be taken to a central office, where all university copying was done. There, upon careful inspection of the text and the form, and after much delay, a copy was finally made. Clearly, a professor (member of the SED) and even an academic department could not be trusted with their own copying machines.[103] In some countries (Romania), typewriters had be registered, and it was forbidden to lend them to others (Gornig, 1987, 80–87). The GDR also had no postal or phone secrecy (Kallinich & de Pasguale, 2002; Obst, 1983, 108).

Article 23 of the 1949 Constitution, as well as Article 16 of the 1968 Constitution, declared that private property was protected and could be abridged only on the basis of law and against adequate compensation. This is not how the conversion of private to state ownership has worked—whether in agriculture, industry, or business. As noted, the Constitution of 1949 also guaranteed the right to strike in explicit language (Art. 14). The second Constitution stated only that "nobody may limit or obstruct" labor union activities (Art. 44.2). Either way, there have been no legal strikes in the GDR.

Article 35 of the first Constitution guaranteed an equal right to education to all citizens. The fact is that children of middle-class parents were systematically denied admission to higher education. The two (three) constitutions also guaranteed free expression of opinion, freedom of the press, freedom of assembly, freedom of religion, and other standard rights associated with liberal democracies. Practice, however, tended to deviate widely from these constitutional pieties. Frey (1987, 170), in a generally sympathetic account of the GDR, was forced to acknowledge that "despite some measure of relaxation, the GDR is still ruled by one of the most repressive dictatorships in Europe, a regime that grants no political freedoms to its citizens and constantly violates their basic human rights."

In sum, the several GDR Constitutions were elaborate documents with extensive civil rights guarantees, including those regarding a free press and the free flow of information. They were, however, irrelevant. They existed merely for show. Party policy always broke constitutional guarantees.

The Special Case of Antifascism

The conversion of the Soviet Zone of Occupation (and later the GDR) into a police state started early and never let up. The early efforts to establish a communist dictatorial police-state system were camouflaged by two types of veils: democracy and antifascism. As noted in Chapter 2, Walter Ulbricht famously said in May 1945: "It must look democratic, but we must have everything in our hands." This line lasted to the very end: the GDR is the only true German democracy; only socialism can bring about a truly democratic system.[104] For a selection of these types of propaganda efforts from the last decade of the GDR, see Felfe, 1987; Gleissner, 1981, 1985; Honecker, 1981, 353–361, 1987; Krolikowski, 1988; Poppe, 1980, 1984, 1985; Prokop, 1986; Schulze, 1980; Weichelt, 1982b; and the fundamental volume of Schuessler and Weichelt, 1977. Of course, the first three decades of the GDR also produced a large number of similar endeavors. To cite only a few: Ulbricht, 1947, 1961, 1966; Honecker, 1974.

The second and most effective masquerade was that of antifascism. To be sure, the communists of the SZ/GDR were genuinely opposed to fascism. This, however, was the opposition to a competing ideology and movement. With few exceptions, it was *not* an opposition to the dictatorial and totalitarian features of fascism and national-socialism. In an early and insightful essay, Norbert Muhlen (1951) identified the communists of East Germany as the "new nazis."[105] GDR antifascism was little more than Stalinism. It is also useful to remember at this point (which, of course, is perceived as an appalling heresy by the academic Left) that concentration camps, such as Buchenwald and Sachsenhausen, saw continued use after the war under Soviet direction until 1950. Thereafter the inmates came under East German control. The inhumane treatment of the inmates, in any case, well resembled that of the camps under nazi command (Agde, 1994; Greve, 1990; Latotzky, 2002; Mayer, 2002, 21; Mueller, 1991; Paetzold, 1991, 26; Reif-Spirek & Ritscher, 1999; Ritscher et al., 1996). These concentration camps became a major destination for social democrats, after the SED had been transformed into a "party of the new type."

Antifascism had an external and an internal function. Externally, it served to distinguish the GDR from the FRG. A very useful line, dished up at every possible occasion was that the GDR is the true antifascist state (and therefore entitled to international respect and cooperation), whereas West Germany continued various fascist traditions, of which all peace-loving nations should be afraid. The proof was that some former national-socialists came to hold government office in the FRG. Depending on the particulars of the case, that may or may not have been a deplorable development. What GDR propaganda did not mention, of course, was that the same could be found in the GDR. As noted in Chapter 2, a substantial number of high-ranking national-socialists came to occupy important positions in the upper echelons of state and society in the GDR (Investigating Committee of Free Jurists, undated; Joseph, 2002; Kappelt, 1981; Muhlen, 1951, 9–10; Schwarze, 1973, 25; Stadtmueller, 1963, 230–231; Wiesenthal, 1968; Zank, 1987, 55). Also, the SED founded a political party primarily for former nazis, the National Democratic Party of Germany (NDPD) (Reichelt, 1997). In addition, it has been estimated that at least a quarter of the SED members were formerly members of the Nazi Party or of one of its subsidiaries (Eppelmann et al., 1996, 186). Furthermore, it is not at all clear that the denazification process was more thorough and complete in the East than in the West[106] (Kappelt, 1997; Roessler, 1994; Weinke, 2002). With the possible exception of the judiciary, it is highly doubtful that denazification was substantially more successful in one section of Germany than the other (Vogt, 2000, 232–234, 244). In any case, as late as 1989, Kurt Hager, the GDR's chief ideologist, sought to justify the separate existence of the GDR by claiming for it an internationally acknowledged "deeply ingrained humanism and antifascism" (Epplemann et al., 1996, 56–57).

Internally, antifascism was the club with which to beat all other groups into submission to communist policies[107] (Brueckl, 2001; Hell, 1997; Knuetter, 1994; Kupferberg, 2002; Leo & Reif-Spirek, 1999, 2001; Pritchard, 2000; Sichrovsky, 1999). Persons and organizations that would have remained indifferent or even hostile to unequivocal communist appeals could be brought into line by appeals to antifascism (Wimmer, 1985). It was a common tactic, particularly in the early years of the SZ/GDR, to mark socialist policy not by its true label but by the antifascist tag. Ulbricht's "construction of the antifascist democratic order" was, in fact, nothing other but the construction of socialism. The appeal to the GDR's antifascist tradition served to justify the regime and to paralyze its opponents (Epplemann et al., 1996, 56). Margot Honecker (wife of Erich and minister of education of the GDR) still used the same argument in the Chilean exile in the 1990s (Corvalan, 2001, 39). Communism and antifascism were equated. Since it was good and proper to be an antifascist, one simply had to be a communist.

The GDR's antifascism doctrine also produced the impression that any and all forms of fascism had been eradicated in that country. The writer Stefan Heym (1990, 229) jested that the GDR had dealt with the past (*Vergangenheitsbewältigung*) so successfully that we now count ourselves among the victors of World War II, with scarcely a follower of Hitler to be found. With the typical delusion of the SED leadership, Hermann Axen (an important member of the Politbureau) proclaimed in 1989 that fascism had been forever exterminated in the GDR and would remain exterminated[108] (Axen, 1989; also Fuchs & Hieke, 1992, 108–111; Hager, 1963, 5). The events since 1989 quickly have exposed this piety as a mere conceit. As soon as the heavy hand of the People's Police and Stasi was removed, all sorts of fascist (and other extremists) came out of the woodwork (Billerbeck, 1999; Brinks, 2000; Bugiel, 2002; Friedrich & Foerster, 1996; Harnischmacher, 2001; Koedderitzsch & Mueller, 1990; Krueger-Potratz, 1991; Maaz, 1995; Pordzik et al., 1993; Raendchen, 2000; Rodden, 2002, 365–367; Scherzer, 2002; Sturzbecher, 1997; Walter, 1997; Wassmund, 1991; Wolfe, 1992, 200–201).

THE POLICE STATE

Citizen Surveillance

The GDR had an extensive system of neighborhood and workplace surveillance.[109] Everyone was expected to watch everyone else and to report miscreants (even simple nonparticipation in the mandated rituals) to the authorities. Party functionaries and neighborhood busybodies frequently were eager to earn bonus points by informing on colleagues and neighbors. Sometimes even family members were recruited for this task. Wolfe (1992, 9) notes that "GDR citizens . . . had a legal obligation [Art. 2 of the Constitution] to aid the police in detection of criminal acts and suspects and in gathering evidence." As a "passive" duty, it cannot be faulted, but if interpreted "pre-actively," it leads to a regime of snoops and busybodies.

To be an informer and to be informed upon were not matters of minor importance. Since the state had a monopoly in the distribution of scarce goods, nonparticipants and other offenders could be (and were) denied access to such things as improved housing, job advancement, superior consumer goods, the ability to travel to other countries, and higher education for their children. Of course, there always was the possibility of criminal sanctions. Life could be (and was) made quite unpleasant for the (perceived or actual) malefactor, and it was generally not necessary to employ the more drastic means available to the security apparatus to keep most people cowed and subservient. The informers, of course, obtained special benefits for their contributions to regime security.

The People's Police and "Voluntary" Submission

The GDR People's Police (*Volkspolizei* = VP) cannot be equated with the Special Police of the Ministry for State Security (Stasi). For both police organizations, however, the ultimate authority was not the state but the Party. As with all GDR organizations, Party directives were binding, not the formal law.[110] While the People's Police also had a reputation for arbitrariness, brutality, and terrorist conduct, its main function was that of any police force:

the prevention of crime and the discovery of criminals.[111] Indeed, the GDR was a police state, but not of the worst variety as far as the regular police was concerned (Heidenheimer, 1961, 179–181; Wechsberg, 1964, 133). Terror, actual and potential, was an instrument of government, as were show trials and unspeakable prisons (Richert, 1966, 63ff; Schneider, 1978, 25), but most of these came under the responsibility of the Stasi rather than the regular police.

Whereas in the early years of the GDR totalitarianism, terror, and fear predominated (Luchsinger, 1951, 12), in the latter years, these instruments were more potential than actual (Richert, 1963, 281). At a certain time the population became sufficiently cowed so that the application of naked terror became ever less necessary. It did not matter how frequently or infrequently brute terror and abuse occurred. It was enough to know that it was readily available[112] and that there was no protection or remedy. Coercion became largely internalized (Inkeles, 1954, 106ff; Sperlich, 2002, 179–180). Brute force, however, was readily applied again toward the end of the GDR. The regime became desperate to stop the ever-increasing citizens' demonstrations. The SED encouraged and condoned again a massive abuse of police power, not seen since the very early years of the GDR (Untersuchungskommission, 1991, 15–25; Wolfe, 1992, 89, 98–99, 104–105).

Open coercion can effect short-term compliance, but not the voluntary cooperation and commitment that the regime craved and that are needed in any complex modern society (Dallin & Breslauer, 1970, 191–199). If the leadership comes to believe that more and more citizens have "accepted the values of the regime as their own, the Party can rely more on 'peer-group pressure' and can substitute 'majority tyranny' for overt terror" (Meyer, 1965, 331–332). Any regime wants to shift from coercive to normative power, which is more effective and also less expensive.

What would lead citizens to do more or less voluntarily what is required of them, so that they will not have to be coerced? Dallin and Breslauer (1970, 211–212) list four elements: (1) national identification (for the USSR it was "the great patriotic war"; for East Germany, especially after the Wall, it was the deliberate creation of GDR nationalism); (2) a belief in the system's effectiveness, especially as it regards living standards (the GDR never did well in this respect)[113] (Poutrus, 2002); (3) a positive identification with the regime through participation—even via involvement in ritual ratifications and various forms of consultation and implementation (the GDR made a maximum effort to get citizens to participate and to persuade them that this participation was meaningful); and (4) connecting the citizen to the regime through various types of official organizations (again, the GDR made a major effort; it had an immense number of organizations, each with a large membership).

Even "voluntary" submission and the pretense of regime support could not make the citizen secure. There remained a great degree of "legal insecurity" (*Rechtsunsicherheit*). In a dictatorial police state it is difficult to know the range of permitted conduct. "There remains an uncertainty that engenders insecurity because in large measure the regime is unable or unwilling to define the boundaries of tolerance and deviance" (Dallin & Breslauer, 1970, 203). It has also rightly been said of GDR-type regimes that whatever is not explicitly permitted is prohibited (Laatz, 1983, 122), but this did not remove the citizen's insecurity, because it was never quite clear what was included in the range of the permitted.

In any case, the citizen was subject to whatever the police deemed appropriate. There were no legal protections. There were no administrative or constitutional courts in which to sue for remedies. The police, of course, was well aware that the citizens had no rights that could effectively be asserted. The GDR signed the Helsinki Accords (1975), but even these provisions did not help East German citizens, though many sought to assert rights on this basis, especially the right to emigrate. After Helsinki they were just as much without rights (*rechtlos*) as before. Many police officers, knowing that they were essentially untouchable, did their jobs with "unlimited brutality" (Budde, 2002; Eppelmann et al., 1996, 471). This was a brutality that many of the (very peaceful) demonstrators of 1989 experienced firsthand (Dennis, 2003, 230–232; Koehler, 1999, 404–405; Maier, 1997, 135, 140–142, 145, 148; Wolfe, 1992, 172–176). Wolf, however, writes that "it appears that only a small minority of individual members of the police system used physical force unnecessarily or acted in excess of legal powers" (1992, 5).

The Stasi

The Ministry for State Security (Stasi)[114] was founded on February 8, 1950, less than one year after the founding of the GDR. It was said to be necessary because of the continuing terrorist bombing attacks of the Anglo-American imperialists against GDR facilities (Gieseke, 2001, 21). While operating as a secret organization, by now the Stasi has become rather well known. A large literature has become available, most, of course, post-1989. Prior to 1989 very little was known and could be known about this institution, for which not even an organization chart existed.[115] Erich Mielke, the long-serving head of the Ministry for State Security (MfS) and a key member of the Politbureau (Baestlein, 2002; Schwan, 1997), was immensely successful in keeping this secret police truly secret. Even the statute regarding the MfS was secret. The decisions and directives of the Party (not of the state!) were declared to be the basis of the MfS' activities. State matters, such as the constitution and the laws, were mentioned only secondarily (Eppelmann et al., 1996, 596). The MfS was indeed the "sword and shield" of the Party. It was not, as some have claimed, a "state within the state"[116] (Siebenmorgen, 1993, 6–8). It did not have, and did not seek, functions other than serving the Party, particularly to quell dissent and to crush any opposition to the regime. Mielke was the closest ally of Honecker throughout. Mielke and Honecker used to meet privately after the meetings of the Politbureau and issue various decisions. Only at the very end did he reluctantly support the elevation of Egon Krenz. In any case, without the oppressive exertions of the Stasi, the SED dictatorship could not have been realized[117] (Epplemann et al., 1996, 599; Koehler, 1999, 30).

The MfS had its own military unit, the Wachregiment Feliks Dzerzhinski (also spelled Dzierzynski), named after the founder of the Soviet Cheka. It was well supplied with weapons. In 1989 the Stasi had 100,000 pistols, 55,000 submachine guns, more than 10 million rounds of ammunition, large quantities of explosives, as well as canons and tanks (Arnold, 1995, 164). The Stasi also has its own prisons[118] (especially for prisoners in the interrogation, pretrial phase) (Fritzsch, 1993). There confessions were obtained by various forms of physical and psychological torture,[119] including beating, sleep deprivation, isolation, disinformation (if need be, by way of forged letters from relatives), and denying the right to receive visitors (Sager, 1986). If nothing helped, the interrogation protocols could be falsified. Formally, these were all violations of "socialist legality." The Stasi, however, was not subject to such restraints. Its prisons and activities were not monitored or controlled by the legal authorities of the state, that is, the courts or the public prosecutor (district attorney).

The offenses that could land a person in the arms of the Stasi were wide-ranging—and often incredible. For example, a theology student was charged with (and convicted of) "incitement hostile to the state." He had obtained a copy of Orwell's *1984* from a West German acquaintance and lent it to some of his East German friends[120] (Dennis, 2003, 62). One other person sought to legally emigrate to the West. He wrote to a friend in West Germany and to Erich Honecker, seeking assistance. This brought a four-year prison sentence. Writing to the friend was judged "establishing an illegal contact." The letter to Honecker was regarded as "public denigration." Similar and heavily sanctioned offenses were "contact with enemies of the state," "engaging in propaganda hostile to the state," "treasonable relaying of information," and "hindering state or social activity." Such nebulous categories, of course, provided vast degrees of discretion for the Stasi (and other police organs) and total insecurity for the citizen. In particular, persons who applied to emigrate immediately became objects of criminal investigation, with all the adverse consequences this implies. Citizens who came to the attention of the regime simply as being "hostile negative" without yet having engaged in any hostile or negative action were subject to a variety of measures designed to discredit and ruin them.[121]

One of these was discrediting public reputation, respect, and prestige by linking true allegations, which could be substantiated, with untrue but believable imputations, which could not be disproven. Others included systematically organizing professional and social failure in order to destroy the selftrust of the individual, creating doubt about personal future, creating mistrust and mutual suspicion inside groups and organizations, using personal weaknesses to obtain compliance, sending anonymous or pseudonymous letters or telegrams, distributing compromising photographs of actual or putative meetings, spreading rumors about individuals, or fostering indiscretions. (Wolfe, 1992, 73)

The case of Wolf Biermann is exemplary. The Stasi brought underage youngsters into contact with him, in the hope of being able to charge him with criminal offenses. Pastors often were victims of doctored pornographic photos and fake reports about extramarital affairs (Gieseke, 2001, 189–191). Such things, it is clear, can devastate a person more thoroughly than a prison term. What defense is there, when your friends come to believe these rumors and fake photographs?

The MfS (Stasi) was remarkably large. From a personnel of about 1,000 in 1950 (the year of its founding), it grew to about 91,000 full-time members in 1989. In addition, the Stasi relied on the services of about 176,000 informers of various types[122] (Dennis, 2003, 90). Higher estimates exist (Wolfe, 1992, 71, 77). The informers were recruited and motivated partly by material and partly by other rewards. Dennis (2003, 97) lists five broad categories of motivations: political and ideological conviction, coercion and fear,[123] personal advantage, emotional needs, and desire to influence official policy. The recruiting officers were masters of psychology. Various dissertations were written at the psychological department of the MfS law college in Potsdam on how best to motivate citizens to become informants.[124]

It should be noted, however, that not all recruitment attempts succeeded. Exact figures, naturally, are hard to come by, but it is estimated that only about one attempt in three worked out (Dennis, 2003, 96). However, the Stasi was quite successful in placing or recruiting spies in West Germany, perhaps as many as 5,000, the most famous case being that of Günter Guillaume, who served as Chancellor Willy Brandt's personal assistant and had access to top-secret foreign and domestic materials. In consequence, Brandt had to resign the chancellorship.[125] The Stasi was also quite successful in influencing the Western media to present a positive picture of the GDR (Knabe, 2001).

Mielke's aim was to know everything about everybody. He came remarkably close to realizing that goal.[126] After the fall of the regime, it was discovered that the Stasi had dossiers on over 6 million persons and that it had records on every second family in the GDR.[127] There were over 120 miles of records in the Stasi archives—and this does not count the many records that were destroyed (Koehler, 1999, 20). The extensiveness and the intensity of the Stasi's surveillance were breathtaking. No persons or organizations were immune. The techniques of surveillance included the customary telephone tapping, the opening of letters,[128] and the surreptitious searches and bugging of dwellings.[129] The most outstanding success of the Stasi, however, lay in its ability to get close to the object of observation. After the Stasi files became available, people discovered that some of their closest friends, sometimes even their spouses, had spied and informed on them. "The end result was to turn citizens against one another and to create an atmosphere of debilitating apprehension. No relationship was immune from the possibility . . . that an informer might be involved. . . . Even some students of the lower schools were active as spies"[130] (Wolfe, 1992, 78–79; also Schell & Kalinka, 1991, 120–121). Not yet content with the millions of informers, the regime "created a law that made the failure to denounce fellow citizens a crime punishable by up to five years' imprisonment" (Koehler, 1999, 19).

The Stasi also collected information about the public's mood, particularly by way of the petitions (*Eingaben*) that it received from disgruntled citizens.[131] It had a department just for this purpose: the Central Assessment and Information Group. "The focus of the petitions was on everyday matters such as poor housing, problems at work, neighbourhood concern," etc. (Dennis, 2003, 217–219). These types of complaints were acceptable, since they did not question the basic features of the system. (More about this in Chapter 6.)

The Stasi had almost complete control over a captive population. According to Christoph Klessmann, Orwell's *1984* was more completely realized in the GDR than even in Hitler's Third Reich. It was "the most pervasive and efficient secret service in history" (Dennis, 2003, 2). It certainly appears to have been the largest one. Not only was it vastly larger than the *Gestapo*, but it also had a more dense net of collaborators[132] (Mitter & Wolle, 1993, 545), and it was even more repressive. In any case, the communists' brutal oppression of the nation by means including murder puts the SED leadership well on a par with Hitler's gang (Gieseke, 2001, 182; Welsch, 1999, 20–25, 141–146). Erich Honecker and Erich Mielke "can justifiably be compared to Hitler and Himmler" (Koehler, 1999, 11). Simon Wiesenthal, who knows something about terror regimes, wrote that the Stasi "terrorized their own people worse than the Gestapo" (Koehler, 1999, 27).

In sum, the citizens of the GDR were entirely subject to Party commands, had to participate in meaningless rituals and pretend that they had real influence, were denied the most elementary civil liberties, were inundated with endless antifascist propaganda, were under constant surveillance by police organizations, and had to be ever apprehensive of Stasi informers. These were not the ways to forge a loyal and supportive citizenry. These were the ways to transform citizens into refugees throughout the existence of the SZ/GDR—and finally, in 1989, into revolutionaries.

NOTES

1. Soviet troop strength in the GDR remained at almost 400,000 soldiers.

2. It was not the first time that the GDR censored Soviet materials. Soviet films with scenes critical of Stalin had these scenes removed before the film could be shown in the GDR (Leonhard, 1990, 133–135).

3. Of course, this worked both ways. There had been earlier prohibitions of GDR magazines in the USSR, presumably because the GDR looked too prosperous for Soviet eyes (Dornberg, 1968, 12).

4. For a discussion of the general reaction of the GDR to perestroika, see Czichon & Marohn, 1999.

5. It is of some interest to note that this was not the first time Honecker allied himself with an occupation power. In the plebiscite of 1935, he agitated for the permanent attachment of the (then French-occupied) Saar to France, rather than for its return to Germany. (Schneider, 1992, 218).

6. The pro-Soviet position did not, of course, have to wait for Erich Honecker. In 1949, for example, Rudolf Herrnstadt (the editor in chief of the Party paper *Neues Deutschland* and member of the Central Committee of the SED) wrote that Germany and the working class will not have a secure future without unreserved and unlimited ties to the Soviet Union (Herrnstadt, 1949, 9; Mueller-Enbergs, 1991). Also see Autorenkollektiv, 1985c; Mueckenberger, 1985.

7. But see Vaillancourt, 1986. For a detailed discussion, see my *Rotten Foundations*, Chapter 3.

8. "Marxism played a gigantic part in the development of all branches of knowledge, inasmuch as it provided a stable scientific foundation and an immensely powerful scientific method for cognition of phenomena—and, in particular, of social phenomena" (Vyshinsky, 1948, 83).

9. In 1981, Erich Honecker began to refer to himself and other top Party members as communists rather than socialists (Wroblewsky, 1990b, 148). Marx (1848), it might be noted, referred to Marxist socialists as "communists" in order to distinguish them from other socialists "but later reverted to the use of the term "socialists," when the German Social-Democratic Party was organized" (Hook, 1955, 31).

10. As Christopher (1985, 21) has pointed out, the dominant role of the SED had to be unconditionally recognized by all other forces of society. "Independent moves or spontaneous initiatives, not to speak of real opposition, are not permitted and the multiplicity of parties and organizations is a mere formality."

11. Regarding the change from Ulbricht to Honecker, see Krenz, 1990, 51–53; Podewin, 1996. About Honecker, see Eberle, 2000; Przybylski, 1991; Spittmann, 1990.

12. Marx (and his successors) romanticized "the masses." It is a fairly common error to assume that the victims also are the virtuous. Marx assumed that the proletariat would be liberal, friendly to learning, the sciences, and the arts because the proletariat had been history's maltreated. Alas, suffering does not generally ennoble, and the masses have been the most consistently anti-intellectual force in history (Feuer, 1959, xv).

13. Democratic centralism was said to have the following characteristics: all Party organs are democratically elected; all those who have been elected must report regularly to those who elected them; all resolutions of the higher Party organs are binding on all lower ones; strict Party discipline must be maintained; the minority must submit to the majority decision.

14. For some post-1989 discussions of the Politbureau, see Jochum, 1996a, 1996b; Uschner, 1993.

15. Günter Schabowski (1991, 24–25), a member of the Central Committee since 1981 and of the Politbureau since 1984 as well as occupant of other important positions, noted that from the perspective of the Party it was better to commit sodomy than factionalism.

16. For histories and general discussions of the SED, see Autorenkollektiv, 1978b; Friedrich-Ebert-Stiftung, 1985, 1988; Kuppe, 1985a, 1985b, 1987; McCauley, 1979;

Meuschel, 1992; Oertel, 1988; Richert, 1963; Schultz, 1956; Spittmann, 1987; Weber, 1974, 1982a, 1985b; H. Weber & Oldenburg, 1971; Weber, 1993.

17. Candidates were provisional members of the Party.

18. Such as following the purges of 1948, 1951, and 1953. The last purge took place in 1980, at which time about 4,000 members were expelled (Krisch, 1985, 31). There were several purges between 1953 and 1980.

19. The VIIIth Party Congress (1971) imposed a ban on nonworkers as new Party members because of grave disproportionality (*gravierender Disproportionalität*). The stop was rescinded at the IXth Party Congress (1976) (Wroblewsky, 1990b, 123). It may also be noted here that in the 1970s the "rules and program of the CPSU no longer refer[red] to the 'party of the working class' but rather to the 'party of the whole people.'" (Medvedev, 1977, 309).

20. *Grundorganizationen* (bases) were formed when there were at least three Party members at a given territory or workplace. *Abteilungsorganizationen* (sections) could be formed when there were 150 Party members at a given territory or workplace. In 1980 the SED had a total of 79,668 *Grundorganizationen* and *Abteilungsorganizationen* (VEB, 1984, 259).

21. Known as the first secretary before 1976.

22. In addition to head of the Politbureau and general secretary of the ZK, Walter Ulbricht and Erich Honecker held the additional positions of chairman of the Council of State (*Staatsrat*) and of chairman of the National Defense Council (*Nationaler Verteidigungsrat*). Egon Krenz also held these offices, but only for a short time.

23. Egon Krenz, it will be remembered, congratulated the Chinese on their Tiananmen Square suppression—a matter that he now denies (Krenz, 1999, 71–73). He also was in charge of the last election in the GDR, the results of which were shamelessly falsified—the responsibility for which he now also denies (Krenz, 1990, 125–128, 1999, 283). These things did not recommend him for the top position in the eyes of most GDR citizens. It did not help that Krenz also was the secretary for security matters in the Central Committee.

24. Party decisions were binding on state organs even without a parallel decision of the executive (*Ministerrat*) or the legislative organs (*Volkskammer*) of the state (Richert, 1961, 11).

25. Zaisser was a member of the Politbureau and the first minister for State Security; Herrnstadt was the editor in chief of the Party newspaper *Neues Deutschland*.

26. Wrong politics toward the GDR was one of the accusations against Beria in 1953 (Rayfield, 2004, 548).

27. For some discussions of the events of June 1953, see Bentzien, 2003; Croan & Friedrich, 1958, 46ff; Dornberg, 1968, 69ff; Hagen, 1992; Hanhardt, 1968, 56–61; Hegedues & Wilke, 2000; Klein, 2002; Leonhard, 1981; Mayer, 2002, 22–27; McCauley, 1983, 63ff; Mitter & Wolle, 1993, 27–162; Ostermann, 2001; Prauss, 1960, 97ff; Strauss, 1982; Turner, 1987, 116ff; Wassmund, 1981, 342ff. The regime characterized the events of 1953 first as a "fascist putsch," later as a "counter-revolutionary putsch"—anything but to acknowledge that the *workers* of the workers-and-farmers state had revolted against their government, which sought to speed up the transformation of GDR society and economy to the soviet model (Prokop, 2003, 15–18). For the Soviet activities, see Berg, 1988, 58–59.

28. In a typical attempt by dictatorial regimes to seek out not only the political but also the moral ruin of perceived enemies, he was also accused of having made ho-

mosexual advances toward his chauffeur. The prototype of this action can be found in the trial of Marie Antoinette before the Convention. It was not enough to charge her with (political) treason; her character also had to be besmirched by accusing her of sexual relations with her small son, the dauphin. It will be remembered that when Hitler ordered the murder of his old comrade Ernst Roehm, he also took great care to portray him as a "homosexual menace." The real issue, of course, was not sex but power. Of course, tables were turned recently with the publication of Machtan's (2001) preposterous book, "outing" Hitler as a homosexual.

29. Schirdewan was a member of the Politbureau; Wollweber was a member of the Politbureau and minister for State Security (the successor to Zaisser); Behrens was a professor of economics, director of the Central Office for Statistics, and member of the Council of Ministers; Benary was a prominent economist, who together with Behrens advocated and developed the New Economic System (for which, see Chapter 5).

30. Havemann had been a recognized opponent of the Hitler regime. In fact, he was sentenced to death at the end of 1943 by the notorious "People's Court" (*Volksgerichtshof*) (Mueller-Enbergs, 2000, 320).

31. Reliance on the military was muted, however. The military as primary regime support would have been "bonapartism," rejected by socialists since the days of Marx and Engels. In at least one matter the rulers of the GDR followed the example of Napoleon Bonaparte: the abolition of the traditional regional frontiers in favor of new administrative units (departments).

32. For the SED bases of legitimacy, see Fricke, 1974, 954ff; Kuppe, 1985, 207; Rausch, 1985, 317; Sontheimer & Bleek, 1975, 46; Weber, 1985b, 213.

33. As Dean Acheson observed, the GDR was "without any legal validity or foundation in popular will [since it was] created by Soviet and Communist fiat" (as quoted in Scharf, 1984, 10).

34. Not only the SED but also the other parties and the mass organizations became subject to the cadre model (Brandt & Dinges, 1984). The same is true, of course, for the state (Glaessner, 1977).

35. For an early discussion of this claim, see Eastman, 1940.

36. This has not prevented GDR theorists from claiming that socialist regimes are *necessarily* democratic: "Democracy is the only possible organizational form for socialism. It is no accident that the first state in the history of the world which has been erected on truly lawful foundations (the USSR), is a state of the socialist type" (Institut für Theorie . . . , 1986, 28).

37. The continued reliance on Soviet support "extinguished [the] last remaining parts of legitimacy" (Scharf, 1984, 9–10). Contrary to communist pretenses, the GDR was not established by way of a proletarian revolution but was imposed by the Red Army and its German helpers on a Stalinist model (Hilger et al., 2001; Minnerup, 1982, 12; Weber, 1993). The Soviet military presence in the GDR amounted to twenty divisions (nearly 400,000 soldiers) (Croan, 1976a, 48).

38. At times the Party emphasized its (supposed) working-class origins even more heavily than (presumed) policy-making expertise.

39. In fact, even to ask for a choice was dangerous. Berg (1988, 45) reports how he was "elected" first SED secretary of a Bezirk. The leadership submitted his name (and only his name) to the electoral body. Four of the members of that body wanted the list to include an alternative candidate. They were expelled from the Party because of a violation of democratic centralism.

40. It was none other than Stalin, in his speech on the draft constitution, who declared: "It may be said that silence is not criticism. But that is not true. The method of keeping silent, as a special method of ignoring things, is also a form of criticism" (Wolfe, 1961, 175). Another way of stating the same principle is Hitler's insistence that "he who is not for us, is against us" and that to show support for national-socialism, it was not enough to say, "I believe." Supporters had to demonstrate their support by their actions. These are principles with which the GDR regime heartily agreed (Richert, 1961, 29). So did the Soviet regime (Spechler, 1982, 1). For a general discussion of the similarities of Left and Right totalitarianism, see my *Rotten Foundations*, Chapter 6; see also Vahlefeld, 2002. For a post-1989 East German rejection of the comparability thesis, see Elm, 2001, 10.

41. The story of having overcome all conflicts is essentially a camouflage for socialist system's inability to deal with conflicts (Bollinger, 1996; see also Sperlich, 2002, 181–191).

42. As Minnerup (1982, 24) rightly observed, the GDR had a legitimacy deficit not only on democratic but also on national grounds.

43. For discussions of the Abgrenzung to West Germany, see Barm, 1971; Childs, 1985, xi–xv; Christopher, 1985, 26–28; Croan, 1976a, 33; Dornberg, 1968, 234, 1974, 198; Krisch, 1985, 74–75, 81–83; Spanger, 1982.

44. Contrary to the formulation of two states of German nationality, the GDR sought to foster not "state consciousness" but "national consciousness" (Schweigler, 1975, 130).

45. Some examples are keeping the old title of the railroads, *Reichsbahn* (imperial railroad) and the "goose-stepping" tradition in the military as well as the massive military parades (Otto, 1961), none of which could be found in the FRG. Honecker went as far as declaring that the "goose step" was the GDR's way of "honoring the victims of fascism, militarism, and imperialism" (Staadt, 1995, 82).

46. This gave rise to a joke. Question: name three countries that begin with "u." Answer: USSR, USA, and Unsere DDR.

47. Quite early the GDR developed a separate dictionary of the (GDR's) German language; the use of FRG dictionaries was forbidden (Paetzold, 1991, 17; see also Fleischer, 1987; Gudorf, 1981; Joensson, 1985; Leske et al., 1982; Ludz, 1980, 113–182; Schmitt, 1993).

48. A "national socialist" German culture?

49. See, for example, Bartel, 1981, 4: 90, 1984; Brinks, 1992; Deiters, 1983, 2: 96; Laube, 1982, 2: 104; Wimmer, 1984. On the general problems of GDR historical science, see Iggers et al., 1998 and Neuhaeuser-Wespy, 1996.

50. Krisch (1985, 83–87) refers to this as "selective incorporation." It follows the Soviet pattern. As Van den Bercken (1987, 264) points out, "By re-interpreting and annexing the past, the Soviet government wishes to represent itself as the legitimate heir of Russian history."

51. Stalin was more insightful and lastly right when he remarked that imposing communism on Germany was like trying to put a saddle on a cow—it works only as long as strong force is applied. Of course, that is precisely what was done. See McElvoy, *The Saddled Cow*, 1992.

52. The GDR saw it differently, at least in its public pronouncement. For the SED regime, *Ostpolitik* was "an assault against the community of socialist states through anticommunism and nationalism, seeking ideological weakening of the socialist states, and wanting to increase the effectiveness of imperialism" (Rausch, 1974,

14; see also Sarotte, 2001), none of which, of course, prevented the GDR from taking advantage of the many economic benefits that *Ostpolitik* offered. It should be acknowledged, however, that prior to *Ostpolitik* the FRG sought to isolate the GDR (Gray, 2003).

53. In 1988, one year before "We are one people," perceptive observers, such as Rupert Scholz (1988, 79), came to the conclusion that the attempt to develop a separate national identity "has failed." On the question of national identity—East and West—since reunification, see Veen, 1993.

54. "*Arbeite mit, plane mit, regiere mit!*" (Art. 21. 1, Constitution of the German Democratic Republic, 1974).

55. Wolfgang Weichelt (1982a, 768), the director of the SED Institute for the Theory of the State and the Law and chair of the Judiciary (Legal) Committee of the Parliament (*Volkskammer*), even called it an "essential" feature of socialist democracy.

56. Grigorenko, a leading Soviet dissident, put it this way: "The elections are a mere farce, necessary to those in power so that they can demonstrate to the outside world that the entire nation stands behind them" (as quoted in Lane, 1976, 105).

57. See Brandt, 1983. Erich Honecker, however, had the cheek to declare in 1992 that the choice between the parties of the FRG was only a "seeming" election (*Scheinwahl*), not a real one (Corvalan, 2001, 216).

58. At the last GDR elections (May 7, 1989), it seems that the regime added between five and twenty percentage points to the turnout and between five and sixteen percentage points to the votes for the government slate (National Front) to achieve the customary 98.5% support (Maier, 1997, 132–133; Wolfe, 1992, 106).

59. For some reasons, see the section on "Nonsecret, Compulsory, and Collective Voting" in Chapter 3.

60. As GDR observers noted from the beginning, the meetings of officials with their constituents were devoted mostly to praising the regime (Croan & Friedrich, 1958, 53).

61. Even the draft for the new constitution of 1968 was submitted to public consultation and discussion. It made very little difference (Schulz, 1968, 11–12, 58–60).

62. In recognition of their great theoretical and practical importance, the social courts will be at the center of the third, forthcoming volume of this study: *Popular Justice in a Marxist-Leninist Society: The East German Social Courts and Other Aspects of GDR Law*.

63. For a comprehensive listing of the social organizations of the GDR, see Autorenkollektiv, 1980. For a briefer overview, see Schulze, 1985, 67–68.

64. Laypersons sitting with the professional judge(s) on the same bench and deliberating with the professional judge(s) to find the verdict.

65. *Zivilgesetzbuch*. See Flinder (1999) for a detailed account of its development.

66. *Strafgesetzbuch*.

67. *Strafprozessordnung*.

68. *Gerichtsverfassungsgesetz*.

69. *Gesetz über die gesellschaftlichen Gerichte*.

70. *Konfliktkommissionsordnung*.

71. *Schiedskommissionsordnung*.

72. This is the conventional, but not entirely accurate, translation. The more precise term would be *societal* courts.

73. For a general discussion, see Scharf, 1984, 136–137.

74. Including a monthly magazine just for lay judges: *Der Schöffe*.

75. Also see Table 2.1 with selected participation figures in Krisch, 1985, 41–42.

76. This is the famous routine of self-criticism and mass criticism most heavily practiced in the People's Republic of China (e.g., Dittmer, 1974).

77. An unremitting effort was made in the GDR to show that the working class and the artists were partners in the building of socialism. See Rauschek, 1984.

78. At the SED's Party Congresses, the participants were instructed at which places of the general secretary's report they should break into shouts of joy (Loeser, 1984).

79. Lack of participatory interest is not solely a problem of the socialist states. Wildavsky (1979, 253) has pointed out that citizen participation is in general not highly esteemed—and for a good reason: "Most of us do little and know less; most people are not interested in most public issues most of the time. Why should they be? To take an interest means having to spend time that might be more profitably devoted to the job or a hobby." Wildavsky (1979, 255–256) also noted that public participation can serve moral development, good citizenship, and better public policy—but only if there is participatory "autonomy." That element, however, was sorely lacking in the GDR.

80. For a similar scenario regarding the USSR, see Nelson, 1980, 216.

81. Needless to say, the correct understanding of the state (and of law) can be found only in socialism. "The genius of Marx-Engels-Lenin-Stalin provided a correct understanding of the nature and essence of the state" (Vyshinsky, 1948, 4). Hilde Benjamin ("red Hilde"), who held several important legal offices in the early years of the GDR, declared that Vyshinsky had been the great teacher in the construction of law in the GDR. One suspects that she was right. While GDR law was not as bloody as Soviet law, much of it resembled Vyshinsky's 1924–1938 pursuits (Henrich, 1990, 179).

82. See, for example, Meyer, 1955, 384.

83. It might be noted here that there has long been a German tradition (quite independent of socialism) of using the state's administrative machinery to bring about social and economic change.

84. Vyshinsky (1948, 40) called the withering-away position a Trotskyist-Bukharinist perversion. Heuer (1989, 359), in his otherwise first-class essay, calls the thesis of the early withering "revisionism." Other characterizations of that position (according to the *Philosophisches Wörterbuch*) were opportunism, pacifism, formalism, cosmopolitanism, and social democratism.

85. The same authors also let it be known that it is a lie that Marx assigned only a short period of time to the dictatorship of the proletariat (Autorenkollektiv, 1985c, 151).

86. Of course, the state as such was no more than a branch office of the Party (Misselwitz, 1993, 105).

87. See also Fedoseyev, 1979, 30.

88. One is reminded of Erich Mielke's pathetic declaration in the GDR parliament on November 13, 1990: "[B]ut I love you all." Mielke, of course, had been the greatly feared minister for State Security (the head of the dreaded Stasi) and one of the most extreme hard-liners in the Politbureau (Baestlein, 2002).

89. It takes considerable brazenness and shamelessness to produce assertions of the following type. *USSR*: "Article 3 of the Constitution of the USSR provides that 'all authority in the USSR belongs to the toilers of the city and country, personified

by Soviets of the Deputies of the Toilers,' confirming the fact of world history in our country that authority is actually in the hands of the toilers—they in reality govern the state and all the affairs of the state" (Vyshinsky, 1948, 164). *GDR*: "Its Programme, its practical activities and social composition show the SED to be a genuine Party of the working class, which at the same time represents the interests of the entire people. . . . The over-riding principle underlying the work of the SED [is]: We know but one aim that permeates the entire policy of our party: to do everything for the well-being of man, for the happiness of the people, for the interest of the working class and all working people. . . . The relationship of trust between the party and the people has grown further as a result. The overwhelming majority of the people in the GDR consider the leading role of the SED in the state and the economy to be one of their most important achievements (Autorenkollektiv, 1977, 32–34).

90. The fact of an undemocratic application was, of course, denied by the GDR. See Klenner, 1967.

91. For general reviews, see Mampel, 1982 (West) and Weichelt, 1984 (East).

92. GDR commentators, nevertheless, manage to pose as champions of civil liberties, protesting, for example, the conservative attacks on civil liberties in the United States of America. See Doetsch and Laemmerzahl, 1987, 188. Also see Childs, 1985, 172–173.

93. These unities are constituent parts of the superiority of Marxism-Leninism. As the incomparable Andrei Vyshinsky tells it: "For the first time in human history there is eliminated the conflict between social interest and personal interest, society and the state, and between society and the state (on the one hand) and individuality and individual interests (on the other)" (Vyshinsky, 1948, 76). It is also a reason that socialist science is superior: "In contrast to the methodology of bourgeois science, which rends an object into two unconnected parts—form and substance—dialectical materialism insists that form and substance are one and contemplates phenomena from the standpoint of that unity" (Vyshinsky, 1948, 85).

94. In fact, political pluralism was regarded as "anti-socialist." See Roeder & Weichelt, 1981; Winkler, 1969.

95. For a more detailed discussion of the socialist unity claims, see my *Rotten Foundations*, Chapter 5.

96. When citizens felt that their rights had been violated, they could not bring suit. They had to rely on the weak and inadequate step of filing a complaint (*Eingabe*) with those responsible for the violation.

97. For a discussion of the development of a "socialist morality," see Bittighoefer & Schmollack, 1968; Mansilla, 1984.

98. Regarding the lack of administrative law and administrative courts (until 1988), see my forthcoming *Popular Justice in a Marxist-Leninist Society: The East German Social Courts and Other Aspects of GDR Law*. See also Ritter, 1971, 1973.

99. It should be noted that the censorship was comprehensive and not limited to evidently political topics. It included all the forms of artistic expression (Agde, 2000; Deiritz, 1993; Dietzel, 2003; Lucchesi, 1993; Muhlen, 1951, 8; Offner & Schroeder, 2000; Rother, 2001; Schiller, 2001; Schwarze, 1973, 18; Stuber, 1998). Even Margot Honecker had to admit that artists were often treated unfairly by the regime (Corvalan, 2001, 76–77). For the likeness of socialist and nazi art censorship, see my *Rotten Foundations*, 118–127; see also Bielefelder Kunstverein, 1997; Muhlen, 1951, 8; Schwarze, 1973, 18. Official publications, of course, had nothing but praise for GDR

cultural developments (i.e., Struetzel & Petzold, 1985). Censorship even extended to natural catastrophes and accidents. This has led some people to believe that such events never happen in socialist systems (Berg, 1988, 99; Heym, 1990, 73; Kolakowski, 1981, 3: 150).

100. In a splendid example of totalitarian brazenness, Soviet propagandists declared: "Anyone can write what he wants here—even complaints about government policies. If such articles don't appear, it's because people are contented with Soviet life" (Lee, 1984, 15).

101. For example, the GDR press published much information on Western military expenditures. The equivalent figures for the USSR, GDR, and other socialist nations, however, were nowhere to be found, creating the impression of one-sided and rampant Western militarism as against the peace-loving socialist camp (Pfaff, 1968, 283). This, of course, is particularly brazen in the context of an increased military orientation and training of the GDR schools (Fricke, 1982; Pfaff, 1968).

102. Questions about freedom of the press were typically answered by pointing to the many organizations in the country—from youth and sports clubs, to technical and scientific associations—that did (or could) publish periodicals or newsletters. But this misses the point. These organizations and their publications were under strict Party control. Prepublication censorship was the rule (for an example, see Novosti Press Agency, 1978, 34).

103. It is also worth pointing out that visitors could not enter the university by themselves. Whenever I visited Humboldt University, I had first to go to a control station to identify myself. From there they would contact the professor on whom I wanted to call. The professor then would send an assistant to get me. Whenever I was in this university, there would always be close supervision. This procedure was the same for all academic institutions and other types of organizations (Wechsberg, 1964, 4–5). In some years, foreign citizens were altogether prohibited from visiting Humboldt University (Mehls, 1998, 201).

104. This was supplemented by the claim that only socialism is truly peace-loving. See Honecker, 1981, 175ff, 1984, 1989.

105. For a detailed discussion of the nazi and the communist version of totalitarianism, see my *Rotten Foundations*, Chapter 6.

106. See the discussion in Chapter 2.

107. This line of argument was also used to recruit Stasi agents who did not respond adequately to the socialist appeals (Dennis, 2003, 98).

108. It should be noted here that anti-Semitism was not a regime priority. Also, the GDR did not pay reparations to Israel (Zuckermann, 2002).

109. As had the other socialist countries. See, for example, Bobkov, 1987.

110. This is not to say that the formal law had no influence on police conduct. But when the Party had an interest in a matter, that interest prevailed. A good example of this is the issue of personal identification. "The police statute (§12, *VP-Gesetz*) stipulated that a policeman could require documentary identification of a person only when absolutely necessary in order to fulfill a police duty" (Wolfe, 1992, 37). It was, however, an interest of the Party to know who among the citizens had contact with foreign embassies. Thus, the police frequently demanded identification of persons coming out of a foreign embassy (including that of the FRG). This also, of course, had the purpose of discouraging such contacts.

111. In the socialist system of the GDR, the police had additional "social" and "ed-

ucational" functions. It also had to play a class mission, that is, to serve the interests of the working class (Wolfe, 1992, 24–25). The last statement would be more forthright if it talked about the interest of the Party.

112. It is of significance in this respect that the visible presence of the police was very high. One could not walk very far in the streets of the GDR without encountering police patrols (Wolfe, 1992, 43).

113. In the USSR it can be seen in the post-Khrushchev shift from ideology to material incentives.

114. A fuller account of the Stasi will be found in my forthcoming *Popular Justice in a Marxist-Leninist Society: The East German Social Courts and Other Aspects of GDR Law*.

115. For a detailed analysis of the organizational features of the MfS, see Henke et al., 1996.

116. Even at the local level, the respective first secretary of the SED could give orders to the local MfS office, albeit usually expressed as a recommendation (Wolfe, 1992, 69).

117. In typical SED manner, the massive surveillance was denied. Only three days before the Wall fell, Mielke's number two, Rudi Mittig, declared: "The Ministry of State Security does not keep people under surveillance." This exists "only in the imagination of the Western media" (Dennis, 2003, 234). A typical product of Eastern imagination was the idea that there cannot be crime in socialism; when criminal acts occur, they evince remnants of bourgeois mentality or the direct influence of the "class-enemy" (Zeng, 2000, 47).

118. The Stasi had prepared lists of tens of thousands of persons who were to be arrested and interned in special camps in case of emergency or war (Eppelmann et al., 1996, 598–599). There also were a variety of underground facilities (bunkers) in various places of East Germany (Wolfe, 1992, 62, 84–85).

119. Taking a leaf from the KGB, the Stasi also made use of psychiatric institutions to deal with dissidents (Behnke, 1995; Schell & Kalinka, 1991, 171–174; Suess, 1998). Psychopharmacological methods to make people literally crazy were also used (Siebenmorgen, 1993, 201). On the Stasi's collaboration with the KGB, see Fricke & Marquardt, 1995.

120. The sentence was twenty-eight months of imprisonment.

121. The Stasi had a special division for disinformation. Its primary purpose was to spread false and damaging information about persons in disfavor with the Party.

122. By one estimate, the Stasi had about 250,000 full-time staff and 600,000 unofficial cooperators (informants) between 1950 and 1989 (Dennis, 2003, 90; Miller, 1999).

123. The threat of exposure was also prominently used. This included misdemeanors that had not otherwise come to light, as well as certain sexual inclinations and drug habits.

124. Including a dissertation on how to recruit homosexuals. The Stasi also used prostitutes to get information from them or to compromise foreign visitors—in the GDR and elsewhere (Dennis, 2003, 94–96, 203–204).

125. It should also be noted that the Stasi actively supported the terrorists of the "Red Army Faction," who had committed murder and arson in the West (Schell & Kalinka, 1991, 225–250; Siebenmorgen, 1993, 225–235; Wolfe, 1992, 80–84).

126. To hide certain activities, the MfS also had its own banking system, with some

4,000 accounts. It had no connection to the GDR state bank or to any other bank (Wolfe, 1992, 62).

127. There was a joke: How do you know that your taxi driver works for the Stasi? He knows your address before you tell him.

128. In East Berlin alone, there were 600 Stasi employees checking the mails.

129. There also was the kidnapping of opponents, particularly in West Berlin. For the discussion of a number of cases, see Epplemann et al., 1996, 599–600; Gieseke, 2001, 182–184. For a general discussion of Berlin during the Cold War, see Smith, 2002.

130. This was another aspect of the deliberate education to an "irreconcilable hatred" of the "class enemy" (Welsch, 1999, 119–122). For a general discussion of the misuse of children and young people, see Behnke, 1998.

131. *Eingaben* could be made to any agency of the state, including the highest offices. They had the purpose of reducing the irritation and feeling of helplessness in the population. This did not succeed, because what really ailed the GDR could not be the subject of *Eingaben*. Only fairly superficial matters could be addressed in this way. Nevertheless, it has been estimated that each year there were about 70,000 *Eingaben* (Muehlberg, 2000, 233).

132. It has been estimated that at the universities, for example, at least 25% of the academic staff worked for the Stasi (Childs, 2001, 39).

Chapter 5

Economics: Reforms, Rigidity, and Failure

THE PRINCIPAL QUESTIONS

Two questions have received much attention in the last few years: (1) What was the real nature of the GDR economy? (2) What caused the rapid collapse of the communist regime of East Germany? Much has been learned since 1989, but the final word may not yet have been spoken in all respects. Additional information keeps emerging out of state and Party archives; individuals (former officials as well as ordinary citizens) are beginning to talk freely about their experiences. This chapter focuses predominantly on the first question, with only an occasional comment regarding the second. The two questions, of course, are closely related. Information about "economics in the GDR" has much to say about "the causes of the regime's demise," though, of course, there were other factors that contributed mightily to the downfall (see Chapters 6 and 7).

Life in the GDR made it difficult for the regime to persuade its people that it was legitimate (i.e., having gained power by lawful means), popular (i.e., freely accepted and supported by its citizens), and competent (i.e., successful in satisfying the needs and wishes of its citizens). Lack of regime legitimacy, support, and competence was the first set of causes of the collapse of communist rule—the internal one. The second set—the external one—was the regime's opposition to Gorbachev's reforms (much desired by the citizens of the GDR),[1] the increasing estrangement of Moscow and Berlin, and steady decline in Soviet willingness to support and shore up what was seen by them as a rigid and doomed leadership. Moscow's correct perception of the increasingly unstable and even desperate political, social, and economic conditions of the GDR in the late 1980s contributed substantially to the evolution of Gorbachev's policy of nonintervention. These developments found their culmination in November 1989, when Soviet tanks would not roll into the streets of the East German cities in defense of the regime—as they had done in 1953.[2] What Gorbachev hoped the East German upheavals would bring, of course, was not the end of communist rule in the GDR but its reform: the advent of a new and better communist government. He was to be disappointed.

A thorough discussion of life in East Germany and of the causes of the regime's collapse would fill several books. This chapter and the next two can deal with only some of the issues and aspects of the GDR's social, economic, and political conditions and circumstances. References, however, will be provided to facilitate more detailed and extensive inquiry.

GDR FICTIONS AND WESTERN CREDULITY

The economic achievements of the GDR were vastly overstated by the regime's propaganda machine but widely believed in the West—even declaring that the "East Germans, too, produced their own 'economic miracle'"[3] (Shlaes, 1991, 3). As late as 1988, Western observers could be found proclaiming that the GDR had become "one of the world's stablest and most advanced economic powers" (McKenna, 1988, 79). Indeed, according to the same author (91): "The East German government has proved that it is possible to build a productive communist state." Or as Bryson (1989, 177; see also Kuhrt, 1996a, 11) formulated it: "Given the natural advantages of socialism (job security, price stability, and the absence of poverty), the system is economically viable if it can maintain its productive momentum and current consumer-friendliness." As anyone who had even just once visited the GDR knew, if there ever was a system that was *not* consumer-friendly, it was that of East Germany.

Even after the opening of the Wall and the new availability of factual economic information, some commentators clung to their earlier misjudgments, such as that "the East German economy did actually work—until its collapse with the opening of the borders in 1989" (Fulbrook, 1992, 191). It may not fit into the dream picture of socialist economics, but the opening of the border was the consequence of the regime's collapse, which was the consequence of the collapse of the economy. It is to be afflicted with unrelieved blindness to believe that the GDR economy collapsed because of the opening of the border. The U.S. Central Intelligence Agency (CIA) also was duped. "As late as 1987 the [CIA] was estimating the per capita Gross National Product (GNP) to be somewhat higher in East Germany than in West Germany . . . [in fact, of course, it was] vastly lower" (Eberstadt, 1993, 47).

Not only was the East German GNP substantially lower than the West German GNP, but, worse yet, the East German economy was primitive, inefficient, largely in ruins, and near collapse in the 1980s, enduring beyond its natural life span only because it was shored up by massive West German aid. The GDR infrastructure and industrial plant, in many ways, had barely made it into the twentieth century. In effect, East Germany resembled a developing country, perpetually needing to import goods, services, and know-how. Even the workers were dissatisfied, commenting that the work in the factory still proceeded as in the year 1800 (Heym, 1990, 97). There is the often-told joke about the Japanese delegation, having visited GDR factories, thanking their guides for the very interesting museum tour and asking to see the actual factories now.

The admirers of the East German "economic miracle" tend to be strangely silent on the vast subsidies received by the GDR from the FRG. Hannes Adomeit (1991, 533), for example, refers to the GDR's "comparative advantage" but does not mention with a single word the Western subsidies that were responsible for this advantage. Adomeit was right, however, to conclude that in the 1980s the "East German economy . . . was in good shape in comparison to the economies of its Eastern neighbors" (see also Baylis, 1989, 34; Bryson, 1989, 174; Francisco, 1989, 189, 195). The GDR did indeed look quite good in comparison to the other members of the Soviet Bloc. The economic shortcomings of the GDR were obvious in comparison to the West. The GDR was quite able to hold its own relative to the other socialist states.

As in other socialist countries, GDR production figures (like other economic indicators) were frequently concealed and regularly falsified[4] (Brzeski, 1970, 193). This was done not only by reporting false figures. Some "true" figures, for example, were generated via the atypical work conditions of "models" and "activists" (Demantowsky, 2000). The GDR was not alone in employing deceptive practices. Heng and Shapiro (1986, 220) reported these People's Republic of China (PRC) practices: "The model workers worked with special tools on specially prepared projects . . . , the model plants received special allocations of raw materials and production machinery . . . , and the model villages received special allocations of seed and fertilizer." The quality of the goods produced also was greatly exaggerated. The GDR even took a leaf from capitalist systems, where a "new and improved product" generally means no more than a "higher price" (Stahnke, 1986, 5). In the GDR a "product was considered 'new' . . . even if only a quarter of its 'use-value' was substantially upgraded. Hence, slight changes in colour, equipment, or other characteristics qualified the producer for higher returns" (Bryson & Melzer, 1991, 25; Thiessen, 2001, 19). In the end, there hardly was a GDR product for which regime propaganda did not claim that it met international standards (Falk et al., 1969)—especially in the fields of microelectronics, optics, and robots[5] (Geipel, 1988; Stoph, 1968, 20)—but for most of them this was a false claim.[6] Gerhard Schuerer (1968, 40), chairman of the State Planning Commission, however, proclaimed electronics and other advanced technologies not only GDR success stories but also part of Marxism-Leninism: "Socialist economic management is part of the economic system of socialism and at the same time the major instrument of its implementation as a whole. This management is based on the Marxist-Leninist science of organization, chiefly on the use of cybernetics, operational research and the application of electronic data processing."[7]

As will be seen later, the primary reason for the poor performance of the GDR economy must be sought in the weaknesses and misjudgments of the planned economy, particularly in its incredible waste of capital, labor, machinery, energy, and raw materials (Hoffmann, 2002; Pirker et al., 1995; Schwarzer, 1999; Wenzel, 1998b). The GDR regime, of course, never tired of asserting that it was contrary to the nature of communism to waste public funds, to underutilize the contributions of science and technology, and to take less than full advantage of the creative initiatives of individual workers and collectives (Institut für Theorie des Staates und des Rechts . . . , 1986, 296). The regime also vigorously asserted that Western claims that its centralized planned economy was unable to satisfy the material needs of its people were "contrary to all facts" (Autorenkollektiv, 1985c, 127).

There certainly was no lack of attention to economic performance. As Kopstein (1997, 1) has pointed out, the SED hierarchy was literally obsessed with improving it. Some nonsystemic reasons for the poor performance of the GDR economy are found in the GDR's obligation to serve the economic needs of the USSR and the COMECON bloc and in the loss of professional and skilled labor before the building of the Wall in 1961. The GDR's own explanations for low economic performance focused on its relative lack of raw materials and energy sources. These explanations are correct as far as they go. Yet other countries with similar paucities (one thinks of Japan) have done very much better. Kopstein (1997, 2) lists three major *political* reasons for the economic decline of the GDR: its dependence on the Soviet Union, its bureaucracy, and the "veto power" of its own working class. The first two are conventional; the third is unusual and surprising. It is considered later.

THE ECONOMIC SYSTEM

Early Economic Policies

The distinguishing characteristic of a socialist economy is the comprehensive transfer of the means of production from private to public ownership. The private owners are expropriated but, typically, not compensated. The chief instrument of ownership transfer is confiscation. As noted, the early policies of the Soviet Union in its Zone of Occupation were not radically Leninist-Stalinist. For tactical reasons, particularly because of the hope to bring all of Germany under Soviet domination, SMAD and Ulbricht took the slow road toward Soviet politics and economics (Matschke, 1988). The expropriation of the owners of the means of production proceeded slowly and through a number of stages. Only the largest industrial and agricultural enterprises (and those owned by persons associated with the national-socialist regime) were socialized immediately after the war. Furthermore, at first, most property was transferred to regional or communal jurisdiction, rather than to central (zonal) control.

The *farm policy* of the Soviet Zone and the GDR went through three basic steps. First was the quite popular land reform program of 1945, which increased the number of independent farmers and privately owned farms by distributing to refugees, farm laborers, and small farmers the acreage of more than 7,000 large estates, that is, those with more than 100 hectares. These new farms tended to be quite small. There are reasons to believe that this was a deliberate creation of uneconomical farms in order to prepare for the collectivization (combining small farms into larger units) to come (Stadtmueller, 1963, 236). In any case, for the time being, the small farms needed much assistance. The "mutual farmers' help organization" (*Vereinigung für gegenseitige Bauernhilfe*) was set up in 1946, and common machine parks in 1947.

In the second phase (1952–1960) farmers were pressured to "voluntarily" deed their land to agricultural collectives or (somewhat later) to state farms. In exchange, they were promised better machinery and supplies as well as lower production quotas. The proportion of farmland in collective or state ownership increased from about 25% in 1952 to 45% in 1959. The third stage, drawn up at the Vth SED Party Congress in 1958, began in 1960: all voluntaristic pretense was dropped, and collectivization became mandatory.[8] By the mid-1960s, 85% of the land had been collectivized. Not long thereafter, the figure approached 100%. Not surprisingly, many farmers responded to the loss of independence by joining the flight to the West (Biehler, 1994; Childs, 1983, 14–15; Kluge et al., 2001; Steele, 1977, 45, 79–80, 115; Wassmund, 1981, 339).

The collectivization of the East German agriculture was not without malice and brutalities. It included expropriation without any compensation, expulsion from homes, arrests, and incarcerations. Soviet officers played an important role in these actions. When the leadership of the CDU manifested some opposition in 1945, its leaders—Andreas Hermens and Walther Schreiber—were quickly removed from their positions (Eppelmann et al., 1996, 131–133). East German collectivization did not, however, entail the deliberate killing of millions of people, as it had in the USSR.[9] Farm productivity, however, sank and remained low throughout the existence of the GDR. In 1967 GDR farm productivity was about 66% of that of the FRG. By 1984 this percentage had declined to about 43% (Thalheim, 1988, 67). By April 1953 about 40% of the larger farmers had fled to the West, and much of the GDR's productive land was lying fallow (Kopstein, 1997, 35). By the end of the 1970s, at the latest, it had become clear that the attempt to engage in agriculture on an industrial model was an abject failure. There were food shortages. An adequate supply of even the most basic food staples never was fully assured during the life of the GDR. None of this, however, deterred socialist propagandists from proclaiming that the cooperative (collectivized) farmers had acquired a socialist consciousness, that they were firmly allied with the working class, and that they felt at home in their socialist villages and liked to live there, which, however, did not stop them from trying to escape to the West. In the words of an Autorenkollektiv (1984, 244):

> The cooperative farmers accept the leading role of the working class and its Marxist-Leninist party; they accept the role of the working class to strengthen socialist attitudes among the cooperative farmers; they comprehend the historic mission of the working class, which leads to a better understanding of socialist achievements and personal identification with them, and to deeper awareness of one's own responsibility for socialist society and in the class conflict with imperialism.

The cooperative farmers, if this testimony is to be accepted, were long on socialist consciousness; too bad that they were so short on productive accomplishments. In June 1948, SMAD authorized the organization of the Democratic Farmers Party of Germany (DBD = *Demokratische Bauernpartei Deutschlands*). The party's functionaries largely came from the SED, as was the case with the other alternative parties. The purpose of the DBD was to secure the collectivization of agriculture and to organize farmers to support SED policies. In 1963, finally, at the VIIth Party Conference of the DBD, the DBD dropped all pretenses of independence and formally adopted the program of the SED as its own (Eppelmann et al., 1996, 153–155).

The conversion of the *industrial means of production* to public ownership also proceeded in stages but advanced more rapidly. The process began with SMAD Order No. 1 of July 23, 1945, which ordered the expropriation of all banks and insurance companies. SMAD Order No. 124 of October 30, 1945, ordered the expropriation of some industrial enterprises. Further orders covered everything: from stores, restaurants, and drugstores, to mining operations. By 1972 practically all enterprises had been socialized, leading to the SED's proud proclamation of the "victory of the socialist mode of production in the DDR" (Eppelmann et al., 1996, 181–183). The private sector, which had been predominant until 1945, was reduced to 25% of all enterprises in 1950, to 5% in 1959, and to about 3% in the last years of the GDR. The goal of comprehensive public ownership was reached in several ways. Outright expropriation was one of them. Other means were more subtle, such as destroying the economic viability of the private firm by failing to supply raw materials for production and capital for modernization and by imposing excessive taxation and mandatory (unprofitable) purchasing and marketing contracts (Thiessen, 2001, 5). If these were not enough, it was always possible to discover rule infringements (entirely unavoidable in East Germany) and put legal (criminal) and administrative pressures on the owners to convert their firms into wholly or partially state-owned entities. The dominant new form was the "people-owned" enterprise (VEB = *Volkseigener Betrieb*), which presumably sounded better than "state-owned." At first, these enterprises were relatively independent operations. By the end of the 1970s, however, most of them had become part of combines. The idea was that larger industrial units would be more efficient. This turned out not to be the case (Eppelmann et al., 1996, 664–666; Schramm, 2001, 66–67). The key effect of conversion to public ownership was, as intended, the elimination of classes other than the regime-supporting proletariat and the collective farmers.

By 1972, middle-class groups such as independent entrepreneurs, shopkeepers, artisans, and farmers in large proportions had left the GDR. The absence of these groups was a major cause of the economic problems of the 1970s and 1980s. The regime, blinded by a rigid Marxism-Leninism, was not about to acknowledge the important economic contributions of these groups.[10] Reflecting the confusions of socialist class theory, official GDR comments on class relations consisted of little more than the wishful drivel: harmonious relations prevailed between the classes of workers and farmers and the stratum of the intelligentsia because the ideology of the working class had become the ideology of the entire people, because the working-class personality had become the model for the development of all classes and strata, and because two prime social problems had essentially been solved: (1) the distinction between physical and mental labor and (2) the distinction between industrial work and agricultural work. Instead of exploiting and exploited classes there was now "the ever closer, creative collaboration of all classes and strata under the leadership of the working class and its Marxist-Leninist party" (Grundmann, 1984, 217–221).

Class collaboration, according to GDR sources, was not based on a "pluralistic compromise among competing interests" but on the "alliance of forces with identical interests" (Autorenkollektiv, 1980, 39–45). In any case, there were no "conflicting class interests" among the classes and strata of the GDR. Whatever differences might exist had "no significant social or political consequences" because there was a "fundamental identity of interest among all classes, strata, and persons" (Panorama-DDR, 1976, 58). All remaining differences between GDR classes and strata belonged to the category of "nonantagonistic conflicts," that is, variances resulting from (still remaining) social and cultural differences, rather than from different relations to the means of production (Autorenkollektiv, 1978a, 24–25; Schuessler, 1981b, 435). Such fantasies reflect, of course, the socialist mirage of comprehensive dialectical unities (for a discussion of which, see my *Rotten Foundations*, Chapter 5).

The GDR had to admit, however, that it had not yet achieved complete uniformity in respect to people's relations to the means of production. Even in the last days of the GDR, there still existed three forms of ownership of the means of production, two major and one minor. The obviously preferred major form was the "socialist ownership of the means of production by the whole society," for example, enterprises, combines, and state farms, which were *the property of the entire people*—one of the more humorous locutions of socialist discourse. The second major form was the "cooperative socialist ownership," for example, agricultural, fishing, and handicrafts cooperatives, where the members of the cooperative, *as a group*, retained ownership (Ahrends & Luft, 1988). The third and minor (and heartily disliked) form was the capitalist remnant of traditional *personal and private ownership*, largely in the form of small service and retail businesses (Cramer, 1988; Grundmann, 1984, 220).

The true classless society was very much wished for but was not anticipated to arrive in the near future. Its advent was envisioned to require developments such as (1) a level of productivity high enough to bring an end to scarcity, allowing goods distributed "to each according to his needs,"[11] (2) the full industrialization of agriculture, (3) the abolition of the distinction between mental and physical work,[12] (4) the change of all property relations to full socialist ownership, and (5) the international victory of socialism. On the last point, Grundmann (1984, 221) writes that the creation of communism (the classless society) "is an international task . . . because relations in one country cannot be called classless as long as on the international level classes still exist that are different from or even hostile to one another." This, of course, is the old issue of "socialism in one country." It is difficult to see why the economic organization of one country should be dependent on that of other countries. One could equally well say that a country cannot be a republic until all countries are republics (until all monarchies have been abolished). This would cause much laughter among people with even the slightest notion about historical developments.

"Discredited" officeholders—that is, civil servants of the Weimar and national-socialist eras—had been removed immediately in 1945, especially those in education, the administration of justice, and the police. Even the learned professions were restructured, that is, nationalized and collectivized. Attorneys, physicians, engineers, architects, and other professionals typically in private practice had to become state employees or, at least, members of special *professional collectives*. According to SED doctrine, the collective is the organic tissue between individual and society. It is the basic form of human existence. Each individual naturally and necessarily is a member of a great variety of collectives, within which practically all his or her activities take place: from work to social life, to hobbies and sport, and to political and civic engagements. Of course, organizing all of a person's activities within collectives makes the surveillance, manipulation, and indoctrination of citizens rather easier—which the regime, of course, knew perfectly well (Becker, 1999).

Teachers, lawyers (Lorenz, 1998), journalists, editors, and artists also joined the ranks of state employees since private employers had largely disappeared. The crucial consequence of the loss of self-employment and private-sector employment was an enormous increase in the power of the state, that is, of the Party, which controlled the state. As Wassmund (1981, 339) rightly pointed out: "The new rulers were perfectly willing to accept economic losses, governmental mismanagement, and a lowering of educational standards through expelling the people they distrusted [even] before they were able to replace them with experts of their own choice." The regime had no qualms about incurring economic losses for the benefit of political gains—particularly since the new ruling class did not have to share in the people's material deprivations.

Strong and *public* support for the new state and for the prevailing Party line became a condition for finding appropriate (or any) employment (Laatz, 1983, 127). Article 24 of the 1974 GDR Constitution included the right as well as the duty to work. The right to work, however, was not interpreted as the right to work in one's profession. Societal necessities prevailed against individual preferences (Ludz, 1974, 190). Of course, dissident physicists and such merely had the right to work as janitors or street sweepers. What Roy Medvedev (1977, xvi–xvii) observed in the USSR also was true in the GDR:

> As everyone knows, in the Soviet Union the state is not just the principal but for all practical purposes the *only* employer; this creates an extremely simple and enormously effective means of putting pressure on individuals who may be totally competent professionally but insufficiently "loyal" in the view of some powerful functionary or other. An attempt was made to influence scientists and scholars by depriving them of well-deserved titles and degrees.

What emerged in place of the traditional heterogeneous multiclass society was the new "worker-and-peasant" state, consisting of a single (if dualistic) class and the hodgepodge stratum of Party functionaries, government officials, and the conglomeration of the various manifestations of the intelligentsia.[13] But the Party functionaries were the real rulers of the GDR, the new "ruling class" (Solga, 1995, 54–55).

For members of the real proletariat, the new developments were a step up in the social order; for the members of the traditional middle and upper classes, it was a decline. Initial GDR policies were designed to advance the interests of the working class. For example, they favored the children of *real* workers in respect to state-controlled benefits, such as access to higher education and scholarships[14] (Berg, 1988, 70; Eichhorn, 2001, 300). However, it became obvious quite quickly to the new elite of functionaries and intellectuals that this produced disadvantages for their own offspring (Maaz, 1995, 11–12). Since it was not possible to simply rescind the well-advertised pro-proletarian policies, other mechanisms were needed to route state benefits to the new ruling class and its scions. The solution was found in expanding the definition of "worker" to include generals, ministers, professors, party functionaries, Stasi operatives, police officers, and sundry other members of the governing order. By this transfiguration, their offspring became the "children of workers" and eligible for favorable treatment under previous policies. The access of *true* working-class children to higher education always remained much lower than that of the offspring of the functionaries and the intelligentsia (Page, 1985, 60). The ceaseless paeans to the identity of interests of all classes and strata failed to notice, of course, this and many other discrepancies.

While it was beneficial for the members of the intelligentsia to be counted among the *workers*, and while it was asserted that intelligentsia and working class had an identity of interests, the GDR regime never formally defined the intelligentsia as being part of the working *class*, at least "not yet." But since the interests of the working class and the intelligentsia were said to "further converge"—no word on how there can be further convergence under conditions of identity—and since the intelligentsia was also alleged to become "more and more like the working class," total integration was confidently expected to occur (Grundmann, 1984, 227–230). This integration would be the result of the unsurpassed political-ideological work of the Party. The PRC, by the way, was way ahead of the GDR in this matter. Already in 1978 Deng Xiaoping had declared "that intellectuals belonged to the working class" (Dittmer, 1988, 21).

Members of the working class or not, the primary beneficiaries of the "rule of the proletariat" were the members of the "new ruling class." They had their own shops (filled with Western products not available elsewhere), medical services (using the most advanced Western medical technology and pharmacology, not available to the ordinary GDR citizen), recreational facilities, and service agencies. The greatest benefits were available to the members of the *nomenclature*[15]: from better housing and transportation, to better shops and medical care, to better education for their children, to tickets for special events, and to the rare privilege of foreign (Western) travel (Eppelmann et al., 1996, 477–478). Indeed, they copied the lifestyle of the traditional ruling classes to the extent of securing for themselves private forest reserves to indulge in their newly acquired aristocratic passion for hunting. These luxuries and privileges remained largely invisible to the general public, of course. They did not comport particularly well with the unending glorification of the equality of all citizens in the GDR, much less with the old socialist notion that elected officials should be paid "no more than the regular workingman's wages" (Sharnoff, 1983, 195). Preaching equality and living in luxury were a feature of communist rule, not just in the GDR but also in the other socialist countries (Hornbostel, 1999; Matthews, 1978).

> While profound differences continue[d] to exist in lifestyles between the new elite . . . and the masses, these systems [were] usually quite successful in diminishing the appearance of disparity. Total control of the media, incessant claims of shared austerity, and inconspicuous, that is, hidden consumption . . . [made] it possible to foster the image. (Taylor, 1993, 95–96)

Elite extravagances and privileges remained mostly hidden in East Germany until after the end of the communist regime—when the country's citizens were dismayed and dumbfounded by what they learned about the lifestyle of their leaders.[16]

Exploitation, Work Ethics, and Productivity

The real workers of the GDR neither owned nor controlled their factories, nor, leaving aside rare exceptions, do the workers in *non*socialist systems. Regardless of the country's economic system and regardless of the formal ownership of the means of production, the company's internal processes and external relations are under the control of the managers—whether these are the agents of the state, of the stockholders, or (as is increasingly the case in the West) merely of their own interests. What really stuck in the throat of the East German workers was not the fact that they were not in control but the pretense that they were[17] (Badstuebner, 2000, 13). What replaced ordinary (private) capitalism in the GDR was not the mythical "socialist mode of ownership and production" but *state capitalism*—not an improvement, according to those who experienced it[18] (Fromm, 1961, vii; Sontheimer & Bleek, 1975, 110). Marx focused on the iniquities of capitalist society, but, as Hook pointed out (1955, 44), he

> never seriously examined the possibility that the workers might be just as much, or even more, exploited under a system of collective ownership where they faced one big boss, panoplied in the armed powers of the state, as under a system of private or mixed ownership in which there were many bosses often at odds with each other.

Communism did not bring the workers' paradise but a "militaristic autocracy exploiting the masses" (Schumpeter, 1950, 404). Not to be overlooked are the analogies to the national-socialist system in respect to the demands made on workers, from comprehensive regulations of work and life, to the granting of privileges as rewards for system conformity[19] (Tenfelde, 1998, 894). Whatever privileges and securities the workers of the GDR enjoyed, they were purchased at the cost of a heavy conformity (see note 32).

What replaced the many partial monopolies found in capitalist economies was the substantially more powerful, comprehensive, and restrictive and, lastly, the worst *single* supermonopoly of the state/Party. Kautsky (1964, 26), as so often, anticipated correctly:

> The absolute rule of bureaucracy . . . leads to arbitrariness and stultification, but a system of production like capitalism, in which each producer is dependent upon numerous others, needs for its prosperity the security and legality of social relations. The absolute State gets into conflict with the productive forces, and becomes a fetter on them. It is, then, urgently necessary for the executive to be subjected to public criticism, for free organizations of citizens to counterbalance the power of the State, for self-government in municipalities and provinces to be established, for the

power of law-making to be taken from the bureaucracy, and put under the control of a central assembly, freely chosen by the people, that is a Parliament.

Such concepts of Marxism-Leninism as "the rule of the working class" and "the dictatorship of the proletariat" were no more than convenient covers with which to camouflage socialist realities.[20] These notions were perceived by most workers as what they were: the insulting prevarications of a single-party regime that controlled the state, the economy, and everything else and that exploited the working masses at least as much as any contemporary capitalist. In a lighter vein, there is the much-cherished response to the GDR teacher's question to his students about the difference between capitalism and socialism. Answer: *in capitalism man exploits man; in socialism it is the other way around.*

The year 1958 was witness to some extraordinary socialist flights of fancy. First, Walter Ulbricht promised that by the year 1961 the citizens of the GDR would have a higher standard of living than the citizens of the FRG and that the GDR would overtake the FRG in per capita consumption of consumer goods and food (Kopstein, 1997, 73–75; Minnerup, 1982, 20–25). The GDR, of course, never even came close to achieving parity, much less superiority, in the quantity or the quality of its products; nor was parity/superiority achieved in respect to other indicators of worker welfare, such as the number of working hours per day or vacation days per year (Gohl, 1986, 90, 135, et passim). By 1960 the GDR's failure was evident. Ulbricht requested Soviet aid. He was turned down. He now requested closing the open border to West Berlin, which allowed GDR citizens to vote with their feet and show which system they thought was the superior one. On August 13, 1961, Ulbricht got his way; the Soviets acceded.

Second, Ulbricht proclaimed the "ten commandments of socialist morality," with the purpose of defining and clarifying the attributes of the "new socialist man." This new man was said to (1) demonstrate international proletarian solidarity, (2) show love for the GDR, (3) fight against exploitation, (4) do good for the cause of socialism, (5) respect the collective and its criticisms, (6) protect and increase the people's property, (7) improve productivity and socialist work discipline, (8) raise children in the spirit of socialism, (9) evince clean living and respect for the family, and (10) give support to national independence movements (Dornberg, 1968, 228–229; Richert, 1966, 114–115). None of these injunctions appear to have been particularly effective, certainly not commandments 4–7.

As an aside, however, it should be noted that, while falling far short of true *ethical* excellence, communist officials tended to be paragons of *petty bourgeois proprieties* (Wroblewsky, 1990b, 120–121). The fevered imaginations of the American Religious Right that communists are sexually promiscuous, want to destroy the family, and have no standards of personal conduct are about as far removed from reality as one can get. The CPSU regularly denounced such failings as drunkenness, hooliganism, parasitism, moneygrubbing, and servility (Congress of the CPSU, 1986, 58). In the GDR, Ulbricht was known to complain that children did not spend enough time with their parents. The regime provided extensive subsidies for families and children. Any type of pornography was strictly outlawed. Party members had to adhere to strict rules of moral conduct. Promiscuity and (even) divorce were frowned upon by the Party. Contact with prostitutes led to disciplinary Party proceedings, as did venality and corruption. The flaws of socialist societies were many, but they were *not* disorder, disrespect, and debauchery.

East German work habits, however, were notoriously lax. Many workers were negligent and uninterested; few put in a full day's work. Much of it was wasted in bureaucratic barrenness, a mere spinning of useless wheels (Heym, 1990, 205). Cardplaying on the job was quite common, as was plain goofing-off. This was reflected in a well-known East German saying: In the West the unemployed loiter about in the streets; in the GDR they loiter about in the factories. There also was much drinking during working hours. Indeed, the GDR developed a rather high and counterproductive tolerance for drunkenness on the job (Wroblewsky, 1990a, 42). Going shopping and running errands during worktime were everyday events. The origins of the GDR's poor work habits cannot, in the first instance, be attributed to character flaws of the workforce. Key causes of the sweeping lack of work discipline were the frequent shortages of raw materials and the equally frequent breakdowns of machinery, together with the great difficulty of getting repairs done.[21] The regime was aware of the problem, as numerous publications about the necessity of "socialist work-discipline" manifested (e.g., Kunz & Michas, 1975).

Quite often, workers simply were unable to perform any work. Unfortunately, inadvertent idleness quickly turned into habitual sloth. The other basic cause of the lack of work discipline was the inadequate supply of nearly all consumer goods, including any kind of food beyond the most basic staples. If, per chance, a department store received a shipment of lightbulbs or a grocery store a crate of lemons, these would long be gone when the work shift came to its close[22] (Witt, 2001). Since in nearly all families both spouses were employed full-time, there really was no choice but to leave the workplace in order to purchase scarce goods. Not surprisingly, the procurement of consumer goods became an East German preoccupation (Grunert-Bronnen, 1970, 35). In any case, after about two decades of GDR socialism, wages had lost their disciplinary and stimulative functions, and the traditional German working-class virtues had largely disappeared. By 1960, East Germany even had a higher rate of absenteeism than any other East Bloc country (Kopstein, 1997, 39).

In a moment of candor, Erich Honecker (1984, 112–119) delivered himself of these comments:

> [W]e find a lack of order and discipline. We must succeed in reversing the damaging trend of increasing time losses. Everywhere we need an atmosphere of high work

> discipline. . . . There must be an absolute end to meetings and programs during working hours [as well as] to the many small discussions.

Honecker was forced to acknowledge that meetings and discussions were not really the main causes of time and production losses. Rather, the real causes were "technical interruptions and damage, missing parts, and interrupted deliveries by suppliers." Honecker did not acknowledge explicitly the scarcity-caused need to go shopping during working hours. He did admit, however, that consumer goods in greater quantity and higher quality were needed and that consumer goods production could no longer be treated as "the fifth wheel on the cart." Verging close to heresy, he even suggested that consumer goods should be "attractive and fashionable" and should be produced according to actual "demand."

Honecker's speech, as one could have predicted, had no effect. GDR labor productivity remained low and continued on its path of lagging ever more behind that of the West.[23] Post-GDR studies show East German productivity was maximally between 40% and 50% of that of West Germany. In some industries it was much lower. The processing of vegetables (canning), for example, reached only 11% of West German productivity (Dietz, 1991, 2; Hitchens et al., 1993, 2; Thalheim, 1988, 89). It gave lie to the statement of the chair of the Council of Ministers and the chair of the Council of State, Willy Stoph (1968, 6), that the GDR has the "task of proving the superiority of socialism over capitalism on German soil in the economic field."[24] Yet, year after year, the GDR went further into arrears compared to the FRG (Obst, 1983, 8). The other socialist economies exhibited similar problems and deficiencies (Bergson, 1989; Hough, 1988, 6–14; Wiles, 1988). Necessarily, low productivity came to be reflected in the need for greater efforts and in the cost of lower rewards. GDR citizens had to put in substantially more working time for about one-half of the real income of an FRG citizen[25] (Francisco, 1989, 196; Hitchens et al., 1993; Obst, 1983, 47). None of these problems, of course, stopped the regime from singing its own economic praise and announcing to the world that the GDR's economic system had proven itself to be "productive, dynamic, and flexible" (Bryson & Melzer, 1991, 8).

Workers and the GDR Labor Union

The workers of socialist states did not have independent labor unions committed to work for their welfare. Labor unions, like practically all other organizations, were wholly owned subsidiaries of the Party (Eckelmann et al., 1990). The union members had effectively no say in the selection of the union functionaries (Heym, 1990, 67). This dependency, of course, was not acknowledged; sophistries and fallacies were the daily menu (Panorama-DDR, 1981, 61–64; Tisch [head of the FDGB], 1989). The USSR's Novosti

Press Agency (1978, 33), for example, provided this proof that Soviet trade unions were truly independent:

> Over the past 60 years there has not been a single law passed in this country that has curtailed or aimed to curtail the rights of trade unions in the slightest degree. Trade unions do not have to register with any government body and neither their activities nor their budget are subject to government control.

Membership in the GDR's single authorized labor union, the Free German Labor Union[26] (*Freier Deutscher Gewerkschaftsbund*—FDGB) was, in effect, mandatory (Heinecke, 2000, 80–81). The statutes of the FDGB were written in the language of voluntarism, yet FDGB membership, for all practical purposes, was compulsory. Few could afford to remain outside the organization, not even members of the scientific and technical elite. For example, by the 1980s, 98.5% of all scientists were members of the Science Division of the FDGB (Beyme & Zimmermann, 1985, 340).

The FDGB never truly represented the interests of the workers (O'Hara, 1982, 25) but assisted management (i.e., government and Party) in instituting speedups and higher production quotas (Belwe, 1979, 217–221; Schwarze, 1973, 36; Slider, 1986, 415) and in organizing additional exploitation opportunities, such as "socialist competitions for greater productivity" and "subbotniks"[27] (Bavarius, 1990, 82; Eppelmann et al., 1996, 689–690). Subbotniks were the "voluntary" and unpaid weekend work invented in the USSR in May 1919 (Yakovlev, 1982, 71). It included street sweeping and other community work as well as additional production efforts (Pravda & Ruble, 1986).

The FDGB was not entirely ineffective in protecting workers' rights at the workplace—but only as such rights were granted by the Party and only in ways that were authorized by the Party. There were no independent FDGB efforts to provide benefits and protection to its members.[28] There was no appreciable effort to safeguard the health of the workers, just as there was no real protection of the environment and the health of all citizens. The work environment often was "filthy," and protective measures were minimal (Wroblewsky, 1990a, 44–45). In the chemical, fiber, mining, and metallurgical industries, workers' health was knowingly and deliberately sacrificed (*verheizt*) to production goals (Paetzold, 1991, 11). Not surprisingly, at the June 1953 unrests, the FDGB supported not the striking workers but the regime. As far as the FDGB was concerned, its really important task was to increase the "socialist state consciousness" (*sozialistisches Staatsbewusstsein*) of the workers, not to assist them in advancing claims against the state (Autorenkollektiv, 1968, 42–44; also see Lehmann & Schulz, 1976, 155). What happened was that the government had imposed a 33% wage reduction, including higher work norms. In response, the workers at several Berlin construction sites walked off the job (June 16, 1953). By the next day, the famous

June 17, 1953, the protests had spread to 272 cities and towns throughout the GDR. Wage demands quickly turned into political demands for free elections and for unification with Western Germany. Public order and SED rule could be restored only with Soviet tanks (Kopstein, 1997, 35–36).

This is not the place for a detailed review of the GDR's environmental policies and their consequences, but this much should be pointed out: there was a monumental indifference to the consequences of the country's nature-destroying industrial and agricultural practices (Kuhrt, 1999). Entirely lacking in shame, an official publication of the SED declared, as late as 1988, that ecological problems are entirely a product of capitalist profit-striving and that "under our socialist productive relations, it is a priori impossible to have anti-ecological policies" (Kosing, 1988, 193; see also Benser, 2000, 275; Dlubek & Merkel, 1981, 395–398; Helmbold, 1989). For reports on the massive degradation of the East German environment, see Rueddenklau, 1992; Scholz, 1988.[29] It was not, to be sure, that the GDR did not adopt laws to protect the environment. It promulgated a large number of rules and regulations, even elevating environmental protection to a constitutional principle (Art. 15 of the 1968/1974 constitution) (Friedrich-Ebert-Stiftung, 1985; Lammich, 1987). The problem was lack of implementation. As in so many other areas of East German life, lofty principles and squalid practices went hand in hand (Kuhrt, 1996b). Citizens who publicly expressed concern about the decay of the East German environment or about the lack of workplace safety measures quickly found themselves subject to unpleasant Stasi attention (Rueddenklau, 1992).

There were no FDGB-organized strikes in all the years of the GDR's existence. Formal labor contracts, which did exist, remained unenforced if they came into conflict with Party policies. As Bendix (1969, 200) observed, socialist collective labor agreements are not so much enforceable contracts but "declarations of loyalty to the dictatorial Party, which pledge each group and individual to the utmost exertions and to eternal vigilance against the 'enemies' of the regime." The FDGB's *primary* functions were prodding the workers to higher levels of productivity and loyalty, as well as operating as one of the Party's channels of surveillance and control. The FDGB's *secondary* tasks included the allocation of vacation slots to the employees of the firm, the administration of the social security system, and the nomination of the members (judges) of the workplace social courts. It was the furthest from the minds of the FDGB functionaries (typically also members of the SED) to fight for the welfare of the union's members.

Of course, the GDR's workers enjoyed a high (practically perfect) degree of job security, and they did not have to compete seriously with one another.[30] The frequently organized "socialist competitions" were contests not for gaining or keeping jobs but for extra material rewards, titles, and medals. As in the other socialist countries, titles and medals were of considerable importance.[31] The GDR had an array of approximately 8,000 medals, decorations, and awards, often linked to monetary (onetime or periodic) payments. The highest award was the Karl-Marx-Medal, which also brought a stipend of 20,000 East German marks. The next highest decorations were the "Hero of the GDR" and the "Hero of Work." Toward the end of the GDR, there was no area of life that did not have its special medals and awards, from "Meritorious Teacher of the People" to "Outstanding Scientist of the People." The honors were awarded not only to persons but also to collectives and enterprises, for example, "Enterprise of Socialist Work" (Eppelmann et al., 1996, 88–89; Richter, 1980).

Outside observers routinely pointed to the lack of competition as one of the major causes of socialist economic backwardness and inefficiency. The regime, of course, saw it differently. The absence of competitive pressures in socialist production, they claimed, favored the development of all creative abilities and, thus, of scientific advancement, technical innovation, high productive quality, increased production, and superior morality (Koch, 1988, 150). History has not been kind to these fantasies.

The 1949 constitution guaranteed to the labor unions and their members the right to strike (Art. 14.2)—as noted, this right never was exercised. The 1968/1974 constitution, in any case, no longer included this right, stating only that labor unions were independent and that no one was permitted to restrict or hinder their activities (Art. 44.2). The FDGB, however, already had anticipated Party policy (with some prodding, one assumes) and declared that there could be no strikes in the socialized sector of the economy (i.e., in practically all of the East German economy), since the workers would, in effect, be striking against themselves.[32] Labor law knows only the "coherence of the political, material, and cultural interests of the workers and their collectives with the societal necessities" (Ludz, 1974, 185).

In spite of the weakness of the FDGB, the East German workers were not without power. The regime had been gravely scared by the events of 1953, when large numbers of workers in various localities laid down their tools to protest the GDR's early (Taylorist) economic policies. As Kopstein (1997, 11) pointed out: "To assure the goodwill of the proletariat, the SED had to give its workers a virtual veto power over wages, prices, and work norms."[33] In the face of labor resistance and power, the regime settled on premium pay for piecework, but with low production norms ("soft plans").[34] The consequences were excessive wage bills, with wages rising much faster than productivity (Kopstein, 1997, 31, 38). High wages plus highly subsidized basic consumer goods did not, however, satisfy the workers of the GDR. After all, there was little that could be bought with those wages. In any case, the high-wage policies did not last. In their place came ever higher production norms. The regime, drawing on the Soviet Stakhanov (Aktivist) movement, recruited Adolf Hennecke and other East German workers to raise quotas. In 1948, Hennecke mined 387% of the normal mining quota on the first anniversary of SMAD Order No. 234.[35] (More about No. 234 later.) The norms for the average workers increased, but not to the Aktivist level—if only because the general workplace chaos made it difficult to set proper norms.

In any case, the norm and wage adjustments of early 1953 amounted to a wage cut of about 33%. Workers' unrest was soon to follow—and persisted (even in the form of wild strikes) throughout the existence of the GDR. From this the regime drew the lesson that not too much should be demanded of its workers and that workers should be given the maximum possible economic benefits. Accordingly, the basic consumer goods—food, apartments, energy, transportation, and so on—were highly subsidized in East Germany. Indeed, many were sold below production cost. Kopstein (1997, 81) reported that the annual subsidies for such goods grew from 8 billion East German marks in 1970 to 53 billion in 1988. This was a tremendous drain on the GDR treasury and contributed greatly to the GDR's high level of (a finally unmanageable) debt (Volze, 1999). The GDR's indebtedness to the West grew from 2.2 billion to 46 billion West marks in the same time period. By the early 1980s, the GDR no longer was able to service even the interest on its debt.

In effect, the workers gained a form of veto power in the 1950s. It enabled them to resist necessary and salutary reforms at later dates, much to the detriment of the GDR economy. The various proletarian privileges, together with the rigidities of the planned economy, contributed greatly to the economic difficulties and decline of the GDR. The price of labor peace, like that of the general calmness of the population, was the comprehensive stagnation in all areas of East German existence and, thus, lastly the ultimate failure of the system. There are reasons to think, however, that the much-praised workplace stability of the GDR was considerably less stable than generally thought. For detailed discussions, see Huertgen and Reichel, 2001.

NES and ESS: The Failure of Early Reforms

In the early 1960s, Walter Ulbricht came to understand that the GDR had to become a more attractive place for its population. At that time, the people (particularly the better educated and more skilled) still had an exit option; the Wall had not yet been built. Since increased political freedom was not a gift the regime would distribute, only economic improvements could be promised to a dissatisfied people. Croan and Friedrich (1958, 50) speak of a two-pronged strategy in effect since 1953: improving economic benefits while perfecting totalitarian controls.

There can be no doubt that the regime sincerely sought to improve the material well-being of its citizens (Dornberg, 1974, 201; Scharf, 1984, 69, 92–95, 116–120; Stuermer, 1986, 229; Weymar, 1985, 80). The problem was that the planned economy turned out to be incapable of doing that. While consumer goods and services were never in adequate supply (with the exception of the most basic foodstuffs), the regime did offer its citizens a fair amount of economic security. The GDR had no starvation or similar deficiencies. The economic benefits were not all that great, but there was real security regarding them, in other words, it was the dependability of benefits rather than the magnitude or quality.

Not to be overlooked is that the citizens did not need to compete for the benefits, which certainly made for a less stressful life. GDR citizens most certainly wanted political change, but not at the cost of social security (Dahrendorf, 1967, 409). The chief East German postunification complaint is precisely that the new freedoms have come at the cost of the many securities that the old regime offered (Boyer & Skyba, 1999).

Various policies were tried, importantly those of the New Economic System (NES). There were two phases in the reform attempts. The first (1963–1967) was designated "the new economic system of planning and management of the people's economy" (NES); the second (1968–1970) was called "the economic system of socialism" (ESS). The ESS was, in fact, a partial retreat, particularly in respect to the decision-making abilities at the economic base (Erbe, 1979, 21).

NES was advocated by Fritz Behrens and Arne Benary and first implemented in 1963–1964. The "guidelines" for the New Economic System (*Richtlinie für das neue ökonomische System der Planung und Leitung der Volkswirtschaft*) were issued on July 11, 1963. NES was based in part on the Liberman discussion of 1962 in *Pravda* (Leptin, 1975, 43). But Moscow resisted very strongly, though it introduced reforms itself in 1965 (Jeffries & Melzer, 1987, 27). Some members of the SED Politburo were also strongly opposed, perceiving it (correctly!) as undermining comprehensive Party control. Or, to speak with Marx, as rephrased by Gregor (1968, 47): "Existing relations of production find their advocates in the members of the economic class that profits from them." In respect to the GDR, however, it might be better to speak of the *political class* that profits from them.

In any case, only some of the NES reform proposals were ever implemented. There were attempts to introduce some measures of decentralization, less rigid plan directives, and more performance premiums and other monetary incentives. It was at least a partial retreat from central planning (Bryson, 1995). The reforms, however, remained halfhearted.[36] They failed to make any real difference. On September 8, 1970, the Politburo decided to abandon the reforms almost in toto (NES and ESS) and to return to a strictly centralized economic system and rigorous plans[37] (Leptin, 1975, 54, 72; Steiner, 1999). For a summary of the economic and noneconomic reasons to abandon the reforms, see Jeffries & Melzer, 1987, 34–35.

It was not only the economic disappointment. It had also become clear that some of the NES/ESS technocratic reforms threatened the interests of the Party and state apparatus. However sincerely the leadership desired economic improvement, the economy had to take second place when it came to the preservation of the political power arrangements.[38] Notwithstanding the socialist pieties about the importance and significance of the economy, in societies like the GDR, the political system has a dominant and central place, and in that system the Party, of course, plays the key role[39] (Lane, 1976, 73–75). Fred Oelssner, member of the Politburo and close comrade of Ulbricht, made a speech at the 30th Plenum of the Central Committee of the SED in which he strongly attacked the ideas of Behrens, characterizing them as petty-bourgeois individualist-anarchical revisionism that came dangerously close to capitalism[40]—which, of course, was strongly denied by the supporters of NES, who also asserted that NES was in no way opposed to Marxism-Leninism and, in fact, served the further strengthening of democratic centralism (e.g., Heuer, 1965, 14–16). But it was not far-fetched for the opponents to say that

> [r]eformists are endlessly propagating all sorts of "models" of a "socialist market economy" or recommend the "complete independence" of enterprises and industrial [combines], that is a so-called self-administration which does not fit into a framework of central management but is opposed to it with a view to eliminating it. (Panorama-DDR, 1981, 59)

The real point of the attack, then, was that Behrens and Benary's ideas would lessen the role of the state in the economy and, thus, the role of the Party (Oelssner, 1957, 324–325; see also Schuerer, 1968, 42; Selucky, 1972, v). Ulbricht, who had always remained a Stalinist, finally decided that the reforms were not fully "socialistic." His successor, Erich Honecker (1984, 111–118), habitually called for the strictest Party control of all aspects of the economy, from the lofty objective of achieving the plan goals to the more mundane matters of staffing shift work. For political and economic reasons, then, the reform efforts were relinquished. At about the same time the regime invented what probably was the silliest of its many silly slogans: *ueberholen ohne einzuholen* (to overtake without catching up). It was, of course, the FRG that was to be overtaken in this fashion. Direct comparisons with FRG performance were anathema to the regime. Whatever comparisons could be made showed that the FRG pulled ever farther away.

Job and Other Securities

Under Honecker, GDR economic policies of the 1970s and 1980s could be termed "conservative consumer socialism," but there was little actual improvement.[41] The regime invented a new slogan, proclaiming "the unity of economic and social policies." What this meant in practice was that some more attention would be paid to consumer needs (Erbe, 1979, 47–48; Manz et al., 2001). The regime's basic ideology, as well as the country's extraordinary (even by socialist standards) bureaucratic and labor rigidities prevented meaningful and effective reforms. In addition, the international economy changed to the detriment of the GDR, especially the higher prices charged by the USSR for oil and the recession in the Western markets. As Kopstein (1997, 12) rightly says, by the end of the 1970s, the GDR was effectively insolvent. As noted earlier (and as will be discussed again later), it was the FRG payments and credits that kept the regime afloat in the international arena and domestically.

On the positive side, at least from the perspective of the workers, it must be noted that there was no unemployment in the GDR. Yet, this was a matter of politics, not economics. For example, the right to work (to employment) was elevated to a constitutional principle via Article 24 of the 1974 version of the 1968 constitution. However, except for the early years, when the GDR experienced true labor shortages, the much-vaunted full employment of the GDR basically was fraudulent. Immediately after the war, the Soviet occupation forces took over a substantial part of the zone's workforce for purposes of industrial demontage (Karlsch & Laufer, 2002), construction of Soviet troop bases, and so on. In addition, Soviet SAGs and companies producing reparation goods had first call on the available labor force—this in the aftermath of high wartime casualties and in the context of significant population losses via flights to the West. Manpower shortages were further magnified by low production rates, due to poor supply of food and clothing and the generally poor health of most of the workforce (Zank, 1987, 84–85).

After the initial difficulties, just described, it became a matter of Party policy that the country simply would have available as many jobs as there were persons to be employed—at the cost of considerable inefficiency. The population was not fooled for very long. Popular sarcasm found expression in another famous East German saying: "All of our unemployed hold full-time jobs." To prevent visible unemployment, enterprises were obligated to keep (and pay) more workers than they needed. Also, enterprises were motivated for their own reasons to keep larger workforces than actually needed. They literally "hoarded" workers (Zank, 1987, 179–188). Most often this involved supplying false figures about employment needs to the State Planning Commission. Since the enterprises could not go bankrupt, the excessive employee cost was not a problem—at least for them. Post-1989 research has shown that about 15% of the workers (1.4 million persons) were part of the "hidden unemployment" (Eppelmann et al., 1996, 68; Guertler et al., 1990; Mayer, 2002, 36).

Yet, all employable persons had jobs and received *wages* rather than welfare. Though many of the employed worked full schedules only on paper, the economic costs of overemployment probably were no higher than those associated with underemployment: unemployment compensation and social assistance, *and* the policy of overemployment avoided the indignities of being without a job and having to depend on unemployment and/or welfare payments. Given the importance of meaningful work to self-respect and basic happiness (surely, Marx was right about this), the GDR's policy of guaranteed employment for all should not be faulted too quickly. Large-scale public works projects probably would have been a more salutary use of manpower, but for such undertakings the GDR tended to lack the requisite resources and flexibility. From a humanitarian (and perhaps even an economic) perspective, the overemployment policies of the GDR should be viewed with considerable charity.

In addition to guaranteed employment, the GDR provided each citizen with the security of not having to worry about the cost of such necessities as education, medical care, and retirement wherewithals. The quality of these services tended to be poor, and the amounts often were inadequate, but they were there. There was a certain minimum below which no citizen had to fear falling. Nevertheless, Ardagh (1987, 328) errs in thinking that the GDR created "an effective and generous welfare state [and that it] ironed out major inequalities of class and income." As retired East Germans well knew, there was nothing generous about the pensions of ordinary citizens.[42] As noted, the inequalities in income and economic privileges always were substantial in the GDR, and they kept increasing[43]—though not among the workers of the same enterprise, where a considerable "wage egalitarianism" prevailed (Kopstein, 1997, 35, 38).

Ardagh is right, however, in remarking that severe poverty had largely been eradicated in the GDR. While the system foundered on its inability to overcome the drastic scarcities in housing and consumer goods, and while the supplies of food, clothing, and shelter remained inadequate to the very end, no one in the GDR had to starve or live in the streets. The disappearance, following German reunification, of the "right to a job," the "right to medical care," and so on has been one of the most difficult aspects of East German readjustment (Cattani, 1993, 29). It is the citizens' deep attachments to comprehensive entitlements that now haunt the efforts of the former socialist countries to change from a planned to a free-market economy (Breslauer, 1991, 10; Gerdes et al., 1997).

The Planned Economy

The development of an apparatus for a planned economy began early in the Soviet Zone of Occupation. The foundations were laid by SMAD Order No. 138 (June 27, 1947). It established the German Economic Commission (*Deutsche Wirtschaftskommission*) as the central agency for the zone's economic affairs. The commission was in charge of developing the first economic plans. It also was responsible for coordinating the reparations to be paid to the USSR. In 1949, the commission became the provisional government of the GDR. This was followed by SMAD Order No. 234, October 13, 1947, which introduced Soviet-style labor relations into East Germany, such as "socialist competition" and People's Control Committees.[44] These committees, it should be noted, worked poorly. They tended to be made up mostly of busybodies. They were corrupt and amateurish and entirely overwhelmed by their tasks. As always, Erich Honecker (1984, 120) was moved to heap praise on socialist institutions, whatever their performance might be, for example: "[A]lready some time ago inspections by the Workers' and Farmers' Inspectorate uncovered usable reserves of materials and secondary raw materials worth almost a billion [East German] marks." In any case, with the introduction of Soviet economic programs, wage and price policies became entirely the domain of the state. They no longer obeyed economic rationales, but political ones. As Bryson (1971, 395) pointed out, "prices played no allocative role" in the GDR economy. As noted, the NES reforms also were intended to return an allocative role to prices, but these reforms could not come to fruition in light of the political opposition they generated. In 1964 there was a serious attempt at industrial price reform, but "rises in the prices of consumer goods were ruled out" (Melzer, 1987, 144).

The move to a comprehensive and centralized socialist economic system, that is, to the *full* Soviet model,[45] came in 1948. There was a half-year plan for 1948, succeeded by a two-year plan for 1949–1950. At that time the State Planning Commission (SPK) came into being, which produced two five-year plans, the second of which was in effect for but three years. Adopting the Soviet time frame, the GDR shifted to a seven-year-plan period, the first of which was to run from 1959 to 1965. Also during these years, the economy of the GDR became ever more closely integrated with the economies of the USSR and the other East Bloc countries. Of course, ever since 1945, the USSR had shaped East German economic reconstruction and development for its own purposes. The economy of the GDR was, in fact, guided less by the needs of its own people than by the strategic requirements of the Soviet Union (Frowen, 1985, 32–43). Matters became yet worse when in 1952, with the escalation of the Cold War, the GDR had to commit major sums for armament and defense industry development. Kopstein (1997, 35) speaks of 1.5 billion East German marks. These had to be financed by higher taxes and reduced social spending. For these and other reasons, the GDR experienced considerable industrial unrest by the end of 1952. The seven-year plan, in any case, failed drastically. It was abandoned in 1962, and an interim plan was put into its place (1963–1970). Beginning in 1971, the GDR returned to using five-year plans.[46] Regardless of the time frame, plan goals generally could not be met—except by way of Western credits and assistance.

Leninist systems require not only the public ownership of the means of production but also a rigorously implemented central direction and control of all economic activities and institutions (Gerhardt, 1997). The chief instrument is the *plan*. The plan, so it is claimed, takes into account not only societal requirements but also the "objective laws of development" (Panorama-DDR, 1977, 12). The stated purposes of the plan were to eliminate the economic causes of conflict, to prevent (the capitalist) discrepancies of supply and demand; and thereby the resulting misuse of capital (financing unneeded plants and unwanted goods), and to preclude periods of high unemployment and general misery. As it turned out, the planned economy, in actuality, was less efficient and more wasteful than the free market.[47] There was heavy and persistent waste of raw materials and labor—and also of capital, which socialist planners somehow regarded as being free of cost (Scharf, 1984, 70–71).

East German economists (presumably on Party instructions) included in their cost and price calculations only production but not reproduction costs. Thus, the enterprises did not accumulate funds to replace worn-out machinery and decaying buildings. Strangely, the miserable state of the GDR's industrial infrastructure, after reunification, came as a great shock to the West Germans, who could and should have anticipated these problems. One suspects that the bad news was partly or fully suppressed because it would have contradicted Chancellor Kohl's euphoristic pretense that reunification and the integration of the two economies would be without significant cost to West Germany. In the meantime, the cost has escalated to about $100 billion per year since 1991 (Goos & Kneip, 2004, 62)—sums that, of course, the West German taxpayers have had to contribute.

It was one of the prouder claims of the GDR to have eliminated economic crises and inflation from its territory (Deutsches Institut für Wirtschaftsforschung, 1984, 120; Kuechler, 1989, 145). Like most official pronouncements, this was largely prattle. For example, during most of the GDR's existence, the plan goals could be reached only on the basis of massive overtime work and the obligatory "voluntary" performance of extra shifts for the "overfulfillment" of the plan (Minnerup, 1982, 38; Pirker et al., 1995). This, of course, remained unacknowledged. It should also be noted in this context that the GDR simply stopped publishing import/export figures, when in the mid-1970s its trade deficit with the West as well as with the USSR increased greatly. (Chapter 1 of my forthcoming *Popular Justice in a Marxist-Leninist Society: The East German Social Courts and Other Aspects of GDR Law* includes a general discussion of the availability and reliability of official socialist data.)

The problems and crises caused by economic malfunctioning do not necessarily take the same form in socialist as in free-market economies. In capitalism they appear predominantly as overproduction, unemployment, inflation, and business failures (bankruptcies). In socialism they appear primarily as shortages of industrial and consumer goods, lagging technological development, innovation deficits, foreign debt, and the inability to compete in the world's markets.[48] It takes more than a little disregard of the obvious to assert that there was no lack of financial discipline in the GDR. The system suffered from large increases in the money supply, high budget deficits, and excess demand over supply (Kopstein, 1997, 39). Only with the massive help of the West German "uncle sugar" did the system survive as long as it did.

Regarding inflation, there was a steady increase in prices throughout the GDR's existence—though not of the double-digit magnitude experienced at times in the West. The somewhat lower rates of inflation were less of an accomplishment, however, than it may seem: the prices of all goods (including rents) were directly controlled by the government and could, thus, be set at any politically desired level. GDR publications took great pride to announce that in East Germany "price stability [was] legally guaranteed" [Panorama-DDR, 1977, 24]. But all that this meant was that inflationary pressures found their outlet not in prices but in salary levels, tax rates, the quality of goods, the availability of government services, and so on. Socialist countries, just like capitalist countries, have not found ways to *outlaw* inflation. All any of them can do is (re-) direct their effects. Taking a page from the "class enemy," the GDR adopted such measures as making some purely cosmetic changes in certain goods but labeling them as "new and improved" and discontinuing other goods in their old forms altogether and bringing them to the market again as "new products," in each case charging higher prices for them. Since the increases in price (presumably) were not for the same product, they did not enter into any measure of inflation and permitted the government to claim that GDR consumer prices were stable (Eppelmann et al., 1996, 384–386; Weiss, 1998). Some of the price increases of 1979 actually led to popular protests, and some had to be rescinded by the regime (O'Hara, 1982, 24). It was a chief complaint of East German citizens that there was nothing to buy for one's money—or at least nothing one would want. Too much money always was chasing too few goods.[49] Had the government not controlled prices, the GDR would have had very high rates of price increases indeed.

Except for that small part of the population that constituted the new ruling class, the East Germans had to endure forever standing in line to obtain even basic necessities. Worse, often they were not available at all—including, at times, matches—or when available, of very poor quality. The waiting time for a car was between ten and twenty years;[50] it was between two and four years for taking a course in driver's education. There are reports that even the State Bank had to wait eight years for a new typewriter (Singer, 2001, 58). The effects of such deficiencies on the GDR economy are not difficult to imagine.

The essential good in worst supply was housing. The scarcity of housing and the poor quality of the housing stock were a constant embarrassment to the regime, generating endless (and always unkept) promises to solve the problem by a certain date[51] (Childs, 1973, 270; Gohl, 1986, 134; Schulze, 1985, 65; Tesch, 2002). At the beginning it had been deliberate policy to neglect housing in preference for industrial buildings. Later, when housing became a matter of great concern, the disastrous policies regarding the GDR's building industry took their toll. Private enterprise had effectively been eliminated. In their stead, the GDR now had a system of massive conglomerates, all state-owned enterprises, that simply were not able to satisfy the need for housing. It also did not help that the regime had favored massive concentrations in the suppliers of building materials. For example, there was but one producer of cement in the GDR, a gargantuan combine with 16,000 workers. There also was a very poor supply of trucks and machinery and of all the other things needed by the building trade. No particular surprise, then, that the productivity of the GDR's building trade was but 54% of that of the FRG. In addition, the regime had a policy of simply letting the existing housing go to ruin. There were neither workers nor materials for necessary repairs. Even today, the results of this policy can be seen in the comprehensively ruined inner cities of East Germany.

Given the general scarcity of desirable goods and services *and* a system of tightly controlled prices, the allocation effects were predictable: a vast system of illicit favor-doings, under-the-counter sales, and barter transactions. (These instances of corruption and lawbreaking were not, of course, reflected in the economic and criminal statistics of the GDR.) It was quite impossible to get one's car repaired or one's leaking faucet fixed if all that one could offer was payments in the GDR's own currency. Only the West German mark or quid pro quos could secure the services of auto mechanics and plumbers and the purchase of desirable products.

The East German government displayed its squalid character most clearly when it proceeded to cash in on the scarcities and inadequacies that its policies had caused. It opened a series of luxury stores in which all types of quality goods (often imported) could be obtained at astronomical prices ("Delikat" shops sold food items; "Exquisit" shops marketed clothing, cosmetics, and similar items). This was economic exploitation taken to a very high level. In addition, the GENEX Gift Service (*Geschenkdienst*) of the GDR delivered any item immediately, even cars, against payment in *West German* currency—usually obtained by GDR citizens from Western relatives (Paetzold, 1991, 16–22). Not surprisingly, the existence of GENEX contributed greatly to the discontent of large numbers of East German citizens—namely, those without contributing Western relatives[52] (Mertens, 2002a, 61, 72–79; Zimmermann, 1979, 71–73).

Returning to the State Planning Commission (SPK), which in the GDR had the status of a ministry, it should be pointed out that the economic objectives for each plan were given to the SPK by the People's Chamber—which is to say, by the SED. The State Planning Commission had no more independence from Party commands than the official labor union. Erich Apel was head of the SPK from January 1963 to December 1965. He was one of the chief architects of the GDR's New Economic System (NES), an attempt to make socialism competitive with capitalism, even at the cost of jettisoning some ideological ballast. Apel committed suicide on December 3, 1965, when he could not prevent the imposition of a very unfavorable trade pact with the USSR, and when it seemed already that his reform efforts (the NES) would fail (Dornberg, 1968, 88; Gohl, 1986, 91–92; Obst, 1983, 93).

As noted earlier, the New Economic System embodied greater planning flexibility, increased reliance on incentives, greater manager responsibilities and decision-making powers, a realistic price structure, and genuine worker participation in economic and political affairs. It was, in the words of one of its supporters, not just an attempt to repair some deficiencies in the administration of the economy; it was to be a

> thorough and comprehensive qualitative change which will allow the planned direction of the economy to divest itself of the character of purely administrative acts and to take on the character of a necessary scientific activity, which will improve the organization of our economy, and will comprehensively mobilize the creative initiatives of the workers. . . . The point is the creation of a new system." (Heuer, 1965, 9–10)

It lasted in various ways from 1963 to 1970. The subsequent years saw a large-scale abandonment of economic reform policies and a return to Stalinist certainties and rigidities (Christopher, 1985, 20; Hanhardt, 1968, 89–100; Steiner, 1999; Wassmund, 1981, 346–348).

Among the tasks of the SPK were the development of plans for the production and consumption of goods, the formulation of long-range designs for the economic development of the GDR, producing economic forecasts, securing the economic basis for military objectives, organizing cooperation with the other COMECON[53] nations, directing and controlling economic activities, and conducting research to improve economic planning. Reflecting shifts in East German economic policy, the responsibilities of the SPK were modified a number of times. In 1961, for example, some of its functions were transferred to a newly formed People's Economic Council (*Volkswirtschaftsrat*). The SPK regained these functions when the People's Economic Council was abolished in 1965.

Socialist theory assumes and socialist declamations assert the primacy of economics and the supremacy of the plan. These stances reflect the old hope of scientific management and the Marxist goal of replacing the governance of people with administration of things. The realities of socialist states, of course, have been otherwise. There never was a higher good or more primary goal than preserving the rule of the Communist Party. Political needs drove economic planning. The primacy of politics was never abandoned in the GDR or the other socialist countries. Socialist regimes knew perfectly well that, in the words of Sidney Hook (1962, 9), "it is not the mode of economic production but the mode of political decision which is of decisive importance." They merely wrapped political fact into thick layers of economic rhetoric.[54] The system was driven by "the grubby reality of the politics of power and of bureaucratic routine" (Rutland, 1985, 237).

Planning was part of the GDR's official creed not because it worked economically (in both meanings of the term) but because it worked (or seemed to work) politically. There are many examples of the economic malfunctioning of the planned economy. Particularly instructive is the grain/bread price ratio. GDR price policies were such that a loaf of bread at the bakery cost less than its grain content. Farmers were quick to notice. They sold their feed grain to the state (for the higher price) and fed store-bought bread to their livestock (at the cheaper price). As another example, animal breeders could sell a rabbit to the state as a wholesaler for fifteen marks and buy it back from the state as a retailer for five marks—all that in the same store and only minutes apart (Wroblewsky, 1990a, 216). For socialist regimes, "the advantages of political stability and concentration of power outweigh the disadvantages of economic sluggishness and inefficiency" (Rutland, 1985, 260). Socialist regimes, of course, are not alone in favoring political over economic considerations. As Aaron Wildavsky (1986, 36) pointed out, all hierarchical regimes prefer stability and order to fluctuations and deviance. They will sacrifice efficiency and prosperity to increase political stability and to reduce the threats of pluralism and opposition.

Comprehensive economic planning satisfies important needs of dictatorial/totalitarian regimes: no surprises, no uncertainties, no conflicts, no contradictions. Unfortunately, "no information" is also part of the package. The information pathologies associated with central planning significantly limit the attainable degree of the satisfaction of the stability needs. "[I]f central planning is emphasized, information processing costs soar, uncertainty is great, and problems of data collection are often insoluble" (Wilensky, 1967, 113). In addition and most importantly, those at the lower levels quickly learn that the transmission of accurate, but unfavorable, data upward will be penalized rather than rewarded. As a result, only substantially "adjusted" information will reach the decision-making levels. The utility and benefits of policies based on such data decline accordingly. Central planning, then, is stupendously short in economic merit, but it does provide the comforting illusion that the Party is engaged in the scientific management of economy and society. Most importantly for the new ruling class, it also provides justification for an ever-expanding Party rule since the development and the implementation of the plan require close and comprehensive supervision and control of all aspects of society (Voigt et al., 1987, 19).

REFORMS IN COMMUNIST SYSTEMS

USSR and GDR Reform Policies

The reform attempts of the 1960s have been discussed previously. It will be remembered that they fell well short of their economic goals while at the same time seeming to endanger centralized Party control. Thus, NES and ESS did not survive the needs of Party politics.

Whether and to what degree Mikhail Gorbachev's perestroika and glasnost improved life in the USSR, provided a reasonable prospect for an improved life, or would have improved life with better luck at implementation are matters for debate.[55] The GDR regime, in any case, rejected Gorbachev's reform proposals *before* they had been put to any real test in the Soviet Union.

The East German leaders spurned these reforms not because it seemed so unlikely that they would truly lead to economic betterment but rather because it seemed so certain that they would lessen the regime's totalitarian controls. Of course, they were right.[56]

Western academic reception of perestroika and glasnost was mixed, ranging from high enthusiasm to deep skepticism. Western business was nearly unanimous in its warm welcome of perestroika and glasnost, viewing them as promises of first-rate profit opportunities (Malcolm, 1984, 104–105). As Sleeper (1987, 333–334) noted:

> Not surprisingly, detente always occurs when the Soviets need it most desperately. Due to a catastrophic decline of productivity caused by the general backwardness of the Soviet economy, they cannot successfully compete militarily with the West, nor can they support their ever-growing empire. These are the real reasons for periodic outbursts of detente or, to take the most recent example, the reasons behind Gorbachev's well-advertised economic reforms. . . . Meanwhile, several hundreds of American businessmen rushed to Moscow eager to improve "East-West economic relations." Credits and technology, goods, and loans are ready to be poured into the Soviet Union.

The conduct of Western businessmen has supported Lenin's well-known assessment that, when the time comes to hang the capitalist class, the international capitalists will compete with one another to sell the Soviets the rope with which to accomplish the hanging (Finder, 1983, 8). Lenin, of course, did not anticipate the full measure of capitalist avarice and shortsightedness: Western businessmen and their political associates (e.g., Franz-Josef Strauss) have been willing not only to sell the rope by which they were to be hanged but also to finance their executioners' purchase of the rope—and at the most favorable rate possible (Hollander, 1987, 39–42).

Franz-Josef Strauss, having arranged in 1983 an unrestricted FRG loan to the GDR of $380 million (1 billion deutschmarks [DM]), was flattered by the attention and praise (what else?) that he received in the GDR and actually bragged that Erich Honecker regarded him as a "statesman of high rank" (Pucher, 1984, 118)—a remarkable metamorphosis of the "principled anticommunist" who had consistently denounced all dealings with the "oppressor/extortionist regime" of the GDR. The loan had absolutely no human rights conditions attached—contrary to the principles of Strauss' own party (CDU/CSU), which had always demanded an East German quid pro quo in humanitarian measures. In the meantime, evidence has become available to indicate that Strauss received benefits in the millions for arranging the GDR credits (Uniewski & Lambrecht, 1994, 124). Susceptibility to socialist flatteries and benefits appears to have been a widespread Western weakness. Armand Hammer (1987, 401) for example, reported with obvious satisfaction:

Under the umbrella of a growing rapprochement between President Nixon and General Secretary Brezhnev, conditions for trade between the two countries, in which I played a prominent role, improved dramatically. In 1978 the Soviet government honored me with the Order of Friendship Between Peoples for my efforts to establish friendly relations and economic cooperation between the two countries—it had never been given to a foreign businessman before.

Opposition from East Germany's Party and government functionaries to Gorbachev's reform proposals was fierce and unrelenting,[57] though there was considerable support from the technical intelligentsia. The ability of socialist functionaries to resist reforms had been manifested before—such as with the GDR's NES and Khrushchev's proposals in 1964 (Brzezinski, 1968, 255). It is important to remember, however, that Gorbachev's reforms did not primarily aim at political freedoms, as these would be understood in the West (e.g., an end to one-party rule), but at making the economy work. Communism as such was not being called into question—at least not intentionally—nor was there a desire to adopt Western political and economic institutions. This was not always clearly perceived by Western observers, who, easily seduced by "mellifluous words" (Lebahn, 1988, 108–110, 124), envisioned an intent to revolutionize the system where there merely was the wish to reform it. Perestroika was designed not to abolish communism but to create an improved and more efficient version thereof.

In systems such as the GDR and the USSR, policy reforms (including the adoption of market mechanisms and the embrace of detente) were most likely to be undertaken when conditions had deteriorated to such an extent that economic and technological change became imperative and unavoidable. Social and political reforms, however, not being ends in themselves, were to be taken no further than absolutely necessary. The dilemma faced by the socialist regimes was that what barely was enough economically (perestroika) was far too much politically (glasnost)—improving citizens' life but endangering Party rule.[58] As noted, when the choice was between efficiency and hierarchy, the latter usually trumped the former (Bechtold, 1988, 133; Goldman, 1987, 251–252; Roberts, 1956, 58–59).

The best of all possible worlds for communist leaders would, of course, have been one in which they maintained full dictatorial powers *and* had a flourishing economy. One might note in this context that the reform policies of the People's Republic of China appear to aim at precisely this objective. However, as Rusinow (1977, 345) foresaw,

> [A] compromise economic model, which seeks to gain the incentives and flexibility of capitalism by inserting a few market mechanisms into an otherwise largely unreconstructed "command economy"—introducing profit-orientation, still largely administered prices which come closer to reflecting relative scarcity values and some independent entrepreneurial decision-making in the enterprise—may be inherently unstable and eventually untenable.

The East German leadership, as will be seen later, was not always opposed to economic reform. At crucial moments, however, the GDR and the USSR were at odds in this respect. They were at odds in the 1960s (regarding the NES—favored for a time in the GDR), and they were at odds again in the 1980s (regarding Gorbachev's reforms—rejected by the GDR). It was at the very end of its existence, when opposing Gorbachev's reforms, that the communist regime of the GDR rediscovered the thesis of the right to national self-determination of the socialist states. The East German leadership declared that the "old thesis" of the convergence of socialist systems was false (and that in addition to the path taken by the USSR there was also an equally valid German path to socialism). This, unfortunately for Honecker and his cohorts, was precisely the moment when the citizens of East Germany began to believe in the slogan that "to learn from the Soviet Union is to learn victory" (Bryson & Melzer, 1991, 19–20).

The New Economic System

As discussed previously in several places, the GDR experienced a form of perestroika in 1963–1967 with the introduction of the New Economic System (NES)—later (1968–1970) changed and reformulated as the Economic System of Socialism (ESS)—which incorporated market-economic elements and a certain measure of decentralization. It also included experimentation with half-nationalized/half-private enterprises. Walter Ulbricht, together with Erich Apel and Günter Mittag, was the driving force of the reforms. The reforms were not received well in Moscow, particularly not by Leonid Brezhnev, who succeeded Nikita Krushchev in 1964 (Podewin, 1999, 33–34). "The Soviets considered this ownership arrangement . . . a violation of the principles of socialist property relations" (Bryson & Melzer, 1991, 14–15).

The NES was the GDR's response to years of economic stagnation and severe production difficulties. It was based on ideas developed by Fritz Behrens, Arne Benary, and their associates in the GDR (Behrens, 1958, 1965) and Evsei Lieberman in the USSR (Lieberman, 1973; *Pravda*, September 9, 1962). It quickly became clear, however, that the innovations called into question the unlimited rule of democratic centralism and the unlimited scope of Party dictatorship.

> [T]he development of the NES as ideology brought with it dangers not fully anticipated by the party bureaucratic elite, residing in its ambiguous implications for the structure of political rule itself. . . . [The regime tried] to save [NES] as an instrument of legitimacy while stripping it of its potential for producing unwanted changes in the organization of political power. (Baylis, 1971, 216)

GDR and (especially) USSR hard-liners brought pressure to bear on Walter Ulbricht to reverse the course. Ulbricht was uncertain. "On the one hand he supported the dogmatists, who had grown more powerful [since the deaths of the pragmatists Apel and Leuschner]; but on the other he wanted to retain some of the recent [economic] gains" (Ludz, 1966, 23).

To no one's surprise, preservation of Party rule turned out to be the more important objective. The chief architect of the decentralization aspects of NES—Uwe-Jens Heuer—was removed from his professorship at Humboldt University (Berlin). Heuer as well as Behrens were charged with revisionism and with aiding the imperialists. The Party, in its usual wisdom, decided that the right solution to the GDR's economic problems was to further increase political centralization rather than to reduce it (Baylis, 1971, 224). For the remainder of the Ulbricht era, economic policies fluctuated in minor ways. After Ulbricht's fall, however, the Honecker government quickly returned to the orthodoxy of a fully planned economy (Turner, 1987, 176–177; McCauley, 1979, 129–131; Ludz, 1977, 18–19). The answer to the problems of the planned economy was again to be found in the more perfectly planned economy. Erich Honecker declared unequivocally and unvaryingly that economic advancement would not, and could not, be achieved by copying capitalist methods but only "by perfecting the socialist planned economy itself" (Honecker, 1983, 24).

Comprehensive and centralized planning was the GDR's operating procedure almost to the very end. It produced the inevitable inefficiencies, scarcities, and waste. It perpetuated the well-known weaknesses of socialist economies: "widespread sluggishness in innovation, weak managerial and labour motivation, insufficient competitive forces, . . . a rigid, noncompetitive supply structure, . . . scarcity in energy, materials, investment, and consumer goods supplies, distorted price structures, and so on" (Bryson & Melzer, 1991, 41). The theoretical foibles of the planned economy had been exposed time and again.[59] The practical failings also were obvious. The chief point of the enterprise was not preserving the purity of Marxism-Leninism or improving the welfare of the people. It was to preserve the power of the ruling class. In comparison to this objective, all else was of little importance.

ASSESSMENTS

The Subsidized Economic System

The new *Ostpolitik* (Eastern Politics, Eastern policy) of the FRG had its beginning in the mid-1960s during Willy Brandt's mayorship of West Berlin. It moved to Bonn with the *Grosse Koalition* (Grand Coalition) of CDU/CSU and SPD in 1966 and substantially burgeoned and accelerated with the accession of the *Sozial-Liberale Koalition* (social-liberal coalition) of the SPD and FDP in 1969 (Bender, 1986, 135–143). It was continued by the new CDU/CSU and FDP coalition of 1982—though with somewhat less fervor. It was suprising that this change of government did not worsen FRG/GDR relations (Zelikow & Rice, 1995, 77). CDU/CSU rhetoric had raised different expectations. As Sichelschmidt (1992, 119) rightly noted, however, Adenauer and his heirs had a strong aversion to the people of the Eastern lands of Germany. Stabilizing the SED regime headed off the nightmare of Adenauer and the other Catholic Francophiles, who dominated the FRG, of having more Prussians and Protestants join their satrapy. It is well known that Adenauer regarded Berlin as a "heathen city." He is also reported to have always closed the curtains of his railroad compartment on trips from Cologne to Berlin as soon as the River Elbe had been crossed because he could not endure the view of the "Eastern steppe."

Fundamentally, the new *Ostpolitik* meant acknowledging and accepting the reality of the division of Germany, accommodating the communist system of the GDR as much as possible, and trying to obtain humanitarian benefits for the population of East Germany in exchange for economic support of the regime.[60] In effect, the FRG paid ever-increasing subsidies to the GDR. The results were a modest increase in the economic well-being of the East Germans and a very slight improvement in their civil liberties. The doctrinaire supporters of the new *Ostpolitik* went through orgiastic celebrations of its (purely imagined) benefits.[61] Like so many, Fritz Stern (1987, 211) was mistaken on all counts when he wrote that the new "*Ostpolitik* has made a *significant* difference to the well-being of both Germanys—and to the relations between them" (emphasis added). In fact, the new policy provided few benefits for the East Germans (and the Soviet Union) and none for the West Germans. Indeed, the well-being of the West Germans was reduced since they, after all, had to pay for the Eastern subsidies. The improvement in the relationship between the two countries also was little more than a pipedream. GDR hostilities toward the FRG varied, but they never vanished[62] (Moeller, 1988).

On balance the new *Ostpolitik* must be regarded as a failed and, indeed, a counterfunctional policy (Obst, 1983, 112–120; Reissig & Glaessner, 1991, 9). The true economic beneficiary of the FRG/GDR trade relations was the GDR—or more precisely, the GDR rulers. The GDR needed this trade (and the associated subsidies) for its very survival; the FRG did not. In 1978, the trade between the two Germanys amounted to DM 8.8 billion. By 1986 it had nearly doubled to DM 15.2 billion. But the FRG's economic presence was also felt in other ways: travel between the FRG and the GDR, for example, netted (over time) billions of DM. In 1980 the FRG agreed to an annual payment for DM 50 million for West German and West Berlin use of the transit routes between the FRG and West Berlin (Childs, 1989, 4–5). Altogether the GDR received DM 7.8 billion in transit fees up to 1989. There were also numerous other ways of getting DM, for example, the compulsory exchange of West marks into East marks (DM 4.5 billion to 1989) and the buying of the freedom of the GDR's political prisoners (DM 3.3 billion to 1989)[63] (Eppelmann et al., 1996, 196–200). These sums made an important, indeed, essential difference to the functioning of the GDR economy. The FRG's aid to the GDR gave that country a margin of comfort—above and beyond what East German socialism could provide for its own citizens.

The *Ostpolitik* and its trade policies stabilized the GDR and kept its regime in place. In effect, it prolonged the misery of the people of East Germany. "Bonn's policy was almost exclusively focused on the powerholders, and ever solicitous not to 'destabilize' their states" (Ash, 1993, 370). It appears certain—particularly now that we know how run-down the country really was—that without the benefits of *Ostpolitik*, the GDR would have collapsed much earlier than it did. The premises of *Ostpolitik*, in any case, were exposed as illusionary early on. There was no "liberalization through stabilization" (*Freiheit durch Stabilität*), and there was no "improvement through proximity" (*Wandel durch Annäherung*).[64] What happened was stabilization without significant liberalization and without real improvements in inter-German relations. The vast subsidies, ransom payments, tax benefits, and credit favors merely allowed the Honecker regime to tighten its grip and survive until 1989. It can also be argued (e.g., Francisco, 1989, 205) that the FRG came to underwrite the cost of Soviet domination of Eastern Europe—perhaps a not unwelcome development for some of the supporters of the ost-political balderdash.

As part of the new policies, the GDR obtained favored trade relations not only with the FRG but also with the other member countries of the European Community (EC), by way of the FRG. West Germany, under EC rules, was not really entitled to grant such benefits to a non-EC nation, such as the GDR (Frowen, 1985, 45). The instrument used by the two countries was the legal fiction—otherwise strenuously rejected by the GDR[65]—that East Germany and West Germany were part of the same "German nation." The GDR had consistently rejected the notion that there was any special status to German–German relations, insisting throughout that the FRG was *simply another foreign country*. This, however, did not prevent the SPD from seeking a closer relationship with the SED, to the point of issuing a common policy paper in 1987 (Mayer, 1998; Neubert, 2002, 243–275; Reissig, 2002).

But the GDR gladly took advantage of the benefits that resulted from FRG special status grants, such as "a clearing agreement of both states' national banks, a permanent interest-free loan to the GDR (the so-called 'swing,' worth hundreds of millions of DM), and the exemption of GDR products from all duties and tariffs." The FRG exempted goods from the GDR of all duties normally levied on imports and reduced the value-added tax (VAT), which was imposed on domestic trade. The costs of the VAT shortfalls alone amount to DM 290 million annually. These policies help to make East German goods more competitive in the Western markets. FRG policies also provided for the implicit membership of the GDR in the European Community. This meant, for example, that the GDR benefited from being able to sell its agricultural (and other) goods at the artificially high prices of the EC (Frey, 1987, 30; Jacobsen & Machowski, 1988; Nehring, 1974).

The trade with West Germany (and the associated benefits, just discussed) was the lifeline that kept the GDR afloat for most of its existence. This trade was much more important than its proportion of the total GDR external trade—8.3% in 1985—would indicate. It was the source of much of the GDR's hard currency. It was conducted on extremely favorable terms, because it was not treated as "foreign trade" by the West Germans, and it was able to avoid the tariff walls of the EC. Furthermore, the FRG/GDR trade agreements did not obligate either country (in effect, the GDR) to annually balance its trade, due to the availability of the *swing*. The swing was, in fact, an interest-free credit. Of course, there also were the direct credits noted earlier. For example, an FRG credit of DM 1 billion was made available to the GDR in 1983, and there was a further credit of DM 950 million in 1984. As Francisco (1989, 192–203) has pointed out:

> The USSR encouraged its allies in 1971 to borrow in the West in order to finance their technology imports and accelerate their growth. . . . The result was a massive accumulation of Western debt. . . . When several CMEA countries finally faced the prospect of default, beginning in 1981, there was no Soviet rescue. . . . West Germany stepped in to rescue the GDR. . . . The East Germans . . . experienced a serious cash problem in the early 1980s . . . the West Germans stepped in with government-guaranteed loans totaling almost 2 billion marks [DM] in 1983 and 1984. The GDR needed funds badly. Its credit rating had plunged . . . and it was unable to secure loans in the open market.

The FRG paid annual subsidies of about DM 1.5 billion (ca. $1 billion) to the GDR. By 1986 the trade between the two Germanys amounted to DM 15.2 billion (ca. $10 billion). GDR trade deficits did not have to be settled in convertible currency. Travel between the FRG and the GDR, as noted, provided to the GDR use-payments of billions of DM. In addition to benefits obtained through governmental channels (such as paying for political prisoners—which the regime steadfastly denied it had), there was a substantial revenue flow from private sources to the GDR, including hard currency sums from West German church organizations and from the mandatory currency exchanges imposed on Western visitors to the GDR. West German citizens also gave generous hard-currency donations to their East German relatives[66]—which explains the existence of the many hard-currency-only Intershops, where items could be bought that were not available in the regular GDR shops.

The GDR never missed an opportunity to point out that it had the most successful economy among the COMECON nations—true as far as it went. What the GDR did not acknowledge was that whatever the actual success of its economy might have been (and official figures were greatly inflated), it was due to a very large degree to West German technology transfers, special trade relations, and subsidy payments. Ash (1993, 373) speaks of "blackmail" payments. His point is well taken, except that certain West German politicians practically begged to be blackmailed. In any case, by the 1980s, the USSR and the other socialist countries had become massively dependent on the West for technology, raw materials, and credit. The question became one of economic and, even, political survival[67] (Seiffert, 1983). However much the East Bloc leaders wanted to build walls against the capitalist world and its destabilizing influences, survival needs dictated openings to the West. Only Gorbachev seemed to be under the illusion that communism could survive glasnost and perestroika.

The Failed Economic System

The first economic plans of the SZ/GDR emphasized the reconstruction and development of heavy industry. This caused significant shortages in basic consumer goods. While rationing was eliminated in the FRG in 1948, the GDR continued to ration basic consumer items until 1958. Shortages remained a problem throughout the existence of the GDR. The regime continued to emphasize central planning and always was in need of hard currencies. To obtain these, it exported many of its better products to the West—much to the disgust of its own people (Goldman, 1987, 149; Weymar, 1985, 79–80; Ulrich, 1984, 104–108). The East German standard of living improved over the years, but it always lagged behind that of West Germany, with an ever-increasing difference (Obst, 1983, 8; Nawrocki, 1967, 6). Wage increases, such as those of 1988, did little to improve the actual standard of living, because few quality products could be purchased with East German marks.

Estimates were that the standard of living of a "worker household" in the GDR was about one-half that of the FRG in the 1970s and 1980s and less than that in the earlier decades (Cornelsen, 1988, 251; Ulrich, 1984, 152–153). A Swedish analysis of the mid-1980s characterized the GDR standard of living as substantially lagging behind that of the FRG and the nature of GDR housing as "unbelievably low" by any standard of comparison (Bergmann-Weinberg, 1987, 387). The East German boast that the socialist mode of production would allow the GDR to overtake the FRG in the consumption (by 1961) and the production (by 1965) of basic consumer goods and foodstuffs was far from being realized even in 1989. In 1971 the regime proudly proclaimed that it had reached the level of "real existing socialism," as well as established the "unity of economic and social policy." Other than "more consumer goods," the meaning of these phrases remains nebulous, but one matter was crystal-clear: the GDR was unable to finance these policies without FRG subsidies (Epplemann et al., 1996, 196–200; Wenzel, 1998a).

In the context of the Soviet Bloc (COMECON), however, the GDR had a relatively successful economy.[68] The advantage over the USSR, for example, was sufficiently large to lead to circulation curtailments (since 1971) of East German pictorial magazines in the Soviet Union. The higher standard of living in the GDR simply was too obvious when viewing these publications. Indeed, while comparisons of GDR production indexes and standards of living with those of the West showed the GDR at a substantial disadvantage, comparisons with the other countries of the Soviet Bloc generated a distinctly more positive picture (Bryson, 1989, 178).

Three factors typically are cited to account for the GDR's relative advantages within the Eastern Bloc: (1) a survival of the traditional German work ethic and workmanship, (2) massive West German aid, and (3) the system of enterprise organizations known as combines (*Kombinate*). There are important reasons to doubt that the work ethic, work habits, workmanship, or combines were major factors.

Regarding the *work ethic and work habits*, the East German workers did work more hours than their West German colleagues. In the 1980s, the average work hours per year were 1,770 in the FRG and 2,100 in the GDR (Obst, 1983, 47). More than 80% of East German women of the appropriate ages were employed full-time, and many women worked beyond the official retirement age of sixty years (Bundesministerium für innerdeutsche Beziehungen, 1985, 447; Witt, 2001, 83).[69] This gives the GDR the highest workforce-to-population ratio in the world, with essentially no unused labor potential. Proportionately more people being employed and the employed reporting more hours on the job did not, however, add up to more work being done or better products being produced. As noted earlier, substantial parts of the official work time were spent in idleness and in pursuing personal projects, such as running errands, going shopping, visiting the beauty parlor, playing cards, and attending to one's hobbies. The traditional German work ethic certainly was marred by the presence of idle workers in the factories and by the nonpresence of those pursuing personal ventures.

The work ethic, however, also was greatly impaired by nonworker factors, for example, breakdowns of machinery, lack of raw materials, and energy scarcities, which prevented the workers from working. In the end, GDR workers had become thoroughly unaccustomed to working a full eight-hour day. As Melville (1990, 5) reported: "There was growing alienation, apathy, and cynicism. People saw that an enormous and ineffective 'welfare state' had been created that was excessive and inadequate. As a result, the work ethic itself was being eroded." The conditions in the GDR were essentially the same as those recounted by Wildavsky (1983, 34–35) for the Soviet Union: "Workers begin late, leave their jobs, get drunk, steal, and otherwise perform badly. But they ordinarily do not struggle as a group; instead they engage in private evasive behavior."

The GDR's official "performance principle" (*Leistungsprinzip*)—those who produce more also may consume more—had little effect on the workers, who knew perfectly well that the goods that they really wanted could not be purchased in any case. Workers also showed little interest in making products of high quality. The many defects in GDR-produced goods were notorious. The wasteful practices of the planned economy—in respect to labor, equipment, energy, raw materials, and capital—limited the productivity of the GDR to a meager 43% of the productivity of the FRG[70] (Obst, 1983, 50). The unproductive and wasteful use of capital was a particularly sore point. The theorists of socialist production never seem to have understood that capital is a *cost* factor that needed to be included in their calculations. Not surprisingly, many capital expenditures were pure waste. Seldom did they produce an increase in quantitative or qualitative productive capabilities. For example, in 1987 "investment expenditures grew by six percent. [But this was] a negative development, since the expansion of capital did not increase productive capacity at all" (Bryson & Melzer, 1991, 23). In the end, even the heavy—and un-Marxist[71]—use of shift work, including night shifts, could not overcome the deficiencies of the planned economic system.

The *combines* (*Kombinate*) were a form of industrial organization that linked production facilities, suppliers, plant construction capacities, sales and delivery organizations, and research institutes in vertical (and, sometimes, horizontal) quasi monopolies (cartels). Developed in the late 1960s and early 1970s, they became the dominant production units of the East German economy by the late 1970s.[72] In the late 1980s, they employed nearly 4 million workers and generated about 80% of the total national product[73] (Bryson, 1987, 52; Friedrich, 1988, 157–158). The purpose of organizing combines was to achieve a more "effective utilization of productive resources and a systematic reduction of materials and energy in production" (Bryson & Melzer, 1991, 6). The combines remained subject to the overall plan but were given considerable managerial autonomy—and more in the GDR than in the USSR. The GDR combine directors general had substantial flexibility in allocating and dividing the total plan obligations among the combines' individual enterprises. The directors general of the combines participated in the development of plans and had some influence on the plan figures (goals). They were seen as occupying a dual position, that of an enterprise manager and that of a ministerial agent. Only the minister responsible for the combine (as opposed to his staff) could give direct orders to a combine director general (Bryson, 1989, 176). In certain respects the combines functioned almost like free-market companies (Autorenkollektiv, 1987; Bryson, 1987; Goldman, 1987, 167–170; Obst, 1983, 29–32, 38). In certain (limited) respects they functioned as a counterforce to the East Berlin ministries.

As it turned out, however, the combines were unable to overcome the deficiencies and defects of the planned economy (Hamel & Leipold, 1987, 302). The organizational benefits were available only to the combines as such, not to the individual enterprises, their constituent units. This contrasts with the more substantial reorganization in Gorbachev's USSR, where a certain autonomy went even to the level of the individual enterprises. Soviet restructuring was substantially more progressive than the changes adopted in the GDR (Bryson & Melzer, 1991, 6–7). The managers of the individual enterprises within the combines remained subject to plan commands, just like any other enterprise. They had no influence on plan development and combine management and little autonomy in enterprise management and production decisions. The directors general of the combines, for example, could (and did) transfer successful production units to enterprises under their personal direction, leaving the other enterprises with the inefficient units. The enterprise managers "were without voice as the assortment of consumer goods diminished, as the size of production units continued to grow, and as enterprise decision prerogatives were reduced" (Bryson & Melzer, 1991, 6–7).

It is unclear whether the combines could have improved East German economic output to a significant degree if autonomy and flexibility had been greater and had reached down to the individual enterprise. It is also unclear whether the combines could have become centers for the innovation of more attractive products for the Western markets if their own scientists[74] had been less subject to bureaucratic controls and to the need of solving immediate production problems. Finally, it is unclear whether the virtual monopoly position of each combine served to dampen any incentive to modernize production and improve products. For whatever reason (probably all), the combines could not halt the East German economy's slide into deterioration and bankruptcy. Nevertheless, Erich Honecker, ever the wishful doctrinaire, declared as late as 1986 (at the XIth Party Congress) that the combines were the determining factor in the success of the East German economy. He affirmed that they were the basis of the "well-functioning, efficient, productive, dynamic, and flexible system of the GDR's socialist planned economy." Of course, he did not fail to point out that this great accomplishment was due to the "extensive theoretical and practical work of the Party" (as reported in Friedrich, 1988, 158–160).

What he did fail to point out was that the GDR's international competitiveness had declined drastically. Most export sales required substantial price reductions, even to levels below the cost of production. Like so many things in the GDR, decisions about combines often were made on political rather than economic grounds. For example, one of the most famous combines—the brown coal and gas production combine *Schwarze Pumpe*—showed an annual net loss of about 500 million East German marks. The Party supported it not because of its productivity or efficiency but because it was a "prestige" enterprise. In some ways, the GDR was located at the level of a Third World country. In fact, GDR building technology (organized, of course, in combines)[75] was not even able to build first-class hotels. When these were needed (particularly from 1970 on), they had to be ordered *complete* from foreign companies (Klingst, 2001, 227).

Even the pride and joy of the GDR regime, its computer industry, was but a pale imitation of Western technology. In fact, as Francisco (1989, 197) pointed out:

> the computer industry . . . is one of the largest areas of GDR dependence on the West. The GDR produces mid-size mainframe computers for the CMEA under a division of labour introduced by the USSR in 1970. East German computers are among the

best available in the CMEA. . . . [But] being the best in the CMEA does not amount to much. The vaunted East German computers are basically copies and revisions of IBM's mid-1960s 360 series of mainframe machines, and its microprocessors are much slower than those available in the West.

What kept the GDR above water for so many years were not the combines or hard work. What sustained the GDR were, as noted, the direct subsidies and other benefits obtained from West Germany—and, in earlier times, from the USSR. It is important to note that the USSR had bailed out the GDR a number of times in the 1950s and 1960s. In later decades the USSR was unwilling to continue this policy. Indeed, in 1981 the USSR greatly hurt the GDR economy by reducing its oil deliveries. The GDR had been earning hard currency by selling some of that oil to the West at a higher price. In this context, the USSR was forced to approve of (previously opposed) new GDR credits from the West. These credits were arranged at the secret Strauss/Schalk-Golodkowski meeting in 1983. West German credits, however, were not the only form of GDR indebtedness. As of 1984, the GDR's trade debt to the USSR was 4 billion rubles. At the same time, the GDR's total Western debt had reached a per capita level of $710 (as against a CMEA average of $230). The GDR "was forced to allocate 58% of every dollar or mark gained from the West simply to satisfy its debt service obligations" (Francisco, 1989, 199). The USSR and the (non-German) West could not be looked to for additional credits. Only the (much hated and denigrated) FRG remained as a possible source of funds. As seen, under the driving force of personal interests and the illusions of *Ostpolitik*, West German politicians practically fell over each other to provide the needed credits and to stabilize the GDR regime. The citizens of the FRG had to bear the material costs; the citizens of the GDR had to endure a hateful regime for longer than was necessary.[76]

It should be pointed out, however, that the inefficiencies of centralized planning and socialist production, low work motivation, insufficient combine and enterprise autonomy, and the emphasis on heavy industry were not the only causes of the GDR's economic difficulties. There also were the matters (noted earlier) of the massive dismantling of the industrial stock and the takeover of remaining plants by the Soviets in the years following World War II, the imposition of highly unfavorable trade agreements by the USSR, the paucity of natural resources, and the flight from the GDR of skilled labor and technical/scientific professionals. The Berlin Wall was meant to be a remedy for the last problem. It never worked perfectly, and in the end it did not work at all. It should be noted in this context that technical experts always were valued less than ideological experts in the GDR. Contrary to Weberian expectations, the technical experts never gained real power; nor did they receive greatly superior salaries, as compared to skilled manual labor. Their (presumably) greater efficiency and rationality might well have improved the economic well-being of the country and even increased regime legitimacy. Weber's technocratic regime legitimization expectancy was, of course, based on the model of the natural sciences. Leninist regime legitimization—contrary to all socialist scientific pretenses—by contrast was based on a teleological fantasy. As Harry Nick (1994, 5), a prominent GDR economist, concludes in his (not unsympathetic) review of the GDR's economic system, it not only failed but also was ill-advised from the very beginning.[77]

The regime sought to replace those who had escaped with a new type of citizen, one who "owed his advantages" to the GDR and who, thus, would be grateful and loyal and remain in the country. In this way the regime sought to solve the traditional dilemma of choosing between the most competent and the most loyal. It led to the development of the (Stalinist) cadre and nomenklatura politics, seeking to combine technical competence with ideological commitment and Party loyalty. After 1971 there was a concerted effort to reverse any inroad that technocrats had made in the preceding decades. Indeed, there was a sharp attack on Peter Ludz, who had presented a technocratic view of the party cadres. His analysis was regarded as "slander."[78] Regularly and endlessly, the GDR's citizens were told how much they owed to the new socialist state. This argument was viable only in respect to the upwardly mobile Party and state functionaries—a rather small proportion of the population. Few workers ever believed that the GDR was a "workers' republic." Indeed, there was more opposition to the regime among ordinary workers than among most other population groups (Prauss, 1960, 205). The uprising of June 1953, for example, was carried out almost entirely by members of the (real) working class.[79] The "revolution" of 1989 was more broadly based, but the Party and state functionaries as well as most academics did not play an important part. They rewarded the Party with loyalty for the opportunities that they had been given.

The Leninist rulers of the GDR did not subscribe to Lenin's notion that anyone, even those with but a grade school education, would be able to perform all societal tasks, from governance and control, to development and production. Leninist lip service, of course, could, and would, not stop. The official GDR line always was that ordinary workers, not only a well-educated elite, were able to administer the state, manage factories, assume leadership functions in social organizations, and command the military (Grundmann, 1984, 223). There was, however, a constant and real effort to create a new type of scientific, technical, and managerial elite from among the workers and peasants. The members of the new elites enjoyed heightened status and improved material rewards—which provided good reasons to display at least the outward signs of loyalty to the system. In addition to the Party cadres—political activism being the foremost avenue of upward mobility—the new professionals were the prime beneficiaries of the socialist state. Nevertheless, discontent increasingly affected even them.

Few of the *workers* in industry and agriculture of this *Arbeiter und Bauern Staat* (worker-and-peasant state) enjoyed high status or superior material rewards—with the exception of a few "activists." Activist workers occupied a special place in the socialist economies. The first Soviet activist was the well-known Aleksei Stakhanov, who on August 30, 1935, on his own "spontaneous initiative" mined 102 tons of coal instead of the customary 7 tons (Heller & Nekrich, 1986, 282). The first GDR activist was the coal miner Adolf Hennecke (as previously noted), who achieved a 387 percent overproduction of the existing norm on October 13, 1948 (Bundesministerium, 1985, 185). The activists received substantial rewards, but their accomplishments amounted to much less than official accounts pretended. The high production rates—risking the assumption that the figures were genuine—were not achieved by ordinary workers laboring in normal settings but involved special preparations, superior tools, first-rate working conditions, and various other forms of assistance. Nevertheless, activist overfulfillments were used to increase the production norms for *all*. This contributed greatly to the discontent and cynicism among the ordinary workers, who knew perfectly well how overproduction had been achieved. Among the consequences of years of persistent and unsustainable rises in the production norms were a substantial increase in escapes to the West as well as the revolts of June 1953 (Hanhardt, 1968, 51–59).

The primary causes of the alienation of the new technical *professionals* were the lack of decision-making autonomy regarding even technical matters, the lack of civil liberties, the dearth of real political influence, and absence of trust. The Central Committee and the Politburo, as well as the lower-level party offices, remained entirely in the domains of the ideological and organizational specialists—most of whom also tended to be quite elderly. Kopstein (1997, 125) reports that in 1987 the average age of Bezirk Party first secretaries was over sixty years. Their chief interests and responsibilities lay in the areas of ideology, myth creation, language control, and the performance of rituals. Most fundamentally, the new technical professionals were alienated from the regime by the obvious failure to be trusted. For example, permission could occasionally be had to attend professional meetings in the West. Family members, however, were not permitted to join in the trip. They had to remain in the GDR as a safeguard against the defection of the whole family and as a guarantee for the traveler's own return (Luebbe, 1980).

The discontent of *ordinary citizens* was yet broader. Few of them ever were trusted to travel to the West before reaching retirement age (at which point the regime was glad to see them go and to live at the expense of the FRG). Even grave family emergencies did not engender travel permits. For most GDR citizens there were few reasons to regard the regime as legitimate, to work hard, or even to remain in the country. The Berlin Wall and the rest of the fortified border made it almost impossible to escape, of course. Virtual imprisonment, however, did not enhance loyalty, reduce discontent, or improve lax work habits. Indeed, initiative and extra toil were treated with suspicion in the socialist camp. "In 1969 a Soviet citizen named Ivan Khudenko obtained a plot in Kazakhstan to grow alfalfa using well-paid labor. The experiment was a huge economic success. Yet the farm was declared a capitalist failure and shut down, and Khudenko was arrested in 1973. Shortly after his trial, he died in prison (Kuran, 1995, 208).

Erich Honecker (1984, 121–122) did express dissatisfaction with the GDR's failure to use the full abilities of all people. He was unable, however, to think beyond the planned economy—being entirely captive of the central planning philosophy of the USSR. He suggested that the solution to the GDR's economic problems was to more "properly assign [people] to workplaces and cadres, according to their qualifications." But, of course, he had to assert GDR and SED achievements: "We have not the slightest reason to hide the fact that the [socioeconomic] course we have followed since the beginning of the 1970s has proven correct" (as reported in Krisch, 1989, 29). (The choice of this date is not particularly surprising. Honecker succeeded Ulbricht as first secretary of the SED on May 3, 1971.)

By the mid-1980s, the GDR, like the other socialist systems, had entered into the advanced stages of economic and political disintegration (Bryson & Melzer, 1991; Janson, 1991; Kusch et al., 1991; also Seiffert & Treutwein, 1991). Even the GDR leadership began to notice that there was a problem.[80] Of course, there could be no questioning of the efficacy and rightness of the economic principles of Marxism-Leninism and of the planned economy. The fault was found in the inadequate application and implementation of the principles and the plan. In a volume published in 1984, Erich Honecker declared that these were the primary causes of the GDR's economic problems: failure to fully utilize modern technological developments, failures of the directors of the combines and enterprises to correctly calculate their equipment needs, lack of timely worker training, not enough use of shift work, not working exactly to plan, inadequate use of basic productive capacities, too much lost time in the enterprises, lack of order and discipline, too many meetings during working hours, not enough continuity in the day-by-day organization of production, introduction of new technologies too slowly, too much administrative personnel,[81] inefficiencies in production, low quality of consumer goods, inadequate use of investment capital, not enough coordination between technology and investment plans, not fulfilling contracts, lack of coordination between supply and demand, wasteful use of raw materials, production costs too high, insufficient strictness in plan fulfillment, enterprise selfishness, excessive expenditures, and many other such problems[82] (Honecker, 1984, 109–121). A number of the items listed by Honecker were, in fact, real problems in the GDR economy. Certainly, lost time, lack of worker discipline, and failure to coordinate technological developments and investments are among them. Not strictly following the plan, however, was not a cause of problems but a consequence thereof. There was no way that enterprises could function and be even minimally productive by strictly following the plan. Successful enterprise and combine directors were successful precisely because they had found ways around the plan.

In any case, by the mid-1980s popular discontent was growing, as was the willingness to give it public expression. There were moral and political as well as economic causes for citizens' dissatisfaction and the regime's downfall. In East Germany, as in the other socialist countries, demoralization

> was occasioned both by declining economies and by the privileges granted by separating party members and their favorites from the consequences of the political economy they created. . . . Even the privileged are disaffected. They no longer believe in Marxism-Leninism. [The] state . . . has lost legitimacy. Both those who lied about its operating norms and those who were lied to are disgusted because in all [communist political economies] the system breeds similar effects, either hostility or disbelief. When these hollow states no longer exist in the hearts and minds of their citizens, when someone pushes on them, they collapse. (Clark & Wildavsky, 1990, 16)

As Leonhard (1990, 201) has rightly pointed out, economic reform cannot be successfully undertaken in isolation from the other characteristics of the system: political rule, valuation of law, cultural freedom, religious tolerance, open discussions, freedom to form organizations and parties, and real parliaments. All that, of course, would have affected SED rule. Thus, no real reforms. The regime's reform attempts stayed limited to fiddling with the economy and even then only timidly and only at the margins. In the end, there was no economic basis, as there was no political basis, from which the regime could have derived legitimacy and loyalty.

NOTES

1. This is not the place for a detailed discussion of Mikhail Gorbachev's domestic reforms or of Moscow's general retreat from military intervention in defense of communist governments. Suffice it to say that most of the citizens of East Germany enthusiastically welcomed Gorbachev's reforms and that the failure of the East German leadership to apply them to the GDR greatly increased the citizens' loathing of the regime.

2. For detailed discussions of the East German Revolt of June 1953, see Baring, 1972, 1983; Brant, 1957; *Bundesministerium für innerdeutsche Beziehungen*, 1988; Diedrich, 1991; Friedrich & Friedrich, 1992; Hagen, 1992; Herrnstadt, 1990; Heym, 1990; Pernkopf, 1982; the various contributions in Spittmann & Fricke, eds., 1988; and, from a novelist's interpretive perspective, Heym, 1977. See also later comments.

3. For general discussions of the East German *Wirtschaftswunder*, see Ardagh, 1987. For critical analyses, see Childs, 1988, Chapter 6; Schneider, 1988.

4. Not even all of the members of the Politburo had access to all the economic data (Deutscher Bundestag, 1993, 27–36).

5. Long viewed as vaguely counterrevolutionary, even cybernetics received some recognition as part of the NES efforts. See Ludz, 1968.

6. Atomic energy was another of the GDR's prestige projects that did not come to much (Abele, 2000; Reichert, 1999). It might also be remembered how quickly GDR labs discovered "cold fusion," then in vogue.

7. In Western Germany, such inane and convoluted edicts were called "Party Chinese" (*Parteichinesisch*).

8. Bertrand Russell [1896, 24–38, 152–160] pointed out that the communist program of agricultural collectivization, a policy of extreme cost and few benefits, had its source in Marx's failure to distinguish between rents and profits, both of which he simply understood as nonwages, in contrast to wages. This confusion of farmers and landlords was inherent in the policy of forced collectivization, that is, in the expropriation of the peasants' productive property in the Soviet Union, the GDR, and other socialist states.

9. A recent analysis of Soviet agricultural policies estimates that the collectivization by "dekulakization" of 1929–1932 caused more than 7 million deaths and that the deliberately induced famine of 1932–1933 claimed another 7 million-plus victims (Conquest, 1986, 299–306). Most of the victims were Ukrainians. For one of several available eyewitness accounts, see Dolot, *Execution by Hunger*, 1985.

10. The destruction of these groups also marked the end of "reform socialism" and of any pretense of a "German path to socialism."

11. This phrase was changed in the GDR literature to read: to each according to his performance (Falk et al., 1969, 279). This follows Stalin's revision of the Marxist phrasing to "to each according to his work" (as quoted in Lane, 1976, 178).

12. The pay differential between mental and physical work was not very large for most positions.

13. In addition to the two recognized "classes" of the workers and the cooperative farmers, there was the "stratum" of the intelligentsia. The latter was not recognized as a class because its existence did not derive from a special property relationship (no uniform relation to the means of production) but rather regarded the organization and nature of its work. These were largely highly qualified professionals, often engaged in mentally creative work. They tended to be subservient to the regime (particularly those in the social sciences and humanities), which kept them faithful by way of various privileges, including academic titles and honorary degrees.

14. In the 1950s children of workers received a scholarship of 180 East German marks; children of office employees (Angestellte), only 130. There was no economic justification for this, since the income of office employees was less than that of workers. Party functionaries earned about five times what workers earned. The top leaders received, of course, vastly more (Berg, 1988, 70–71).

15. The nomenklatura had two aspects. First, it was a listing of those positions that (at a given level) party or state functionaries were responsible to staff and, thus, were outside the normal hiring processes. Second, it was a listing of persons eligible to fill these positions. These persons were a stratum of higher functionaries and, while not necessarily incompetent, were qualified for their positions *primarily* by their devotion and loyalty to the party (Wagner, 1998, 11–15).

16. It needs to be said, however, that the great majority of mid- and low-level functionaries were not corrupt. At least in this respect they deserved the appellation *Red Prussians* (Venohr, 1989).

17. A secret (but leaked) report to the top Party leadership showed that "three-quarters of young workers at the Robotron plant in Dresden felt that they had no

say in its affairs, and over 60 per cent said they were afraid to voice any criticism" (Ardagh, 1987, 336). Increasingly, another problem developed (thanks to a successful education/training system): overqualification. Dennis (1986, 61) estimates that about 25% of the workers "were employed in jobs which did not match their level of qualification."

18. Lenin acknowledged this point but gave it a special twist: "[S]ocialism is nothing but state capitalist monopoly made to *benefit the whole people*" (as quoted in Cliff, 1974, 163–164).

19. Regarding the employers in national-socialist Germany, however, it should be noted that they had a considerable autonomy in running their enterprises. The political apparatus gave the business elite much more independence than was the case in the GDR. In fact, Overy (1997, 19) speaks of the "polycratic structure of the Nazi state."

20. "The state was said to embody the proletarian dictatorship, but the ordinary worker . . . was suppressed as never before. Western commentators used to say that Russia of the thirties was not a political democracy but was an economic democracy. This was a total error. It is not just that trade unions were emasculated and free speech vanished. Workers were treated with arbitrariness and brutality" (Nove, 1989, 60–61).

21. This was not a function of complicated, recent technology. Sometimes, simply the right-sized screw could not be obtained, and soft-drink bottling plants often could not operate because there were not enough empty bottles (Klingst, 2001, 229), and when there were bottles, distribution was often faulty. For example, at the Baltic Sea tourist destinations, not enough soft drinks would be available during the summer (Kawohl, 2000, 17).

22. Truly desirable and scarce goods did not enter normal transactions at all. They would be reserved for friends of the sales personnel and for persons who also had scarce goods available for "swapping" (Klingst, 2001).

23. Low productivity of labor, equipment, and capital, of course, was a problem in all socialist countries. As a sympathetic observer noted: "Although the Soviet Union is the world's second industrial power, its labor productivity is relatively low. Compared to the U.S., it is scarcely better than half in industry and less than a fourth in agriculture" (Sharnoff, 1983, 282).

24. The socialist literature arguing the superiority of socialism is endless. For some examples, see Gemeinsame Kommission, 1982; Heuer, 1984; Hummel & Schieck, 1985; Koziolek & Reinhold, 1988; Reinhold, 1985a, 1985b.

25. Since formal working time and actual working time tended to diverge considerably in the GDR, some of the "working time" should be understood as "time scheduled to be at the workplace."

26. Authorized by SMAD Order No. 2 of June 10, 1945, it was completely under KPD/SED control. Its primary purpose was that of another transmission belt for SED policies (Eppelmann et al., 1996, 211–214). In the very early postwar years, there was a real movement toward workers' power in the enterprises (*Mitbestimmung*). It did not survive the ascendancy of the SED (Suckut, 1982).

27. These efforts were given the title "the democratic co-determination (*Mitwirkung*) of the labor unions" (Siewert, 1988).

28. Some of the enterprise councilors [*Betriebsräte*] were more active in these respects, but usually without the help of the FDGB (Kaedtler et al., 1997). Enterprises had a "worker protection overseer" (*Arbeitsschutzobmann*), but his activities had to be in conformity with SED policy (Bundesvorstand des FDGB, 1970).

29. Disastrous environmental policies were a common problem in the socialist countries. See, for example, Kurlantzick, 2004, on the problems in China. This is not to say, of course, that the West is ecologically blameless. It is to say, however, that socialism uniquely combined calamitous policies and an overblown, self-congratulatory rhetoric.

30. What Chi An reported regarding the People's Republic of China applied equally to the German Democratic Republic: "Life in China's socialist welfare state, with its cradle-to-grave job security, was undemanding as long as one did not deviate from the authorities' rigid plan" (Mosher, 1993, 246). In fact, a number of refugees returned to the GDR because they missed the security provided by that country and "the feeling to be looked after and to be taken care of" (Richert, 1963, 288).

31. Over time, the medals lost much of their attractiveness; too many of them were poured into the population (Scholze, 1999, 85, 93).

32. The identity of interests of workers and society (state) was another manifestation of the dialectical unity fantasies explored in *Rotten Foundations* (Chapter 5).

33. In the words of Hans Apel (2000, 133), "wages exploded."

34. Year-end premium payments, initially intended for extraordinary plan fulfillments, became part of the regular worker remuneration, which further increased the cost of labor.

35. Hennecke, it should be noted, became one of the "socialist heroes" of the GDR—a rare honor, typically awarded to antinazi politicians (e.g., Ernst Thälmann) or successful sports figures (e.g., Gustav Adolf Schur). See Satjukow, 2002.

36. Bahro had declared that the GDR was not "*reformfähig*" (able to reform itself). This prognosis earned him eight years of imprisonment (Bahro, 1977). It should be noted, however, that the GDR was the first socialist state even to attempt these types of economic reforms. The point was a reaffirmation of centralism and the protection of SED rule (Erbe, 1979, 15–22). When it came to *political* reforms, it was indeed a fair question to ask (as Daniels, 1988, did in respect to the USSR) whether the system was "reformable." The answer appears to be *no*. Socialist systems do not seem to be able to survive serious political reform.

37. As noted by Rakowska-Harmstone (1979, 1) regarding socialist systems: "Paradoxically, a system designed to change society saw no need for its own adaptation and provided no mechanism for its own change." Until the advent of Gorbachev this was true indeed; and when fundamental political and economic reforms were undertaken, the system collapsed. To the very end, however, the GDR regarded itself as a "revolutionary" system (Opitz, 1988).

38. As Brzeski (1970, 162) has pointed out, "within the structure of the communist polity, any but a trivial reorganization constitutes a political issue." NES, of course, was far from "trivial." Conversely, the reasons for any major overhaul of the economy have always been political.

39. Gerhard Schuerer (1999, 90), head of the State Planning Commission, stated after the demise of the GDR that there had always been in East Germany "a primacy of politics over economics" (see also Kuhnert, 1980, 42; Weinert, 1995).

40. At the October 1968 Plenary Session of the Central Committee of the SED, Ulbricht and Günter Mittag massively attacked NES as a theory of convergence and revisionism (Leptin, 1975, 46). However, the complete abandonment of NES was not what Ulbricht wanted. Ulbricht had been one of the early supporters of the technocrats (vs. the dogmatic bureaucrats) and NES (Leonhard, 1990, 155). Only by rendering Ulbricht powerless in the overthrow of 1971 could they force a return to the

full, centrally planned economy (Hamel & Leipold, 1987, 300; Pirker et al., 1995, 22–23).

41. Confronted with similar problems, Hungary chose the gradual introduction of a market economy. The GDR did not.

42. The 1989 minimum retirement pay was 330 East German marks per month. This contrasted to an average monthly income of 1,300 marks. Since 1971, it was possible to pay into a fund for some additional retirement income. This did not greatly improve matters. The additional income was only 80 marks on average (Epplemann et al., 1996, 492–494).

43. The inequalities in economic privileges were the ones that really mattered. These determined the individual's "lifestyle" much more than monetary earnings (Mertens, 2002b, 120; Voigt et al., 1987, 145).

44. The People's Control Committees were to aid governmental agencies in the fight against economic crimes, such as black market activities. In 1963, they were transformed into Worker and Farmer Inspections (*Arbeiter- und Bauerninspektionen*), and their organizational status was significantly upgraded. Their purpose remained the same. Their competency was increased to include the leveling of disciplinary penalties (Eppelmann et al., 1996, 69–70; Mummert, 1999; Stief, 1988).

45. The comprehensive system of central planning is, of course, of Leninist-Stalinist rather than Marxist derivation (Jordan, 1985, 305–311).

46. Actually, there were concurrent plans for different time periods, some of them as long as twenty years, others as short as one year.

47. For early criticisms of the planned economy, see Friedrich von Hayek (1935, 1944, 1948, 1988); Ludwig von Mises (1932, 1937, 1944, 1947); Lionel Robbins (1937, 1939); Wilhelm Roepke (1942, 1943, 1947); Adolf Weber (1929, 1930, 1944, 1949, 1950).

48. It should not be imagined, however, that socialist economies are immune to business cycles. See Paraskewopoulos, 1985. However, it was with much glee that GDR writers reported about Western business cycles (particularly in their down phase) (Reinhold, 1984) and about such matters as the American indebtedness to other countries (Burg, 1985). For general discussions of the GDR views of the United States, see Grosse, 1999; Schnoor, 1999. On the issue of mutual perceptions, see Buckow, 2003.

49. This is also reflected in the rather extraordinary amount of personal savings, which in 1989 amounted to about 160 billion East German marks (Eppelmann et al., 1996, 379).

50. This was also the waiting time for a private telephone connection. Here it should be noted, however, that the regime certainly had no interest in a well-functioning system of communications for its citizens.

51. Falsifying statistics was part of the regime's sugarcoating reality. For example, official GDR statistics paraded 2.8 million apartments as having been built between 1975 and 1989. The actual figure was 1.7 million—an overstatement of 65%. It is of interest to note in this connection that the official statistics of the GDR were not generated independently of the Party but were controlled by the Central Committee of the SED (Eppelmann et al., 1996, 98, 612–615). There was no free access to economic (or any other) statistics. Even economic specialists, professors at GDR universities, did not have access, which surely handicapped their work (Luft, 1992, 36).

52. Including, interestingly, most Party functionaries, who were not permitted to have Western contacts.

53. The COMECON was founded in 1949 to organize economic cooperation and the division of labor among the socialist nations. It was strengthened in 1971, with particular attention to science and technology. COMECON was less effective than it might have been, because the central COMECON office could issue only recommendations, and not all of them were carried out (Eppelmann et al., 1996, 478–480).

54. Occasionally, the wrapping fell apart. While the principle of the primacy of economics was officially adopted as SED doctrine in the fall of 1962, the VIth SED Party Congress of 1963 admitted to the actual primacy of politics, that is, of Party rule.

55. It was, in any case, a needed reaction to the stagnation of the Brezhnev years (Shlapentokh, 1988).

56. To the end, however, they continued to emphasize the importance of close economic cooperation with the Soviet Union as well as other countries (Scharschmidt, 1989).

57. The homegrown reformers—the various NES supporters as well as such functionaries as Schuerer, Wittkowski, and Krolikowski—lost whatever influence they had already in the 1970s.

58. Thomas Baylis (1987), focusing specifically on the GDR, thought that significant economic reforms could be achieved even without fundamental political changes. The actual developments did not support this assessment. See also Hough, 1988, 14–45.

59. The classic critique of planning remains Hayek's Road to Serfdom (1944). An important recent analysis of the problems and difficulties of a planned economy is Rutland's The Myth of the Plan (1985).

60. For discussions of the development and consequences of the *Ostpolitik*, see Ardagh, 1987; Ash, 1993; Bender, 1986; Griffith, 1978; Kroemke, 1998; Merkl, 1993, 59–62; Mitter & Wolle, 1993; Roesler, 1998; Zelikow & Rice, 1995.

61. In particular, members of the SPD were quite unrestrained in their efforts to curry favor with the East German regime. They went as far as to demand the closing of the Salzgitter Office, which kept a record of regime crimes, especially the killing of refugees crossing the border. The GDR had long demanded the abolition of the Salzgitter Office (Koop, 1996, 351). About the work of the Salzgitter Office, see Sauer, 1993.

62. For the GDR, Brandt's *Ostpolitik* "meant a barefaced attempt at subversion of communist rule and principles by the agent of imperialism." The GDR saw it as an "attack on the socialist community of nations, exemplifying anti-communism and nationalism, with the goal of destroying socialism" (Merkl, 1993, 61; Rausch, 1974, 14).

63. East German audacity had almost no limits. At a meeting with Willy Brandt in 1970, GDR premier Willi Stoph had the nerve to demand a payment of DM 10 billion in reparations from the FRG for the pre-1961 loss of the East Germans who had escaped from the GDR, as well as for FRG discrimination of the GDR (Merkl, 1993, 59–60).

64. This was the motto of the West German SPD politician Egon Bahr and an example of SPD attempts to curry favor with the East. Honecker, however, never accepted the idea that there should be a closer relation between the peoples of the two Germanys (Nawrocki, 1986, 58). In any case, whenever the GDR found itself in a particularly difficult economic situation, it could find some virtue in *Ostpolitik* and greater openness in foreign relations (Bethkenhagen et al., 1980; see also Mallinckrodt, 1972; Schulz et al., 1982; Siebs, 1999).

65. See, for example, Honecker, 1981, 389–398, 415–417. As late as 1986, in an interview with the (West German) paper *Die Zeit*, Honecker declared that the existence of two German states was an "essential element of European stability." Anyone who seeks to change that "jeopardizes the peace" (as quoted in Nawrocki, 1986, 7).

66. West German citizens also gave generous gifts in kind to their Eastern relatives. Each year approximately 25 million parcels and packages were sent from the FRG to the GDR (Kaminsky, 2001, 158). These gifts have been estimated to have been worth several billion DM.

67. For a full discussion of the SED's motives to agree to the FRG's *Ostpolitik*, see Sarotte, 2001, 164–170.

68. For summaries of economic indicators, comparing the GDR to COMECON and Western countries, see Merseburger, 1988, 44–48.

69. For discussions of the function of women in the GDR economy and society, see Hauser, 1996; Hieblinger, 1984, 247–263; Krisch, 1985, 146–153; Mueller-Rieger, 1997. On the problems encountered by women seeking to combine family and work, see Joost, 2000. There also is the problem of the "glass ceiling," well known in the West. Doelling (1986, 81) reports that whereas women constitute 84% of the student body at technical colleges, "only 7.4% of the professors and lecturers are women." For a feminist analysis of GDR literature, see Linklater, 1998; also of interest are Buehler, 1997; Hauser, 1994; D. Muehlberg, 2000, 681. On the political persecution of women, see Schacht, 1984.

70. Estimates of GDR productivity range from 1/3 to 1/4 of that of the FRG (Verkade, 1991, 7; see also Hitchens et al., 1993; Wenzel, 1998b).

71. Marx (1933, 272–273) was particularly opposed to night shifts. Honecker (1984, 110–118), on the other hand, held that the "inadequate use of shift work" prevented the full blossoming of socialism's economic benefits. The remedy, as always, was stricter Party control of the economy: from the lofty objective of achieving plan goals, to such mundane concerns of how to staff shift work.

72. Certain large enterprises had been called "combines" since the 1950s, but these were merely *horizontally* integrated production units. The key feature of most of the latter combines was their vertical integration (Bryson, 1987, 53–54).

73. Kopstein (1997, 96) reports that by 1986 over 90% of all industrial production took place in 133 centrally managed combines, with an average of twenty to thirty enterprises and about 20,000 employees. In addition there were ninety-three smaller combines, organized at the Bezirk level.

74. Each combine had its own research and development divisions. Nevertheless, they greatly lagged in technological progress.

75. At the end there were twenty-one building combines in addition to the 126 industrial combines.

76. Without FRG assistance, the GDR could not have survived into the 1980s. Eppelmann et al., 1996, 198.

77. For general discussions of the failure of the GDR economy, see Apel, 2000; Gerhardt, 1997; Hoffmann, 2002; Huertgen & Reichel, 2001; Kocka & Sabrow, 1994; Kuhrt, 1996b, 1999; Nick, 1994; Schabowski, 1994; Schalck-Golodkowski, 2000; Schwarzer, 1999; Thiessen, 2001; Wenzel, 1998a.

78. Ludz was not seeking to slander the SED or the GDR regime. However, he was mistaken—as was Thomas Baylis, 1974—about the rise of technocratic rule in the GDR and the other Soviet Bloc countries. For a (GDR) discussion of problems with cadres in industry, see Poeschel & Tripoczky, 1966.

79. This was much less true in the 1989 revolution (Fuller, 1999).

80. It was not only a material but also an ideological problem. GDR leadership had frequently announced that economic advances were of "decisive importance in the further shaping of the developed socialist society" (Honecker, 1984, 122).

81. This was a particularly problematic area of the GDR economy (and of the state in general): too many administrators and functionaries per worker (Haase, 1980, 45). Exact figures, not surprisingly, are not available (Ludz, 1974, 584).

82. This, however, did not prevent Honecker in 1986 (reporting at the XIth Party Congress about the fulfillment of the 1981–1985 Plan) from claiming dramatic increases in productivity and income and an internationally leading role for the GDR in fields of science and technology (as reported in Bryson, 1989, 173–174).

Chapter 6

Persuasion and Nonpersuasion: Public Opinion and Public Discourse

PUBLIC OPINION

General Conditions

Public opinion in the German Democratic Republic was an enigma. Since there were no published, systematic opinion polls, one must depend on various nonsystematic indicators: personal impressions, reports of travelers, letters to the editor, a West German telephone poll (much objected to by the regime), and such occasional public opinion data as released by the regime for its own purpose. The overall impression from such sources is one of significant discontent and a deep malaise. While certain aspects of life in East Germany found appreciation in the population (especially the extensive social security system) (Apel, 1967, 20), most citizens were profoundly unhappy about the politics and (even) the economics of their society. The constant messages received from the regime that they were not trusted[1]—from the unavailability of correct information, to the inability to visit the West—did not improve the mood. Free and complete information for the citizens was not wanted, thus no free flow of information. Informed citizens were a danger to the dictatorial regime. The purpose of the GDR information system was not to inform but to strengthen the power of the Party and socialist ideology[2] (Gornig, 1987, 80–82). Living in the GDR was like being locked up in the charge of an ill-tempered governess, without any hope of emancipation.

The GDR regime, of course, was not unaware of this negative state of public opinion. The top leadership, however, did not always receive an accurate picture of the unfavorable developments of public opinion, anymore than they received accurate reports on economic developments. As in all dictatorial systems, workers and agents at the base preferred to send up rosy pictures (Heym, 1990, 66), but it is also true that the leadership managed to ignore unfavorable news—until the very last (Krenz, 1990, 37–38, 68–69). When the well-informed Secret Service (*Staatssicherheitsdienst* = Stasi) reported on the disaffection of the East German citizens, often it was not believed. This was one of the consequences of the top leaders residing in their own blocked-off village of Wandlitz, where nothing was amiss, where all goods and services were abundantly available, and where ordinary citizens never were seen (Schmidt, 1999; Schell & Kalinka, 1991, 88–91).

As noted, no opinion polls were published in the GDR (Schweigler, 1975, 131), except for occasional favorable (and possibly fraudulent) ones that showed very high regime approval.[3] Opinion polls were conducted with some regularity by the GDR Institute for Opinion Research[4] (*Institut für Meinungsforschung*) on order of the Politburo, the Central Committee, or other top institutions, but always under strict Party control. The results were closely guarded (Krisch, 1976, 399). Not even all of the higher SED functionaries had access to them. It was only after the fall of the GDR that some of the data became known. Most of them are not very complimentary. For example, asked toward the end of the GDR to rate economic conditions, only 35% answered "very good" or "good," 48% "so-so," and 16% "not good" and "bad" (Niemann, 1993, 4). Asked whether they were satisfied with the working conditions at their place of work, 45% answered "satisfied," 52% "not satisfied" (Niemann, 1993, 6). However, when the question touched on a clear Party line, the answers tended to follow it.[5] Asking to which system belonged the future, about 80% opted for socialism and only about 3% for capitalism (the rest "don't know") (Niemann, 1993, 20). Given the political environment of the poll, with no real assurance of confidentiality, 80% for socialism seems rather low.[6] In any case, the SED received only limited votes of confidence. The question was, "I have confidence in the SED." The three possible responses were "entirely," "some," and "almost none & none." The respondents all were young people (apprentices). Percentage figures are available for three years:

Year	*Entirely*	*Some*	*Almost None None*
1970	24	53	23
1986	26	53	21
1989	10	37	53

Source: Foerster & Roski, 1990, 44.

Private opinion polls were not permitted in the GDR. Indeed, the regime thought it to be an outrage when a West German opinion research organization conducted a telephone poll with GDR citizens. The SED sponsored a variety of public opinion polls.[7] While findings were not published in the general media or even widely circulated among Party and state functionaries, they typically were available to most of the top leadership, which, thus, should have been reasonably well informed about the state GDR public opinion (Connor, 1977; Niemann, 1993; Schweigler, 1975, 131). But, as noted, they were not always correctly informed, and they did not always believe it when they were. This is one of the consequences of living in a total falsification system that falsified the past, the present, and the future (Henrich, 1990, 209). It is impossible to know what to believe, including the truth.

An important focus of GDR opinion research was the views of young people. There was a special research institute in Leipzig dedicated to "youth research" (Friedrich et al., 1999). It did not help much. At the end of the GDR, the leadership still was under the mistaken impression that it had the full and enthusiastic support of the youth of the country. In any case, it is not clear that the "official" data deserve serious discussion. Such discussion necessarily assumes that the data gathered were an accurate reflection of the public's state of mind. This, however, is not an easy assumption to make in the quasi-totalitarian system of the GDR[8] (Welsh, 1981, 9–12).

Control and Manipulation

Public expressions of opinion were tightly controlled in the GDR as in all countries of the Soviet Bloc.[9] Public opinion also was massively manipulated. There was the effort to report only favorable news: prominent visitors from abroad coming to pay homage to the GDR, a new delivery of tractors from the Soviet Union, the overfulfillment of the plan in various industrial plants, record harvests of potatoes and grain, great progress on the road to mature socialism, the fabulous and beneficial resolutions of the last SED Congress,[10] and, last but not least, further creative advances of socialist theory on account of the great wisdom of the leadership. The picture of the GDR presented to the citizens was one of unrelieved sanguinity. Any reports about the West (especially the FRG) took on the opposite flavoring. Western nations were corrupt, crime-ridden, militaristic, unable to meet the needs of their people, and on the verge of collapse. Unfortunately for the SED regime, most GDR citizens had access to West German television. The attempts to misinform became obvious. This could not but increase popular discontent and the loathing of the regime.[11]

Occasionally, something unpleasant would be reported about their own country. Usually, it amounted to pronouncements of official *and popular* outrage at certain counterrevolutionaries and ingrates who would not follow the Party line. Here is a prominent example from the USSR: in 1948 the Central Committee of the CPSU condemned the music of Shostakovich, Muradeli, and others as antipeople formalism, whereupon:

> Meetings and gatherings were held everywhere, in factories, communal farms, industrial cartels, and places of public food consumption. And the workers discussed the document with enthusiasm, since, as it turned out, the document echoed the spiritual needs of millions of people. These millions were united in their rejection of Shostakovich and other formalists. (Volkov, 1980, 144)

Workers and farmers in the socialist countries, obviously, have rather peculiar and special spiritual needs, including the need to condemn formalism in music. It is unlikely that many people were fooled by this. Certainly, the participants knew how the "enthusiastic discussion" had been arranged. The others, as citizens of a totalitarian system, will have had their own experiences of being manipulated and coerced to give enthusiastic support to whatever the Party stipulated at the time.

The Dishonest Style of GDR Communications

The style of East German official communications was one of unrelenting repetitions of the vilest nonsense, presented with deafening shrillness, and the frequent use of the "big lie" technique. The regime knew itself to be nonlegitimate by any of the commonly accepted standards of legitimacy, and it knew itself to be unsupported by the great majority of its citizens. This knowledge caused official speech to mutate into *shouting*. Messages were not spoken but screeched. As with second-rate opera singers, top-of-the-voice was the only known dynamic level. As is typical for those who lie and know that they are lying, *repetition* was joined to loudness as a key characteristic of GDR discourse—and the bigger the lie, the more deafening and insistent the repetitions (Almond, 1954, 377; Bothe, 1983, 66; Deinert, 1983, 49; Grunert-Bronnen, 1970, 35, 123; Meyer, 1967, 84; Smith, 1969, 63). For any sort of criticism or skepticism (great heresies) the Party always had the same remedy: more, stronger, and better indoctrination (Helwig, 1968, 212).

Other key features of the regime's communication efforts were unlimited self-praise and self-congratulation, limitless dissimulation and hypocrisy, and an obvious contempt for the targeted recipients of the Party's messages (Apel, 1967; Grunert-Bronnen, 1970, 34; Richert, 1966, 121; Stuermer, 1986, 240; Uledow, 1964). GDR citizens could not help but notice that "their Party" had a rather wretched estimate of their intelligence and of their ability to observe GDR realities. The constant repetition of stock phrases and of known lies soon came to be understood for what they were: expressions of disrespect and disdain for the people of the GDR (Deinert, 1983, 49; Prauss, 1960, 203). Among the best known of the "big lies" can be counted Ulbricht's assurance until the very last moment before building the Berlin Wall that no wall would be built.

Involuntary Enthusiasm

In the Soviet Bloc, Hegel's historical optimism had been raised to a new level, in the form of endless claims of an ever-greater perfection in and of the countries in question. A key phrase of GDR regime proclamations was *weitere Vervollkommnung* (further improvement of perfection).[12] Everything is perfect already, but the Party is going to make it more perfect yet. What other response could there be than jubilation? Unfortunately, for most of the citizens of the GDR the cheers did not come naturally; they were not genuine. After forty years of involuntary enthusiasm, the citizens had had enough of it: 1989!

To return to the "further improvement of perfection," how would this happen? The "still further successes" will become possible by way of proper (more) political agitation. The Party is, of course, eminently successful, "but its functionaries can still do much more in tapping the underutilized resources of the country, and the hallowed initiative of the masses" (Bendix, 1969, 205). Or, as Erich Honecker characterized the road to increased perfection: "*Vor allem kommt es darauf an, das bestehende Vertrauensverhältnis zwischen Partei und Volk weiter zu vertiefen*" (The most important matter is further to deepen the existing relationship of trust between Party and people [Machalz-Urban, 1985, 56]).

Of course, there was very little trust. There were endless "discussions" and "consultations," but they did not lead in the direction of the people's wishes. They were merely other forms of persuasion and manipulation. The subject class of the totalitarian state (i.e., the potential opposition to the ruling class)

> is unable to organize itself; there is no freedom of coalition. Whatever conflicts exist are therefore forced to remain latent or under cover. Yet even the "official" structure of political authority provides this subjected quasi-group with channels of expression. In order to recognize these, we must remember that "discussion" is one of the crucial features of totalitarian government. Nowhere is there as much "discussion" as in the one-party countries of the modern world: meetings in one's factory or office, street or house, trade union, cooperative society, choir or football club, school, etc., serve the one purpose of "discussing" things. These "discussions" are not, to be sure, opportunities for a free exchange of ideas. They are, above all, attempts at indoctrination and at soliciting that brand of "voluntary cooperation" so peculiar to modern totalitarian states. But *inter alia* and in a minor way, the meetings and "discussions" which loom so large in the life of every subject of totalitarian government provide a chance to voice, cautiously and in the accepted language, criticisms of individuals and policies, suggestions and demands. From the point of view of the ruling class, this fact is both "functional" and "disfunctional." On the one hand, the party organization and its varied affiliations serve as a gigantic institute of opinion research which, through meetings and "discussions," tries to explore the "wishes and feelings of the people." On the other hand, the same meetings and "discussions" . . . bring into contact the otherwise scattered members of the subjected quasi-group and form the nu-

clei of actual and future conflicts. It is no accident that the revolts in Communist countries originated among those who meet most often in large numbers: building workers, steelworkers, students.

Undoubtedly, meetings and "discussions" as channels of conflict are, from the point of view of the ruling class, largely a pretext. It may well be that state parties explore their subjects' wishes and feelings not in order to incorporate these in their policies, but in order to see how much further they can push their own plans. (Dahrendorf, 1959, 312–313)

The manipulation of public opinion and the endless bogus consultation cannot forever remain shrouded from the citizens. Once the fraudulent nature of the regime becomes a matter of common knowledge, only fear and force keep it in power. The manipulative efforts backfired. When the fear is surmounted and the force proves ineffective or unavailable (as in the last months of the GDR), the regime is doomed.

THE SPECIAL CASE OF LETTERS TO THE EDITOR

Topics, Targets, Attention, and Replies

It was of great importance to the regime to be seen (by its own people as well as by the West) as encouraging input from its citizens, even when of a critical nature. With a wholly controlled press and a strictly supervised public life, this was not difficult to arrange, of course. Letters to the editor were a major form of that input. The regimes made a great show of wanting such letters and of taking them seriously.

Alexandrov (1977, 74–75) informs us that in the USSR[13] even the heads of government's agencies and of state institutions were obliged to reply within a fixed and rather short period of time, not only to letters that were published in the press but also to criticism included in the regular "Summary of Letters" column, and to letters that were forwarded to them by newspapers or magazines but that were not published. Failure to reply to criticism or giving a merely routine reply that avoided the issue raised was considered a violation of the rights of working people and was subject to censure.[14] Thus, "by publishing critical remarks sent in by readers concerning shortcomings in society, the newspapers help to eliminate such shortcomings" (Alexandrov, 1977, 71–72).

It is likely that Soviet-style governments, including that of the GDR, did indeed attach substantial importance to the letters to the editor and to the criticisms they contained. Given the general lack of freedom of expression in such systems, the top leadership often finds it useful to take some reading of the people's pulse in this way (Merkel, 1998, 13). A massive battalion of secret informers was, of course, the primary information source. But the letters to the editor could also serve to bridge the information gap existing in unfree societies.

Alexandrov (1977, 77) also informs us that new forms of considering and handling critical remarks, as a way of drawing working people into state administration, were constantly being developed. Unfortunately, some of the "critical remarks" would consign the authors to the "new forms" of the Gulag and mental hospitals (Bukowskij, 1973; Sichel, 1974). Letters reporting shortcomings could be genuinely welcome, as long as such shortcomings did not regard basic features of GDR socialism. Letters that crossed the line between welcome and unwelcome criticism could always be suppressed.[15]

In 1976, we further learn from Alexandrov (1977, 77), the CPSU Central Committee passed a resolution calling "on the editorial staffs of central and local newspapers to make more effective use of the letters they receive, to publish more letters dealing with the urgent topics of the day and report more fully instances of bureaucratism and red tape in dealing with people's just complaints."[16] What developed in the GDR, as elsewhere, was a "culture of complaints" instead of a "culture of citizen rights." No doubt, the CPSU and SED were interested in reducing bureaucratism and red tape at the lower echelons. This, surely, was a good thing in the heavily bureaucratized communist systems. The interest just was not as high-reaching and comprehensive as the official line would like us to believe. Hollander's (1972, 46) analysis of letters to *Izvestiya* and *Zarya Vostoka* showed that while 75% were negative, "most complaints were made about economic management and bureaucracy, public services, and technical development." Socialism, Party, and leadership, of course, are missing from this array.

The Communist Party as an institution and the top leaders of Party and state did not have to worry about seeing their actions criticized in the newspapers or elsewhere—indeed, in certain respects, such criticism would have been a criminal offense. The following will be instructive: During most of the GDR years, East Berlin boasted of a political cabaret: *Die Stachelschweine* (the porcupines). It was paraded with great pride to Western visitors as proof of the existence of true freedom of speech and of the regime's willingness to be criticized.[17] When visiting the GDR, I made a point of attending. The cabaret, it might be noted, was immensely popular, and tickets were difficult to get. The typical program took this form: lengthy glorification of the Party and the top leadership; two sharp attacks on Western policies and politicians; one rather mild criticism of a minor GDR problem (e.g., one village post office was too slow in processing the mails); two sharp attacks on Western policies and politicians; one rather mild criticism of a minor GDR problem (e.g., the traffic lights at a certain intersection were still not functioning properly—and on and on in the same cycle[18] [Henrich, 1990, 201; Kloetzer & Lokatis, 1999, 241–263; Petzold, 2001; Revel, 1977, 44; Wechsberg, 1964, 136–139; Wolle, 1998, 154–155]).

Yes, it was possible to make fun of GDR officials in the GDR, as long as the official was of lower rank and as long as the problem was portrayed as a matter of personal failing, not as a consequence of Party policy. Indeed, more often than not, the storytellers were sure to point out that the problem arose in the first instance because the functionary had ignored the clear wishes and instructions of the Party. A post office teller could be lambasted for being slow and ineffective. No criticism, however funny, ever was leveled at the general secretary, the Party, or the Soviet big brother.

What happens when newspaper content aims at more highly placed targets emerges in the reports on China by Heng and Shapiro (1986, 14). They found that either newspaper criticisms of state and Party officials received little attention at the top, or the attention was negative: "Far more often, the journalist himself was criticized or transferred. . . . Journalists were instructed that they were 'tools to express the voice of the party,' or, as it was also put, 'conveyers of the party spirit to the masses, and collectors of the opinions of the masses for the party.' It was little wonder that most reporters chose to remain silent about the abuses they uncovered." Writers of letters to the editor could generally be counted among those who were aware of the limits to permissible criticism.

The Up and Down Functions of the Fakes

Letters to the editor had at least two basic functions: to provide a channel for complaints and criticisms "from below" but also to provide a channel for instructions and persuasion "from above." Inkeles and Geiger's study of the Soviet press (1952, 694) focused on the "from below" aspect and reported that:

> the party permits and indeed encourages a significant amount of popular exposure and criticism of defects in the functioning of Soviet institutions and personnel. The main channel provided for the expression of this criticism "from below" is in the critical letters to the editors of the Soviet press.

Chu and Chu (1983, 214–215) report the same regarding the PRC and emphasized the letters' integrative and safety-valve functions. These descriptions, no doubt, are accurate as far as they go. They do, however, give short shrift to the "from above" functions of letters to the editors. As seen, writers (of letters or otherwise) were expected to be "tools to express the voice of the party" and "conveyers of the party spirit to the masses." The party spirit, of course, is not easily conveyed to the masses by way of genuine letters from ordinary citizens complaining about things. Here is where the *fake* letters came in.

Not all the letters to the editor in the GDR and other Soviet Bloc countries were true expressions of the views of their authors, nor did they even originate with the supposed authors. Letters were ordered to be written and even were manufactured by interested officials. Bogus letters might be solicited or manufactured by the newspaper editors themselves or (and more likely) by functionaries of the state, the Party, or Party-controlled organizations. The simple manufacturing of letters was the easiest process. Solicitation of letters was not a difficult task either, even when the subject matter was obscure and incomprehensible. In totalitarian systems, citizens are accustomed to comply with Party requests, whether they understand them or not, and help with the actual writing was easily available.[19]

As previously noted, in the late 1940s, when Shostakovich was in Stalin's disfavor, "the newspapers were full of 'letters from workers' condemning his music" (Volkov, 1980, xxxvi–xxxvii). Similarly, when the newspaper *Komsomolskaya pravda* published an article attacking Yevtushenko, it received more than 1,000 letters in response. According to Sergei Pavlov (Komsomol head), only fifteen of them defended Yevtushenko (Johnson, 1965, 51). As an illustration of the same process working in the GDR, the matter of the letters contra the GDR writer Stefan Heym is instructive. Erich Honecker reported that the workers had written many letters denouncing Heym because of his negative-critical views of the GDR. As Heym shows, this was highly unlikely, indeed, impossible, given certain publication dates (Heym, 1990, 126). In addition to the issue of letters ordered to be written, it is perfectly obvious—and sometimes provable—that unfavorable letters were suppressed—from publication, as well as from the official tallies of supportive and nonsupportive letters. Johnson (1965, 72–73) provides a number of examples.

The question is: Why bother with bogus letters? Clearly, solicited and manufactured letters could not serve to channel real views, complaints, and criticisms "from below," up to the elite level. The functionaries knew this. To bother at all with such letters, then, other purposes had to be served. One was simply to show great popular support for the regime's policies and positions—be they about politics and economics or about musical and literary styles. The second and most important purpose was to instruct, manipulate, and persuade—the "from above" function of the fake letters.

The activation of this second function produced the remarkably high volume and the surprisingly uniform tone of the letters supporting some official position (Loeser, 1984, 74–76). In a major study of GDR letters to the editor, Ellen Bos (1993, 3) also concluded that the letters had the purpose of legitimating Party policies via approving letters from the citizens. The government, of course, pretended to take the letters very seriously.

In spite of the various limitations placed on the letters to the editor and in spite of the pure fakery involved in such letters (and in other expressions of public support for socialist regimes), in some of the Western literature the integrative and safety-valve functions of such letters were greatly overestimated. Chu and Chu (1983, 214–215), for example, wrote:

> Letters to the editor . . . have become a major institution in China. In a system as closely coordinated as China's, in which dissent does not receive active encouragement, the letters column provides a legitimate channel for citizens to send messages to the central leadership. Through this channel the central leadership orients itself

> toward the divergent views and conflictual issues at the grassroots level. By airing *minor grievances*, the letters serve as an outlet, or safety valve, for releasing some of the latent tension before it accumulates to an intolerable degree. But more importantly, the letters help focus public attention on substantive areas of contention and conflict that must be resolved in order to maintain the adequate functioning and viability of the system. (emphasis added)

In the GDR, as in most other socialist systems, adequate functioning and viability were not maintained, of course. The permission to air *minor* grievances could not save entities that did not function well economically and denied the most basic liberties to their citizens, to whom the lies and manipulations had become transparent.

Permissible Inferences

No doubt, a careful and systematic analysis of the letters to the editor in the socialist press can supply important information and fascinating insights. There are, for example, the questions of how many letters were written,[20] who wrote these letters, and whose letters got published.

Inkeles and Geiger (1953, 13) report that only 13% of the letters in their sample of several Soviet papers were written by women and conclude: "These figures hardly give strong evidence of a high degree of participation by women in the socio-economic processes in Soviet society." Such inferences also were made regarding other groups. The authors write: "Considering the proportion of the total population in the intelligentsia category and the proportion of the workforce holding responsible positions . . . these figures indicate a strikingly disproportionate preponderance of people in those categories among the letter writers" (14). (Would that not be true in any country?)

Inkeles and Geiger are willing to generalize from their letter samples not only to demographic but also to cognitive and behavioral categories (1953, 16):

> Of the 239 letters which attached responsibility to any source, 42 per cent criticized one or more organizations without designating responsible individuals, 37 per cent criticized one or more individuals, and 21 per cent criticized both individual and organizational targets. It would appear, therefore, that there is no clearly marked tendency to personalize responsibility.

Similarly, Inkeles and Geiger (1953, 18) concluded that

> the slight attention given to the trade unions and other "public" groups and associations reflects their relative atrophy in contemporary Soviet society, involving loss of function and power as well as lack of interest on the part of both regime and people.

This type of analysis is subject to at least *three flaws*: lack of representativeness, self-censorship, and the presence of fraudulent letters.[21]

In respect to the *first* flaw, this type of analysis overlooks that the letters actually printed are not, by all odds, a random sample of letters received. Editors (West and East) typically select only a few of the letters received for publication. The criteria of selection will vary. They may be idiosyncratic or systemic; the letters may be chosen for entertainment value or for their correct political line. Whatever the criteria, the selection is not likely to be random, and the sample is not likely to be representative. Thus, no inferences can legitimately be drawn about the universe of letter writers (or worse yet, about society at large) based on the set of letters printed. It may well be, for example, that intellectuals write more letters than others (indeed, this seems likely), but it may also be that their letters simply get published more often. It is simply not permissible to make inferences about the role of women, about the people's interest in labor unions, or about the atrophy of labor unions in a given system from letters selected for publication in a controlled press. Inferences about the regime's attitudes, however, may be more solid (see later).

The *second* flaw, self-censorship, reflects the understanding of the citizen that acceptable criticism in a totalitarian system is limited to a certain range of persons, conditions, and events. The permissible range has a permanent and a temporary component. The permanent component makes available the bungling of low-ranking officials, a "few remaining" remnants of capitalist mentality, Western influences, and uncontrollable forces of nature. Excluded are high-ranking officials, Marxist-Leninist ideology, and the basic features of socialist government and economy. The temporary component includes leaders and doctrines that have fallen out of favor and, thus, have become "fair game."

Citizens of totalitarian countries know well that criticism directed at targets outside the currently authorized range will bring certain retribution if the writer can be identified. Inkeles concluded (1950, 207):

> One cannot, of course, find any letters printed which attack the Soviet system, the policies of the party, or its highest leaders. . . . Obviously, no individual in the Soviet Union who had any grasp of the system under which he lives would write a letter, or at least a signed letter, in which he attacked the top leaders or the Soviet system.

In any case, should citizens be brave enough to engage in unauthorized criticism and/or deal with proscribed topics, at the very least, "their letters are effectively screened out by the editors" (Inkeles & Geiger, 1952, 700).

The *third* flaw, the fraudulent letter, occurs in two basic forms: the solicited and the self-manufactured. As discussed earlier, through personal contacts and/or Party-controlled organizations, editors can cause letters to flow in whatever quantity desired, addressing whatever topic is at issue, and taking whatever position is required.[22] Chu and Chu's (1983, 176–177) analysis of letters to the editor of the PRC's *People's Daily* repeats the paper's reports regarding the number of letters received, without giving any evidence of even the slightest suspicion that these numbers might be manipulated. Inkeles (1950, 208) is equally trusting in his report of the number of letters received by *Pravda*.

The solicited or self-manufactured letter often was an important tool in factional struggles, when one set of officials sought to undermine the position of another set by way of a campaign of "grassroots criticism" or when it had been decided to place the blame for a disaster of some magnitude on a specific official or organization. Even Inkeles (1950, 208), who is not particularly skeptical of the letter-writing mechanism, reported:

> There is some evidence to indicate . . . that on matters of really major importance, or in cases affecting responsible officials, the party organization on the corresponding level will request or designate some members to write the necessary critical "letter from a reader."

Some Western authors, however, give little evidence of being aware of this problem. Chu and Chu's study of the PCR's *People's Daily* (1983, 185), for example, conveys an entirely voluntaristic interpretation to the finding that there were a large number of letters in 1967–1968 from peasants, workers, intellectuals, and the revolutionary masses "all attacking class enemies and capitalist roaders along the line of the Party's sixteen point directives." This in spite of the fact that only a few pages earlier Chu and Chu (1983, 177) themselves had reported, "During this period, the Party . . . encouraged the mass of people to participate in a nationwide campaign against Liu Shao-Ch'i and his followers."

Chu and Chu (1983, 185) further write: "Also noteworthy were the conflicts [in the letters] between workers and intellectuals, mostly because the workers did not agree with the way the intellectuals were handling things concerning them." The authors might have been less impressed by the workers' expressions of disapproval if they recalled that they were talking about the period of the Cultural Revolution and the Party-directed persecution of intellectuals. Indeed, Chu and Chu in one place acknowledge the problem, without, however, drawing the obvious inferences about the rest of their findings: "Letters published [during the Cultural Revolution] appeared to be more a chorus than a genuine expression of public concern"[23] (215).

Predictive Values and the Berlin Wall

It is the third flaw, however, *fraudulence*, which, while demolishing the letters' use as an inferential base for conclusions about citizens, enables us to draw inferences about *elite* concerns and policies—and even to predict likely actions. One of the key tasks of the mass media in a totalitarian system is, of course, to persuade the population of the rightness and necessity of government conduct and policies. Such campaigns tend to start with ever-increasing messages about a (supposed or actual) problem and how it is getting worse, followed by statements that it can no longer be tolerated and, finally, by a suggestion for its solution. If the solution is likely to be not well liked by the public, the regime will attempt to make it appear to be the popular choice nevertheless, by the use of various persuasive mechanisms, such as letters to the editor calling for the regime's favorite solution. Then the regime will claim that its policies merely respond to, and are following, popular demand, which is, of course, precisely what happened at the building of the Berlin Wall[24] (Leonhard, 1990, 116).

This is exactly what happened in the weeks before the construction of the Berlin Wall. Not being able to express their true preference at the polls, increasing numbers of GDR citizens voted with their feet. While the zonal borders had been heavily fortified, making it nearly impossible to cross them, Berlin still had an open border, allowing people to escape. The GDR, of course, was greatly concerned about this drain of workforce and talent[25] and wanted to stop it, even if this meant breaking Four Power agreements regarding Berlin and having to admit to the utter failure of the regime to persuade its people of the advantages of living in a socialist society.

Knowing how unpopular the Wall would be, the regime engaged in a number of preparatory actions. As Mueller and Greiner (1969, 59, 63) demonstrated, the East German press played a major role in preparing internal and external publics for the construction of the Wall, by presenting arguments to justify and legitimate such action and by printing letters to the editor (supposedly) from citizens and collectives calling on the government to stop the outflow and to close the border. The government, ever serving the will of the people, stood ready to satisfy these demands.

Mueller and Greiner (1969, 28–30, 48–50) have shown that the publication of steeply increasing numbers of letters to the editor (and other forms of communication) calling for a certain action is one of the best predictors that such an action is about to take place. If Western leaders, who professed to have been surprised by the Wall, had paid attention to the letters and articles in such papers as the party organ *Neues Deutschland*, which increasingly addressed the "problem of the open border" and demanded that it be closed, they need not have been quite so flabbergasted. The number of letters and articles, particularly with calls to action, increased sharply in the two months preceding the construction of the Wall (August 13, 1961).[26] All this fits well, of course, with the socialist theory of mass communications. The relevant decree of the SED Politburo states: "As collective agitator, propagandist, and organizer, each publication not only has the duty to influence and change the people's thoughts and attitudes, but also to elicit and organize actions in all areas of socialist revolution" (as quoted in Mueller & Greiner, 1969, 52).

There can be no doubt that letters to the editor in the GDR were instruments of communication not only "from below" but also "from above." The most important letters (i.e., those not dealing with routine complaints) may often have been fraudulent, but even as such, they did not necessarily lack instructive value. If approached with the right frame of mind, there was much to be learned from an examination of letters to the editors—even in the context of a thoroughly controlled press—particularly about what policies the regime favors and what actions are likely to be taken. One function the letters to the editor in the GDR and other socialist countries cannot serve, however, is to provide reliable data about the views and attitudes of the people of these countries.

Party Control and Retribution

It should be noted that the decision to print a letter may not even have rested entirely with the paper's editors. Chu and Chu (1983, 177) report: "There were times when the *People's Daily* sought clearance from a higher unit . . . before a letter was published." As Inkeles (1950, 213) has pointed out:

> the director of any letter department of a Soviet newspaper sends a copy of all letters that might require their action to the appropriate justice or control agencies in the government and the party. This includes, of course, letters which the editors feel are written by people who are "hostile" to the regime.

In respect to ordinary (low-level) complaints, it is likely that the agencies receiving those letters, given limited space, simply filed and forgot many of them. Regarding "hostile" letters, however, such laxity was unthinkable. The extraordinary level of regime paranoia in the GDR would quickly have involved state security agencies and significant retributions applied to the hapless author, if he or she could be identified.

Strangely, Inkeles and Geiger (1952, 701) take a lack of ideological references (high-level criticism) in the letters as evidence that "the newspaper editors do not excessively re-write or tamper with letters during the editing process." It may be useful to entertain the alternative hypothesis, that editors were not idiots and knew what a "genuine" letter looked like. In any case, there is no particular reason to doubt that a substantial proportion of "low-level" letters were more or less spontaneous communications from ordinary citizens.

With rather wide-eyed astonishment, Chu and Chu (1983, 191) write that toward the end of 1966 the regime urged the Red Guards to go back to school, many of whom, however, refused to do so, whereupon: "A number of letters attacked this position and urged the stray Red Guards to return to school. None of the letters supported the [Red Guards]." It is not clear why this should at all be surprising when dealing with a regime-controlled press.

The citizens of such countries are less likely to be fooled than some Western observers. The internal utility and effect

> of such publications [are] limited by the fact that the citizens of totalitarian regimes know perfectly well how such letters and public resolutions can be generated. Involved here is a cynicism which knows that the lie will be recognized as a lie, but which does not care as long as there is an external effect. Citizens of non-totalitarian systems often cannot conceive of the possibility that people can be pressured to write such letters. (Mueller & Greiner, 1969, 60)

In the case of the building of the Berlin Wall, the media campaign was, in fact, successful. There was no revolt internally, and foreign leaders quickly came to adopt the arguments of the GDR regarding need for, and the legitimacy of, the Wall. In the longer run, of course, the lies about the "anti-fascist defense barrier" necessarily added to the citizens' contempt and cynicism about the regime.

PERSONALITY CULTS AND PUBLIC ADORATION

Adoring the Leaders: GDR

The citizens of the GDR, like the citizens of the other socialist countries, were expected to be loyal and appreciative members of their society and to admire the great successes and the perfection of socialist doctrine and institutions. But this was not yet enough. They also were expected to adore and admire their brilliant and selfless leaders, particularly the one at the very top. Almost from the moment of birth of the GDR in the late 1940s, the country was converted into a Stalinist personality-cult state. The first GDR-specific cult was that of Walter Ulbricht. No speech, article, or book was complete without an appropriate quote of his, however obscure. The thoroughly servile adulation reached a new high at the first secretary's seventy-fifth birthday in 1968. The director of the Dresden *Staatstheater* praised Ulbricht as one of "the most active and knowledgeable theatre-goers in the GDR." Others of the academic and literary establishment (including Arnold Zweig) added their tributes, and one professor of the fine arts thanked Ulbricht "for his tips on painting" (Childs, 1973, 268).

Under Ulbricht's successor, Erich Honecker, the cultic extravagances continued and even increased. Honecker's personality cult manifested itself not only in the mandatory textual accolades but also in the pictorial representations of the great leader. Hardly any edition of any newspaper was without at least a few Honecker photographs, always showing him to the best possible effect. As a typical example, the issue of May 25, 1989, of the *Neues Deutschland* (the chief GDR newspaper and organ of the SED) consisted of a mere eight pages but nevertheless included five pictures of Honecker. When there were major events, such as conferences or trade fairs, yet more was done. For example, the issue of March 13, 1989, of the *Neues Deutschland*, also consisting of only eight pages, presented a full thirty-nine pictures of Honecker. In the last years of the GDR, twenty pictures of Honecker per issue were not at all unusual (Wroblewsky, 1990a, 157). The matter was not limited to newspapers. In the early 1980s, one of the official publishing houses brought out a splendidly produced, fine-paper coffee-table book *Afrika im Aufbruch* [African Beginnings]. Its price was seventy marks (expensive by GDR standards). It "turned out to be largely concerned with Erich Honecker's two trips to Africa in 1979" (Davis, 1984, 45).

The GDR, of course, needed more than one personality cult. As a USSR subsidiary, it had to develop a dual-cult system, one prong focused on Moscow, the other on Berlin. As an example of the former, the East German Writers Congress resolved in 1950 that Stalin was "the greatest writer of all ages" (Muhlen, 1951, 8). Subsequent Soviet leaders also received their share of East German accolades—at least until the time of Gorbachev's reforms.

Stalin and Brezhnev: Soviet Examples

The beginnings of Soviet personality cults can be found in the adoration of Lenin. It was a relatively mild form.

> Under Lenin [the] cult of personality—as opposed to the cult of the Party—was muted and couched in modern, scientific terms as the ability to understand and apply the laws of history to concrete situations. Even though, it was powerful enough to subvert the principles of collective leadership. (Janos, 1976, 9)

The full flowering of sycophancy was not reached until Stalin.[27] Stalin, according to his devotees, was simply the finest human being that ever lived and the greatest genius of all times (Vyshinsky, 1948, 53). The celebration of Stalin's fiftieth birthday in 1929 provided a major impetus toward the Stalin cult: he was assigned every human and superhuman virtue in the book (Childs, 1973, 122). The world was spared no detail about the great man. Stalin was, inter alia, the greatest philologist, the greatest economist, the greatest philosopher, and the greatest historian of the world (Kolakowski, 1969, 194). He was "the greatest genius, scholar-scientist of all lands and all times" (Wolfe, 1961, 100). Stalin's seventieth birthday was similarly celebrated. It was declared "that people of the future would call Stalin's time the 'epoch of justice' and might choose his birthday as the beginning of a new calendar, calling it 'the Day of Thanksgiving' of the Year One" (*Pravda*, December 18, 1949, as quoted in Medvedev, 1989, 819).

One of the early models of totalitarian socialist hagiography can be found in Lavrenti Beria's *On the History of the Bolshevik Organizations in Transcaucasia*. It is subtitled *Stalin's Early Writings and Activities*. The subtitle is the message: all the Transcaucasian achievements had been the personal work of Stalin. Before Beria's book, there was uncertainty about Stalin's role in the events and developments. The book dispelled all doubts and confusions. As Wolfe (1954, 266) points out, in Beria's book the history of Transcaucasia was established, coordinated, streamlined. All important Transcaucasian organizations, it turned out, had been formed, all strikes led, all key thoughts thought and key articles written, by the youthful Joseph Stalin. Whoever remembered otherwise ended up with a bullet in the base of the brain and a footnote in later editions of Beria's book, reading: "So-and-so has since been exposed as an enemy of the people."

Stalin's own writings (i.e., the volumes published under his name) were, of course, the finest ever produced and wholly indispensable to the instruction of socialist citizens. A prime example is Stalin's *Short Course of the History of the Communist Party of the Soviet Union*.[28] An excerpt from V. Il'enkov's novel *The Great Highway* can illustrate the status of the *Short Course*:

> Father Degtyarev brought in a small volume and said: "Everything is said in here, in the fourth chapter." Vinkentii Ivanovich took the book and thought: "There is no book on this earth that contains everything that a man needs . . ." But Vinkentii Ivanovich . . . soon realized that he was wrong and accepted Degtyarev's view which was that of all advanced people: "This book contains everything a man needs." (Tertz, 1960, 34)

Of course, American religious fundamentalists feel the same way about the Bible.[29]

Stalin was the extreme case, but his successors also were happy to be the objects of cultic adoration, particularly Leonid Brezhnev.[30] For example, the 1979 May Day Parade was graced by a "particularly impressive float . . . made in the shape of two huge red books that held a gold-lettered poster between them. The books represented volumes I and II of Brezhnev's *Real Issues of Communist Work of the Communist Party of the Soviet Union*. The poster read: THE BOOKS OF L. I. BREZHNEV—A MAJOR CONTRIBUTION IN THE THEORY AND PRACTICE OF IDEOLOGICAL WORK" (Lee, 1984, 209). Further, a review of Leonid Brezhnev's book *On the Foreign Policy of the CPSU and the Soviet State* in a Soviet social science journal was full of effusive praise for his "profound scientific analysis," his "vivid and convincing" demonstrations of the scientific nature of socialist policies, and the "outstanding significance" of his meeting with other statesmen (Note, 1979, 7–12).

Mao Tse-tung and Kim Il-Sung: The Cult in the Far East

Personality cults rivaling that of Stalin also have made their appearance in the China of Mao Tse-tung and the North Korea of Kim Il-Sung (Chu & Chu, 1983, 54, 58–59). Since the death of Stalin, Mao Tse-tung, we are told, had assumed the role of the principal theoretician of Marxism-Leninism.[31] No doubt was left in PRC pronouncements "that the immortal group of Marx, Engels, Lenin, and Stalin had now been increased by one to include Mao Tse-tung" (Meyer, 1969, 97). The *People's Daily* of September 28, 1959, was happy to let the world know that "Comrade Mao Tse-tung is the most outstanding exponent of the heroic proletariat of our county, the most distinguished representative of our superior traditions in the entire history of our great nation, . . . and the most outstanding contemporary revolutionist, statesman, and theoretician of Marxism-Leninism." But Comrade Mao[32] had skills not even imagined by Marx and Engels and the other members of the socialist pantheon. Mao was not only, as one would expect, heroic, lofty, magnanimous, affectionate, modest, gentle, kind, sincere, and warm but also was "able to swim mighty rivers and plow astonishingly straight furrows" (Walker, 1960, 34–35). Mao had become an infallible God-figure but one "whose fallibility has been amply demonstrated to all who care to see" (Meyer, 1969, 156). One suspects that most did not care to see, infallibility being an essential component of religious belief. As the hymn had it: "The East is Red / The Sun Rises / On the Horizon of China Appears the Great Hero Mao Tse-tung . . . / He is the Great *Savior* of the People."

Kim Il-Sung was not one to hide his many virtues either. Robert Scalapino (1988, 2) noted, regarding Kim, "Nowhere in these times has the cult of personality been carried to such length." The "fatherly leadership" of Kim Il-Sung "was viewed as a wellspring of sustenance." He was regarded as the "ever-victorious commander, peerless patriot, and founder and guide of the nation" (Bunge, 1981, 216–220). Of course, Western commentators are not always sufficiently skeptical when it comes to socialist laudatories. Savada (1994, 275) observes that Kim Il-Sung, "by all indications, truly is admired and supported by the general population." Yes, just as the general population admired Mao's plowing proficiencies and Ulbricht's painting skills.

The Fame Is Fleeting

Socialist personality-cult fame tended to be rather fleeting. Walter Ulbricht came to be a nonperson after his departure from office, even more so than Stalin. GDR publications since the early 1970s gave little indication that he ever existed, much less how important he was in the founding of the GDR and the establishment of one-party rule[33] (Weber, 1988, 78). Ulbricht quotations were removed from official publications and replaced with those of Honecker (Loeser, 1984, 59–60). A GDR social science textbook, written only three years after Ulbricht's death, managed to discuss the development of the SED and the National Front, as well as the founding of the GDR, without once referring to Ulbricht (Schulze, 1978, 18–50). Ulbricht's writings—once the most essential texts of GDR socialism—were no longer cited. Very few streets or buildings still bore his name a few years after his departure. His picture did not appear in otherwise well illustrated volumes. A popular discussion of the GDR Constitution (Weichelt, 1984), for example, included (in addition to the obligatory Honecker photos) pictures of such early GDR figures as Pieck, Grotewohl, and Dieckmann, but not of Ulbricht.

This, of course, was a rather general procedure in socialist systems: the predecessor became a "nonperson" (Villain, 1990, 53).

Honecker was Ulbricht's protégé, but Ulbricht became a nonperson even in Honecker's own books. For example, *The German Democratic Republic: Pillar of Peace and Socialism*, published in 1979, shows Honecker with Soviet dignitaries, such as Brezhnev and Gromyko, and even with a number of Americans, such as Gerald Ford, Angela Davis, and Gus Hall, but not with Walter Ulbricht. It does not surprise, thus, to learn that after Ulbricht's death a specific defamation campaign was arranged by his former protégé Honecker[34] (Loeser, 1984, 50).

The rapid decline of adoration was not limited to the GDR. It was a characteristic of all the socialist countries. Except for Lenin, who is needed as the legitimating founding father, personality cults did not extend beyond the lifetime of the object of adoration. The old leaders quickly became *un*persons as the new leader sought to establish his own superlative credentials.

To a considerable degree this is true even for Stalin. In 1982, for example, Yegor Yakolev managed to publish a biography of Lenin without any reference to Stalin. In an official history of the CPSU, published at the time of Brezhnev, there are only two references to Stalin and none to Khrushchev (in spite of the inclusion of a discussion of the XXth Party Congress). Here is how the person of Khrushchev disappeared in the text: "A report *was made* 'On the Cult of Personality and Its Consequences,' and the Congress categorically condemned the Stalin personality cult which had arisen" (emphasis added; Novosti Press Agency, 1977, 57). The only additional reference to Stalin is a cryptic remark that he was elected general secretary in 1922 (Novosti Press Agency, 1977, 37). The volume, however, provided generous samples from the pen of Leonid Brezhnev. Brezhnev's invaluable contributions to Marxism-Leninism, however, were quickly forgotten after his death. One may well conclude that it is a characteristic of Marxism-Leninism that invaluable contributions to Marxist-Leninist theory retain their value only during the lifetime of the contributor.

Was the Adoration Genuine?

Did anyone actually believe all this fulsome praise? On the example of the GDR, one must conclude that only very few of the ordinary citizens gave the accolades full credence, and so did very few Western spectators.[35] Regarding the USSR, some Western observers, particularly in the 1930s, were easily taken in. Feuchtwanger (1937, 85), for example, noted that the worship of Stalin "is one of the first things that strike a foreigner visiting the Soviet Union." He continued:

> There can be no question that in the great majority of cases this idolatry is genuine. The people feel the need to express their gratitude, their infinite admiration. They

do in truth believe that they owe to Stalin all they are and have, and, however incongruous and at times distasteful this Stalin-worship may seem to us of the West, nowhere have I found anything to indicate that it is in the least artificial or ready-made. (Feuchtwanger, 1937, 86)

To the contrary, Feuchtwanger (1937, 93–95) determined that it was "manifestly irksome to Stalin to be idolized as he [was]. . . . If he tolerates all the cheering, he [Stalin] explained, it is because he knows the naive joy and the uproar of the festivities afford those who organize them."

Stalin's fine character and the Soviet people's gratitude also were noted in a rather more likely source, the *Daily Worker*, the organ of the British Communist Party. The *Daily Worker* wrote at Stalin's death (but before the XXth Congress of the CPSU) that time could never efface his luster.

"Never the dictator, never one to lay down the law, always eager and willing to listen, to understand another's point of view. . . . No words, no monuments, no tributes can ever do justice to the revolution in people's minds and actions, in changing world history, in freeing millions from darkness, oppression, poverty and misery that have been brought about by the work of Comrade Stalin. . . . Eternal glory to the memory of Joseph Stalin." (as quoted in Childs, 1980, 22–23)

How many citizens of the Soviet Union truly felt that way about Stalin and the other leaders I cannot say. But it is quite clear that very few people in the GDR thought of Ulbricht or Honecker as the finest human beings that ever lived and as superhuman heroes who deserved eternal glory.

A Strange Aspect of Socialism?

As Baylis (1989, 91) rightly pointed out, it is particularly ironic that the most extreme personality cults developed in the socialist countries, that is, in systems that stress the inexorable and impersonal forces of history rather than the role of the "great man." The personality-cult aspect of socialist regimes is, or should be, an embarrassment to a movement whose decisions, supposedly, are guided by the scientific principles of Marxism-Leninism.

Communist doctrine is adverse to dependence on leaders. Hierarchical practice, however, cannot avoid it. Marxists, thus, have a remarkably difficult time dealing with their leaders. Whereas their counterparts on the Right have raised personal leadership to the highest principle of government (the *Führerprinzip*), orthodox Marxists must deny it. The Engels-Plekhanov substitutability view (if a given leader had been killed prematurely, another would have taken his place, pursuing the same policies), however, already gave way with Lenin and Trotsky (Stojanovic, 1981, 38–43).

Ecstatic adoration ebbed somewhat after Stalin, but, as seen, by no means did it disappear. Until the time of Gorbachev, it remained mandatory to present the current leader as the fountainhead of all wisdom and the incarnation of all goodness. Every speech and publication had copiously to refer to him.

All accomplishments in Party and state, in economy and society, had to be credited to his unceasing labors, untiring energy, profound learning, exceptional intelligence, and unsurpassed devotion to the people. In the style of royal court news, to mention the leader's name required a listing of all of his many titles (Otto, 1983, 79). Of course, there could be no public criticism of his political ideas, administrative actions, or personal conduct, no matter how poorly things were going.

These habits of fundamental dishonesty and stunning sycophancy, however, did take their revenge. As seen, when the object of worshipful praise departs from power and/or from among the living, his name disappeared from public discourse with breathtaking speed. After the death of Stalin and particularly after the XXth Congress of the CPSU, students had to revise their dissertations and scholars their manuscripts to eliminate the wisdom of Stalin and replace it with quotations from Khrushchev and Lenin[36] (Feifer, 1976, 12; Prauss, 1960, 165–166).

In the GDR at least, the fundamental dishonesty and hypocrisy of the communist approach to present and past leaders did not escape popular notice. They added substantially to the citizens' contempt for the regime and to their withholding of support.

Personalities and Correct Understanding

As discussed at some length in Chapter 4 of my *Rotten Foundations*, Marxism-Leninism resembles traditional religion in many ways, not the least in its multifaceted interpretive possibilities. The scriptures are complex and confusing. True doctrine is not self-evident; it must be determined and proclaimed.[37] This is one of the tasks of the prime leader. There cannot be correct policies without the correct understanding of the holy texts.

There is, of course, no necessary relationship between "correct understanding" and political success. The trust that a given leader possesses "correct understanding" of the classics of the particular belief system is likely to improve his political standing. But, as Meyer (1970, 79–80) points out:

> more often ideological "correctness" flows from a firm position of political superiority. The successful leader is able to proclaim with authority, his superior understanding of contemporary problems as well as future developments as a result of the superior power position he enjoys relative to his rivals or potential rivals within the ruling elite. While ideological "correctness" may be a function of the political strength of the leader, rather than the reverse, nevertheless the rhetoric of political power struggles in a communist system is always framed in terms of the ideological correctness or superior scientific understanding of the combatants.

It was necessary, said Mao, that one's understanding

> of the Communist classics be the "correct" understanding, and that the application of these ideas be both "profound" and "scientific" if they are to be of any real use. . . .

This assertion obviously sheds very little real light on the question of what, precisely, is the correct understanding or valid application of the writings of Marx, Engels, Lenin, and Stalin. This determination must ultimately be a subjective one, and there is no doubt that the sense of Mao's statement . . . affirmed that the determination would be made by the Party center, and that the valid and correct interpretations of the doctrine were embodied in the thought of Mao Tse-tung." (Meyer, 1969, 38)

The ultimate test of "correct understanding," however, is not (and cannot be) found in theoretical discourse but only in political success. With this, we have returned to Hegel: *Die Weltgeschichte ist das Weltgericht*.

What kept the people of the GDR in line for some forty years was not the trust that their leaders had the "correct understanding" of the one "true science" of Marxism-Leninism, nor that their leaders were well-meaning, self-sacrificing humanitarians, nor that their leaders always listened to their complaints and gave them positive responses. What kept them in line were manipulation and power. When the deficiencies of the regime became too severe to be endured and too obvious to be smoothed over by manipulation and propaganda, *and* when Soviet might became unavailable to defend the system, the people dared to demonstrate in the streets, and the regime collapsed quickly and ignominiously as the rotten edifice that it was.

NOTES

1. Wechsberg (1964, 44) reports: "A scientist, a member of the elite, who has a villa, a car, and a high income, told me he is unhappy because he feels cut off. He may visit Western countries as a member of scientific delegations but he is always guarded. He doesn't dare make an application for a passport to travel alone to the West because this might make 'a bad impression.' "

2. Marx was generally in favor of freedom of the press, but not in socialist states. There the press had the function of "ideological guidance and furtherance of socialist conscience" (Gornig, 1987, 82, 87).

3. Western visitors also fell victim to fake data, for example, Hans Apel, who reported the following ever-increasing percentages for regime "loyalty": 1962: 37%, 1964: 51%, 1966: 71% (Schweigler, 1975, 121).

4. Strangely, this institute was closed in 1978. It seems that the Party preferred its illusions to the facts (Foerster & Roski, 1990, 15; Niemann, 1993, 55–56).

5. It should be noted, however, that some studies of Soviet *exiles* produced some rather favorable responses. For example, when asked what aspects of the Soviet system they would want to keep, only between 19% (intelligentsia) and 33% (ordinary workers) said, "[K]eep nothing" (Inkeles & Bauer, 1959, 244–245).

6. There are some indications that outright noncooperation with the poll takers was low. Walter Friedrich's (1997, 97) estimate is a refusal rate of about 2% to 3%.

7. It also sought to collect information about the citizens' state of mind in other ways, for example, through informants of various types—much as had been done by Hermann Göring's office during the Third Reich.

8. About respondents' "clamping down" in the presence of another East German (when interviewed by a foreigner), see Wechsberg, 1964, 12–13.

9. This included *all* of the media (Riedel, 1994). Films, for example, could be made only by a single organization (the DEFA), which was under strict Party control (Opgenoorth, 1984).

10. Stefan Heym (1990, 75) parodied the falsity of the supposedly ecstatic popular reaction to regime declarations when he wrote this satirical press release: "The GDR Press Service reports: *Die Witwe Pietsch in Hinterkötzschenbroda erklärt, daß sie über die letzten Beschlüsse der Regierung überglücklich ist.*" Roughly translated: The widow Pietsch of Upperlowerbackwoodside said that she is overjoyed at the latest resolutions of the government. This, one must say, comes uncomfortably close to the actual press reports, published by the dozens in any newspaper, that some ordinary citizens experienced great joy at the latest resolutions and decisions of Party and government.

11. On the censorship of the news, see Pucher, 1984, 234; Richert, 1966, 118.

12. The phrase made its way into innumerable publication titles, usually of articles seeking to tell the audience how something that was already perfect in the GDR was now in the process of being further improved (e.g., Lehmann & Pohl, 1986; Reinwarth & Schlegel, 1966; Siegert, 1970).

13. The fountainhead of all wisdom, which the GDR regime slavishly tried to copy—until almost the very end.

14. This is unlikely. Lower-level functionaries may well have been subject to the rule of an "early and satisfactory reply." Agency heads were likely to be exempted from this requirement. The example provided to support the claim, in any case, was that of a complaint about a store selling hard liquor after closing hours—not likely a matter of concern for a government agency head.

15. Johnson (1965, 72–73), giving various examples, concluded that "it is perfectly obvious—and sometimes provable—that unfavorable letters are suppressed not only from publication, but from the official tallies." Of course, unwelcome criticism could always be (and were) sent anonymously (Merkel, 1998, 13).

16. Newspapers were said even to have special reception rooms where members of the staff and lawyers received people and considered their complaints (Alexandrov, 1977, 75). It would be interesting to know how many citizens came in to complain about Khrushchev or Brezhnev or, for that matter, Erich Honecker—not to speak of Joseph Stalin. Alexandrov, of course, provides no figures regarding the targets of complaints.

17. The GDR also had a satirical magazine: *Eulenspiegel*. It labored under the same constraints as the cabaret. In addition, only a small number of copies were printed. One had to be good friends with the salesperson to be able to buy a copy—when its sale was not prohibited altogether (Klessmann & Wagner, 1993, 400).

18. Leipzig also had a political cabaret: *Die Pfeffermühle* (the pepper mill). As with all such institutions, the program had to be approved by the authorities. In one case the authorities did not pay close attention. A program was performed "which was critical of the politics of Party and state, which contained slander and hostility regarding the Party and its policies." The matter went up all the way to Honecker. The program was canceled, the local authorities received a severe admonition, and a new control committee was instituted (Klessman & Wagner, 1993, 500–501; Sommer, 2002, 250).

19. Heym comments knowingly on the processes by which low-ranking Party members and ordinary workers were impelled to send these missives to the newspapers (Heym, 1990, 283). In the fall of 1989, the *Neue Deutschland* still published letters to the editor that accused the Western media of attempting to recruit GDR citizens to

the West (Menge, 1990, 117). This demonstrates the utter helplessness of the GDR leadership in view of the mass escapes. Surely, they must have known that it was not the Western media who motivated so many of their citizens to work for their escape via the occupancy of West German embassies or by way of the Hungarian/Austrian border.

20. Chu and Chu's analysis of letters to the editor of the PRC *People's Daily* repeats the paper's reports regarding the number of letters received without giving evidence of even the slightest suspicion that these numbers might be manipulated (1983, 176–177). Inkeles is equally trusting in his report of the number of letters received by *Pravda* (1950, 208).

21. The first flaw (nonrepresentativeness) also, of course, is found in the newspapers of the West. The second and third flaws (self-censorship and fake letters), however, appear to be unique features of the press in totalitarian systems.

22. As noted, should such an outreach not be practicable, editors can always write the letters themselves—signed: "a concerned citizen."

23. To be fair, the problem also has invaded American politics. The political leaders of this country have become quite adept at inviting friendly organizations to generate floods of supportive mail, which then is used as evidence for the existence of popular support for the favored policy.

24. This tactic was tried once more in the revolutionary days of the fall of 1989. An attempt was made to produce large numbers of letters calling on the government to put down the demonstrations. It no longer worked. People knew how the system worked (Natter, 1994, 22).

25. It was disproportionately the highly educated and highly skilled who left the GDR.

26. In the week June 12–18 there were five such pieces; in the week August 7–13 there were fifty-one. The weeks in between these dates saw steady increases.

27. Stalin could glory in the appellation "the greatest human being who ever lived" (Getty, 1992, 118). Hitler, by contrast, had to be satisfied with the more limited designation of "greatest general of all times" (*größter Feldherr aller Zeiten*)—which, furthermore, the always witty Berliners quickly converted into the acronym GRÖFAZ, a rough alliteration of "greatest imbecile."

28. In the GDR, too, the *Short Course* had the function of a "substitute bible" (*Ersatzbibel*) (Uschner, 1995, 8).

29. For a discussion of the affinities of fundamentalist religious and secular totalitarian thought, see my *Rotten Foundations*, Chapter 4.

30. "Brezhnev's vanity was gargantuan and he was happy to nurture his own 'cult of personality'" (Shevchenko, 1985, 25). The Brezhnev cult, rather maliciously, has been called a personality cult "without a personality" (Doder, 1988, 48–49; Lewis & Whitehead, 1990, 203).

31. Khrushchev, of course, also aspired to that role, and conflict ensued. In 1959 "Mao wanted to leave no doubt that it was he, not Khrushchev, who rightly wore the mantle of Lenin and Stalin. It was he, Mao Tse-tung, who was the most outstanding contemporary 'theoretician of Marxism-Leninism'" (Meyer, 1965, 486–487). This compares, of course, to Stalin's laying claim to being Lenin's best student. Mao's claim that he was Stalin's most outstanding student became a matter of "some concern to the Chinese leader in 1956 following Stalin's fall from grace in the CPSU" (Meyer, 1969, 58).

32. Meyer reports that the thought of Mao Tse-tung was advertised as "the brilliant peak of contemporary Marxism-Leninism" (Meyer, 1969, 133). Meyer (1969, 90) also speaks of the "enormous personal vanity of Mao Tse-tung."

33. A biographical GDR volume (*Names and Dates of Important Persons of the GDR*), published in 1982 in its third edition, contains no entry for Walter Ulbricht (Buch, 1982; see also Leonhard, 1990, 157).

34. It should be noted that Ulbricht was not an easy partner for the Soviet Union. Brezhnev complained bitterly to Honecker about Ulbricht's presumptions (Kopstein, 1997, 71–72). Except for the very end, Honecker was a more obedient partner. Not surprisingly, the USSR did have a hand in engineering Ulbricht's fall (Croan, 1976a, 10–11, 29, 46, 1976b, 369–372). Interestingly, the Soviets continued to support Honecker, rather than his opposition in the Politburo, in the late 1970s/1980s, when there developed a split regarding the relations with the West, which, for example, forced the cancellation of the Honecker trip to FRG planned for 1984. Honecker's trip finally did take place in 1987.

35. With the usual exceptions of the academic Left and of the left wing of the SPD.

36. However, it should be noted that the de-Stalinization efforts in the GDR were undertaken slowly and reluctantly (Berg, 1988, 89).

37. Just like religion, Marxism-Leninism has had to deal with a wide variety of heresies. Of course, the determination of what is a heresy is a matter of great flexibility. In principle, orthodoxy corresponds to the current opinion of the maximum leader; everything else is heresy, including the leader's prior views.

Chapter 7

Life in East Germany: Some Vignettes

LIFE AND LIES IN SOCIALISM

What Is Truth?

There were many reasons to be dissatisfied as a citizen of the GDR. Life in East Germany was "drab, dull, dark, shabby, scruffy, somber, ragged, neglected and listless" (Dornberg, 1968, 13). Some of the more prominent economic and social factors have been explored in the previous chapters. The present pages deal with some additional social factors and, in particular, with the effects of the social and political (civic) circumstances on the personality (psyche) of GDR citizens. The mandatory participation and the coerced enthusiasm of the official parades, the hypocritical pretense of citizen influence, the fraudulent and manipulated elections, the severe restrictions on any kind of private sphere, the endless and intrusive censorship, and the lack of most forms of freedom (speech, press, association, travel, and many others) left their marks. They produced timid, dependent, insecure, and subservient persons. The socialist state, as Wolfe (1992, 11) rightly remarks, was paternal in nature; citizens were being kept in a state of wardship. Persistent wardship produces wards, not self-reliant and autonomous citizens.

The system also produced persons who did not know whom to trust and what to believe. As regards *trust*, everyone had to distrust everyone else. Only in the smallest circle of friends did people feel safe to speak freely (Wroblewsky, 1990a, 84), and even that could be a mistake. The Stasi was everywhere. As regards *believing*, GDR citizens knew that the regime frequently lied, but absent a free press and open discussions, they could not know which were the lies and what might be true. Some of the falsifications, of course, were so preposterous that only a few "true believers" and pathetic ignoramuses would accept them as the truth.

One of the most flagrant pieces of historical falsification was the official name for the Berlin Wall. This abomination, the sole purpose of which was to force the East German citizens to remain in the GDR, was called the "antifascist protection wall" (*antifaschistischer Schutzwall*). Official explanations for the existence of the Wall were in consonance with the name: the purpose of the Wall was to keep out the Western imperialists and militarists who would otherwise infiltrate and subvert the GDR. According to the regime, by building the Wall on August 13, 1961, the GDR secured its borders against imperialist aggression (Hexelschneider & John, 1984, 55). Even a very sympathetic observer, Dornberg, writes that in spite of Ulbricht's pretenses, "no sane observer . . . would doubt that the Wall had but one purpose: to interdict once and for all the gushing hemorrhage that . . . had deprived the country of its lifeblood—the mass exodus of 3,500,000[1] workers, farmers, merchants, physicians, engineers, intellectuals, housewives, and children" (Dornberg, 1968, 4).

Then there was the often repeated assertion that the GDR did not conduct political trials and had no political prisoners, at the same time that political prisoners were sold to the FRG for about DM 60,000 per head (Bath, 1981; Bechert, 1995; Beckert, 1995; Fricke, 1986; Haase & Pampel, 2001; Lammich, 1980; Pucher, 1984, 225; Rehlinger, 1991; Sauer & Plumeyer, 1993; Skribanowitz, 1991; Staadt, 1995, 81; Werkentin, 1997). The number of political prisoners has been estimated as 200,000 (per year between 4,000 and 5,000), together with about 10,000 executions for political reasons (Fricke, 1986, 22; Welsch, 1999, 17, 135).

What also deserves mentioning are the endless falsifications of historical truth. For example, according to GDR sources, all the German resistance to Hitler was communist (Stadtmueller, 1981). This statement would have surprised not only social democrats and religious opponents, as well as the members of the Kreisau circle (*Kreisauer Kreis*), but also Hitler, who termed the assassination attempt of July 20, 1944, the "conspiracy of the counts" (*Grafenverschwörung*). Further, as Wechsberg (1964, 58–59) has pointed out, in respect to World War II

> one looks in vain for any mention of the United States. The only indication that Americans fought and died in the war is contained in the sentence: "The anti-Hitler coalition comprised countries with different social systems, and united many nations threatened by the Hitler regime, under the leadership of the Soviet Union."

There is no mention of the Hitler–Stalin Pact, which, at least for a while, made the Soviet Union Hitler's ally. There was a comprehensive GDR silence about the details of Stalinist rule in the USSR (Benser, 2000, 89–90). With the customary double standard, the GDR loudly and persistently (and falsely, one might note) criticized the FRG for not being more informative about the Hitler years—notwithstanding that to the very end of the system there was practically nothing in GDR education and public discourse about Stalinism, whether in the Soviet Union or in East Germany (Wechsberg, 1964, 56).

The treatment of GDR history and its leaders was equally untrustworthy.[2] When Carola Stern (1965, vi–vii) undertook to write a biography of Walter Ulbricht, she found that

> [t]he volumes of Ulbricht's speeches and articles that have been published in East Berlin thus far are edited with a political eye; articles are missing that Ulbricht would like forgotten—for example, those in which he equates Nazis and Social Democrats, hails the terrible Soviet purges, or praises Stalin to the sky. . . . [Further,] many of the speeches and articles that *are* included . . . have been "abridged" or "revised" without comment.

None of this will be surprising to anyone familiar with the editing of photographs of Soviet leaders that deleted persons no longer in the good grace of Stalin (Jaubert, 1989). Nor will it surprise anyone familiar with the deliberate inaccuracies in GDR and USSR cartographic materials (Unverhau, 2003).

These are some of the more glaring examples of regime falsehoods. Perhaps even more grating were the untruths about daily life in the GDR, the veracity of some of which the citizen could easily test. In any case, on the Soviet model, history is forever being rewritten. The "rewriting" of Soviet history extends beyond the written text to historical artifacts. Not only do persons become *un*persons, but objects become *un*objects. Bertram Wolfe reported on the 1952 purges of the museums in the non-Russian republics:

> During the past spring even objects began to become *unobjects*. . . . The Lithuanian museums were rebuked for failing to show the influence of Great Russian culture and the struggles and longings of their peoples for the extinction of their independence, while the Kazakh museums were condemned for the nostalgic splendor of their daggers, guns, harnesses, bridal costumes, and for failing to display any objects showing Great Russia's civilizing influence and the "progressive" character of her annexation of Kazakhstan. (Wolfe, 1954, 263)

The aims of historiography change from an accurate description of earlier times to the justification of current policies by way of selected or, even, invented "facts" or "documents" of the past. As Wolfe rightly observed, the past has always been subject to changing interpretation, but in socialist historiography "the past loses its pastness and firmness at a rate that is as dizzying as the changing policies of the Soviet Government" (Wolfe, 1954, 264). This takes its toll on the historians as well as on the general public. The former risk reputation and life;[3] the latter must cope with perplexity and disillusionment.[4]

Security versus Freedom

Those who found themselves (for whatever reasons) at odds with the regime had nowhere to go within the system. For most of GDR history there was only a unified political and economic power, no countervailing forces. For all the years of the existence of the GDR there were no competing elites, no checks and balances, no competitive elections, no party-independent associations, no separation of powers, no alternative paths to advancement (Scharf, 1984, 26, 142). Even quite casual observations of life in the GDR (particularly of the younger generation) left no doubt about the existence of a significant need for individualistic expression and differentiation from the gray uniformity of official harmony scenarios.

Nor did it increase citizen satisfaction with their lives to be told that they had the "good fortune to exist in a country of peaceful harmony" (Urban, 1981, 147). Altogether there was little positive attachment to the SED regime. The majority of the citizens were against it (however secretly)[5] (Bothe, 1983, 64; Picaper, 1982, 225; Scharf, 1984, 41, 200). The (seeming) stability of the GDR and the continuity of the leadership (Croan, 1976b, 165–166) should not have been confused, as they often were, with popular regime acceptance and legitimacy, though, of course, some degree of accommodation was inevitable. A substantial proportion of the population was quite content with these facets of the system: economic and social security[6] (Dornberg, 1968, 20). Among these security dimensions were universal medical care and pensions, a relatively high standard of living (compared to that of the other COMECON countries), state subsidies for basic necessities (food, housing, transportation), a high degree of job security, a strong sense of solidarity (in housing units, in schools, at work, etc.), reasonable equality of opportunity in education (Glaessner, 1989, 322–323), no great disparities in income,[7] lack of great private wealth, and emancipation of women and extensive birth and child-care benefits.

Reality, of course, was at some variance with the official picture. The top jobs went only to men (Ansorg & Huertgen, 1999; Langenhan & Ross, 1999); education was often a matter of indoctrination; political activity was more important for advancement than job performance; elite benefits were vastly superior to those of ordinary citizens, including remuneration (in money and in kind), access to education and to desirable jobs, and so on (Wassmund, 1981, 339–341). But it cannot be denied that GDR citizens had a fair amount of social security and (exempting the elite) a respectable measure of social equality. On these grounds many citizens did indeed take pride in their socialist system.[8] But the things that were missing, personal freedoms and autonomy, turned out to be more important and consequential.

The GDR was vehement in the rejection of the "totalitarianism" label, for itself and other communist regimes. It saw in the use of this term nothing but "the spearpoint of anticommunism" (Funke, 1988, 57) and an "anticommunist distortion of history" (Loesdau & Lozek, 1984, 357ff). Totalitarianism theory was, from the perspective of the GDR, no more than a product of Cold War hostility, with the intent to rehabilitate fascism—particularly in West Germany (Jesse, 1985, 70, 75). It did not fit into the GDR worldview that a country (e.g., the FRG) might be opposed to communist *and* to fascist totalitarianism.[9]

In any case, by its ideological claims and daily practices, the GDR must be regarded as a totalitarian state. As regards *ideology*, the regime never abandoned the principles of Party monopoly and the rule of no limits to the scope of the Party. Nothing was excluded from Party purview, with only the partial exception of the church. This exception, however, was a matter of necessity, not a change of doctrine.

As regards *practice*, the early years of the GDR were Stalinist and unrestrainedly totalitarian (Weber, 1994, 1–4). The last years saw a certain relaxation of some of the totalitarian practices. Again, this was not because doctrine had changed. It was because the population of the GDR had become thoroughly cowed. Coercion had become internalized. In general, brute force was no longer necessary. Also, many of the coercive procedures had become institutionalized in the form of social control agencies. This, of course, was less expensive, and more satisfactory from a public relations perspective.

It may be argued, therefore, that the GDR had been transformed into a "quasi-totalitarian" system. But this is quibbling about words. The people of East Germany knew perfectly well that totalitarianism—with its lies, intimidation, lack of freedom, coercion, and terror—had not vanished from their "guardian state" (Henrich, 1989).

CULTURAL LIFE

Education

In some ways, the school system of East Germany was exemplary. The regime devoted much attention and substantial funding to it. As the Party knew, the campaign to win minds began in the schools.[10] "Youth and education formed the two pillars of the GDR utopia. . . . there was ceaseless ritualistic SED sloganeering" (Rodden, 2002, xxv). The Party took very seriously the old slogan: Storm the citadel of learning. It celebrated the new school system as a "historical accomplishment" (Oppermann, 1989). While the teaching of technical subjects could be quite good[11] (though never free of Party propaganda), the primary goal of GDR education was to form the "socialist personality." In the last analysis, GDR education sought to create "nothing less than a higher human being, the 'new socialist man' who would 'build socialism,' i.e., the utopia known as 'the better Germany'" (Rodden, 2002, 379; see also Brandis, 1974, 527–528). "The primary commandments in schools, whose goal was a ruthless leveling of individual qualities, potentials, and abilities, were: always fit into the collective whole, and subordinate yourself to the collective rules" (Maaz, 1995, 20).

Precollege education was comprehensive, free or low-cost, and (at least in the lower stages) equal-access. Crèches were provided for children up to three years old. This was followed by kindergarten for the three-to-six-year-olds. The care included not only play activities but also regular physicians' visits and a hot midday meal. For both systems, the cost to the parents was about 1 East German mark per day. The actual cost run from about 200 marks for the crèches to about 300 marks for kindergarten per month. The government heavily subsidized preschool education (like all other education).

The motivation for this, however, should not be thought to be simply to provide the best possible care for young children. The GDR always was short of workers (partly self-induced). It simply needed every man *and woman* to be in the workforce. As was seen earlier (Chapter 5), more than 80% of East German women were employed full-time, and many of the others part-time. This level of female employment, obviously, could not be sustained without relieving women of the burden of caring for their children during the working hours—thus, the extensive preschool programs.[12] There also were extensive after-school programs in the high schools (see later) to keep the pupils safe and occupied until the parents got off work.

The next ten years of schooling were provided by the polytechnical high schools. The education was strongly oriented toward the sciences and technology. This education was free of charge, including most of the textbooks. Eight years of this school were compulsory; that is, pupils could leave the school at age sixteen. For those who did not continue with formal education, there were apprenticeship programs and vocational training schools (the *Berufsschulen* of the traditional German model). The polytechnical high schools were comprehensive institutions in the sense that *all* pupils attended them[13] (Waterkamp, 1983, 119–123). This differed from the traditional German model, which separated pupils at age ten into general and higher (college preparatory) schools. The GDR schools followed that model in the last four years of high school (the *Oberstufe*), which was primary college-preparatory and fairly exclusive (Hearnden, 1974, 20). Wilhelmi (1983, 71) reports that only two or three pupils in each class had the chance to sit for the *Abitur* (the school-leaving examination, qualifying for university admission).

> The goal of the high schools was to make the children grasp what goes on in the production processes in an advanced socialist society, and prepare themselves not only for making a contribution to this later on, but for playing an active part in society generally, including in the sphere of intellectual and cultural activities. The political and moral aspect of teaching is directed towards bringing up people who are not only committed to the communist future, but who are already developing communist patterns of thought and behavior. . . . Such an education not only means that they will

be reliable vis-a-vis their fellow man, but that they will also have a high level of class consciousness. (Panorama-DDR, 1976, 196–197)

As in all aspects of GDR life, socialist conviction trumped professional expertise. Underdeveloped socialist conviction—manifested, for example, by way of a small cross on one's lapel—was a reason not to admit a student to the *Oberstufe* (Fuchs & Hieke, 1992, 12).[14]

The "high level of class consciousness" was the sore point of GDR education. Many hours were spent on "*Staatsbürgerkunde*" (civics), which was little more than watered-down Marxism-Leninism and rigorous socialist indoctrination. It was presenting justifications for Party policies (Wroblewsky, 1990a, 107). It has rightly been characterized as the "horror subject" of GDR education (Bothe, 1983, 60). Wilhelmi (1983, 78) calls it the "key subject" of the high school curriculum.[15] Performance in this subject was an important factor for any further educational opportunity.[16] Any questions or ideas of their own were not welcome (Schuster, 1999). It was strictly parroting the party line—an activity, it was agreed, that one cannot learn early enough. As in other socialist (totalitarian) systems, students were certainly not taught *to think*. For example, Liang Heng reports after visiting the "best school" with "excellent facilities" in a Chinese city in the early 1980s:

I expected to see great differences between the education these post-Cultural-Revolution-era young people were receiving and my own "Revolutionary" education, which had been so narrow and so burdened with slogans. But to my surprise, little had changed. The blind obedience that had made the Cultural Revolution possible was being fostered still. No one was being taught how to think. On the contrary, the same old empty banalities were everyday fare. (Heng & Shapiro, 1983, 289)

A politics examination included these questions: "Why do we say Communism will inevitably be realized and Capitalism wiped out? To obey the Party and be the Party's good sons and daughters, what do we have to do? In our nation, some people say 'Without the leaders of the Party, we can still realize the Four Modernizations.' Please criticize this incorrect viewpoint" (Heng & Shapiro, 1983, 290).

In the lower grades of the GDR schools, when the "only scientific ideology" was presented for the first time, most students were reasonably receptive and interested. This changed very quickly into large-scale disbelief and utter disdain. Of course, it was still necessary to do well in the course. One's academic advancement and future career depended on the mastery and (seeming) agreement with the lessons. Therefore, the material could not be tuned out altogether. It had to be memorized and parroted, however reluctantly and unwillingly.

What GDR civics did was to contribute to the wide-ranging schizophrenia of the country. GDR citizens had to have two sets of consciousness: a public one and a private one.[17] In public discourse one professed the official ideology; in private discourse one revealed true beliefs and actual experiences (Bothe, 1983, 61). Those who experienced it called communism the "eight-hour ideology," that is, the cognitive set on which one drew only during school hours and (later) working hours.[18] As much as possible, the official ideology was screened out even during the eight public hours. In the end, indifference to the official ideology became all-pervasive in the GDR (Sontheimer & Bleek, 1975, 45). More than being indifferent, the students hated it.[19] They sought to avoid it and similar happenings whenever they could (Fuchs & Hieke, 1992, 103).

There also was a strong and influential presence in the schools of the Young Pioneer and the Free German Youth (see later), which meant additional efforts at indoctrination. A student who appeared loyal to state and Party could count on much help and ready promotion. It was very difficult, however, to make much progress in the system if a student did not bend to the constant pressure of the collectivity and the constant control by the community.[20] Outsiders and individualists were not wanted. The system did not have a place for them (Heyen, 1972, 97). The regime was greatly concerned with generating loyal socialist citizens of the GDR. There is a very large GDR literature dealing with this problem.[21] The indoctrination was not as effective as the regime had hoped. A substantial portion of the younger persons in the GDR were significantly alienated from their society, state, and Party.[22]

Those who completed twelve years of high school and passed the *Abitur* were eligible to apply to institutions of higher learning. Regardless of major, Marxism-Leninism was compulsory (and very time-consuming). "A socialist intellectual and professional sector thus emerges, one which has close ties with the working class and indeed with the whole of the working population" (Panorama-DDR, 1976, 202). Marxism-Leninism, however, tended to be just as unpopular at the universities as it had been in the high schools—except, of course, for those who were preparing for a career with Party or state.

The GDR universities and other institutes of higher learning were entirely under Party and Stasi control (Connelly, 2000; Voigt & Mertens, 1995). In no sense were there *Lernfreiheit* and *Lehrfreiheit* (freedom to learn, freedom to teach). Dissertations could be circulated or published only with Party approval[23] (Bleek & Mertens, 1994). Academic life was strictly regimented—from the mandatory Marxism-Leninism, to the saturation of every subject matter with socialist dogma, to the military obligations, and to the obligation to spend some time in the productive process (in factories or on farms) (Stoecker, 2000). The social sciences (Voigt, 1975; Schimunek, 2002), history (Kuczynski, 1994), and philosophy (Herzberg, 2000) one could have expected to come under close scrutiny. But so did all field and any research undertaking (Macrakis & Hoffmann, 1999; Pasternack, 1999). Science had to be ideologically pure and serve the working class; it also had to make its contribution to the economic well-being of the GDR. Professors (Jessen, 1999) were just as much governed and regulated by the Party as students, some of whom resisted, but to no effect.[24] When the GDR finally collapsed, education was still completely under Party control.

Intellectuals

It is difficult to know who should be counted as an intellectual[25] (Natter, 1994, 9; Voigt et al., 1987, 148). It is not a matter of formal education. In the West, the typical physician might not qualify; the typical professor might. Socialist countries used a fairly expansive definition. "Counted among the intelligentsia are scholars and scientists, writers, artists, teachers in schools and institutions of higher education, doctors, engineers, lawyers, as well as certain others—individuals whose work embraces more complicated kinds of mental labor demanding considerable independence, creativity, and a high level of general or specialized preparation."[26] With this definition, the only groups not qualifying are the workers (in industry), peasants (in agriculture) and those white-collar workers who carry out repetitive and mechanical forms of mental work that do not demand a high level of education. This still leaves some intermediate groups unallocated, for example, technicians and nurses. "In socialist society it is particularly difficult to define the social boundaries of the intelligentsia because of the efforts being made to overcome the distinction between mental and physical labor" (Medvedev, 1977, 302–303).

> One can say that the intellectuals are all those whose profession is to create and communicate cultural values—scientific information, an outlook on the world, works of art, knowledge of current society, political opinions—in short, scientists, teachers, artists, journalists, propagandists, and the like. In particular, however, we are concerned here with people professionally engaged in theoretical work in fields relating to the organization of the life of society. Now the spiritual dominion of any ruling class over the people, far more than its material domination, depends on its bonds with the intelligentsia. That is why those in power in all social orders strive to maintain the closest possible cooperation with their intellectuals. (Kolakowski, 1969, 179)

The intellectuals tend to have special concerns and needs. They tend to be more attached to the "open society" than other classes and strata. This is partly a matter of greater sensitivity to justice and freedom and partly a matter of being able to do one's job. Censorship and close Party control of creative activities are a grave detriment to the intellectual's work. Intellectuals (academics) were overrepresented among the political prisoners in the GDR (Fricke, 1986, 23). Medvedev (1977, 301) makes the point from a socialist perspective: "The intelligentsia is the section of our society most sensitive to violations of democratic rights and freedoms. Representatives of different subdivisions within the intelligentsia have been the most energetic advocates of a genuine development of socialist democracy."

This brings us to a problem. On the one hand, intellectuals are particularly concerned with freedom; on the other hand, they were among the most reliable supporters of the socialist regime of the GDR. Is there an explanation? Feuer (1959, x) offers this interpretation: "The appeals of Marxism (as against Christianity, for example) have always been first to the intellectuals. . . . To intellectuals it has appealed as no other doctrine has because it integrated for them most fully discordant psychological motives. In Marxism we find for the first time a combination of the language of science and the language of myth—a union of mysticism and logic." This, at best, describes a certain type of intellectual, one with priestly tendencies (such as certain present-day physicists who are discovering deities in their materials).

Feuer (1959, xi), however, has more to say: "Here was a science which at the same time gave intellectuals a cause, a sense of mission, a conviction that their lives were worth while because history needed them. Here was a system that was both science and ethics, which called itself historical materialism and demanded idealistic commitment." But it was not only a matter of "idealist commitment." It was also a matter of power or, at least, of being needed by power:[27] "Marx offered the intellectuals leadership in the new world. Feudal society had been ruled by military lords, capitalist society by money-minded businessmen, but in the socialist society the intellectuals would rule in the name of the proletariat" (Feuer, 1959, xii). Or, in the words of Konrad and Szelenyi (1979, 3): in Eastern European state socialism "for the first time in the history of mankind,[28] the intelligentsia is in the process of forming a class. Intellectuals there are a dominant class in *statu nascendi* . . . while pretending to carry out the 'historical mission of the proletariat,' in fact gradually established its own class domination over the working class."

In the GDR, the intellectuals were not the actual rulers. Taking the top leadership, Ulbricht was a cabinetmaker by profession, Honecker a roofer, and Krenz a mechanic. The next rank did not look much different: Mielke (minister for State Security) was trained as a shipping agent, Mittag (economic czar) began as a agricultural worker before entering upon his SED career, Pieck (president of the GDR) was a cabinetmaker, and Grotewohl (prime minister of the GDR) was a printer. Only Kurt Hager (the ideology czar), who in his early years worked as a journalist, can be counted among the intellectuals.[29] The GDR intellectuals did not rule. The vast majority of them occupied much lower ranks[30] (Erbe, 1982, 72). The GDR intellectuals, however, importantly assisted the rulers—also a matter of considerable satisfaction.[31]

Marxists rulers take their ideology seriously, much more seriously than Western elites. The contribution of the intellectuals, however, is not the working out of the theory's actual guidance of practice (as is the official doctrine) but in "the persistent attempts . . . to maintain the *appearance* of ideological consistency" (Bauer, 1954, 151). Theory, then, is taken seriously not as a guide to practice but as a legitimation device. For this, the intellectuals are crucially needed. The intellectuals, thus, have a much greater importance in socialism than in other systems. They can fall out of favor, but sooner or later they have to be called back.[32] While particular individuals may be persecuted, intellectuals as a group tend to do rather well in socialism. They are needed, usually quite well rewarded, and they can feel important.

The crucial point, then, is that in socialist systems intellectuals are taken seriously, and much attention is paid to them. In the West (with very few efforts at censorship), intellectuals can pretty much say and write whatever they want—and nobody pays them much attention. Under socialism the situation is reversed. Intellectuals cannot say and write whatever they want, but what they say is given much attention and taken very seriously. In this sense, censorship is a *compliment*; it contributes to a high sense of self-esteem. In the West, writers are seldom taken seriously; generally they are regarded as entertainers. In the East, however, the writer's product is a societal force, a factor in public life, and a weapon in the struggle for a better future. The socialist writer is an important person.

Intellectuals in the GDR had to confront many troublesome situations. For some of them the trouble was so great that they left the country. But the majority of intellectuals were not dissidents. Those who could endure the cumbersome and obnoxious aspects of the system were ultimately among the beneficiaries of the system.[33] Support for the system, thus, should not come as a surprise. But it was not just benefits and the feeling of power; it also was the opportunity to do something significant with their lives. The intellectuals "offered their loyalty and their services to the new social system because they were profoundly excited by the opportunities which it seemed to offer them" (Konrad & Szelenyi, 1979, 203).

Of course, there is the position, most strongly expressed by Julien Benda (1955), that intellectuals should serve only the truth, not power. This is a very high-minded idealism, but it is asking too much. Very few intellectuals have (and can have) the self-sacrificing dedication of a Socrates. We will have to be satisfied if in every generation there are at least few dissenters who are willing to speak truth to power, regardless of cost. Of those, the GDR had quite a few.[34]

Censorship

Various earlier passages have touched on the subject of censorship, particularly in Chapters 4 and 6. This section, therefore, can be relatively brief. Censorship was just as total as the state. GDR totalitarianism existed in different degrees during the forty years of the country's duration, but it was never absent. The enormous apparatus of the Stasi was to observe just about everyone's sentiments and views, even when expressed in an intimate circle.

GDR censorship, being total, was concerned with all possible manifestations of thought and conduct. It ranged from literature and the arts, to musical styles and cabaret performances, to matters of dress and grooming. There was nothing that was not of public (official) significance. Any deviation from the given line was readily interpreted as "negative-hostile" and, therefore, as a danger to the regime. For a long time, only the dreary "socialist realism" was an acceptable art style.[35]

As noted before, the regime realized that some criticism had to be permitted. Criticism of minor policy details and low-level functionaries was not only permitted but encouraged (Prauss, 1960, 179; Scharf, 1984, 128–136; Schwarze, 1969, 257; Wechsberg, 1964, 37–57, 135). It provided a safety valve and was the source of useful information. Criticism of the leadership, the general policy lines, the theoretical foundations (Marxism-Leninism) of the GDR, and its bond to the Soviet Union was *not* tolerated, however. Under East German law, such criticisms counted as criminal offenses (Luchsinger, 1951, 13). However, there was much uncertainty as to the exact border between permitted and prohibited criticism (Gornig, 1987, 90). This gave prosecutors much discretion and contributed to the legal and political insecurity of the citizens.

A commentary on the GDR Constitution was explicit: "There can be no freedom for ideological diversion in a socialist society" (Gornig, 1987, 84). Only the correct view could be expressed; there was no need for a variety of outlooks—all but one of which were false anyhow.[36] The Party stood always ready to inform the citizen of the correct opinion, which, of course, had to be class-based (Gornig, 1987, 81–83). A great variety of new criminal offenses were introduced,[37] including such matters as Treasonanable Relaying of Information and Treasonable Agent Activity (contacting Western embassies to inquire about immigration: up to two and a half years hard labor),[38] Propaganda Hostile to the State (referring to border fortifications as "nonsense": a year and a half at hard labor), Interference in Activities of the State or Society (showing a poster that said, "[W]e want to leave, but they won't let us": sixteen months prison)[39] (Koehler, 1999, 18–19; see also Skribanowitz, 1991, 120–125; Weber, 1994, 23–50). As noted, a citizen who had lent Orwell's *1984* to a friend was found guilty of state-hostile agitation (*staatsfeindliche Hetze*): two years and four months prison (Vollnhals & Weber, 2002, 141). A perusal of the Criminal Code is instructive: §98: transmitting information that might be used against the GDR: two to twelve years of prison; §99: entering into connection with foreign organization hostile to the GDR: prison of at least two years and in particularly severe cases: life sentences or capital punishment;[40] §106: writings that harm the reputation of the state, the political, or economic system of the GDR: one to five years in prison; and many other such paragraphs. These offenses lacked precision. Almost any form of conduct or speech could be ruled criminal.[41] This use of the criminal code was not limited to the GDR. It could be found in all socialist states, for example, the USSR:

> The terms of the Soviet law against slander (Art. 70 of the USSR Criminal Code) are extremely vague and imprecise; they are frequently applied to works containing

even completely justified criticism of particular aspects of the political structure, usually survivals from the Stalin years which contravene the basic principles of socialism and the Soviet system. Materials intended to strengthen socialist democracy are thus denounced as "anti-Soviet agitation and propaganda." Similarly, entirely reasonable spoken or written criticism of the various shortcomings of Soviet life are made out to be "slanderous fabrications." (Medvedev, 1977, 153)

Soviet sources are always instructive. The GDR certainly attempted (except at the very end) to be a good student of the socialist motherland. These are the pronouncements (in question-and-answer form) of the official Novosti Press Agency (1978, 94–95):

QUESTION: Who has the right to criticize and who may be criticized in the USSR?
ANSWER: Each citizen is entitled to criticize the activities of any government and Party body and of any executive regardless of office.

This right is extensively exercised in diverse ways. . . . It would be hard to find a copy of a newspaper or magazine which did not carry critical letters, articles and other items. . . .

Criticism is expressed not only through the medium of the press. One will possibly hear more criticism at the various trade union and Party meetings than anywhere else, on both affairs of state as well as local issues. Executives at any level, from shop superintendent to minister, are obliged to provide a satisfactory answer to any critical remarks addressed to them and report what has been done or will be done to remove the shortcomings. . . .

The Soviet citizen feels that he takes part in the running of his country, and this in turn fosters within him a feeling of responsibility, of intolerance for anything that still stands in the way of normal life and work, that hampers Soviet society's advance towards the accomplishment of its communist ideals.

The last part is the important one. It is the attempt at comprehensive surveillance: the ordinary citizen must not tolerate anything that hampers communist advancement. The citizen has the obligation to defend the socialist order. Not defending—that is, not reporting deviant speech or conduct—was in itself a criminal offense (Gornig, 1987, 85).

Orwell's *1984* was, of course, prohibited in the GDR, as were countless other Western literary works. Even university professors could obtain literature from the West only with special permission—this included medical texts (Braun, 1994, 15). Lacking such a permission made acquiring Western literature a criminal offense (Berg, 1988, 34). But non-Western products shared this fate. The prohibition of Sputnik has been mentioned. There also were a variety of other Soviet publications that were banned in the GDR (Plock, 1993, 165; Rein, 1990, 121–122). The possession of Polish labor union materials brought, in 1980, an East German student fifteen months in prison (Mayer, 2002, 47). Even Karl Marx was censored:[42] For a time the early manuscripts of Marx were not included in the complete works of Marx and Engels published in the GDR (Gregor, 1974, 25; Lauterbach, 1954, 287).

Organizations were just as much coerced as individuals.[43] No public statement could be made that reflected anything else but the demands of the Party. Stefan Heym (1990, 66), for example, reports that on June 17, 1953, a resolution, full of tired slogans and phrases, was put before the assembled members of the writers association (*Schriftstellerverband*). At about 3:00 P.M., the editing committee sought to make some changes. The secretary-general of the association lost patience and declared that the resolution (in its original form) had already been approved by the Central Committee of the SED and thus could not be changed. In other words, the approval of the resolution preceded the vote of the members. Heym asked rightly, What is the meaning of resolutions that are imposed from above?[44] It was the party line, or nothing (or even criminal penalties). Writers and artists, professors and journalists, musicians and entertainers—none were free to follow their interests or creative instincts (Kaiser & Petzold, 1997). What else, then, could the GDR be, but a drab, dull, and dreary country?

Youth

The GDR regime knew perfectly well that its long-term survival depended on its ability to win the country's youth to its cause. No efforts were left undone toward this goal. The objective was to produce citizens who would be truly and fully devoted to the ideas of socialism, who would want to strengthen socialism, and who would defend it against all enemies. As the Party saw it, it was the duty of all young citizens to work, learn, and live socialistically, always to act unselfishly for the greater good of their socialist fatherland, to strengthen the friendship-alliance with the Soviet Union and the other socialist brother-countries, and to strive for the comprehensive cooperation of the socialist community of nations (Klessmann & Wagner, 1993, 458).

The FDJ (*Freie Deutsche Jugend* = Free German Youth) was founded in 1946. While the FDJ was formed on the basis of the Komsomol model, initially it was a semi-nonpartisan organization. By 1952, however, it had become thoroughly Stalinized, like almost everything else in the GDR (Maehlert, 1994, 73–78, 1995, 282–326). It also became a monopoly; no other youth organizations were tolerated (Walter, 1997, 29). Its purpose was to provide an organizational frame for fourteen- to twenty-five-year-olds[45] and to make certain that the next generation would be convinced socialist and loyal citizens of the GDR. As Wassmund (1981, 333) writes, the function of GDR youth organizations was "making young people convinced socialists, preparing them for jobs, giving them a pre-military training, and preaching to them intolerance towards class enemies and the imperialist camp."

These goals, or so the regime thought, required not only socialist indoctrination but also keeping the youth protected from the nefarious influences of the West, that is, capitalism, imperialism, fascism, and general decadence.[46] In fact, simple protection soon was found not to be enough. It became an explicit purpose of the FDJ, the SED's youth organization, to teach youth *to hate the class enemy* (Rodden, 2002, xxviii). As noted earlier (Chapter 3), the FDJ always received a number of seats in the People's Chamber (*Volkskammer*), the national parliament. For the 1986 session, the FDJ held sixty-one seats. The FDJ was similarly represented in the lower legislative bodies. The FDJ, however, had no autonomy vis-à-vis the SED. Accordingly, the much acclaimed youth involvement in politics and government remained purely formalistic (Walter, 1997, 267).

GDR youth, however, found some aspect of Western life quite attractive, for example, blue jeans and rock music (Hoernigk & Stephan, 2002; Wicke, 1988). The Party had no explanation for this other than that there must be deliberate Western efforts to undermine socialism by subverting socialist youth and making them puppets of monopoly-capitalism (Klessmann & Wagner, 1993, 467). It did not enter the heads of the GDR leadership that young people simply wanted a different style of dress and music than what was available in the GDR (namely, drab and dowdy). Place of origin probably was not a major consideration. Chances are that if the alternative musical styles had originated in the Soviet Union, they would have been taken up just as readily.[47] For the regime, however, counterrevolutionary efforts were the only conceivable explanation.

The FDJ events tended to be manipulative, wholly politicized, staid, and stolid; the participants (quite rightly) had the feeling that they were patronized. The individual was regarded as inconsequential and treated with disdain. Only the collective was esteemed; the individual was valued only as a member of a collective. At public events they had to appear in their uniforms (blue shirts) and demonstrate their great joy and enthusiasm for their Party and wise leaders[48] (Possner, 1995). The prescribed cheers, of course, had the opposite effect of what the Party wanted: a deep listlessness and a thorough disgust with the officially demanded hypocrisy. Nevertheless, most members of the FDJ (and of the other organizations) conformed to the totalitarian behavior expectations, which, of course, are always "easier to secure than conversion" (Kirkpatrick, 1983, 124). There was much lip service but very little internalization (Smith, 1969, 44). The only persons in the parades who genuinely cheered were the FDJ functionaries, most of them far beyond the age of their charges and already well on the way to a bureaucratic career.

The SED had two youth organizations. In addition to the FDJ, there were the Young Pioneers (*Junge Pioniere*) for the age group ten to fourteen.[49] The Young Pioneers were founded in 1948. Their purpose and function were the same as those of the FDJ, just adjusted for the younger age. Just like the FDJ, they were a monopoly organization. No other youth organizations were permitted.[50] The majority of the leaders of both youth organizations were members of the SED. Any change in the higher leadership had to be approved by the parallel Party organ—for the top leadership this meant approval by the Politburo of the SED (Ansorg, 1997, 46). The Party took youth work very seriously, indeed. Not only was there the issue of a comprehensive loyalty to Party and state, but these were also the *Kaderschmieden* (cadre forges), which were to produce the next generation of leaders. Ideological work was foremost (Autorenkollektiv, 1980, 58; Gotschlich, 1999, 94). Much like the nazi youth organizations, however, FDJ and Young Pioneers offered activities naturally popular with youngsters, particularly sports, but also camping, weapons training, and parades. Membership was not compulsory, but in 1989 FDJ membership was about 76% of the age cohort (Ansorg, 1997, 10). Still, in spite of considerable pressure not everybody joined, and those who did become members often joined as a matter of opportunism. Most of the ordinary members resented the mass indoctrination and the attempt to have all of their existence organized on the official socialist model. There were much indifference and loathing (Ansorg, 1997, 208).

The GDR collapsed not unimportantly for this reason: the regime was unable to gain the support and loyalty of its younger people. The young people, it became obvious by the 1980s, had not become the "new socialist personalities," as had been hoped by the regime (Hollander, 1992, 7; Voigt et al., 1987, 57). The leaders had to recognize that they had not raised a generation of loyal little helpers for the Party but that instead many of the young people lacked attachment and solidarity with the "party of the working class" (Gries, 1994; Gruber, 1997). "The FDJ failed to reach the goal of tying young people to ideology and state; the organization was unable to win their loyalty" (Walter, 1997, 266).

GDR youth recognized the constant manipulation to which they were exposed, and they saw quite clearly the difference between the endlessly and pompously repeated regime slogans and the desolate, confined, and unpleasant reality in which they had to live. GDR youth were dissatisfied with the conditions of their lives, and they were apathetic because (until the very end) they could see no way to change it: it was the devastating apathy of futility (Buescher & Wensierski, 1984; Childs, 1985, 126–129; Mason & Nelson, 1987; Picaper, 1982, 168, 287).

Religion

The socialist regime of the GDR hoped that religions would disappear altogether. With Marx and Engels (1953, 12; 1976, 54), they viewed religious responses to human problems as illusionary and irrational and, most importantly, as counterproductive. Religion can divert attention from misery (if only temporarily), but it leaves the *causes* of human misery unaffected. As Lenin said (1960, 19: 83), religion can be no more than an "opium for the people." Lenin's initial approach to the matter was not, however, militantly atheistic. He did not want to waste energy on a moribund institution. Religious sentiments would simply wither away, unable to compete with the *science* of socialism that provided correct analyses and real solutions to human misery.

The leaders of the GDR more or less followed this general pattern. Policies regarding religion fluctuated between stern opposition and begrudging tolerance.[51] The policies were dominantly antagonistic in the earlier years of the GDR. The regime was quite successful in separating the majority of the population from their traditional churches.[52] It also was successful (in 1969) to get the Protestant Church of the GDR to sever its formal organizational ties to the Protestant Church in the FRG (Joas & Kohli, 1993, 250). However, there always remained a remnant of believers. In the later years the regime adopted a fairly conciliatory stance toward them, particularly since the event of the "Luther Year" in 1985 (500-year celebration), when Luther was rehabilitated[53] (Stackhouse, 1984, 131–166; Wolle, 1998, 133).

Only toward the end (second half of the 1980s) did the Protestant Church[54] provide a relatively protected space in which peace groups (Pollack, 2000, 77), ecological groups (Bastian, 1996), and, finally, protest groups (Grix, 2000) could meet and organize[55] (Alsmeier, 1994; Daehn, 1984, 1993; Hartweg, 1995). The regime hoped, of course, that the new "leniency" would not increase the number of church followers, rather that even those people who joined in church services would remain proper socialists. For most, this was indeed how it worked. Participation in church events did not generally lead to religious conviction. In any case, church participation did not (until very late) cause explicit antagonism to Party policies.[56]

In about the last decade of the GDR, the Protestant churches experienced an increasing influx of young people. The church youth organization *Junge Gemeinde* (Young Congregation) became a very attractive place for young people to visit. Participation was quite easy, since there were no formal membership requirements. One simply showed up. It did not require, and generally it did not produce, religious belief. It was basically a place where people could talk freely about what concerned them, without having to worry about the correct line and without having their interests and cares directed into safe channels by official functionaries—as always was the case in FDJ meetings (Klessmann & Wagner, 1993, 457). However, the Stasi did have its agents and informers in just about every church group (Lasky, 1992, 14; Vollnhals, 1996). It still required some courage to speak freely even at the *Junge Gemeinde*.

Since 1989, the Protestant Church has become subject to considerable criticism. While by its own lights, the church tried to find a balance between opportunism and opposition (Henrich, 1990, 228), the critics found that it had moved too far toward opportunism and accommodation and that it did not take a sufficiently clear and strong position against the regime—on the example of the *Bekennende Kirche* and Dietrich Bonhoeffer during the nazi period. There is no doubt that a major concern of the church was self-preservation, and for the church bureaucracy it also was retaining certain privileges, for example, travel to the West and the ability to receive DM in the form of FRG donations—estimated at about 400 million (Maaz, 1995, 50). Indeed, some church officials were exposed as Stasi collaborators after the fall of the GDR. Most of the regular pastors seem to have opposed the regime as best they could under very difficult circumstances. There was one prominent martyr. On August 18, 1976, Pastor Oskar Brüsewitz unfurled a sign in the central square of Zeitz, protesting against the persecution of the churches and against the discrimination of young Christians in the GDR. Brüsewitz doused himself with a flammable liquid and set himself aflame. He suffered severe burns and died four days later (Fricke, 1984, 192–193; Mueller-Ensberg et al., 1993).

But it cannot be denied that in spite of all good intentions (working for conscientious objectors[57] [Koch & Eschler, 1994], for ecological measures, for greater openness of debate), which necessarily required some collaboration with the regime, in the last analysis the church (just like *Ostpolitik*) became system-supportive. The church hierarchy proclaimed that they intended to be a "church in socialism," not a "church against socialism" (Schroeder, 1990, 149–159). Critics, of course, see in this a continuation of age-old Protestant praxis: support for, and collaboration with, the secular authorities, whoever they might be. This charge cannot be denied. On the other hand, the existence of the church in the GDR was a positive factor, particularly in providing the protected space of the *Junge Gemeinde*. This would not have been possible, or so it appears, if the church had simply gone into general opposition (Joas & Kohli, 1993, 249–255). Nearly everyone in the GDR found some form of accommodation; the church was no exception (Besier, 1993; Fulbrook, 1995, 87–127).

The *Jugendweihe*

One mechanism of weaning people away from the churches was to provide alternative rituals for the important episodes in life. There were, for example, socialist-secular rituals for marriage and funerals. But, of course, one "needs to get them young." Religious organizations have long supplied rites of passage from childhood to adolescence (adulthood). They served to tie the young person securely to the religion in question. Bar mitzvah and confirmation are obvious examples of such ceremonies. The GDR provided the *Jugendweihe* (Youth Consecration).

The *Jugendweihe* (hereafter "JW") was instituted in 1954 for the thirteen to fourteen-year age group.[58] Participation was not compulsory, but, of course, a good socialist participated. Not joining in the official rituals and organizations could have serious consequences for the young person's future opportunities. Pressure could also be brought on the parents, of course.[59] It would be an error to believe that all JW participation was truly voluntary

(Becker, 1999, 164–165; Braun, 1996, 83; Eppelmann et al., 1996, 319–320). However, there was not much resistance to the new rite. By the end of the 1950s participation had already reached 90%. In 1989 it was 97% (Terwey, 1997, 182). Church confirmation, in contrast, became the ritual of a small minority (Becker, 1999, 163).

The JW was preceded by an intensive political and ideological series of instructions. The JW ceremony took place in a municipal auditorium, splendidly decorated for the occasion. There would be speeches by prominent functionaries of Party or state, there would be a musical program, the youngsters would recite a vow to be proper GDR citizens and receive a certificate, showing that they had done so, there would be an official gift (usually a book), and there would be private gifts from family and friends. Very little distinguished the JW from a church confirmation, except the missing religious component. Parents and kids were just as concerned with the question of proper dress and how to feed all the guests as they had been when there were confirmations (Klessmann & Wagner, 1993, 456–460).

The JW began as a socialist ritual to supplant church ceremonies. As seen, in this it was very successful. It seems, however, that over the years the socialist component became less prominent in the minds of the participants, and the JW became simply a widely accepted ritual of transition. There is no other explanation for the fact that the JW has survived the fall of socialism. A majority of the youngsters, in the areas of the former GDR, still participate in the rite (Braun, 1996, 86).

Swords to Plowshares

In 1980 the Protestant Church initiated a movement, *Frieden schaffen ohne Waffen* (Create Peace without Weapons). The increasing militarization of East Germany was one of the causes[60] (Grunenberg, 1990, 130–138). Another one was the concern about the stationing of atomic weapons on both sides of the Iron Curtain. In January 1982, Pastor Eppelmann and Professor Havemann issued the "Berlin Appeal," which asked that all of Europe should become a nuclear-free zone.

The SED had in the past advocated nuclear-free zones themselves, and peace was one of the most prominent mottos in the Party literature. But, of course, the thrust of the SED's peace efforts had always been Western disarmament. Anybody who advocated bilateral disarmament had to be an agent of imperialism and an enemy of the GDR. Instead of integrating the church endeavors into the official peace movement, the church activities were criminalized and the participants were harassed by the Stasi (Childs, 2001, 43).

The church peace movement took to wearing a badge, showing a man with a hammer smashing a sword. It also carried the text: *Schwerter zu Pflugscharen* (Swords to Plowshares). This badge became a red cloth to the regime. It exposed the wearer to endless harrying by the Stasi. Students were expelled from the school; others were brutally beaten and sent to prison (Schwarz & Schwarz, 1997, 110). The peace movement, however, continued to grow, particularly since the churches made their facilities available for meetings and organizing (Maier, 1997, 174).

Sports

More than most nations, the GDR transformed sports into an instrument of national and international policy.[61] Success in sports was to bring the GDR the international recognition that it craved. Domestically, it was to instill in GDR citizens a new pride in their country. The regime hoped, of course, that this pride would translate into a greater loyalty toward Party and state. Indeed, there are indications that it succeeded to a considerable extent (Seppelt & Schueck, 1999, 20, 31, 365). It goes without saying that the GDR athletic successes also were promulgated as further proof of the superiority of socialism over capitalism (Knecht, 1978).

In typical GDR fashion, East German commentators criticized the West because it "use[s] the mass appeal (mass effects) of sport to spread their ideas" (Elm, 1986, 365). The leaders of Western sports organizations also came in for criticism because they seek to "increase the function of the political effectiveness of imperialist champion sports to stabilize the social system in the interest of monopoly capitalism" (Elm, 1986, 373). This describes to the dot the GDR's use of sports, needing to change only "monopoly capitalism" to "dictatorial socialism."

Except for the bottomless hypocrisy of GDR pronouncements, East Germany simply followed the pattern of other sports-obsessed nations. Top athletes received great benefits. While active, they did not have a job; their finances were well taken care of. Good cars (scarce in the GDR) were readily available, as were better apartments. The state bore all the expense. They also had the opportunity regularly to travel to the West (a rare privilege). When the time came to retire from active competition, a good job would be waiting for them.

Selection of promising athletes began very early, sometimes as early as kindergarten. The system was well organized, and the state invested substantial resources in the selection and training of athletes. Those athletes who reached international standards and won medals in international competitions, particularly the olympics, became national heroes and were well rewarded. Thus, even though the training was demanding, there was never any dearth of youngsters wanting to get into the program (Hartmann, 1997).

The sports program of the GDR did, however, have a dark side: *doping*.[62] Doping, of course, is not an unknown practice in other countries. Certainly, U.S. athletics, from college programs to professional leagues, are heavily contaminated. The distinction of the East German program is found in these facts: one, that the doping started at a very early age, two, that the athletes did not know that they were ingesting various powerful drugs,[63] and three, that it was state-organized. Children as young as nine years old were doped with steroids (Seppelt & Schueck, 1999, 15). They were not much older when they were subjected to testosterone injections. "In the three decades, when the GDR's secret [doping program] was in effect, more than ten thousand unsuspecting young athletes were given massive doses of performance-enhancing anabolic steroids. They achieved near-miraculous success in international competition,[64] including the Olympics.[65] But for the most, their physical and emotional health was permanently shattered." The various pills were distributed by the coaches. It was forbidden (on pain of leaving the program) to refuse them (Ungerleider, 2001, 7). The young athletes also could not see physicians outside the program. They also had to guarantee that they would not talk to anyone about the nature of their training (Seppelt & Schueck, 1999, 42–43).

The drugs were primarily anabolic steroids and testosterone preparations, but amphetamines were also tested for athletic use (Ungerleider, 2001, 22). The supervising physicians (of whom there were many) knew what was happening to their charges. Most of them did not care (Seppelt & Schueck, 1999, 64). Parents who noticed the physical and emotional changes in their children were lied to. Yet many parents did not ask questions in spite of very visible changes. They did not want to make problems for their kids, whose future would, after all, be well taken care of as star athletes (Seppelt & Schueck, 1999, 62; Ungerleider, 2001, 14–15).

The consequences often were devastating. Boys and girls produced a number of abnormalities, but it was particularly bad for the girls, who developed overly broad shoulders, enormous muscles, great increases in body hair, and deep voices. They also became very aggressive. They became the object of ridicule at international meets. But this was not the worst. There were significant injuries because there developed a disparity between muscle mass and the tendons. Many athletes developed liver cancer. Kidney tumors appeared. There also were severe depressions and "angst" conditions (Seppelt & Schueck, 1999, 61). There was paralysis because of an overload of testosterone. There also were deaths, for example, ruptured hearts from anabolic overload (Ungerleider, 2001, 187–189, 198).

It will not surprise anyone to learn that the Stasi also had their fingers in the sports programs.[66] The East German government was deeply involved in elite athletics, which it controlled by way of the Stasi (Seppelt & Schueck, 1999, 23; Ungerleider, 2001, 20, 27). The findings of GDR sports medicine (which was also a well-financed and favored area) were strictly secret. The Stasi classified them at the same level of secrecy as military or nuclear secrets (Seppelt & Schueck, 1999, 36).

These athletes were not treated as human beings but as "engineering experiments" (Ungerleider, 2001, 11). The whole program was not only a gigantic fraud but also a form of state-sponsored crime. However, very little happened to the perpetrators. After the end of the GDR, some trainers and physicians were charged with crimes, having done great damage to underage children. They had the perfect defense: doping was not illegal in the GDR. They got away with suspended sentences and fines. As a final irony, it may be noticed that International Olympic Committee (IOC) chairman Juan Antonio Samaranch awarded the medal of the Gold Olympic Order (a high award for selected officials who uphold the "perfect ideal of sports and humanity") to Erich Honecker, the man ultimately in charge of this exploitation and abuse of young athletes (Ungerleider, 2001, 24).

Self-Criticism and Other Indignities

Life in a bureaucratic police state brought daily indignities. Some were just petty annoyances, such as the unavailability of business cards (Smith, 1969, 46) or having to stand in the right queue (see later). Others were deeply troubling, particularly when viewed in conjunction with other detriments, such as endless regimentation, the need to continuously applaud the wisdom of the latest Soviet or SED pronouncements, the lack of cultural and political freedom, the constant need to dissemble, and the pervasiveness of arbitrary actions and coercive methods.

Self-criticism was a particularly demeaning mechanism by which the Party enforced discipline: the submission to today's truth, even if it is the exact opposite of yesterday's gospel, and the confession of personal errors and failings, even when there are not any (Richert, 1966, 215; Prauss, 1960, 168–178). The periods of the Soviet show trials of the 1930s (Deutscher, 1984, 72–121; Leites & Bernaut, 1954) and of China's Great Proletarian Cultural Revolution of the 1960s (Dittmer, 1974, 297–358) are the past high points in the use of the self-criticism device.

The GDR did not take the method to the Soviet or Chinese high points, but it certainly knew how to use it. It was not so much a weapon against ordinary citizens as a weapon against higher Party and state functionaries, whose loyalty and following the strict party line had come to be doubted. They had to write endless reports (the first versions of which usually were deemed unacceptable) about their (often wholly imaginary) failings and offenses. These reports had to have just the right portion of facts and fantasy and of groveling and remorse to find the favor of the accusers. Far worse than a criminal trial, the self-criticism ritual left the accused with no personal dignity or honor (Benser, 2000, 327; Stillman, 1959, xxxi).

The New Socialist Personality

It was a major craving of the GDR regime to shape a new human being as it was shaping a new society. This was the "new socialist personality." The idea was an old one. It can be traced back to Marx and Engels (Dlubek & Merkel, 1981, 391–395), but it was not original with Marx and Engels. Just about every new *Weltanschauung* felt the need to alter human nature as well as to introduce new ideas and mold new societal relations. It can be seen quite clearly in Christianity, where "the old Adam" had to be driven out in favor of a new one. To use a more recent example, Hitler was gravely concerned with creating a "new German youth."

The SED had a clear idea what socialist youth should be like: loyal to socialism, patriotic, healthy, and cheerful. The 1974 *Jugendgesetz* (Youth Code) had as its goal the "development of youth to socialist personalities." Paragraph 1, Article 1 said:

> In the formation of the developed socialist society, it is a primary goal to make all young people into citizens who are loyal to the ideas of socialism, who think and act as patriots and internationalists,[67] who will strengthen socialism and protect it against all enemies. Youth itself has great responsibility for its development to socialist personalities. (as quoted in Ahrberg, 1996, 7)

The Party was also quite clear what should *not* be a part of the new socialist personalities: individualism, violence, criminality, and religion.[68]

Where such things surfaced, the Party became extremely agitated, suspecting an assault of the class-enemy (especially the FRG) on the youth of the GDR. The Party took every possible step to screen out "hostile" influences, including fashion trends and musical styles. It was not wholly successful in this. West Germany was too close, and FRG citizens might send blue jeans to their young GDR relatives. West German television could be received almost everywhere in the GDR (Hesse, 1988), and Western music (rock, beat, etc.) was immensely popular.[69] Up to a point, the Party simply had to live with rock music, but there were other matters that simply could not be tolerated to any degree. These were promptly criminalized. The official *index prohibitorum* is very long. Some examples are to doubt the correctness of the policies of the party and government; to discuss and advocate enemy arguments, interpretations, and theories; to bring contempt to ("*verächtlich machen*") the policies or orders of the party and government; to read or exchange corrupting literature, including anticommunist publications; to produce by oneself "hostile-negative" views, such as "political-negative" jokes, songs, and slogans[70] (Ahrberg, 1996, 13). The list goes on. Not surprisingly, many young people, as well as older ones, got themselves into significant trouble on these issues. Prison was a not uncommon price to pay.[71]

THE CUSTOMER IS ALWAYS WRONG

Restaurants

The treatment of customers in the GDR was uniformly disagreeable and offensive. The problem was, of course, lack of motivation and of control. Salespersons, waiters, clerks, and so on had no incentive to be pleasant or to make an effort. Their remuneration would be the same. They did not have to worry about losing their jobs because customers might stay away, and the managers of the establishments had neither enough authority nor the inclination to call the employees to order. The possibility of getting tips was no incentive either. As remarked earlier, money had lost its motivating power in the GDR. Wolle (1998, 213) speaks of the "managers of scarcity." The customer is king when there is a surplus of goods and when vendors have to compete for customers. In the GDR, it was the opposite. A permanent scarcity of goods made the vendors into kings, for whose favors and considerations the customers had to compete. The GDR citizen had to endure not only the dictatorship of the Party but also the dictatorship of the distributors.

Waiters in restaurants were known to be particularly unpleasant. In Europe it is customary that guests seat themselves; not so in the GDR. There always was a prominent sign saying: "Please wait; we will seat you," except that there was no one to direct the guest to a table. The restaurant might be empty, and the waiters just standing around gossiping, but no one would dare to call the waiters or simply to sit down at an empty table—and if a person did sit down, he or she would certainly not be served. Often it would take a very long time before being seated. Also, as was well known, waiters, fearing the amount of work of a full restaurant, would place "reserved" signs on the tables and turn away potential guests, telling them that no tables were available.[72]

When finally seated, the service would be plainly bad and incompetent. Most of the items listed on the menu would not be available. This would be communicated to the guest in a tone of voice that suggested that the guest must be a moron or troublemaker even to have asked for an unavailable dish. When agreement could be reached on an item that was actually available, the service would be sloppy and surly, and the food certainly would not be of the right temperature. Yet, almost nobody complained. The waiter clearly was doing the guest a favor by serving him or her at all. Complaining would only have led to the complete cessation of service.[73]

I remember one instance. I was having dinner with the chairman of the judiciary committee of the *Volkskammer* (parliament)—a "Prof. Dr." and holder of several high political and academic positions. We were in one of the "better" restaurants of East Berlin. After some unremarkable main dish, we had an appetite for some dessert. Nothing was listed on the menu. The chairman asked the waitress what might be available. She was clearly vexed that he would ask such a question; could he not see there was nothing on the menu? This was communicated in the rudest possible tone of voice. Here, then, was a young woman (in her early twenties, I would guess) who literally dressed down a distinguished older gentleman who had the temerity to want some dessert. She most likely did not know who he was, but his appearance should have told her that he was a man of some importance. It made no difference. Demanding customers had to be put in their place.

Shops

Restaurants were exemplary, but other service situations were no better. Rather amusing was the *Körbchen* (basket) procedure in bookstores. Upon entering a bookstore, customers were obligated to equip themselves with a basket in which to place their selections. At one visit, I told the saleslady that I just wanted to browse and would not need a basket. This did not impress her; I was to take a basket anyhow. So far only a minor annoyance, *but* there never were enough baskets. Still, one could not proceed without one. Customers were told to wait at the entrance until a basket became available; only then were they permitted to go to the shelves. Of course, these orders were issued in a tone of voice that clearly suggested that the lacking basket was the customers' fault. The sales staff, accordingly, was irritated and provoked with the customers. Similar practices prevailed in other stores. See also Bavarius, 1990, 19, 50.

The sales personnel did have a difficult job. There were many things wrong with the retail shops in the GDR, but whatever it was, the customers tended to treat it as a failing of the personnel. Unavailable merchandise, long lines, or poor quality of goods—it always was seen as the fault of the personnel. The sales staff was not well paid, and working conditions tended to be poor, so no wonder there was a total disinterest in serving the customer. In fact, the personnel saw in the customer primarily an unwelcome disturbance. It was one of the standard tales of GDR retail stores that, if a piece of merchandise was in the storeroom rather than upfront, the sales staff would declare, "[W]e don't have it," rather than make the trip to the storeroom to get it. However the faults of GDR retail merchandising are to be allocated, shopping in East Germany often was a very unpleasant experience—and frequently the customer did not even obtain the desired goods[74] (Kaminsky, 2001; Merkel, 1999).

Bureaucracy

Bureaucrats—petty and otherwise—also had a habit of demeaning and degrading those who had to appear before them[75] (Philipsen, 1993, 9). At my many visits to the GDR, only once did I encounter a border control officer who was pleasant. One more personal example: in 1990, one day before the end of all border controls, I went to East Berlin by train. There was very heavy traffic at the railroad station at Friedrichstrasse, the official rail crossing place into East Berlin. Hundreds of persons crowded into a fairly small basement room. There were three processing counters, with lines in front of each of them. Naturally, I joined the shortest line. A bad mistake. At each counter there was a sign (not visible from a distance) that specified what kind of person was to be processed there. When the sign finally became visible and I found myself in the wrong line. I had been standing in that line for quite some time and did not feel like going to the back of another line. After all, in but a few hours there would be no control at all. What harm could it do if an American citizen went through the West Berliner station? The whole procedure consisted merely of presenting one's pass. No records were made; no lists were examined. Well, I was about to be corrected. Language and tone of voice were highly unpleasant, and, of course, I had to go to the back of another line. The officer in charge visibly enjoyed our little interaction. I suffered no harm except some lost time. But what must it be like to endure bureaucratic arrogance and insolence every day, without being able to do anything about them?

Dependent and Timid

The overall effect of all these humiliating and degrading experiences was a thoroughly cowed population. Berg (1988) has characterized the typical comportment of the GDR citizens as "forestalling" or "preventive submission" (*vorbeugende Unterwerfung*). When the Wall fell, the people of the GDR were pathologically timid and dependent. They were unwilling and unable to assert themselves (Schedlinski, 1991, 27–35). They waited for others (particularly persons perceived to be in some authority) to tell them what to do. Thus, while the signs about waiting for a table disappeared quite soon (now tips again had meaning), the brave citizens of the GDR would wait at the entrance anyhow, literally afraid to seat themselves (Klessmann & Wagner, 1993, 407–409).

RÉSUMÉ

There were few truly contented citizens in the GDR. Public life was largely unpleasant—from the constant need to be on one's guard against the omnipresent Stasi informers, to the rudeness of waiters, retail personnel, and socialist bureaucracy. There were the matters of mandatory participation in state and Party rituals and the coerced enthusiasm for the wise leaders. There was the pretense of economic success, while life was scruffy and desirable goods scarce. Censorship was omnipresent (including even some writings of Marx), elections were fraudulent, history was falsified, and there was no freedom of speech, press, association, and travel. Education was indoctrination. Advancement depended more on political criteria than professional accomplishments. Even the universities were closely controlled, with little opportunity for creative work. As became widely known, steroids brought the many international medals to the GDR: better sports through chemistry. There was, in the end, very little of which the GDR citizen could be proud.

There were no political alternatives. Opposition was not permitted. Political trials (while officially denied) were ubiquitous. New political crimes were invented with regularity. Churches provided some free space, but it was tolerated grudgingly, and the policy was subject to reversal at any time. There was a hypocritical pretense of citizen power and influence, and there was the ever-present celebration of antifascism to disguise the long-lasting Stalinism of the GDR. There was the official antagonism to militarism, while at the same time there was paramilitary instruction into the schools. Young people were endlessly regimented in the Party-affiliated youth organizations. Grown-ups were forever intimidated by the security forces. Both had to suffer endless indignities.

Not surprisingly, there was a general turning from the public arena to the private one (Fulbrook, 1995, 87)—except that the totalitarian regime could not accept a truly private sphere. Withdrawal to a private niche was understood to be "state-hostile." There were two countermeasures. First, normally private activities were marshaled into Party-controlled organizations—from hobby gardeners to stamp collectors (Ludwig, 1999, 11). No collaborative activity could be hidden from the eyes and ears of the regime. It was a sound assumption that within each group there was at least one Stasi informer. Second, even the most intimate relationships (families, friends) were infiltrated by the Stasi. Spouses and close friends were in the service of the Stasi—not discovered in most cases until after the fall of the system. "Many East Germans were appalled when they realized how badly they had been treated during the GDR regime. They had been controlled, manipulated, and impoverished by their own leadership. Their anger and resentment resurfaced when the press reported that their neighbors, friends, and professional colleagues had been spying on each other for years" (Ungerleider, 2001, 18).

There were, however, also certain advantages. The dictatorship of the Party was a "welfare dictatorship" (Wierling, 2002, 10). The rewards for not asserting oneself, for being an obedient citizen, were comprehensive material security arrangements. The basic foodstuffs were highly subsidized, as were rents and public transportation. Education and medical care were free, and, quite importantly, no one had to worry about losing one's job and joining the ranks of the unemployed. The government, in fact, took care of *everything* (Glaab, 1993, 123; Meckel, 1993, 123). The quality of the GDR goods and services was less than one might have desired, but most basic ones were available.

Only the "new class" could be truly satisfied with life in the GDR. This new class consisted mainly of two types of persons. First were those who benefited materially, who lived the life of true luxury (including, as noted, hunting reserves), and who had available to them not only the best Western goods but also the finest (most advanced, i.e., Western) medical care. Second were the "true believers," whose commitment to Marxism-Leninism was so strong that the realities of East German existence either did not register or enabled them to "dialectically" explain them away. My judgment is that the two groups together constituted about 20% of the GDR population.[76] These groups, of course, also overlapped, but my impression is that the members of the second group were not typically also the top material beneficiaries of the system.

In any case, this leaves about 80% of the population exposed to the "real GDR." What kind of people is such a system likely to create? In the first instance, *dependent and diffident* persons, unable and unwilling to take responsibility for themselves. Autonomous and self-reliant people were exceedingly rare. The system also created thoroughly *confused and perplexed* persons. The lack of reliable information and the constant prevarications of the regime produced people who did not know what or whom to believe. Furthermore, the system generated *suspicious and untrusting* persons. In the GDR no one could trust anyone; the long arm of the Stasi had seen to that. The inability to trust contributed to the general unhappiness and discontent. Finally, it will not come as a surprise that the GDR citizen was deeply *apathetic and schizophrenic*—everything but "the new socialist man."[77]

The GDR was a country of "sullen monotony." It was dull and drab, listless and shabby, gray and scruffy, unfriendly and inimical. It was a country under comprehensive coercion by a regime that lacked legitimacy. Accommodation to what one could not change became the principle for most, but there were always some who sought change: some by internal resistance, more by fleeing the country.

Given the nature of life in East Germany, it is not surprising that from the very beginning (as the Soviet Zone of Occupation) to the very end (as the sovereign German Democratic Republic), people sought to leave the country—often at a very high cost to themselves and their families. The story of the East German exodus is reported in the next chapter.

NOTES

1. The GDR had inhabitants of about 17 million after the Wall had stabilized the population, so 3.5 million is, of course, a very substantial loss, given the total size of the population.

2. As seen earlier, GDR historiography was ever-changing socialist rewritings of history, particularly in regard to the figures and events of German history. See Chapter 4; see also Klein, 2000.

3. Commenting on the persistent crisis in Soviet historiography, Bertram Wolfe (1954, 262) wrote:

> Histories succeed each other as if they were being consumed by a giant chain smoker who lights the first volume of the new work with the last of the old. Historians appear, disappear, and reappear; others vanish without a trace. . . . One day a given statement of events or interpretations is obligatory. The next it is condemned in words which seem to portend the doom of the historian who faithfully carried out his instructions.

4. Soviet rewriting of history did not end with Stalin's demise. In 1982, Yegor Yakovlev managed to publish a biography of Lenin wholly devoid of references to Trotsky (the old *un*person) and Stalin (the new *un*person).

5. The dissidents in the socialist system generally were found among cultural, not

technical elites (Dallin & Breslauer, 1970, 202). This is less true as it regards the GDR, where the technical elites chafed under the lack of trust on the part of the Party.

6. What Chi An reported regarding the People's Republic of China applied equally to the German Democratic Republic: "Life in China's socialist welfare state, with its cradle-to-grave job security, was undemanding as long as one did not deviate from the authorities' rigid plan" (Mosher, 1993, 246).

7. With the exception of the "new class" and their offspring, of course (Schell & Kalinka, 1991, 93–94).

8. As Czeslaw Milosz (1960, 19) remarked about the Soviet Union, "[I]t is likely that [those] who want freedom and justice find themselves in conflict with most of their fellow countrymen." In the GDR, however, it would not, however, have been "most" of their countrymen.

9. For a detailed discussion of comparative totalitarianism, see my *Rotten Foundations*, Chapter 6.

10. It should be noted, however, that the regime also was attentive to adult education, very much in the tradition of the German workers' movement (Hering & Luetzenkirchen, 1995).

11. Nevertheless, Pätzold (1991, 13) notes "significant educational deficiencies."

12. In addition, there was the goal of the Party to form the "new socialist personalities" as early as possible. Parental influence and involvement were seen as counterfunctional (Gries, 2001, 26–32).

13. There were few exceptions. There were some special schools for exceptionally gifted students, for example, in music or sports (see later), and some special schools for students who had mental or physical handicaps. These, however, affected only a small proportion of the students.

14. Ungerleider (2001, 15) writes that to continue after the standard ten years, "you had to have connections." Heym (1990, 286) reports that "the progress of the students often depended on the conduct of the parents." The teachers, of course, also found themselves in a difficult position. Most of them wanted to teach the subject matter but had to pay close attention to the ideological demands (Internationale Erich-Fromm-Gesellschaft, 1995; Weber, 1997).

15. Furthermore, the materials of the other classes were well coordinated with civics. This was most obvious when it came to history and geography, but even music was affected: class-based songs that proclaim loyalty to socialism were the favorites (Heyen, 1972, 74).

16. Another subject was participation in paramilitary instruction, since 1978 a regular part of the curriculum (Koch, 2000). Many students did not care for it (Rein, 1990, 115–119), perhaps because they took the official antimilitarist line of the Party seriously or perhaps they came from a religious family. But here is the statement of a student in support of it: "Military instruction and competitions are great, not only because they contribute to a meaningful use of our leisure time, but also because they help us in the forming of our socialist personality" (Symposium, 1982, 1112). Of course, this statement has all the characteristics of the fake letters to the editor discussed earlier (Chapter 6).

17. Of course, from the perspective of the regime, there could be no border between the public and the private. Unfortunately, even in the West, there have been groups proclaiming that "the private *is* the public" (Nastola, 1999, 107).

18. Scharf (1984, 127, 167) speaks of a "prudent hypocrisy." Walter (1997, 268) characterizes it as "double-think," which joined outer opportunism to inner detachment. See also Wechsberg, 1964, 135.

19. In my many interviews with GDR citizens of various political persuasion, before and after 1989, I could not find a single person who would speak positively of his or her civics classes. At the very most, Party and state officials would argue for the necessity of such instruction.

20. Collectives, which are everywhere (school, job, neighborhood, etc.), "function on the principle of mutual assistance . . . working and learning in a collective environment helps the individual to activate his potential [and] to stimulate his energies and abilities" (Klein, 1980, 77). Or more precisely (about university student collectives): "The 'collectives' live and work together and the members watch one another, politically and scholastically, so that the student is almost never on his own" (Wechsberg, 1964, 64).

21. A small selection from just one year: Bauer, 1960; Engelstaedter, 1960; Hoerz, 1960; Sauermann, 1960.

22. It was estimated that at least 15% of the GDR youth showed severe disturbances, including apathy and refusal of societal participation. They were, of course, not left to themselves but became "patients" of the *Jugendhilfe* (Youth Help), whose purpose was the application of an "early corrective influence when there were signs of derelict social development. The Youth Help had about 25,000 cases a year" (Helwig, 1983, 279–281).

23. As further testimonies to regime paranoia: no personnel registers or course catalogs could be published (Mehls, 1998, 162).

24. For student resistance, see Schmiedebach & Spiess, 2001. For the resistance of other young people, see Dellmuth, 1999.

25. While considering the matter of great importance, even the SED was not able to settle on a single, uniform definition (Heider & Thoens, 1990, 5).

26. As seen earlier (Chapter 5), to increase the number of workers in the "workers' party" and to be able to afford the offspring of the intellectuals' working-class benefits, ministers, professors, generals, and so on were reclassified as "workers." It was a key characteristic of the new GDR elite to think of itself as part of the working class (Huebner & Tenfelde, 1999, 12).

27. As Kolakowski (1969, 179) points out, "an organized communist movement was inconceivable without the participation of people who belonged to the bourgeois intelligentsia," such as Marx, Engels, and Lenin. On the other hand, socialist regimes typically manifested considerable suspicions about their intellectuals (a "love/hate" relationship), unsure how much they could really be trusted (Mehls, 1998, 242).

28. "For the first time" seems to overlook the priestly class of intellectuals, who for centuries dominated all other groups to the point of deposing emperors. The church drew the intellectuals to itself and was their great patron, at the same time that it mercilessly burned those intellectuals who would not hew the party line. Thus, it trained the intellectuals to forgo independent thinking—a tradition much alive in modern socialist dictatorships.

29. The other persons listed were obviously highly intelligent, but that is not the crucial criterion.

30. As the Polish writer Andrzej Szczypioski declared: "Intellectuals are always weak people, therefore I always say, I am not one of them" (Mittenzwei, 2001, 9).

31. As Gramsci noted, every social class needs its own intelligentsia. Intellectuals must choose with which social class they are going to ally themselves.

32. In the mid-1980s, Heng and Shapiro (1986, 9) observed that "Deng Xiaoping's policies, emphasizing the contributions that intellectuals could make to the modernization drive, had gone far to reverse Maoist prejudices toward people with professional abilities." It is of importance to note, however, that the initial recall regarded technicians rather than the literary or philosophical elite. A regime might well be able to do without the latter, but it cannot do for long without technical experts (Konrad & Szelenyi, 1979, 189).

33. This is particularly true for the philosophical and social science intellectuals. It is less true for the technical intelligentsia.

34. For some discussions of intellectual dissent in the GDR, see Bialas, 1996; Geulen, 1998; Krisch, 1985; Land & Possekel, 1994; Torpey, 1995; Wolle, 1998, 235–246.

35. See my *Rotten Foundations*, 118–127.

36. Article 125 of the Soviet constitution of 1922 guaranteed Soviet citizens freedom of speech *but only in order to strengthen the socialist system*. "And it is the party which decides what does, and what does not, serve this end" (Childs, 1973, 137–138).

37. Of particular interest was the use of the currency law (*Devisengesetz*) to prevent unauthorized publications in the West. Initially, the penalty for unsanctioned publications in the West was a fine of 300 East marks. Then unauthorized publication was redefined as a crime. It carried sanctions of up to ten years' imprisonment and a fine of up to 10,000 marks (Heym, 1990, 167–175).

38. On the criminalization of Western contacts, see Richter, 1995b, 122–123.

39. It should be noted that GDR prisons were extremely unpleasant places; physical brutality and other mistreatments were common occurrences. See Heyme, 1991.

40. Capital punishment was abolished in 1987.

41. For general discussions of GDR intolerance and censorship, see Bothe, 1983, 64; Finn & Julius, 1983, 51; Scharf, 1984, 128, 163–167; Schwarze, 1973, 32; Turner, 1987, 102; Thielbeer, 1985, 277.

42. As he was in the USSR. See Lauterbach, 1954, 287; Wolfe, 1954, 271.

43. The GDR PEN-Club, in a show of rare courage, passed a resolution asking for the release from prison of Vaclav Havel. This resolution could not be made public in East Berlin (Heym, 1990, 254).

44. At another time, the writers voiced the willingness to "support with their whole being those things which are devoted to the rise of the proletariat and the rise of a new humanity" (Bollinger & Vilmar, 2002, 107).

45. However, since 1981 there was no upper age limit (Walter, 1997, 24).

46. There is, however, much to be said for some decadence instead of communist totalitarianism (Aron, 1977). Certainly, the youth of East Germany would have welcomed it. In the 1980s they made some stabs in that direction—heavily sanctioned, of course.

47. Of course, it also did not enter the heads of the GDR leadership that young people anywhere tend not to be particularly tasteful in matters of dress and grooming and, in particular, tend to have truly dreadful musical tastes.

48. In the early years of the GDR, members of the FDJ were sent to West Germany as agitators, with the hope of influencing FRG elections. This was not the smartest move Erich Honecker ever made. The FDJ in later years was also active in recruiting (in fact, pressuring) young men for the military (Berg, 1988, 54–57).

49. The parallels to the nazi youth groups—*Deutsches Jungvolk* 10–14 and *Hitlerjugend* = HJ 14–18—were remarkable in substance, purposes, and organization. The *Hitlerjugend* obviously was to be loyal to the *führer*; for the FDJ it was faithfulness to Stalin. The slogans were very similar, including the one to be "hard as steel." The FDJ was expected to march just as smartly (*zackig*) as the HJ. Both groups provided intensive paramilitary training. (For the FDJ, see Berg, 1988, 43, 62–63; Maehlert, 1995, 306–309; for the HJ, see Koch, 1972; Lewis, 2000; for a comparative analysis, see Ansorg, 1997, 176–182; Bolling, 1950, 395; Grunert-Bronnen, 1970, 120; Haeder, 1998, 18–34; Rodden, 2002, 369).

50. Between 1945 and 1946 a variety of youth groups were founded in East Germany. Their demise came early. In 1946, SMAD integrated them in the official Antifascist Youth Committees, where they still had a certain amount of independence, however. But shortly thereafter, they became a branch organization of the FDJ, known as the Children-Groups of the FDJ. In 1948, finally, the Children-Groups became the Young Pioneers. While still closely collaborating with the FDJ, they became an organization with their own line to the Central Committee of the SED (Ansorg, 1997, 28–49).

51. One of the more amusing antireligious occurrences (which I personally experienced while in the GDR) was the transformation of Santa Claus into the "little solidarity man" (*Solidaritätsmänchen*). This happened at Christmas 1945 in Saxony, where the local authorities organized a festivity for children.

52. In 1950, 81.6% of the GDR population were members of the Protestant Church. By 1988, this figure was 23% (Joas & Kohli, 1993, 254). It should also be noted that the "religious renaissance" observed in the Soviet Union has not yet had an equivalent occurrence in the GDR (Seide, 1984).

53. He used to be, in GDR language, a "prince's lackey" and a "butcher of the peasants."

54. The GDR was largely a Protestant country (the home territory of Luther). The dispute between Party and church, therefore, was predominantly focused on the Protestant Church. There were only a few Catholic enclaves, and the Catholic Church played essentially no role in support of the protest movement. On the state of the Catholic Church in the GDR, see Grande & Schaefer, 1998; Klessmann & Wagner, 1993, 405–407; Raabe, 1995.

55. While the regime came to an arrangement with the Protestant Church (Goeckel, 1990) and, in a way, with the Catholic Church, it was unremittingly hostile to minority denominations. See, for example, Hirch, 2001; Vollnhals & Weber, 2002, 218–286.

56. Toward non-Marxists the Party typically displayed a limited degree of toleration. It did not require ideological conversion, though it did demand adherence to SED policies (Wolfe, 1971, 468; see also Muhlen, 1951; Schwarze, 1969, 331; Wiesenthal, 1968).

57. In addition to the regular armed forces (*Volksarmee*), there were a number of other armed units, most prominently, of course, the various police groupings and the armed section of the Stasi, but there were also the *Kampfgruppen der Arbeiterklasse*, that is, armed groupings organized on an enterprise basis (Koop, 1997). There was no dearth of organized units to protect the system, and this is not yet counting the Soviet troops.

58. The national socialists had a similar ritual, called the *Jugendleite* (Youth Guidance) (Meier, 1998, 11).

59. Parents had to deal with the question: Can I be a good GDR citizen if I don't have my child participate in the *Jugendweihe*? (Griese, 2001).

60. In 1978, compulsory premilitary training for fifteen- and sixteen-year-olds was added to the school curriculum. The church also sought a system of "civil service" as an alternative to compulsory military service.

61. This was quite easy because since 1948 the FDJ (thus, the SED) had a monopoly over organized sports (Maehlert, 1995, 269–272).

62. GDR officials, of course, vehemently denied that there was any doping in East German sports (Seppelt & Schueck, 1999, 47–48).

63. There was a prohibition against letting the children see the original packages (Seppelt & Schueck, 1999, 42, 55).

64. Some of the successes, no doubt, were due to talent and rigorous training, but the overall success of GDR sports must be attributed to systematic doping of the athletes (Seppelt & Schueck, 1999, 12, 19).

65. At the summer games in Montreal (1976), GDR swimmers had eleven out of thirteen first-place finishes. The overall gold count for the GDR was forty, compared to ten for the FRG—extraordinary results for a small country like East Germany. Other international results were similar (Seppelt & Schueck, 1999, 38).

66. As an aside, Erich Mielke, the minister for State Security, was heavily involved in soccer. A real fan, he caused promising players to be transferred to the Berlin team that he favored (Pleil, 2001).

67. The easy linking of "patriot" and "internationalist" is typical for a system in which all opposites form "dialectical unities."

68. The Party also was against such "backward" behavior as egoism, seeking wealth, dishonesty, fraud, hypocrisy, dawdling in one's work, bureaucratic deportment, alcoholism, and other such things. The causes of such behavior all were found outside one's own society—either in the form of current attacks of the class-enemy or as remnants of the old "exploiter society" (Ahrberg, 1996, 11–12).

69. While the playing of Western music could not be prohibited altogether, the Party sought to limit it. There was a law that discotheques could play maximally 40% Western music; the rest had to be homemade (Ahrberg, 1996, 7; Sommer, 2002, 277). This was taken very seriously. There even were informers in the discotheques. I know some East German musicians who got into serious trouble with the Stasi because they exceeded the 40% limit.

70. A student got himself into deep trouble with the Stasi because his roommate had played a tape with songs by Biermann (expelled from the GDR) and *he had not reported it* (Heinecke, 2000, 78–79).

71. This will be treated in greater detail in the forthcoming *Popular Justice in a Marxist-Leninist Society: The East German Social Courts and Other Aspects of GDR Law*.

72. The same could be observed at any retail establishment. There were frequent closings because of illness, inventory, burst pipes, or simply "technical reasons." Also, shops principally opened late for business and closed early (Wolle, 1998, 215). Complaints were not only useless but counterproductive. The GDR citizen knew enough to keep quiet.

73. In some cities, the FDJ had Youth Clubs. Entry was strictly on good behavior. Even a lit cigarette could be reason to refuse admission, if the supervisors were in a bad mood (Klessmann & Wagner, 1993, 472). This policy, of course, does not differ from that of certain clubs in the United States of America—but with this difference: in the GDR there was no place else to go.

74. To be able to obtain first-class (and rare) merchandise, one had to have connections. Either one was a close friend with a salesperson, or one could offer some rare goods or service in exchange, or one was able to pay in West marks (Grohnert, 1999, 113–128). In some ways, the GDR economy returned to a much older form of trade: it became a *bartering* economy, where goods, not money, constituted the primary medium of exchange.

75. Margarita Mathiopoulos (1994, 11) characterizes the speech manners of the GDR officials as "concentration camp tone."

76. Wechsberg (1964, 38) gives an estimate of 15% regime supporters. See also Oehme & Schmidt-Lauzemis, 1993.

77. It is important to note that not every GDR citizen fitted the personality profile here delineated. Still, a substantial majority showed signs of these deformations (Klessmann & Wagner, 1993).

Chapter 8

The End of the GDR: Exodus, Revolution, and Reunification

INCARCERATION AND ESCAPE

Before the Wall[1]

As noted earlier, the SZ/GDR lost a substantial portion of its inhabitants. It has been estimated that about 25% of its people left East Germany—some of them legally,[2] some not (Berg, 1988, 63). Typically, it was the better-educated part of the population (particularly of the indispensable technical elite) who fled. Given the open border in Berlin, ever new waves of refugees escaped to the FRG. The GDR placed substantial restrictions on the free travel of its citizens and instituted rigorous controls of persons traveling from the interior to Berlin. Having all your children with you or carrying much luggage would give rise to immediate suspicion. Most likely, the police would escort you back to your hometown, where then you would be closely watched.

The first constitution of the GDR knew the right to emigrate. This right was no longer to be found in the next constitutions,[3] which, however, still guaranteed free choice of residence with the GDR. This freedom was hollow, too. According to a law of August 24, 1961, citizens' domiciles could be restricted to particular communities. In addition, citizens could be legally prevented from visiting the border region (Mayer, 2002, 28; for a comprehensive account of life in the border region, see Grafe, 2002). People could be doubly imprisoned then: in the GDR and in a particular community.

These measures did not stop the exodus. Between 200,000 and 300,000 East Germans left each year (Mayer, 2002, 27). The total has been estimated to have been more than 3 million persons[4] (Wassmund, 1981, 345). Most escaped by way of West Berlin, which was entirely open until the Wall. The border between the Zones of Occupation (later the FRG/GDR border) had been almost completely closed already on June 30, 1946, and was heavily guarded by Soviet and East German troops.[5] Finally, the GDR was sealed off from the West by the building of the Berlin Wall (August 13, 1961).[6] It seemed to be the only way—short of changing the nature of the regime—to stop the drain (Dornberg, 1968, 17; Gelb, 1986; Plischke, 1961, 211; Richert, 1961, 47–58; Ulrich, 1984, 172–195; Wassmund, 1981, 345). As discussed earlier, the Wall, according to the GDR, was an "anti-fascist protection wall," protecting East Germany from the imperialist aggression of the West.[7] The GDR government also proudly proclaimed that by building the Wall, the GDR saved the peace in Europe and the world, which peace had been threatened by West German militarism (Mayer, 2002, 27).

By the time the Wall was built, many of those who opposed the regime on principle had left the GDR—including high-ranking officials and even Party members (Mayer, 2002, 17; Schenck, 1962). The remaining population had to accommodate itself as best as it could (Fulbrook, 1992, 183). Now, most dangerous to the regime were those who criticized the GDR from a Marxist perspective, individuals like Havemann, Biermann, and Bahro, who had the same communist credentials as the SED leadership (Wassmund, 1981, 344–345).

After the Wall

People now were imprisoned in their own country. Seeking to leave the country *without permission* was made into a crime—fleeing the republic = *Republikflucht*—including the mere preparation or attempt, with prison sentences up to life.[8] Of course, many escapees received a death sentence. The border patrol had orders to shoot when people tried to cross the border.[9] In fact, hundreds of people were killed seeking to cross the border. The estimates (there are no exact figures since the GDR, of course, did not generally publicize the number of victims who remained on their side of the border—which were most) vary between 500 and 900 (Hildebrandt, 2001; Koop, 1996, 353–353). Thousands were gravely wounded[10] and then imprisoned for long periods (Koop, 1996, 7).

There was a way to leave the country *with permission* (Jeschonnek, 1988, 234). The citizen had to file an application with the local authorities. This had the consequences of losing one's job, coming under constant close Stasi observation, and, at times, even losing one's children, who would be placed in youth homes or with foster parents—wanting to leave the GDR was evidence not only for being "state-hostile," but also for being an unfit parent.[11] Of course, the GDR regime could not conceive of anyone leaving the workers' paradise of their own will. The official line was that each departure was the result of a "targeted recruitment" (*gezielte Abwerbung*).[12] This may, on occasion, be believed when it regards an individual case, but it becomes laughable when applied to the thousands of GDR citizens who left the country, enduring great hardships and risking their lives in doing so.

Pragmatic accommodation, acquiescence, dissimulation, evasion, and encapsulation in a private niche became the key axioms of GDR existence (Dornberg, 1968, 230; Haeder, 1998, 341; Hanhardt, 1968, 78; Laatz, 1983, 123; Minnerup, 1982, 52–53; Prauss, 1960, 206; Richert, 1961, 38; Sontheimer & Bleek, 1975, 44; Staritz, 1994, 27; Stuermer, 1986, 230). GDR citizens withdrew into themselves and into their families and close friends. The GDR became a "retreatist culture characterized by a double life: conformity in public, authenticity in private. . . . the prevalence of the retreatist mode, in combination with at least a minimum of material satisfaction, resulted in a degree of domestic political stability" (Fulbrook, 1992, 184). The fate of Shostakovich was discussed in Chapter 6. Here it remains to note his reaction. "After 1948, Shostakovich withdrew into himself. The split into two personae was complete. He continued making occasional mandatory public appearances, hurriedly and with visible revulsion reading confessions or pathos-filled pronoucements he had not written" (Volkov, 1980, xxxvi).

Just as Shostakovich had to keep making some appearances, so did the GDR citizen. As seen earlier, evasion was difficult to practice under the mandatory participation rules of the GDR, mere acquiescence was not enough since enthusiasm was demanded, and withdrawal into the family[13] or a private niche was not allowed, being perceived as a "state-hostile" act (Dahrendorf, 1967, 407; Picaper, 1982, 280). Nevertheless, most people sought to get by with the absolutely unavoidable minimum of involvement (Minnerup, 1982, 49; Wolfe, 1971, 477). In fact, for some people the situation was comparable to the "inner emigration" of the nazi period.

Yet there were oppositional endeavors (Bruce, 2003; Neubert & Eisenfeld, 2001; Pollack & Rink, 1997). The first ones were found in the context of the Protestant Church (see earlier). There were the "Dresden Peace Forum" of 1982, the "Berlin Appell" of Eppelmann and Havemann (which gathered about 2,000 signatures), and the "Swords to Plowshares" movement. The regime response was intense and brutal, as seen in the 1987 forced occupation of the ecological library of the Zion church in Berlin, in the assault of the Luxemburg demonstrators in 1988, and in the aggression against the election-falsification prostesters since June 1989. Finally, there were the mass demonstrations of the fall of 1989, as well as the mass emigrations of the same period. The regime still could (and did) muster brutal force, but the full effect was lacking. In fact, the regime looked helpless and confused, yet it remained opposed to any reform[14] (Prokop, 1994, 12). Because of this confusion and in conjunction with other factors (see later), there came about an opportunity to change[15] the system, which had oppressed its people for more than forty years.

Since the building of the Wall, one could speak of a stabilization of the regime, but not of a full acceptance by its people.[16] Legitimacy still was lacking; loyalty still was in doubt. The regime made great efforts to overcome the legitimacy deficit and to secure citizen support and loyalty. The efforts were largely cosmetic, however, and did not work. Thus, even the Wall could not conceal the basic inner weakness of the GDR (Friedman, 1963; Turner, 1987, 130). Nevertheless, now "the SED could afford to take measures in order slowly to integrate more and more of the people into the social and political system. The SED created mechanisms of consultation and strove, by emphasizing the importance of high standards of living, encouraging pride in the state's achievements and seeking to forge a new national self-consciousness, for an identity of the goals of the population with those of the party" (Wassmund, 1981, 329). But as previous chapters have shown, political integration and consultation were fraudulent, the high standard of living was never accomplished, and the GDR-consciousness remained largely a chimera.

Of course, the "niche society" and the "retreatist culture," even where possible, were not very satisfactory solutions. First, it meant giving up even the pretense of being an engaged and influential member of society. Second, there were the difficulties of doing it, as just discussed. Third, there was the Stasi, which sought to recruit even family members and close friends as collaborators—and with considerable success. Many a person discovered after the end of the regime that his or her spouse and/or trusted friends had been Stasi informers[17] (Arnold, 1995, 91–92; Lengsfeld, 1997, 104; Schell & Kalinka, 1991, 120–121).

Tunnels, Boats, Balloons

With the building of the Wall, the last exit route was closed. People still wanted to leave the GDR. They could apply for permission, which, however, was not usually granted[18] (Dowty, 1987). This left the option of escaping across the border in various ways and by various devices. The first major method was digging tunnels under the Berlin Wall. Quite often these tunnels had their origin on the Western side, where digging was more easily arranged. Several hundred East Berliners escaped in this way. It did not take the Stasi very long to discover the tunneling activities, particularly since some of them were betrayed (Nooke, 1999).

Desperate would-be escapees tried other, highly risky methods (Hollander, 1992, 96; Mueller, 2001). Several East German families escaped via self-constructed hot-air balloons across the border to West Germany. Procuring the necessary materials was very difficult. It was not possible, for example, to purchase the total amount of canvas needed in one place. This would immediately have alerted the Stasi. Small pieces of canvas were obtained in places all over the GDR. These had to be stitched together in laborious efforts over a long period of time, remembering that all the while the work had to be hidden—not an easy task with something the size of an hot-air balloon. (For a complete report of one such escape, see Petschull, 1981.)

The river Elbe formed the border between the GDR and the FRG for a considerable distance. Many tried to flee by swimming across. The GDR border guards were merciless, killing many swimmers with well-aimed rifle fire. The same happened wherever a body of water formed the border, whether river or lake. These attempts were particularly frequent in Berlin, with its many rivers and lakes. One family built itself a submarine, which, however, did not work properly. Many others, living close to the Baltic Sea, sought to escape by boat. Most of them were caught by the GDR coast guard.

There also were many attempts to cross the border on foot. This was a most dangerous undertaking. The border, as noted, was secured by mines and automatic firing devices, in addition to several barbed-wire barriers, dogs on patrol, searchlights, and the heavy presence of border guards. Not many people escaped successfully by this route. Some individuals even tried to climb over the Berlin Wall, which was similarly guarded. Few were able to succeed.[19] Finally, people sought to escape by hiding in vehicles that could cross the border. All sorts of concealing spaces were installed in cars and trucks. The border police discovered most of them.

It is obvious that GDR citizens were desperate to leave the country. They took the risk of being killed or gravely injured. If they did not make it across the border, they would have to spend long years in prison.[20] Different persons, of course, had different motivations to undertake a *Republikflucht* (Lemke, 1991). Two possible reasons, however, can be largely discounted: economics and Western recruitment. As seen above, the GDR was not a shopper's paradise. Many goods were available only sporadically, and often they were of poor quality. But no one had to starve or to live under bridges in the GDR. The basic foodstuffs were inexpensive and readily obtainable. The story that West German firms deliberately recruited East German citizens is plainly absurd (the logistics alone would make this undoable). There is little doubt that the reason in most cases was the desire for more freedom and autonomy than could be had in the GDR. The regimented and coerced life of the average East German citizen simply was more than some could endure.

Ausbürgerung

Imprisonment was the most common way in which the regime dealt with critics who could not be intimidated and who would not keep quiet. But there was yet another weapon in the regime's arsenal: expatriation (*Ausbürgerung*). The expatriation involved the physical removal of the person from the territory of the GDR as well as the retracting of his or her GDR citizenship.

It could proceed in two ways. One was allowing the person to travel to a Western country (most often the FRG) and then denying his or her reentering the GDR. This is what happened to the singer/composer Wolf Biermann. The act had been planned for a long time, involving both the Politburo and the Stasi, but in the years 1971–1975 Biermann did not travel abroad[21] (Borgwardt, 2002, 395–490; Lasky, 1992, 35–50; Pleitgen, 2001, 19). In 1976, Biermann finally visited the FRG (giving a major concert in Cologne), and the regime took the opportunity to withdraw GDR citizenship from him (because of supposed hostility to the GDR) and prevent him from returning to East Germany (which he wanted to do).[22] The case caused much unrest and resistance in the GDR. Many East Germans signed a resolution protesting the expatriation of Biermann, including a number of prominent writers and artists. This was an act of great courage. The Stasi, of course, quickly started investigation of the signatories, making their lives very difficult.[23] As a consequence many of them left the GDR—some voluntarily, some coerced (Pleitgen, 2001, 21).

The second way was to expel GDR citizens. Often there even was a profit in it for the regime. Citizens would first be arrested and imprisoned. Then the FRG would be permitted to purchase their freedom (*freikaufen*) and transfer them to West Germany. Often this treatment was also accorded to their families. The purchase price was about 60,000 West marks. There was an additional profit: citizens who left the GDR had to sell their property (particularly any real estate) to state agencies at dumping prices (Liebernickel, 2000).

THE BLOODLESS REVOLUTION

Expectations

In the mid-1980s there was no expectation of a reunification of the two German states (Obst, 1983, 110). It was literally "unthinkable" (Schoenbaum & Pond, 1996, 3). Any talk of reunification was being dismissed as wildly irrational and possibly dangerous[24] (Bruns, 1989, 194–202; Leonhard, 1992; Zitelmann, 1993, 234–235). Indeed, it ran counter to the fond dreams of *Ostpolitik*, that is, to stabilize the GDR and, if feasible, transform it into a more humane system. *Die Zeit*, Countess Dönhoff's West German newspaper, thoroughly left-wing and rabidly anti-FRG, took the lead in publishing reports about the good, free, and wonderful life in the GDR, which on no account should be disturbed by reunification talks[25] (Lasky, 1992, 55–56). Of course, there were many others who thought the GDR a great success, including a Harvard professor who *in the summer of 1989* could write that the great accomplishments of the GDR would allow it to prosper in the foreseeable future[26] (McAdams, 1989, 14).

Similarly, there was no expectation of an East German revolution or of the general disintegration of the communist system (Hollander, 1992, 3; Minnerup, 1982, 56). People were grumbling, but so had they for a long time. The Party appeared to have matters well under control. No one, it seems, was able to predict revolution and reunification—not even the intelligence services, whose business it was to foresee such developments.

What brought about the change?[27] In retrospect a number of factors can be suggested. First of all, Kuhrt (1996a, 9) is right in saying that "the reasons for the collapse of the GDR are found in the beginning." The GDR began as, and remained, an illegitimate entity, subject to a totalitarian party dictatorship, never viable economically, never supported by a majority of its citizens, and depending on coercion for its survival. When the coercion became uncertain, the edifice collapsed. There were a number of other factors: the crash of the GDR economy[28] (which had become painfully obvious by the mid-1980s: obsolete factories, no capital, an insuffiently qualified workforce, noncompetitive products), the scarcity of goods and housing, the limited social mobility for most of the population, the restrictions on travel, the unwillingness to adopt Gorbachev's reforms, and, very importantly, the loss of the regime's Soviet protection (Muehlen, 2000, 352–35; Wilhelmy, 1995, 23).

Then there was the new "civic movement," largely under the umbrella of the Protestant Church (Motschmann, 1993, 65), which clearly enunciated what heretofore had been taboo subjects: the arbitrariness, fraud, dishonesty, and cruelty of the regime. The falsification of the May 1989 elections did much to discredit the regime. It brought into question the accommodating mind-set of the GDR citizen. Also important were the many new political groups that were founded in September[29] and October 1989.[30] The existence of these associations destroyed the idea that such groups could exist only with the permission of, and in cooperation with, the SED. Their existence also undermined the notion of the "leading role" of the SED. The cry *Wir sind das Volk* (We are the people) was a remembrance and restoration of the much promulgated, but never actualized, concept of *Volkssouveränität* (popular sovereignty). To these many factors must, finally, be added the manifest confusion and helplessness of the regime (from ever-changing policies regarding freedom to travel, to the hasty and inadequate changes in the top leadership, to the inadvertent announcement of the opening of the Wall). The people of the GDR, with much courage, tried their hands at revolution,[31] but also, in fairness, the regime simply imploded[32] (Jarausch, 1999b). In the end, not even the SED functionaries believed in the legitimacy of SED rule (Gutjahr-Loeser, 1998; Wilhelmy, 1995, 11). The central and most symbolic event was the fall of the Berlin Wall, with the people dancing on top of it (Hertle, 1999). It was a world-dramatic episode, comparable to the storming of the Bastille.

Many things happened in the late summer and fall of 1989. The developments were rapid and confusing. Some were strictly German matters; others involved other nations. Following are some highlights.

The Third-Country Route

The first signal of major unrest came on June 8, 1989, in East Berlin, when the office of the West German representative (*ständige Vertretung*) had to be closed after it had been occupied by GDR citizens who wanted to force their right to leave East Germany in this way. This was followed by the occupation of West German embassies in Budapest, Warsaw, and Prague by citizens of the GDR, who hoped to embarrass the system in this way and gain their emigration to the West. The second signal was that many GDR citizens traveled to Hungary in the summer of 1989, hoping to cross from there into Austria and ultimately to West Germany.

A crisis rapidly developed. The embassies were overrun; people had to camp out in the embassy gardens; sanitary conditions were dismal. Hungary found itself with more would-be refugees than it could handle; camps had to be set up for the East Germans. The East Germans authorities looked (and were) utterly helpless and confused. They could think only of the tired old complaint that the FRG was trying to provoke unrest and recruit the citizens of the GDR to leave their country (Zelikow & Rice, 1995, 64).

The Hungarians had a long-standing agreement with the GDR to send the East Germans back home who would not voluntarily return. On August 9, 1989, the Hungarians stopped sending the GDR citizens back. However, they still tried to stop the East Germans from crossing the border into Austria.[33] The West Germans were not, of course, trying to provoke a crisis. Being captive of their own *Ostpolitik*, they were committed to stabilize the GDR, not to undermine it.[34] In previous refugee situations, the West German government had always persuaded the asylum seekers to go back to the GDR and seek legal permission to emigrate (with protections against reprisals). After the payment of considerable amounts of money, the permission was usually granted (Frey, 1987, 118; Zelikow & Rice, 1995, 65).

By the end of August East German refugees were filling the Hungarian detention camps. The Hungarian government was looking for a way out. On August 25, there were secret discussions with Kohl and foreign minister Genscher. In return for DM 500 million to support the Hungarian economy, the Hungarians agreed that they would not return the East Germans to the GDR but would instead allow them to travel to the West (Zelikow & Rice, 1995, 67–68).

The GDR protested vehemently, characterizing the Hungarian policies as treason. Moscow, by the way, did not bring pressure to bear on Hungary.[35] The Hungarians were not impressed with the East German remonstrations. They annulled their pact with the GDR on September 10 and opened the border to Austria. By the end of September about 40,000 East Germans had successfully fled their country via Hungary (Zelikow & Rice, 1995, 68).

By mid-September the GDR cut off travel to Hungary, whereupon the crisis spread into Czechoslovakia. Thousands of refugees scaled the walls of the

West German Embassy in Prague. By late September over 5,000 people were crowded into the embassy, producing severe problems of sustenance and sanitation. The government of the GDR finally agreed that the refugees could go to West Germany, but it insisted that this would have to be done by way of trains that would pass through the GDR.[36] The Czech–GDR border was closed on October 3. Two days earlier, the East German government declared defiantly that no tears would be shed about the refugees who "had removed themselves from our society" (Zelikow & Rice, 1995, 76, 82). By the time the Wall fell, 10,000 East Germans had gotten to the West via the FRG Embassy in Budapest, 17,000 via the FRG Embassy in Prague, and almost 5,000 via the FRG Embassy in Warsaw (Maier, 1997, 131; Schuetzsack, 1990).

Demonstrations in the GDR

The earliest significant demonstration can be dated to the Rosa Luxemburg parade in January 1988. Rosa Luxemburg was a prominent communist (cofounder of the KPD and a comrade/critic of Lenin) who had been murdered in 1919 in Berlin (together with Karl Liebknecht) by right-wing soldiers (Bronner, 1987, 95; Weitz, 1997, 14, 267). She was one of the heroines of the GDR. Each year there was an official march from the center of Berlin to the socialist memorial in Friedrichsfelde (Berlin), in which Honecker and the other leading politicians prominently participated. In 1988, for the first time, some people carried their own (nonapproved) banners. This, of course, could not be tolerated, particularly since the banners proclaimed the most famous saying of Luxemburg: "*Freiheit ist immer Freiheit der Andersdenkenden*" ("Freedom is always the freedom of those who think differently").[37] More than 100 persons (mostly young people) were arrested and brutalized (Menge, 1990, 15). Nevertheless, the nonofficial banners also made their appearance again in 1989 (Rein, 1990, 58–59, 325–326).

After the election falsifications of May 7, 1989, had become known, there had been protests organized by peace groups on the seventh day of every month at 5:00 P.M. at the Alexander-Platz in the center of East Berlin. The first such demonstration took place on June 7. The protesters were few, and the Stasi had no problem to arrest them. But in the following three months the number of participants grew, though the Stasi still was very much in control.[38] October 7 (the next demonstration date) coincided with the celebration of the fortieth anniversary of the founding of the GDR. The officials were nervous. There was a massive show of force on the part of the Stasi (in civilian clothing) and the police (in uniform). When the arrests started, there was resistance. People linked arms, booed the security forces, and shouted, "Freedom, Freedom." The security forces were unable to disperse or arrest all the protesters. This had never happened before in the GDR. Later in the evening the participants set out to march to the Palace of the Republic (some miles away), where celebrations were taking place (see later). The shouts now were, "Gorbi, We are the People, No Force." When it got dark, the protesters dispersed, most of them in the direction of Penzlauer Berg. This was what the security services had been waiting for. With great brutality they picked out particular demonstrators, beat them, and placed them under arrest. This conduct continued for the rest of the night and into the next day (Mitter & Wolle, 1993, 484–488).

On October 7, 1989, the GDR staged the fortieth-anniversary celebration of its existence. There was a massive military review, after which the civilian organizations paraded their members in front of the reviewing stand. The marching East Germans shouted "Gorbi, Gorbi." Honecker was not amused. He saw it as a provocation. Gorbachev, of course, was present in the reviewing stand, as were the leaders of the other socialist nations (Zelikow & Rice, 1995, 83). On the evening of that day, there was a gala reception for the domestic and foreign leadership at the Palace of the Republic in the center of Berlin. Outside the building the citizens assembled to make their displeasures known. There was no end to the "Gorbi" cries.

While in Berlin, Gorbachev met with Honecker and the East German Politburo. Gorbachev, then, made his famous statement that "life punishes those who come too late." He did not criticize FRG Chancellor Kohl, as Honecker had wanted. Instead, he insisted on Soviet "noninterference." There would be, then, no Soviet military aid to quell the revolution, the contours of which had become plainly visible. Honecker came to regard this as a "stab in the back" by his Russian comrade[39] (Lasky, 1992, 114; see also Gedmin, 1992, 97–100; Reuth & Boente, 1993). He certainly regarded the revolution as a counterrevolutionary event[40] (Natter, 1994, 13–15, 28). It should also be noted that a rather fantastic conspiracy theory also has been proposed, that the revolution was organized by the Stasi (Wilhelmy, 1995, 29).

The *general* mass demonstration (against the regime, not in respect to specific causes like Luxemburg or election falsification) began in East Germany on October 9 in Leipzig. About 70,000 citizens participated.[41] The Leipzig demonstration was peaceful, though there had been much fear of a "Chinese solution." In the city of Halle and other places, however, similar demonstrations were met with truncheons. The number of participants increased rapidly. For the week of October 23–30, the Stasi reported that over 130 demonstrations had taken place with more than 500,000 people.

The initial aim of the demonstrators had not been to abolish the GDR but to improve it—the old dream of the East German civil rights activists (*Bürgerrechtler*). In a discussion I had with Wolfgang Harich in 1999, this former victim of the SED regime expressed great concerns that reunification would abolish socialism and the social security benefits of the system.[42] He very much preferred a separate, but improved, GDR. Walter Janka, fellow-victim of the regime but also opponent of Harich, expressed similar sentiments (Lasky, 1992, 101–108; see also Mitter & Wolle, 1993, 542). The basic idea of these dissidents seems to have been that Marxism-Leninism was indeed the correct *Weltanschauung* to lead humanity to a glorious future. Only the leaders of the GDR had made a shambles of it. Many of these individuals have since become active in the PDS, the successor party to the SED. There they work against what they perceive to be the "reunification-injustice" and indulge in "GDR-nostalgia" (Kupferberg, 2002, 172–173; Moreau & Lang, 1994, 87).[43]

The regime had difficulty deciding how to react. It vacillated between hard-line responses and the pious hope that the demonstrations would naturally come to a halt. Honecker at the time was very ill with a severe gall bladder problem and not fully functional. The regime certainly did not want a repeat of the October 7–8 events in Berlin. It had damaged the prestige of the GDR, foreign reporters having been much in evidence. Soon, however, tougher measures were used (especially outside Berlin), particularly in reaction to the protesters who beleaguered the Dresden railroad station, through which passed the trains from Prague. The protesters had hoped to gain access to the trains and join the journey to the West. Similar events happened at several other railroad stations through which the trains had to pass. Indeed, people waited at the tracks, in places where trains usually had to slow down, hoping to be able to jump on the carriages.

Early in October (particularly regarding the October 9, 1989, demonstration in Leipzig) there was considerable police brutality. People were expecting a Tiananmen Square–style massacre.[44] Yet, at the last minute cooler heads prevailed, and the police and other armed units were withdrawn. With the armed units out of the way, the "peaceful revolution" resumed its way.

The situation clearly had become untenable. The SED tried to rescue the system by changes in the top leadership. On October 17, Honecker was replaced by Krenz. Honecker was expelled from the Politburo, as were several of his close associates. It was too late. The revolution could no longer be stopped, particularly not by Krenz, who had very little credence among the East Germans. They remembered him as the Tiananmen Square advocate and the person in charge of the last, falsified election.

Dornberg (1968, 20–21) described the situation in the early 1960s as follows: "Though the majority of East Germans insist they still would like to see Germany reunified some day, they also qualify this hope with the adamant reservation that they would not be willing to pay the ultimate price of reunification which Bonn may demand: jettisoning Communism." Assuming that Dornberg was right (which I am inclined to doubt), in 1989 most East Germans were willing to pay the price of getting rid of their communist regime. The regime, after all, was marked by a gargantuan and largely incompetent bureaucracy, which treated citizens like children without rights. It was a system that was unable to connect to modern technology and unable to provide for the needs of the population. It did not permit a democratic participation of its citizens, nor was it able to satisfy their ethical wants. It was a system that was unable to gain the support of the youth. It was a system that gave the individuals neither hope nor a perspective (Leonhard, 1990, 199). By now, it had become obvious to all but the most devoted and thoroughly blind Marxist-Leninists that no real reforms and improvement could be expected from the present regime. But overthrowing the regime, it now also had become clear, would not be enough. East Germany was simply not a viable state. Its economy was a thoroughly botched mess that could no longer provide even the basic necessities[45] (Mayer, 1991). It had become painfully obvious that the only hope for the East Germans lay in a rapid reunification with the FRG.

REUNIFICATION AND THE END OF THE SOCIALIST EXPERIMENT

Not all West Germans were eager for reunification. In mid-1989, still being committed to *Ostpolitik*, foreign minister Hans-Dietrich Genscher opposed reunification. Chancellor Helmut Kohl, however, now seemed ready to abandon traditional *Ostpolitik* and declared that the German question (i.e., reunification) was "back on the international agenda."[46] Some thirty years earlier, Walter Ulbricht had declared "The GDR stands with the victors of history" (Falk et al., 1969, 286). This, however, was true only for as long as the "class-enemy" was willing to shore up the regime. This willingness now had come to its end.

Events now progressed with unimaginable speed. October 18: forced resignation of Honecker as general secretary of the SED, election of Egon Krenz as his successor; expulsion of Honecker, Mittag, and Herrmann from the Politburo of the SED. October 19: Krenz promised a *Wende* (turning point, change). October 20: Sputnik may be sold again; 50,000 demonstrate in Dresden for free elections. October 21: demonstrations in most of the major cities. October 22: first common public discussion of SED functionaries, theologians, and citizens in Leipzig. October 23: massive demonstrations in Berlin, Leipzig, Dresden, and other cities. October 24: *Volkskammer* election of Krenz into the offices vacated by Honecker (chair of the Council of State, chair of the National Defense Committee); protests against this election in various localities. October 25: demonstrations in Berlin and elsewhere. October 26: first contact between Krenz and Kohl. October 26–31: daily demonstrations in all of the GDR. November 1: Krenz meets with Gorbachev in Moscow. November 1–6: massive demonstrations throughout the GDR; resignation of many state and Party functionaries (e.g., the minister for education, Margot Honecker, the head of the FDGB, the lord major of Leipzig, and many SED first secretaries); Axen, Hager, Mielke, Mückenberger, and Neumann leave the Politburo. November 7: resignation of the government of Willi Stoph; abolition of paramilitary instruction in the schools. November 8: resignation of the entire Politburo; reelection of Krenz as SED general secretary. November 8: Schabowski announces the opening of the Wall for the next day; the same evening thousands of persons stream to the Wall and force the crossing of the border.[47] November 10: massive border crossings to the West, in Berlin, and throughout the GDR; rally of 100,000 citizens in Berlin to discuss reforms. November 11–12: opening of new border crossings; large-scale replacement of SED functionaries. November 13: election of Hans Modrow as head of government. November 14: announcement of a possible membership of the GDR in the EG; forty-eight universities demand the abolition of compulsory Marxist-Leninist instruction. November 15–16: revelation of SED corruption and special privileges; revelation of ecological damages in the GDR; rehabilitation of Robert Havemann and Ernst Bloch; calls for reunification at the Leipzig demonstrations and the singing of the prohibited words of the GDR anthem, including the phrase "Germany, united fatherland"; November 17: Modrow suggests a community-treaty (*Vertragsgemeinschaft*) between the GDR and the FRG. November 18–30: daily demonstrations, resignations, and reform discussions in various locations; estimate that since November 1, 1989, 100,000 GDR citizens have left the country.

December 1: elimination of the paragraph about the "leading role" of the SED from the constitution. December 2: demonstrations of SED members against Egon Krenz. December 3: the Politburo and the Central Committee of the SED resign in their entirety; hundreds of thousands of people participate in a "human chain" across the GDR to support a "democratic renewal." December 4: the CDU leaves the National Front (the unity list of parties); the SPD suggests May 6, 1990, as the date for new elections. December 5: house arrest of Honecker and others; LDPD leaves the National Front. December 6: Krenz resigns his state offices; police take control of Stasi buildings to prevent the further destruction of files and documents (Hollitzer, 1996). December 7: beginning of the "round table" discussions of all the political and social groups seeking to reform the GDR (Elster, 1996). December 8: arrest of Mielke, Stoph, Kleiber, and Krolikowski; special party congress of the SED. December 9: election of Gregor Gysi as head of the SED. Rest of December: massive demonstrations; more resignations and arrests; Lothar de Maiziere elected chair of the CDU; SED changes its name to PDS (Party of Democratic Socialism) (Links & Bahrmann, 1990, 211–223).

The new year brought the dissolution of the GDR. The early months saw much activity on the part of the old, reconstituted parties and the newly funded political parties in preparation for the March elections[48] (advanced from May). The government of the FRG announced that during the year 1989 a total of 343,854 GDR citizens moved to West Germany. There also was a further increase of movements to the West, about 2,000 per day in 1990. February 1: Modrow presents a statement about "the way to German unity." February 6: the government of the FRG announces its willingness to immediately enter into negotiations with the GDR regarding a common currency and common economic organization. February 10: Kohl and Gorbachev meet in Moscow to discuss German reunification (the USSR demands massive German economic aid, and gets it (Pond, 1993, 223). February 14: the foreign secretaries of the United States of America, USSR, Great Britain, France, FRG, and GDR agree to the "four-plus-two" formula to discuss the international aspects of reunification. March 18: *Volkskammer* elections (results are found in Chapter 3). April 12: election of de Maiziere as head of GDR government. May 4: currency union (most of the exchange of East marks to West marks at a completely unrealistic rate of 1:1; 1:4 would have been more appropriate) (Dietz, 1991, 4). May 6: local elections in the GDR. The numerous negotiations between FRG and GDR and between the FRG and other countries need not be listed here. Several excellent volumes deal with them in detail (e.g., Zelikow & Rice, 1995). In July Kohl obtained Gorbachev consent to an all-German North American Treaty Organization (NATO) membership. On October 3, 1990, the Federal Republic of Germany finally absorbed the German Democratic Republic.[49] More than forty years of division and of the communist experiment on German soil had come to an end.[50]

AFTERMATH

The price of unification was high. Externally, it meant the acceptance of the massive loss of German territories to other countries, especially Poland and Czechoslovakia. Kohl's willingness to abandon German rights to these territories touched on treason (for related discussions, see Fisch, 2001, 180; Moeller, 1995). Internally, it committed the old states of the FRG to massive economic aid to the new states.[51] Since 1990 billions of dollars have been transferred to the new states. While this has caused a clear drop in the living standards of the old states, it has not been enough, unfortunately, to solve the former GDR's economic problems (Fisch, 2001, 180). Many enterprises were not viable (particularly not in the context of international competition) and had to be closed (Dietz, 1991, 1–2). As a result, there is large-scale unemployment in the East—a novel experience for the people of East Germany (Keck, 1991, 59–86; see also Gerdes et al., 1997; Windolf et al., 1999). While few East Germans want a return of the communist regime, many miss its social security aspects. Never before did they have to look for jobs or for housing by themselves.[52]

Altogether, reunification has not been a happy experience. The people in the West are not pleased with the sacrifices they had to make (particularly since they have received very little thanks for them). The people in the East are resentful that they have not yet achieved the same degree of prosperity as the West, which, it must be said, West German politicians (Kohl) led them to believe would be theirs in no time[53] (Meuschel, 1992, 335). Most of the difficulties could have been foreseen. It would have been more sensible to proceed at a slower pace. But Kohl's ambition was to be a second Bismarck, the chancellor of reunification. When the opportunity arose, it seemed important not to squander it, and speed became very important in Kohl's mind.

West and East Germans, more than ten years after reunification, are not happy with each other. The East Germans in particular are resentful and bitter.[54] Some feel that their revolution was kidnapped by Western capitalism, when, in fact, it was supposed to lead to a "reformed" socialism (Hecht, 1991; Schneider, 1990; Schreiter, 1990). From the East German perspective, the West Germans always *had* it better, and in postunification they conducted themselves as if they *were* better. It is true that many West Germans feel superior, but the East German inferiority complex does its part in disturbing the East–West relations. The West Germans—not without cause—find the East German whining irritating and annoying. They would rather see some more gratitude for the very substantial sacrifices that they have made and are still making. In my judgment, it will take at least one complete generational turnover before truly harmonious relations will come into being and East and West will no longer have the border "in their heads."[55] Then East and West Germans may indeed be one people again; and they may decide that it all has been worth it.

NOTES

1. The topics of this chapter are well and widely known. Thus, we can be quite brief, highlighting only certain aspects of the refugee difficulties and the final demise of the GDR. Again, bibliographical citations are provided for further investigation.

2. It has been estimated that on average 13,000 persons left East Germany *legally* each year (Scharf, 1984, 15, 182; see also Grunert-Bronnen, 1970, 7–8; Schneider, 1978, 28; Schenck, 1962).

3. The official explanation for the lack of a right to emigrate was that an emigration right is not needed in the GDR since the socialist social system, for the first time in history, guarantees social security, safety, and free and unrestricted personal development to all human beings (Kuhrt, 1996a, 12).

4. Of which about 2.6 million escaped before the Wall was built. Between one-half and three-quarters of a million escaped even after the Wall—at very high risk (Pucher, 1984, 228).

5. The border region also saw the measure of "forced evacuation" (*Zwangsaussiedlung*), whereby the inhabitants of about a three-mile-wide strip of land next to the border were forced to leave their houses and farms. They were given no warning. Police simply showed up in the early morning and told them that they had to leave. They could take along very little. They were moved to substandard habitations in the interior of the GDR. The major evacuations took place in 1952 and 1961 (Mayer, 2002, 19–20). The fear of the regime was, obviously, that people living close to the border would find a way to cross it.

6. It appears that Khruschev briefly considered a blockade of the Western air corridors as an alternative to the Wall. It was dropped because of its potential of a real conflict with the United States of America (Spittmann, 1981, 385).

7. The GDR official declaration was that every country has the right to protect its borders (Wechsberg, 1964, 17).

8. The length of the sentences differed over time. The applicable laws were changed several times. For an account of one case of "fleeing the republic," see Oesterreich, 1988.

9. The GDR order to shoot at persons trying to cross the border dates from the late 1940s. Also, in 1947, the Soviet border troops had orders to shoot (Koop, 1996, 8–9).

10. This was due not only to the deliberate fire of the border police but also to the more than 1 million mines and thousands of automatic shooting devices installed at the border. Children counted prominently among the victims (Koop, 1996, 7, 337–350).

11. In fact, while the GDR had accepted emigration for two "humanitarian" purposes, namely, "uniting families" and permitting pensioners to leave (i.e., shifting the burden of pension payment for retirees to the FRG). All other applications for emigration, however, were regarded as illegal acts and criminalized (Kuhrt, 1996a, 18).

12. In fact, Ulbricht called it a form of "slave trade" (*Menschenhandel*) (Dowty, 1987, 123). The regime went as far as to publish fictional kidnapping stories, for example, the tale of the railroad cook Ferworm, who claimed to have been made unconscious via a menthol cigarette and then carried off (Natter, 1994, 26).

13. The regime, however, held that the family was of primary importance for the happiness of GDR citizens (Kuhrig, 1985).

14. Which is not to say, however, that all of the SED functionaries did not recognize the need for reforms (Uschner, 1995, 15).

15. A majority of the dissidents thought of reforming, rather than replacing, socialism (Philipsen, 1993, 12). Reunification did not emerge as the overwhelming goal until November 1989. As Richter (1995a, 14) correctly remarks, the initial goal of the "revolutionaries" was not revolution but democratic reform. Still in November, GDR intellectuals and artists published an appeal to preserve a separate GDR. The appeals gathered 1,167,048 signatures (Prokop, 1994, 23).

16. Accommodation, however, should not be confused with acceptance, as did McKenna (1988, 89), when he wrote that most East Germans "have accepted the Communist regime that was forced on them."

17. Even children as young as fourteen were sought out to work for the Stasi (Schell & Kalinka, 1991, 121).

18. There were occasional periods when the regime would grant permission to improve its image and to get rid of troublemakers. One such period was the spring of 1984, when more than 25,000 persons were given permission to leave (Mayer, 2002, 13).

19. Peter Fechter, an eighteen-year-old construction worker, did not make it. He had already overcome most of the barriers associated with the Berlin Wall. At the last barrier he was shot by the border police. For nearly an hour he lay on East German territory, moaning and crying for help. He could have been reached from the West. The American lieutenant on duty, however, decided: "It's not my problem." As a con-

sequence U.S. troops were booed for the first time in West Berlin. Fechter bled to death. The East German border police were in no hurry to assist him (Gelb, 1986, 269–270). It appears that the last person shot to death at the Berlin Wall was Chris Gueffroy, on February 6, 1989 (Maier, 1997, 320).

20. It has been estimated that between 1961 and 1989 about 75,000 persons were imprisoned because they sought to leave the GDR without authorization; and nearly 1,000 persons were killed while trying to cross the border (Mayer, 2002, 27).

21. The Stasi records on Biermann consist of sixty-nine volumes. At least 194 Stasi employees were active in the Biermann case, as well as 210 Stasi informers.

22. On the expatriation of Uwe Johnson, see Grunert-Bronnen, 1970. On the expatriation of Rudolf Bahro, see Herzberg & Seifert, 2002. General discussions of the expatriation practice can be found in Finn & Julius, 1983; Guestrow, 1983; Grunert-Bronnen, 1970; Minnerup, 1982; Scharf, 1984; Wassmund, 1981; Wolfe, 1992.

23. In fact, some could not resist the pressure and withdrew their signatures.

24. Former federal president Walter Scheel (1986) could ask just a few years before reunification whether there was anyone who was still pained by the division of Germany.

25. The Germanophobia of some left-leaning West Germans was extraordinary; among them must be counted Günter Grass (1990), Jürgen Habermas, Walter Jens, and Erich Kuby. They, of course, were strongly opposed to reunification, though one suspects they would not have minded if the FRG had become part of the GDR—under the glorious leadership of comrade Honecker. For a general discussion, see Winckler, 1992, 494–499.

26. For some data on the real conditions of the GDR, see Statistisches Bundesamt, 1990.

27. For some considerations, see Wilhelmi, 1996, who regards the collapse as *rätselhaft* (puzzling).

28. Gerhard Schuerer, the head of the Planning Commission, on October 24, 1989, submitted to the Politburo an economic analysis that concluded that simply stopping the growth of the amount of foreign debt would cause a reduction in GDR living standards of 25 to 30% and make the country ungovernable (Prokop, 1994, 20).

29. As late as September 21, 1989, the Interior Ministry refused to license the "New Forum," one of the new civic groups, because it was, so the ministry decided, "state-hostile" (Prokop, 1994, 13). The SED, however, determined that the Ministry should also explain to the unsuccessful applicants that "there was no societal need for an alliance of the type proposed; there already were many organizations in the GDR, who look after the political and social interests of the people" (Gysi & Falkner, 1990, 11).

30. For a listing, see Anonymous, 1990. It is particularly interesting to note that the membership of some of these groups tended heavily toward Stasi informers (Wilhelmy, 1995, 16).

31. A matter at which the Germans are singularly without talent.

32. For some general discussion of the collapse of the GDR (in addition to volumes cited already, e.g., Joas & Kohli, 1993; Keck, 1991; Lasky, 1992; Leonhard, 1990; Links & Bahrmann, 1990; Maier, 1997; Merkl, 1993; Mitter & Wolle, 1993; Pond, 1993; Rein, 1990; Reissig & Glaessner, 1991; Schueddekopf, 1990; Villain, 1990; Zelikow & Rice, 1995), see Hertle & Stephan, 1997; Loew, 1993; McFalls, 1995; Plock, 1993; Stephan, 1994; see also Coleman, 1996.

33. However, already on August 19, about 600 GDR citizens had crossed from Hungary into Austria (Keck, 1991, 113).

34. Opposition social democrat Horst Ehmke, an old partisan of Ostpolitik, attacked the Kohl government on August 15 for having aggravated the crisis *by welcoming the refugees* (Zelikow, 1995, 66).

35. The Soviets had more pressing problems with Poland at the time. There also was turmoil in the Baltic states, as well as in several of the other Soviet republics, for example, the Moldavian, the Georgian, and the Ukrainian republics. But the failure of Gorbachev to aid the GDR in bringing to an end the escape of East Germans via assorted socialist countries certainly was an important factor leading to the dissolution of the GDR.

36. This surely was an absurd idea. As will be seen, it caused only further turmoil in the GDR.

37. A leading SED functionary insisted (post-1989) that the Stasi was not a manifestation of distrust of the people but that its purpose was to protect the people. He did, however, concede that there was a "total intolerance of those who thought differently" (Vietzke, 1992, 145–146).

38. September 7 saw a massive deployment of police and Stasi, which blocked the Alexander-Platz. Only about 200 persons succeeded in entering the square. They were met with exorbitant force. There were many serious injuries. Most of the participants, who had been entirely peaceful, were arrested and taken to the Stasi prison in Rummelsburg (Schueddekopf, 1990, 27–28).

39. Already in 1987, Honecker had received Soviet signals that unification was a possibility. He did not take them seriously (Prokop, 1994, 7; see also Winkelmann, 1992).

40. For others, it was a revolution of a "new type." See Neubert, 1990.

41. There were many other demonstrations in early October. Some examples: October 9: Dresden, 22,000; Plauen, 10,000; Magdeburg, 4,100; Halle, 1,100; October 13: Rostock, 5,000; Erfurt, 850; October 15: Jena, 2,200; Suhl, 1,800. Even small communities saw demonstrations with just a few hundred participants, which took tremendous courage, because they were easily identified by the ever-present Stasi (Mitter & Wolle, 1993, 536).

42. Of course, what Harich and others overlooked was that the social policies (social security expenditures) of the GDR were coming to an end, one way or the other. As Guenter Schabowski admitted: "For forty years we have pursued social policies which we could not afford; they dragged us into bankruptcy" (Pohl, 1999, 34).

43. Many of the original civil rights activists, whether socialist or not, have expressed a strong dissatisfaction with the postunification conditions in East Germany. See, for example, Bollinger, 1999; Eckert & Faulenbach, 1996; Fritze, 1993; Gehrke & Rueddenklau, 1999; Glaser, 1990; Grimm, 1993; Juergs, 1997; Reich, 1996; Richter, 1998; Wieschiolek, 1999.

44. It will be remembered that the regime (particularly in the person of Egon Krenz, soon to be Honecker's successor) had praised the "Chinese solution."

45. Toward the end of the GDR, even basic goods, which previously had been in good supply, had become scarce.

46. The GDR reaction was sharp: any talk about an "open German question" was an attempt of West German imperialism and capitalism to undermine the socialist nations with demagogic and revanchist talk. There was no "open German question"

(Koch, 1989, 274–275). Not all of the foreign powers and leaders were happy either; one thinks particularly of Margaret Thatcher. For a comprehensive review of foreign concerns, see Schulz & Danylow, 1985. For a report of the diplomatic efforts, see Szabo, 1992.

47. Landgrebe (1999) has published an interesting collection of eyewitness reports regarding the fall of the Berlin Wall.

48. For a description of the nearly forty groups and parties, see Anonymous, 1990.

49. Numerous volumes of commentary by former GDR leaders have been published. Most of them are predominantly exculpatory; some of them are exercises in denial. Here are some examples: Apel, 2000; Axen, 1992; Corvalan-Honecker, 2001; Fricke, 1993; Kessler, 1996; Krenz, 1999, 2000; Schabowski, 1991, 1994; Schalck-Golokowski, 2000. A compendium of the postunification careers/fates of 100 GDR leaders can be found in Zimmermann, 1994.

50. The story of that experiment would fit well with Koestler's *The God That Failed.*

51. As was seen earlier, also to the USSR.

52. Here are some examples of critical voices, most of them close to the PDS: Bechert, 1999; Brie, 1996; Gysi, 1995, 2000, 2001; Luft, 1999; Wedel, 1996; Uschner, 1995; Zadek & Zadek, 1998. On the dangers associated with the PDS as a continuation of the SED, see Koschyk & Weiss, 1996.

53. In Kohl's famous phrase: "All will be better off, no one will be worse off." De Maiziere (GDR chief of government) used very much the same words (Hauser, et al., 1996, 10–11). Some East Germans, in the meantime, have adopted the rejection motto of a "West German imperialism" (Decker, 1989).

54. Here are some commentaries on the East German mind-set: Baroth, 1994; Bellers & Bellers, 1997; Decker & Decker, 2000; Dieckmann, 1999; Engler, 1999; Herles, 1990; Hildebrand & Sello, 1995; Hochhuth, 1993; Kopielski et al., 1990; Kuczynski, 1999; Leidecker, 1991; Mackat, 2000; Marcuse, 1991; Rosenlöcher, 1997; Scherzer, 1997; Schneider, 1991a, 1991b; Schroeder, 2000; Segert & Zierke, 2000; Zeller, 2000.

55. The famous "mental wall," which came to replace the Berlin Wall (Betts & Eghigian, 2003, 193). For an early and relatively optimistic account of the future of the all-German economy see, Smyser, 1992. Not all of the prognosis has turned out to be correct.

Bibliography

Abele, Johannes (2000): KERNKRAFT IN DER DDR. Hannah-Arendt-Institut.

Adomeit, Hannes (1991): Gorbachev and German Unification: Revision of Thinking, Realignment of Power. Alexander Dallin & Gail W. Lapidus, eds.: THE SOVIET SYSTEM IN CRISIS. Westview Press.

Agde, Guenter (1994): SACHSENHAUSEN BEI BERLIN. Aufbau Verlag.

Agde, Guenter (2000): KAHLSCHLAG. Aufbau Taschenbuch Verlag.

Agsten, Rudolf et al. (1985): LDPD 1945 BIS 1961: IM FESTEN BÜNDNIS MIT DER ARBEITERKLASSE UND IHRER PARTEI. Buchverlag Der Morgen.

Ahrberg, Edda (1996): MIT GESTUTZTEN FLÜGELN: JUGEND IN DER DDR. Landesbeauftragter Sachsen-Anhalt.

Ahrends, Klaus & Hans Luft (1988): Genossenschaften in der DDR. 43 EINHEIT 894–899.

Akademie für Gesellschaftswissenschaften beim ZK der SED (1981): BÜNDNISPOLITK IM SOZIALISMUS. Dietz Verlag.

Alexandrov, I. (1977): THE RIGHTS AND FREEDOMS OF SOVIET CITIZENS. Novosti Press Agency.

Almond, Gabriel A. (1954): THE APPEALS OF COMMUNISM. Princeton University Press.

Alsmeier, Bernd (1994): WEGBEREITER DER WENDE: DIE ROLLE DER EVANGELISCHEN KIRCHE IN DER AUSGANGSPHASE DER DDR. Centaurus Verlag.

Alter, Peter (1992): Nationalism and German Politics after 1945. John Breuilly, ed.: THE STATE OF GERMANY. Longman.

Amos, Heike (1996): JUSTIZVERWALTUNG IN DER SBZ/DDR: PERSONAL POLITIK 1945 BIS ANFANG DER 50er JAHRE. Böhlau Verlag.

Andert, Reinhold (2001): NACH DEM STURZ: GESPRÄCHE MIT ERICH HONECKER. Faber & Faber.

Andert, Reinhold & Wolfgang Herzberg (1990): DER STURZ: ERICH HONECKER IM KREUZVERHÖR. Aufbau Verlag.

Anonymous (1990): POLITISCHE PARTEIEN UND BEWEGUNGEN DER DDR: ÜBER SICH SELBST. Staatsverlag.

Ansorg, Leonore (1997): KINDER IM KLASSENKAMPF. Akademie Verlag.

Ansorg, Leonore & Renate Huertgen (1999): The Myth of Female Emancipation. Konrad H. Jarausch, ed.: DICTATORSHIP AS EXPERIENCE. Berghahn Books.

Apel, Hans (1967): Wie sie es sehen. 19:1222 DER MONAT 15–23 (March).

Apel, Hans (2000): ZERSTÖRTE ILLUSIONEN. Deutsche Verlags-Anstalt.

Ardagh, John (1987): GERMANY AND THE GERMANS. Harper & Row.

Arndt Verlag (1997): ALLIIERTE KRIEGSVERBRECHEN UND VERBRECHEN GEGEN DIE MENSCHLICHKEIT. [Zusammengestellt und bezeugt im Jahre 1946 von Internierten des Lagers 91 Darmstadt] Arndt Verlag.

Arnold, Karl-Heinz (1995): SCHILD UND SCHWERT. Edition Ost.

Aron, Raymond (1977): IN DEFENSE OF DECADENT. EUROPE. Regnery.

Ascherson, Neal (1967): Progress, Not Politics. NEW YORK REVIEW OF BOOKS March 9.

Ash, Timothy G. (1993): IN EUROPE'S NAME: GERMANY AND THE DIVIDED CONTINENT. Random House.

Autorenkollektiv (1968): LEITUNGSTÄTIGKEIT UND PÄDAGOGIK. Staatsverlag.

Autorenkollektiv (1977): WHAT IS LIFE LIKE IN THE GDR? Verlag Zeit im Bild.

Autorenkollektiv (1978a): DDR: GESELLSCHAFT, STAAT, BÜRGER. 2d ed. Staatsverlag.

Autorenkollektiv (1978b): GESCHICHTE DER SOZIALISTISCHEN EINHEITSPARTEI DEUTSCHLANDS. Dietz Verlag.

Autorenkollektiv (1980): DIE GESELLSCHAFTLICHEN ORGANISATIONEN IN DER DDR. Staatsverlag.

Autorenkollektiv (1984): DDR: BÜRGERINTERESSEN ALS STAATSPOLITIK. Staatsverlag.

Autorenkollektiv (1985a): SOZIALISTISCHE ORIENTIERUNG NATIONAL BEFREITER STAATEN. Staatsverlag.

Autorenkollektiv (1985b): DIE TOTALITARISMUS-DOKTRIN IM ANTIKOMMUNISMUS. Dietz Verlag.

Autorenkollektiv (1985c): ZEHN JAHRE FREUNDSCHAFTSVERTRAG DDR-UdSSR. Staatsverlag.

Autorenkollektiv (1987): KOMBINATE ALS RÜCKGRAT SOZIALISTISCHER PLANWIRTSCHFT. Friedrich-Schiller-Universität Jena.

Axen, Hermann (1989): FASCISM AND MILITARISM HAVE BEEN AND REMAIN EXTERMINATED FOR EVER IN THE GDR. Panorama-DDR.

Axen, Hermann (1992): ICH WAR EIN DIENER DER PARTEI. Edition Ost.

Bacque, James (1999): DER GEPLANTE TOD: DEUTSCHE KRIEGSGEFANGENE IN AMERIKANISCHEN UND FRANZÖSICHEN LAGERN 1945–1946. Ullstein.

Bacque, James (2002): VERSCHWIEGENE SCHULD: DIE ALLIERTE BESATZUNGSPOLITIK IN DEUTSCHLAND NACH 1945. Pour le Merite Verlag.

Badstuebner, Evemarie, ed. (2000): BEFREMDLICH ANDERS: LEBEN IN DER DDR. Karl Dietz Verlag.

Baestlein, Klaus (2002): DER FALL MIELKE. Nomos Verlag.

Bahro, Rudolf (1977): DIE ALTERNATIVE: ZUR KRITIK DES REAL EXISTIERENDEN SOZIALISMUS. Europäische Verlagsanstalt.

Baras, Victor (1975): Beria's Fall and Ulbricht's Survival. 27 SOVIET STUDIES 381–395.

Baring, Arnulf (1972): UPRISING IN EAST GERMANY: JUNE 17, 1953. Cornell University Press.

Baring, Arnulf (1983): DER 17. JUNI 1953. Deutsche Verlags-Anstalt.

Barm, Werner (1971): TOTALE ABGRENZUNG: ZEHN JAHRE UNTER ULBRICHT, HONECKER UND STOPH AN DER INNERDEUTSCHEN GRENZE. Seewald Verlag.

Barnouw, Dagmar (1996): GERMANY 1945: VIEWS OF WAR AND VIOLENCE. Indiana University Press.

Baroth, Hans Dieter (1994): ABER JETZT IST ÜBERALL WESTEN. Dietz Verlag.

Bartel, Horst (1981): A Modern View of Prussia. 81:4 PRISMA 90.

Bartel, Horst & Walter Schmidt (1984): Sozialismus und historisches Erbe in der DDR. 39 EINHEIT 111–116.

Bastian, Uwe (1996): GREENPEACE IN DER DDR. Edition Ost.

Bath, Matthias (1981): GEFANGEN UND FREIGETAUSCHT: 1197 TAGE ALS FLUCHTHELFER IN DDR-HAFT. Olzog.

Bauer, Raymond (1954): The Bolshevik Attitude toward Science. Carl J. Friedrich, ed.: TOTALITARIANISM. Harvard University Press.

Bauer, Rudolf (1960): Der Beitrag der Schule zur Entwicklung des sozialistischen Staatsbewusstseins. Institut für Philosophie der Humboldt-Universität Berlin: DER STAAT SIND WIR: BEITRÄGE ZU PROBLEMEN DER ENTWICKLUNG DES SOZIALISTISCHEN STAATSBEWUSSTSEINS IN DER DDR. Dietz Verlag.

Bavarius, Nikolaus (1990): DDR-DEUTSCH. Tomus Verlag.

Baylis, Thomas A. (1971): Economic Reform as Ideology: East Germany's New Economic System. 3 COMPARATIVE POLITICS 211–229.

Baylis, Thomas A. (1972): East Germany: In Quest of Legitimacy. 21 PROBLEMS OF COMMUNISM 46–55.

Baylis, Thomas A. (1974): THE EAST GERMAN ELITE AND THE TECHNOCRATIC INTELLIGENTSIA. University of California Press.

Baylis, Thomas A. (1987): "PERFECTING" THE PLANNING MECHANISM: THE POLITICS OF INCREMENTAL REFORM IN THE GDR. Paper delivered at the Annual Meeting of the American Political Science Association.

Baylis, Thomas A. (1989): Leadership Structures and Leadership Politics in Hungary and the GDR. David Childs et al., eds.: EAST GERMANY IN COMPARATIVE PERSPECTIVE. Routledge.

Bechert, Robert (1999): DIE GESCHEITERTE REVOLUTION. Babol-Druck.

Bechtoldt, Heinrich (1988): Parallels and Differentiations of Reforms in Peking and Moscow. 39 AUSSENPOLITIK 125–137.

Becker, Arnold (1999): JUGENDWEIHE. Haag & Herchen Verlag.

Beckert, Rudi (1995): DIE ERSTE UND LETZTE INSTANZ: SCHAU- UND GEHEIMPROZESSE VOR DEM OBERSTEN GERICHT DER DDR. Keip Verlag.

Behnke, Klaus & Juergen Fuchs, eds. (1995): ZERSETZUNG DER SEELE: PSYCHOLOGIE UND PSYCHIATRY IM DIENSTE DER STASI. Rotbuch Verlag.

Behnke, Klaus & Juergen Wolf, eds. (1998): STASI AUF DEM SCHULHOF. Ullstein Verlag.

Behr, Hermann (1961): FROM CHAOS ZUM STAAT. Verlag Frankfurter Bücher.

Behr, Wolfgang (1985a): BUNDESREPUBLIK DEUTSCHLAND—DEUTSCHE DEMOKRATISCHE REPUBLIK: SYSTEMVERGLEICH. 2d ed. Kohlhammer.

Behr, Wolfgang (1985b): Politische Willensbildung. Eckhard Jesse, ed.: BUNDESREPUBLIK DEUTSCHLAND UND DEUTSCHE DEMOKRATISCHE REPUBLIK. 4th ed. Colloquium Verlag.

Behrends, Jan C. et al., eds. (2003): FREMDE UND FREMD-SEIN IN DER DDR. Metropol Verlag.

Behrens, Fritz (1958): EINIGE FRAGEN DER ÖKONOMISCHEN ENTWICKLUNG IM LICHTE DER GROSSEN SOZIALISTISCHEN OKTOBERREVOLUTION. Akademie-Verlag.

Behrens, Fritz (1965): NEUES ÖKONOMISCHES SYSTEM. Verlag Der Wirtschaft.

Bellers, Anni & Juergen Bellers (1997): DIE DDR TICKT WEITER: WIE DIE OSTDEUTSCHEN DENKEN. AT Edition.

Belwe, Katharina (1979): MITWIRKUNG IM INDUSTRIEBETRIEB DER DDR. Westdeutscher Verlag.

Benda, Julien (1955): THE BETRAYAL OF THE INTELLECTUALS. Beacon Press.

Bender, Peter (1986): NEUE OSTPOLITIK: VOM MAUERBAU BIS ZUM MOSKAUER VERTRAG. DTV.

Bender, Peter (1992): UNSERE ERBSCHAFT: WAS WAR DIE DDR, WAS BLEIBT VON IHR? Luchterhand.

Bendix, Reinhard (1969): NATION-BUILDING AND CITIZENSHIP. Doubleday.

Benser, Guenter (2000): DDR: GEDENKT IHRER MIT NACHSICHT. Karl Dietz Verlag.

Bentzien, Hans (2003): WAS GESCHAH AM 17. JUNI? Edition Ost.

Benz, Wolfgang (1984): VON DER BESATZUNGSHERRSCHAFT ZUR BUNDESREPUBLIK: STATIONEN EINER STAATSGRÜNDUNG, 1946–1949. Fischer Verlag.

Berg, Hermann v. (1988): VORBEUGENDE UNTERWERFUNG. Universitas Verlag.

Bergmann-Weinberg, Marie-Louise von (1987): WOHLFAHRT, LEBENSNIVEAU UND LEBENSWEISE IM DEUTSCH-DEUTSCHEN VERGLEICH. Swedish School of Economics and Business Administration at Helsingfors.

Bergson, Abram (1989): PLANNING AND PERFORMANCE IN SOCIALIST ECONOMIES. Unwin Hyman.

Besier, Gerhard (1993): DER SED-STAAT UND DIE KIRCHE: DER WEG IN DIE ANPASSUNG. Bertelsmann Verlag.

Bethkenhagen, Jochen et al. (1980): Über den Zusammenhang von ausserwirtschaftlichen Interessen der DDR und Entspannung. EDITION DEUTSCHLAND ARCHIV 3–17.

Betts, Paul & Greg Eghigian, eds. (2003): PAIN AND PROSPERITY. Stanford University Press.

Beyme, Klaus v. & Hartmut Zimmermann (1985): Introduction. Beyme, Klaus v. & Hartmut Zimmermann, eds.: POLICYMAKING IN THE GERMAN DEMOCRATIC REPUBLIC. St. Martin's Press.

Bialas, Wolfgang (1996): VOM UNFREIEN SCHWEBEN ZUM FREIEN FALL. OSTDEUTSCHE INTELLEKTUELLE IM GESELLSCHAFTLICHEN UMBRUCH. Fischer Verlag.

Bibic, Adolf (1970): CIVIL SOCIETY AND THE STATE IN THE WORK OF HEGEL AND MARX. Paper delivered at the World Congress of the International Political Science Association, Munich, Germany.

Biehler, Gernot (1994): DIE BODENKOMFISKATIONEN IN DER SOWJETISCHEN BESATZUNGSZONE DEUTSCHLANDS 1945 NACH WIEDERHERSTELLUNG DER GESAMTDEUTSCHEN RECHTSORDNUNG 1990. Duncker & Humblot.

Bielefelder, Kunstverein (1997): TOTALITÄRE KUNST—KUNST IM TOTALITARISMUS: BEISPIELE AUS DEM NS-STAAT UND DER DDR. Pendragon Verlag.

Bielke, Brigitte (1997): Wahlenthaltung führt zur Stasi-Haft. Juergen Aretz & Wolfgang Stock, eds.: DIE VERGESSENEN OPFER DER DDR. Bastei Verlag.

Billerbeck, Liane v. (1999): GENERATION OST. Ch. Links Verlag.

Bittighoefer, Bernd & Juergen Schmollack, eds. (1968): MORAL UND GESELLSCHAFT. Dietz Verlag.

Bleek, Wilhelm & Lothar Mertens (1994): DDR-DISSERTATIONEN. Westdeutscher Verlag.

Bley, Gotthold & Frohmut Mueller (1979): Gesetzlichkeit und Leitungstätigkeit im Leninschen Sinne. 33 NEUE JUSTIZ 389–391.

Bloch, Peter (1986): ZWISCHEN HOFFNUNG UND RESIGNATION: ALS CDU-POLITIKER IN BRANDENBURG, 1945–1950. Verlag für Wirtschaft und Politik.

Bobkov, F. (1987): Vigilance: A Demand of the Times. 26 SOVIET LAW AND GOVERNMENT 66–79.

Bolling, Landrum (1950): Zone of Silence. Arthur Settel, ed.: THIS IS GERMANY. Sloane.

Bollinger, Stefan (1996): KONFLIKTE, KRISEN UND POLITISCHE STABILITÄT: GEDANKEN ZUR HISTORISCHEN UNFÄHIGKEIT EINES REALSOZIALISTISCHEN KONFLIKTMANAGEMENTS. Gesellschaftwissenschaftliches Forum.

Bollinger, Stefan (1999): 1989: EINE ABGEBROCHENE REVOLUTION. Trafo Verlag.

Bollinger, Stefan & Fritz Vilmar, eds. (2002): DIE DDR WAR ANDERS. Forschungsgruppe Kritische Analyse.

Borgwardt, Angela (2002): IM UMGANG MIT DER MACHT. Westdeutscher Verlag.

Bos, Ellen (1993): LESERBRIEFE IN TAGESZEITUNGEN DER DDR. Westdeutscher Verlag.

Bothe, Matthias (1983): Die Acht-Stunden-Ideologie. Gerhard Finn & Liselotte Julius, eds.: VON DEUTSCHLAND NACH DEUTSCHLAND. Verlag für Wirtschaft und Politik.

Bouvier, Beatrix (1996): AUSGESCHALTET: SOZIALDEMOKRATEN IN DER SOWJETISCHEN BESATZUBGSZONE UND IN DER DDR 1945–1953. Verlag Dietz Nachfolger.

Bouvier, Beatrix W. & Horst-Peter Schulz (1991): DIE SPD ABER AUFGEHÖRT HAT ZU EXISTIEREN: SOZIALDEMOKRATEN UNTER SOWJETISCHER BESATZUNG. Verlag Dietz Nachfolger.

Boyer, Christoph & Peter Skyba, eds. (1999): REPRESSION UND WOHLSTANDSVERSPRECHEN. Hannah-Arendt-Institut.

Brandis, Udo (1974): Politische Bildung in beiden Teilen Deutschlands. 7 DEUTSCHLAND ARCHIV 527–542.

Brandt, Hans-Juergen (1983): DIE KANDIDATENAUFSTELLUNG ZU DEN VOLKSKAMMERWAHLEN DER DDR. Nomos Verlag.

Brandt, Hans-Juergen & Martin Dinges (1984): KADERPOLITIK UND KADERARBEIT IN DEN "BÜRGERLICHEN" PARTEIEN UND DEN MASSENORGANIZATIONEN IN DER DDR. Berlin Verlag.

Brant, Stefan (1957): THE EAST GERMAN RISING: 17th JUNE 1953. Praeger.

Braun, Johannes (1994): MENSCHEN UND MÄCHTE IN DER DDR. Mecke Verlag.

Braun, Johannes (1996): MEIN LEBEN MIT DEN SOCIALISTEN. Mecke Verlag.

Breslauer, George W. (1991): Is the Soviet System Transformable? The Perennial Question. George W. Breslauer, ed.: DILEMMAS OF TRANSITION IN THE SOVIET UNION AND EASTERN EUROPE. University of California, Center for Slavic and East European Studies.

Brie, Andre (1996): ICH TAUCHE NICHT AB. Edition Ost.

Brinks, Jan Hermann (1992): DIE DDR-GESCHICHTSWISSENSCHAFT AUF DEM WEG ZUR DEUTSCHEN EINHEIT: LUTHER, FRIEDRICH II UND BISMARCK ALS PARADIGMEN POLITISCHEN WANDELS. Campus Verlag.

Brinks, Jan Hermann (2000): CHILDREN OF A NEW FATHERLAND: GERMANY'S POST-WAR RIGHT-WING POLITICS. Tauris Publishers.

Brinks, Jan Hermann (2001): PARADIGMS OF POLITICAL CHANGE: LUTHER, FREDERICK II, AND BISMARCK. Marquette University Press.

Brodersen, Ingke, ed. (1990): DER PROZESS GEGEN WALTER JANKA UND ANDERE. Rowohlt Verlag.

Bronner, Stephen E. (1987): ROSA LUXEMBURG: A REVOLUTIONARY FOR OUR TIMES. Columbia University Press.

Bruce, Gary (2003): RESISTANCE WITH THE PEOPLE. Rowman & Littlefield.

Brueckl, Hans (2001): ZWISCHEN BRAUN UND ROT: DER VERORDNETE ANTIFASCHISMUS DER DDR. Edition La Colombe.

Bruns, Wilhelm (1989): VON DER DEUTSCHLAND-POLITIK ZUR DDR-POLITIK? Leske & Budrich.

Bryson, Phillip J. (1971): Liberal Socialism *ohne* Market: Price Reform in the German Democratic Republic. 5 EAST EUROPEAN QUARTERLY 393–405.

Bryson, Phillip J. (1987): PLANNING REFINEMENTS AND COMBINE FORMATION IN EAST GERMAN ECONOMIC "INTENSIFICATION." Center for Russian and East European Studies, University of Pittsburgh.

Bryson, Phillip J. (1989): Enterprise and Association in Soviet Planning: Comparisons with the East German Experience. David Childs et al., eds.: EAST GERMANY IN COMPARATIVE PERSPECTIVE. Routledge.

Bryson, Phillip J. (1995): THE RELUCTANT RETREAT: THE SOVIET AND EAST GERMAN DEPARTURE FROM CENTRAL PLANNING. Dartmouth Publishing Co.

Bryson, Phillip J. & Manfred Melzer (1987): The Kombinat in GDR Economic Organization. Ian Jeffries & Manfred Melzer, eds.: THE EAST GERMAN ECONOMY. Croom Helm.

Bryson, Phillip J. & Manfred Melzer (1991): THE END OF THE EAST GERMAN ECONOMY: FROM HONECKER TO REUNIFICATION. St. Martin's Press.

Brzeski, Andrzej (1970): Social Engineering and Realpolitik in Communist Economic Reorganization. Gregory Grossman, ed.: ESSAYS IN SOCIALISM AND PLANNING IN HONOR OF CARL LANDAUER. Prentice-Hall.

Brzezinski, Zbigniew (1965): ALTERNATIVE TO PARTITION. McGraw-Hill.

Brzezinski, Zbigniew (1968): The Soviet Political System: Transformation or Degeneration? Henry S. Albinski & Lawrence K. Pettit, eds.: EUROPEAN POLITICAL PROCESSES. Allyn & Bacon.

Buch, Guenther (1982): NAMEN UND DATEN WICHTIGER PERSONEN DER DDR. 3d ed. Dietz Verlag.

Buchholz, Erich (1989): Gesellschaftliche Gerichte und sozialistischer Staat. 75 ARCHIV FÜR RECHTS—UND SOCIALPHILOSOPHIE 72–81.

Buckow, Anjana (2003): ZWISCHEN PROPAGANDA UND REALPOLITIK. Franz Steiner Verlag.

Budde, Heidrun (2002): WILLKÜR! DIE SCHATTENSEITE DER DDR. Ingo Koch Verlag.

Buehler, Grit (1997): MYTHOS GLEICHBERECHTIGUNG IN DER DDR. Campus Verlag.

Buescher, Wolfgang & Peter Wensierski (1984): NULL BOCK AUF DDR: AUSSTEIGERJUGEND IM ANDEREN DEUTSCHLAND. Spiegel Verlag.

Bugiel, Britta (2002): RECHTSEXTREMISMUS JUGENDLICHER IN DER DDR UND IN DEN NEUEN BUNDESLÄNDERN VON 1982–1998. LIT Verlag.

Bukowskij, Wladimir (1973): OPPOSITION: EINE NEUE GEISTESKRANKHEIT IN DER SOWJETUNION? Deutscher Taschenbuch Verlag.

Bundesministerium für innderdeutsche Beziehungen (1985): DDR HANDBUCH. 3d ed. Bundesministerium.

Bundesministerium für innerdeutsche Beziehungen (1988): DER AUFSTAND VOM 17. JUNI 1953. Enlarged ed. Bundesministerium.

Bundesvorstand des FDGB (1970): HANDBUCH FÜR DEN ARBEITSSCHUTZ-OBMANN. Verlag Tribüne.

Bunge, Frederica M. (1981): NORTH KOREA: A COUNTRY STUDY. U.S. Department of the Army.

Burg, Helmut (1985): Schuldnerland USA. 40 EINHEIT 1124–1128.

Burrichter, Clemens & Gerald Diesener, eds. (2002): AUF DEM WEG ZUR PRODUKTIVKRAFT WISSENSCHAFT. Akademische Verlagsanstalt.

Buske, Heinz et al. (1981): BÜNDNISPOLITIK IM SOZIALISMUS. Dietz Verlag.

Butz, Otto (1954): GERMANY: DILEMMA FOR AMERICAN FOREIGN POLICY. Doubleday.

Byrnes, James F. (1947): SPEAKING FRANKLY. Harper & Brothers.

Cattani, Alfred (1993): Ein Land verändert sich. 11:6 KULTUR CHRONIK 28–31 (June 1993). Originally published in NEUE ZÜRCHER ZEITUNG.

Childs, David (1969): EAST GERMANY. Ernest Benn.

Childs, David (1973): MARX AND THE MARXISTS: AN OUTLINE OF PRACTICE AND THEORY. Barnes & Noble.

Childs, David (1980): The Changing Face of Western Communism. David Childs, ed.: THE CHANGING FACE OF WESTERN COMMUNISM. Croom Helm.

Childs, David (1983): THE GDR: MOSCOW'S GERMAN ALLY. Allen & Unwin.

Childs, David (1988): THE GDR: MOSCOW'S GERMAN ALLY. 2d ed. Unwin Hyman.

Childs, David (1989): The SED Faces Challenges of Ostpolitik and Glasnost. David Childs et al., eds.: EAST GERMANY IN COMPARATIVE PERSPECTIVE. Routledge.

Childs, David (2001): THE FALL OF THE GDR: GERMANY'S ROAD TO UNITY. Longman.

Childs, David, ed. (1985): HONECKER'S GERMANY. Allen & Unwin.

Childs, David & Richard Popplewell (1996): THE STASI: THE EAST GERMAN INTELLIGENCE AND SECURITY SERVICE. Macmillan.

Christopher, Inge (1985): The Written Constitution: The Basic Law of a Socialist State? David Childs, ed.: HONECKER'S GERMANY. Allen & Unwin.

Chu, Godwin C. & Leonard L. Chu (1983): Mass Media and Conflict Resolution: An Analysis of Letters to the Editor. Godwin C. Chu & Francis L. K. Hsu, eds.: CHINA'S NEW SOCIAL FABRIC. Kegan Paul.

Clark, John & Aaron Wildavsky (1990): THE MORAL COLLAPSE OF COMMUNISM: POLAND AS A CAUTIONARY TALE. ICS Press.

Clay, Lucius D. (1950): DECISION IN GERMANY. Doubleday.

Cliff, Tony (1974): STATE CAPITALISM IN RUSSIA. Pluto Press.

Coleman, Fred (1996): THE DECLINE AND FALL OF THE SOVIET EMPIRE. St. Martin's Press.

Congress of the CPSU [27th Congress] (1986): THE PROGRAMME OF THE COMMUNIST PARTY OF THE SOVIET UNION. Moscow: Novosti Press Agency.

Connelly, John (2000): CAPTIVE UNIVERSITY: THE SOVIETIZATION OF EAST GERMAN, CZECH, AND POLISH HIGHER EDUCATION 1945–1956. University of North Carolina Press.

Connor, Walter D. (1977): Opinion, Reality, and the Communist Political Process. Walter D. Connor & Zvi Y. Gitelman, eds.: PUBLIC OPINION IN EUROPEAN SOCIALIST SYSTEMS. Praeger.

Conquest, Robert (1986): THE HARVEST OF SORROW: SOVIET COLLECTIVIZATION AND THE TERROR-FAMINE. Oxford University Press.

Conradt, David P. (1978): THE GERMAN POLITY. Longman.

Constitution of the German Democratic Republic, 1974.

Cornelsen, Doris (1988): Wirtschaftsentwicklung in der DDR: Handlungsbedarf für Reformen? Forschungsstelle für Gesamtdeutsche Wirtschaftliche und Soziale

Fragen: GLASNOST UND PERESTROJKA AUCH IN DER DDR? Berlin Verlag Arno Spitz.

Corvalan, Luis (2001): GESPRÄCHE MIT MARGOT HONECKER ÜBER DAS ANDERE DEUTSCHLAND. Das Neue Berlin Verlag.

Cramer, Werner (1988): Über den privaten Einzelhandel in unserer Volkswirtschaft. 43 EINHEIT 951–954.

Croan, Melvin (1976a): EAST GERMANY: THE SOVIET CONNECTION. Sage.

Croan, Melvin (1976b): The Leading Role of the Party: Concepts and Contexts. Andrew C. Janos, ed.: AUTHORITARIAN POLITICS IN COMMUNIST EUROPE. Institute of International Studies, University of California, Berkeley.

Croan, Melvin & Carl J. Friedrich (1958): The East German Regime and Soviet Policy in Germany. 20 JOURNAL OF POLITICS 44–63.

Curtis, Michael (1969): Retreat from Totalitarianism. Carl J. Friedrich et al., eds.: TOTALITARIANISM IN PERSPECTIVE: THREE VIEWS. Praeger.

Czichon, Eberhard & Heinz Marohn (1999): DAS GESCHENK: DIE DDR IM PERESTROIKA AUSVERKAUF. PapyRossa Verlag.

Daehn, Horst (1984): Die Kirchen im Spannungsfeld von Loyalität und Opposition in der DDR. 22 DEUTSCHE STUDIEN 321–341.

Daehn, Horst, ed. (1993): DIE ROLLE DER KIRCHEN IN DER DDR. Olzog Verlag.

Daehn, Horst & Joachim Heise (1996): LUTHER UND DIE DDR. Edition Ost.

Dahrendorf, Ralf (1959): CLASS AND CLASS CONFLICT IN INDUSTRIAL SOCIETY. Stanford University Press.

Dahrendorf, Ralf (1967): SOCIETY AND DEMOCRACY IN GERMANY. Greenwood Press.

Dallin, Alexander & George W. Breslauer (1970): POLITICAL TERROR IN COMMUNIST SYSTEMS. Stanford University Press.

Daniels, Robert V. (1988): IS RUSSIA REFORMABLE? Westview Press.

Daniels, Robert V., ed. (1962): A DOCUMENTARY HISTORY OF COMMUNISM. 2 vols. Vintage.

Davies, Norman (1984): HEART OF EUROPE: A SHORT HISTORY OF POLAND. Clarendon Press.

Davis, Geoffrey (1984): Erkennt Ihr, warum wir Euch lieben. Ian Wallace, ed.: THE GDR IN THE 1980s. GDR Monitor.

Davison, W. Phillips (1958): THE BERLIN BLOCKADE. Princeton University Press.

Decker, Kerstin & Gunnar Decker (2000): GEFÜHLSAUSBRÜCHE, ODER EWIG PUBERTIERT DER OSTDEUTSCHE. Verlag Das Neue Berlin.

Decker, Peter & Karl Held (1989): DDR KAPUTT DEUTSCHLAND GANZ. Resultate Verlag.

Deighton, Anne (1990): THE IMPOSSIBLE PEACE: BRITAIN, THE DIVISION OF GERMANY AND THE ORIGINS OF THE COLD WAR. Clarendon Press.

Deinert, Wolf (1983): Mutti, wie schreibt man Amerika? Gerhard Finn & Liselotte Julius, eds.: VON DEUTSCHLAND NACH DEUTSCHLAND. Verlag für Wirtschaft und Politik.

Deiritz, Karl & Hannes Krauss, eds. (1993): VERRAT AN DER KUNST: RÜCKBLICKE AUF DIE DDR-LITERATUR. Aufbau Verlag, 1993.

Deiters, Ludwig (1983): The Tradition of Christian Art in the German Democratic Republic. 83:2 PRISMA 96.

Dellmuth, Rainer (1999): AUSFLÜGE IM GROTEWOHL-EXPRESS. Anita Tykve Verlag.

Demantowsky, Marko (2000): GESCHICHTSPROPAGANDA UND AKTIVISTENBEWEGUBG IN THE SBZ UND FRÜHEN DDR. Lit Verlag.

Dennis, Mike (1986): Degradation or Humanization? Work and Scientific-Technical Progress in the GDR. Margy Gerber, ed.: STUDIES IN GDR CULTURE AND SOCIETY 6. University Press of America.

Dennis, Mike (2003): THE STASI: MYTH AND REALITY. Pearson Longman.

Deutscher Bundestag (1993): DIE DDR-VOLKSWIRTSCHAFT ALS INSTRUMENT DER SED-DIKTATUR. Bundestag.

Deutscher, Isaac (1984): THE GREAT PURGES. Blackwell.

Deutsches Institut für Wirtschaftsforschung (1984): HANDBUCH DDR-WIRTSCHAFT. Rowohlt Verlag.

Dieckmann, Christoph (1999): DAS WAHRE LEBEN IM FALSCHEN: GESCHICHTEN VON OSTDEUTSCHER IDENTITÄT. Ch. Links Verlag.

Diedrich, Torsten (1991): DER 17. JUNI 1953 IN DER DDR: BEWAFFNETE GEWALT GEGEN DAS VOLK. Dietz Verlag.

Dietz, Raimund (1991): THE IMPACT OF THE UNIFICATION ON THE EAST GERMAN ECONOMY. Viena Institute for Comparative Economic Studies.

Dietzel, Ulrich (2003): MÄNNER UND MASKEN: KUNST UND POLITIK IN OSTDEUTSCHLAND. Faber & Faber Verlag.

Di Palma, Giuseppe (1990): TO CRAFT DEMOCRACIES: AN ESSAY ON DEMOCRATIC TRANSITIONS. University of California Press.

Dittmar, Peter (1984): Die Nationalhymne der DDR. 17 DEUTSCHLAND ARCHIV 1136–1137.

Dittmer, Lowell (1974): LIU SHAO-CHI AND THE CHINESE CULTURAL REVOLUTION: THE POLITICS OF MASS CRITICISM. University of California Press.

Dittmer, Lowell (1988): Marxist Ideology in China and North Korea. Robert A. Scalapino & Dalchoong Kim, eds.: ASIAN COMMUNISM: CONTINUITY AND TRANSITION. University of California, Center for Korean Studies.

Dlubek, Rolf & Renate Merkel (1981): MARX AND ENGELS ÜBER DIE SOZIALISTISCHE UND KOMMUNISTISCHE GESELLSCHAFT. Dietz Verlag.

Doder, Dusko (1988): SHADOWS AND WHISPERS: POWER POLITICS INSIDE THE KREMLIN FROM BREZHNEV TO GORBACHEV. Penguin.

Doelling, Irene (1986): Social and Cultural Changes in the Lives of GDR Women. Margy Gerber, ed.: STUDIES IN GDR CULTURE AND SOCIETY 6. University Press of America.

Doetsch, Jochen & Rolf Lämmerzahl (1987): Konservative Angriffe auf die Schutzrechte der USA-Bürger vor Willk Ürlicher Strafverfolgung. 41 NEUE JUSTIZ 188–190.

Dokumentation (1990): DER PROZESS GEGEN WALTER JANKA UND ANDERE. Rowohlt Verlag.

Dolot, Miron (1985): EXECUTION BY HUNGER: THE HIDDEN HOLOCAUST. Norton.
Dornberg, John (1968): THE OTHER GERMANY. Doubleday.
Dornberg, John (1974): THE TWO GERMANYS. Dial Press.
Dowty, Alan (1987): CLOSED BORDERS. Yale University Press.
Duffy, Christopher (1991): RED STORM ON THE REICH: THE SOVIET MARCH ON GERMANY, 1945. Atheneum.
Duhnke, Horst (1955): STALINISMUS IN DEUTSCHLAND. Verlag für Politik und Wirtschaft.
Eastman, Max (1940): MARXISM: IS IT A SCIENCE? Norton.
Eberle, Henrik (2000): ANMERKUNGEN ZU HONECKER. Schwarzkopf & Schwarzkopf.
Eberstadt, Nicholas (1993): Mortality Rates and Nations in Crisis. 4:5 THE AMERICAN ENTERPRISE 46–53 (September).
Eckelmann, Wolfgang et al. (1990): FDGB INTERN: INNENANSICHTEN EINER MASSENORGANIZATION DER SED. Treptower Verlagshaus.
Eckert, Rainer & Bernd Faulenbach, eds. (1996): HALBHERZIGER REVISIONISMUS. Olzog Verlag.
Edinger, Lewis J. (1965): KURT SCHUMACHER. Stanford University Press.
Eichhorn, Karin (2001): Vom plankonformen Arbeiten mit Kindern. Friedrich Thiessen, ed.: ZWISCHEN PLAN UND PLEITE. Böhlau Verlag.
Eichhorn, Wolfgang (1985): Gesellschaftliche und individuelle Freiheit in unserer Zeit. 85:3 EINHEIT 212–217.
Elm, Ludwig (1986): KONSERVATISMUS HEUTE. Pahl-Rugenstein.
Elm, Ludwig (2001): DAS VERORDNETE FEINDBILD. PapyRossa Verlag.
Elster, Jon, ed. (1996): THE ROUNDTABLE TALKS AND THE BREAKDOWN OF COMMUNISM. University of Chicago Press.
Engelmann, Bernt (1982): WIE WIR WURDEN, WAS WIR SIND. Goldmann Verlag.
Engelstaedter, Heinz (1960): Zur Entwicklung des sozialistischen Staatsbewusstseins unserer Studenten. Institut für Philosophie der Humboldt-University Berlin: DER STAAT SIND WIR: BEITRÄGE ZU PROBLEMEN DER ENTWICKLUNG DES SOZIALISTISCHEN STAATSBEWUSSTSEINS IN DER DDR. Dietz Verlag.
Engler, Wolfgang (1999): DIE OSTDEUTSCHEN: KUNDE VON EINEM VERLORENEN LAND. Aufbau Verlag.
Eppelmann, Rainer et al., eds. (1996): LEXIKON DES DDR-SOZIALISMUS. Schöningh Verlag.
Erbe, Guenter (1982): ARBEITERKLASSE UND INTELLIGENZ IN DER DDR. Westdeutscher Verlag.
Erbe, Guenter et al. (1979): POLITIK, WIRTSCHAFT UND GESELLSCHAFT IN DER DDR. Westdeutscher Verlag.
Falk, Waltraud et al. (1969): WIRTSCHAFT, WISSENSCHAFT, WELTHÖCHSTSTAND. Verlag die Wirtschaft.
Faulenbach, Bernd et al., eds. (1994): DIE PARTEI HATTE IMMER RECHT: AUFARBEITUNG VON GESCHICHTE UND FOLGEN DER SED-DIKTATUR. Klartext Verlag.

Fedoseyev, P. (1979): Social Science and Social Progress. 10:3 SOCIAL SCIENCES 15–32.
Feifer, George (1976): MOSCOW FAREWELL. Viking Press.
Feis, Herbert (1957): CHURCHILL, ROOSEVELT, STALIN. Princeton University Press.
Felfe, Werner (1987): ALLES MIT DEN MENSCHEN, ALLES FÜR DIE MENSCHEN. Dietz Verlag.
Fernau, Joachim (1997): SPRECHEN WIR ÜBER PREUSSEN. Ullstein Verlag.
Feuchtwanger, Lion (1937): MOSCOW 1937. Victor Gollancz.
Feuer, Lewis S., ed. (1959): MARX AND ENGELS: BASIC WRITINGS ON POLITICS AND PHILOSOPHY. Doubleday.
Finder, Joseph (1983): RED CARPET. Holt, Rinehart & Winston.
Finn, Gerhard & Liselotte Julius, eds. (1983): VON DEUTSCHLAND NACH DEUTSCHLAND. Verlag für Wirtschaft und Politik.
Fisch, Bernhard (2001): WIR BRAUCHEN EINEN LANGEN ATEM. Verlag Neue Literatur.
Fischer, Oskar (1984): The Principles of East German Foreign Policy. Arthur W. McCardle & A. Bruce Boneau, eds.: EAST GERMANY: A NEW NATION UNDER SOCIALISM? University Press of America.
Fleischer, Wolfgang (1987): WORTSCHATZ DER DEUTSCHEN SPRACHE IN DER DDR. VEB Bibliographisches Institut Leipzig.
Flinder, Marcus (1999): DIE ENTSTEHUNGSGESCHICHT DES ZIVILGESETZBUCHES DER DDR. Peter Lang Verlag.
Foerster, Peter & Guenter Roski (1990): DDR ZWISCHEN WENDE UND WAHL: MEINUNGSFORSCHER ANALYSIEREN DEN UMBRUCH. LinksDruck Verlag.
Francisco, Ronald A. (1989): The Foreign Economic Policies of the GDR and the USSR: The End of Autarky? David Childs et al., eds.: EAST GERMANY IN COMPARATIVE PERSPECTIVE. Routledge.
Freund, Gerald (1961): GERMANY BETWEEN TWO WORLDS. Harcourt, Brace.
Frey, Eric G. (1987): DIVISION AND DETENTE: THE GERMANIES AND THEIR ALLIANCES. Praeger.
Fricke, Hans (1993): DAVOR—DABEI—DANACH. GNN Verlag.
Fricke, Karl Wilhelm (1974): DDR-Gründung und Opposition. 7 DEUTSCHLAND ARCHIV 946–955.
Fricke, Karl Wilhelm (1982): Forcierte Militarisierung im Erziehungswesen der DDR. 15 DEUTSCHLAND ARCHIV 1057–1062.
Fricke, Karl Wilhelm (1984): OPPOSITION UND WIDERSTAND IN DER DDR. Verlag Wissenschaft und Politik.
Fricke, Karl Wilhelm (1986): ZUR MENSCHEN-UND GRUNDRECHTSSITUATION POLITISCHER GEFANGENER IN DER DDR. Verlag Wissenschaft und Politik.
Fricke, Karl Wilhelm & Bernhard Marquardt (1995): DDR STAATSSICHERHEIT. Universitätsverlag Dr. N. Brockmeyer.
Fried, Robert (1966): COMPARATIVE POLITICAL INSTITUTIONS. Macmillan.
Friedman, Peter (1963): Ulbricht's Wall. 12:8 EAST EUROPE 2–9.
Friedrich, Armin & Thomas Friedrich, eds. (1992): ES HAT ALLES KEINEN ZWECK, DER SPITZBART MUSS WEG: DER 17. JUNI 1953. Paetec Verlag.

Friedrich, Carl J., ed. (1954): TOTALITARIANISM. Harvard University Press.
Friedrich, Carl J. & Zbigniew K. Brzezinski (1956): TOTALITARIAN DICTATORSHIP AND AUTOCRACY. Praeger.
Friedrich, Gerd (1988): ZUM EINFLUSS DER MODERNEN INFORMATIONSTECHNOLOGIE AUF DIE SOZIALISTISCHE BETRIEBSWIRTSCHAFT. Akademie-Verlag.
Friedrich, Walter (1997): Zur inhaltlichen und methodischen Forschung am Zentralinstitut für Jugendforschung Leipzig. Evelyn Brislinger et al., eds.: JUGEND IM OSTEN. Zentralarchiv für empirsche Sozialforschung.
Friedrich, Walter & Peter Foerster (1996): JUGEND IM OSTEN. Rosa-Luxemburg-Verein.
Friedrich, Walter et al., eds. (1999): DAS ZENTRALINSTITUT FÜR JUGENDFORSCHUNG LEIPZIG 1966–1990. Edition Ost.
Friedrich-Ebert-Stiftung, ed. (1983): MARTIN LUTHER: AHNHERR DER DDR? ZU SEINEM 500. GEBURTSTAG. Verlag Neue Gesellschaft.
Friedrich-Ebert-Stiftung, ed. (1985): DIE GRUNDRECHTE IN BEIDEN DEUTSCHEN STAATEN. 5th ed. Verlag Neue Gesellschaft.
Friedrich-Ebert-Stiftung, ed. (1988): JUGEND IN DER DDR. Verlag Neue Gesellschaft.
Fritze, Lothar (1993): INNENANSICHT EINES RUINS: GEDANKEN ZUM UNTERGANG DER DDR. Olzog Verlag.
Fritzsch, Guenter (1993): GESICHT ZUR WAND: WILLKÜR UND ERPRESSUNG HINTER MIELKES MAUERN. Benno Verlag.
Fromm, Erich (1961): MARX'S CONCEPT OF MAN. Frederick Ungar.
Frowen, Stephen F. (1985): The Economy of the German Democratic Republic. David Childs, ed.: HONECKER'S GERMANY. Allen & Unwin.
Fuchs, Juergen & Gerhard Hieke (1992): DUMMGESCHULT? BasisDruck Verlag.
Fulbrook, Mary (1992): THE DIVIDED NATION: A HISTORY OF GERMANY 1918–1990. Oxford University Press.
Fulbrook, Mary (1995): ANATOMY OF A DICTATORSHIP: INSIDE THE GDR 1949–1989. Oxford University Press.
Fuller, Lina (1999): WHERE WAS THE WORKING CLASS? REVOLUTION IN EASTERN GERMANY. University of Illinois Press.
Funke, Manfred (1988): Erfahrung und Aktualität des Totalitarismus: Zur definitorischen Sicherung eines umstrittenes Begriffs moderner Herrschaftslehre. Konrad Loew, ed.: TOTALITARISMUS. Duncker & Humblot.
Gatzke, Hans W. (1980): GERMANY AND THE UNITED STATES: A "SPECIAL RELATIONSHIP?" Harvard University Press.
Gedmin, Jeffrey (1992): THE HIDDEN HAND: GORBACHEV AND THE COLLAPSE OF EAST GERMANY. AEI Press.
Gehrke, Bernd & Wolfgang Rueddenklau, eds. (1999): DAS WAR DOCH NICHT UNSERE ALTERNATIVE: DDR-OPPOSITIONELLE ZEHN JAHRE NACH DER WENDE. Verlag Westfälisches Dampfboot.
Geipel, Gary (1988): Politics and Computers in the German Democratic Republic: The Robotron Combine. Margy Gerber, ed.: STUDIES IN GDR CULTURE AND SOCIETY 8. University Press of America.
Gelb, Norman (1986): THE BERLIN WALL. Simon & Schuster.
Gemeinsame Kommission der Ökonomen der UdSSR und der DDR (1982):

SOZIALISTISCHES WELTSYSTEM UND REVOLUTIONÄRER WELTPROZESS. Dietz Verlag.

Gerdes, Johann et al. (1997): DAS VERSCHWINDEN DER ARBEITSPLÄTZE—WO BLEIBEN DIE ARBEITSKRÄFTE? Universität Rostock.

Gerhardt, Sebastian (1997): POLITBÜROKRATIE UND HEBELWIRTSCHAFT IN DER DDR. Hefte zur DDR-Geschichte.

Gerlach, Manfred (1984): The Contribution of the Liberal Democrats to the Development of the GDR. Arthur W. McCardle & A. Bruce Boneau, eds.: EAST GERMANY: A NEW NATION UNDER SOCIALISM? University Press of America.

GERMAN TRIBUNE, June 15, 1986, p. 5.

Getty, J. Arch (1992): The Politics of Stalinism. Alec Nove, ed.: THE STALIN PHENOMENON. St. Martin's Press.

Geulen, Dieter (1998): POLITISCHE SOZIALISATION IN DER DDR. Leske & Budrich Verlag.

Geyer, Dietrich (1987): THE RUSSIAN REVOLUTION. Berg.

Gieseke, Jens (2001): MIELKE-KONZERN: DIE GESCHICHTE DER STASI 1945–1990. Deutsche Verlagsanstalt.

Glaab, Manuela (1993): Die junge Generation in den neuen Bundesländern. Werner Weidenfeld, ed.: DEUTSCHLAND: EINE NATION—DOPPELTE GESCHICHTE. Verlag Wissenschaft und Politik.

Glaessner, Gert-Joachim (1977): HERRSCHAFT DURCH KADER. Westdeutscher Verlag.

Glaessner, Gert-Joachim (1989): DIE ANDERE DEUTSCHE REPUBLIK. Westdeutscher Verlag.

Glaser, Hermann, ed. (1990): WAS BLEIBT—WAS WIRD. Inter Nationes.

Gleissner, Guenter (1981): Demokratischer Zentralismus: unveräusserliches Grundprinzip sozialistischer Leitung and Organisation. 81:10 EINHEIT 995–1000.

Gleissner, Guenter (1985): Wo das Volk souverän ist. 85:1 EINHEIT 75–79.

Goeckel, Robert F. (1990): THE LUTHERAN CHURCH AND THE EAST GERMAN STATE. Cornell University Press.

Goetting, Gerald (1984): Christian Democrats, Active Partners in the Shaping of Our Republic. Arthur W. McCardle & A. Bruce Boneau, eds.: EAST GERMANY: A NEW NATION UNDER SOCIALISM? University Press of America.

Gohl, Dietmar (1986): DEUTSCHE DEMOKRATISCHE REPUBLIK: EINE AKTUELLE LANDESKUNDE. Fischer Verlag.

Goldhagen, Daniel Jonah (1996): HITLER'S WILLING EXECUTIONERS: ORDINARY GERMANS AND THE HOLOCAUST. Alfred A. Knopf.

Goldman, Guido (1974): THE GERMAN POLITICAL SYSTEM. Random House.

Goldman, Marshall I. (1987): GORBACHEV'S CHALLENGE. Norton.

Goos, Hauke & Ansbert Kneip (2004): Das Ende der Illusion. DER SPIEGEL 39, 62–72 (September 20).

Gorbachev, Mikhail (1987): PERESTROIKA: NEW THINKING FOR OUR COUNTRY AND THE WORLD. Harper & Row.

Gornig, Gilbert (1987): Meinungsäusserungsrecht und Pressefreiheit nach marxistisch-leninistischem Grundrechtsverständnis. 31 RECHT IN OST UND WEST 79–90.

Gotschlich, Helga (1999): UND DER EIGENEN KRAFT VERTRAUEND. Metropol Verlag.

Gradl, Johann B. (1981): ANFANG UNTER SOWJETSTERN: DIE CDU 1945–1948 IN DER SOWJETISCHEN BESATZUNGSZONE DEUTSCHLANDS. Verlag für Wirtschaft und Politik.

Grafe, Roman (2002): DIE GRENZE DURCH DEUTSCHLAND. Siedler Verlag.

Grande, Dieter & Bernd Schaefer (1998): KIRCHE IM VISIER. Benno Verlag.

Grass, Günter (1990): EIN SCHNÄPPCHEN NAMENS DDR. Luchterhand Verlag.

Gray, Wiiliam Glenn (2003): GERMANY'S COLD WAR: THE GLOBAL CAMPAIGN TO ISOLATE EAST GERMANY, 1949–1969. University of North Carolina Press.

Gregor, A. James (1968): CONTEMPORARY RADICAL IDEOLOGIES. Random House.

Gregor, A. James (1974): THE FASCIST PERSUASION IN RADICAL POLITICS. Princeton University Press.

Greve, Uwe (1990): LAGER DES GRAUENS: SOWJETISCHE KZs IN DER DDR NACH 1945. Arndt Verlag.

Gries, Sabine (1994): MISSLUNGENE KINDHEITEN: ZUM UNSOZIALISTISCHEN AUFWACHSEN VON KINDERN IN DER DDR. LIT Verlag.

Gries, Sabine (2001): Kleine Klassenkämpfer. Lothar Mertens, ed.: MACHT-OKKUPATION UND SYSTEMIMPLOSION. Duncker & Humblot Verlag.

Griese, Christiane (2001): BIN ICH EIN GUTER STAATSBÜRGER, WENN ICH MEIN KIND NICHT ZUR JUGENDWEIHE SCHICKE. Schneider Verlag.

Griffith, William E. (1978): THE OSTPOLITIK OF THE FEDERAL REPUBLIC OF GERMANY. MIT Press.

Grimm, Thomas (1993): WAS VON DEN TRÄUMEN BLIEB: EINE BILANZ DER SOZIALISTISCHEN UTOPIE. Siedler Verlag.

Grix, Jonathan (2000): THE ROLE OF THE MASSES IN THE COLLAPSE OF THE GDR. Macmillan.

Grohnert, Evelin (1999): Es gab nichts, aber jeder hatte alles. Andreas Ludwig, ed. (1999): FORTSCHRITT, NORM UND EIGENSINN: ERKUNDUNGEN IM ALLTAG DER DDR. Ch. Links Verlag.

Grosse, Juergen (1999): AMERIKAPOLITIK UND AMERIKABILD DER DDR 1974–1989. Bouvier Verlag.

Grosser, Alfred (1960): DIE BONNER DEMOKRATIE. Karl Rauch Verlag.

Gruber, Tina (1997): HONNIES ENKEL PACKEN AUS. Verlagsbuchhandel Ch. Schubert.

Grundmann, Siegfried (1984): The Working Class: Main Social Force in the Shaping of the Developed Socialist Society. Arthur W. McCardle & A. Bruce Boneau, eds.: EAST GERMANY: A NEW NATION UNDER SOCIALISM? University Press of America.

Grunenberg, Antonia (1990): AUFBRUCH DER INNEREN MAUER. Edition Temmen.

Grunert-Bronnen, Barbara (1970): ICH BIN BÜRGER DER DDR UND LEBE IN DER BUNDESREPUBLIK. Piper Verlag.

Gudorf, Odilo (1981): SPRACHE ALS POLITIK. Verlag Politik und Wissenschaft.

Guertler, Joachim et al. (1990): VERDECKTE ARBEITSLOSIGKEIT IN DER DDR. Ifo-Institut für Wirtschaftsforschung.

Guestrow, Dietrich (1983): IN JENEN JAHREN: AUFZEICHNUNGEN EINES "BEFREITEN" DEUTSCHEN. Severin & Siedler.
Gutjahr-Loeser, Peter (1998): STAATSINFARKT. Rasch & Röhring Verlag.
Gysi, Gregor (1995): DAS WAR'S NOCH LANGE NICHT. Econ Verlag.
Gysi, Gregor (2001): EIN BLICK ZURÜCK, EIN SCHRITT NACH VORN. Hoffmann & Campe Verlag.
Gysi, Gregor & Thomas Falkner (1990): STURM AUFS GROSSE HAUS: DER UNTERGANG DER SED. Edition Fischerinsel.
Gysi, Gregor et al. (1992): ZWEIGETEILT: ÜBER DEN UMGANG MIT DER SED-VERGANGENHEIT. VSA-Verlag.
Haase, Herwig E. (1980): ENTWICKLUNGSTENDENZEN DER DDR-WIRTSCHAFT FÜR DIE 80er JAHRE. Osteuropa-Institut Berlin.
Haase, Norbert & Bert Pampel, eds. (2001): DIE WALDHEIMER "PROZESSE": FÜNFZIG JAHRE DANACH. Nomos Verlag.
Haeder, Sonja (1998): SCHÜLERKINDHEIT IN OST-BERLIN. Böhlau Verlag.
Hagen, Manfred (1992): DDR JUNI '53. Franz Steiner Verlag.
Hager, Kurt (1963): Some Aspects of Full-Scale Bulding of Socialsm in the German Democratic Republic. 6 PEACE, FREEDOM AND SOCIALISM 2–9.
Hager, Kurt (1996): ERINNERUNGEN. Faber & Faber.
Hahn, Erich (1985): Die sozialistische Ideologie: Triebkraft bewussten Handelns. 40 EINHEIT 598–604.
Hajna, Karl-Heinz (2000): DIE LANDTAGSWAHLEN 1946 IN DER SBZ. Peter Lang Verlag.
Halecki, O. (1978): A HISTORY OF POLAND. Routledge & Kegan Paul.
Hamel, Hannelore & Helmut Leipold (1987): Economic Reform in the GDR: Causes and Effects. Ian Jeffries & Manfred Melzer, eds.: THE EAST GERMAN ECONOMY. Croom Helm.
Hammer, Armand (1987): HAMMER. Putnam's Sons.
Hanauske, Dieter, ed. (1995): DIE SITZUNGSPROTOKOLLE DES MAGISTRATS DER STADT BERLIN 1945/46. Berlin Verlag Spitz.
Hancock, M. Donald (1973): THE BUNDESWEHR AND THE NATIONAL PEOPLE'S ARMY: A COMPARATIVE STUDY OF GERMAN CIVIL-MILITARY POLITY. University of Denver: Monograph Series in World Affairs, vol. 10, nr. 2.
Hancock, M. Donald (1989): WEST GERMANY: THE POLITICS OF DEMOCRATIC CORPORATISM. Chatham House.
Hanhardt, Arthur M., Jr. (1968): THE GERMAN DEMOCRATIC REPUBLIC. Johns Hopkins University Press.
Hanrieder, Wolfram F., ed. (1982): HELMUT SCHMIDT: PERSPECTIVES ON POLITICS. Westview Press.
Harder, Friedel (1988): Unser bewährtes Zusammenwirken mit den befreundeten Parteien. 43 EINHEIT 889–893.
Harder, Friedel et al. (1986): Die Rolle der mit der SED befreundeten Parteien im politischen System der DDR. 35 STAAT UND RECHT 275–287.
Harich, Wolfgang (1993): KEINE SCHWIERIGKEITEN MIT DER WAHRHEIT. Dietz Verlag.
Harnischmacher, Robert, ed. (2001): ANGRIFF VON RECHTS: RECHTSEX-

TREMISMUS UND NEONAZISMUS UNTER JUGENDLICHEN OST-BERLINS. Berlin-Brandenburger Bildungswerk.
Hartmann, Andreas & Sabine Kuensting, eds. (1990): GRENZGESCHICHTEN: BERICHTE AUS DEM DEUTSCHEN NIEMANDSLAND. S. Fischer Verlag.
Hartmann, Grit (1997): GOLDKINDER: DIE DDR IM SPIEGEL IHRES SPITZENSPORTS. Forum Verlag.
Hartweg, Frederic, ed. (1995): SED UND KIRCHE. Neukirchener Verlag.
Hauser, Erich & Harald Hotze (1996): DER ABZOCKER-STAAT. Econ Verlag.
Hauser, Kornelia (1994): PATRIARCHAT ALS SOZIALISMUS. Argument-Sonderbände.
Hauser, Richard et al. (1996): UNGLEICHHEIT UND SOZIALPOLITIK. Leske & Budrich.
Havemann, Katja & Joachim Widmann (2003): ROBERT HAVEMANN: ODER WIE DIE DDR SICH ERLEDIGTE. Ullstein Verlag.
Havemann, Robert (1985): Antworten auf zwei Fragen. Hartmut Jäckel, ed.: EIN MARXIST IN DER DDR: FÜR ROBERT HAVEMANN. Piper, 1980.
Hayek, Friedrich A. von (1944): THE ROAD TO SERFDOM. University of Chicago Press.
Hayek, Friedrich A. von (1948): INDIVIDUALISM AND ECONOMIC ORDER. University of Chicago Press.
Hayek, Friedrich A. von (W. W. Bartley III, ed.) (1988): THE FATAL CONCEIT: THE ERRORS OF SOCIALISM. University of Chicago Press.
Hayek, Friedrich A. von, ed. (1935): COLLECTIVIST ECONOMIC PLANNING: CRITICAL STUDIES ON THE POSSIBILITIES OF SOCIALISM. Routledge & Sons.
Hazard, John N. (1948): Introduction. Andrei Vyshinsky, ed.: THE LAW OF THE SOVIET STATE. Macmillan.
Hearnden, Arthur (1974): EDUCATION IN THE TWO GERMANIES. Basil Blackwell.
Hecht, Werner (1991): DER ABSTIEG IN DEN WOHLSTAND: HARAKIRI DER DDR? Picus Verlag.
Hegedues, Andras B. & Manfred Wilke, eds. (2000): SATELLITEN NACH STALINS TOD. Akademie Verlag.
Heidenheimer, Arnold J. (1961): THE GOVERNMENTS OF GERMANY. Crowell.
Heider, Magdalena & Kerstin Thoens (1990): Vorwort. SED UND INTELECTUELLE IN DER DDR DER FÜNFZIGER JAHRE. Edition Deutschland Archiv.
Heinecke, Barbara (2000): GESTUTZTE FLÜGEL. Krämer Verlag.
Hell, Julia (1997): POST-FASCIST FANTASIES. Duke University Press.
Heller, Mikhail & Aleksandr M. Nekrich (1986): UTOPIA IN POWER: THE HISTORY OF THE SOVIET UNION FROM 1917 TO THE PRESENT. Summit Books.
Helmbold, Martin (1989): Zur Umweltpolitik der DDR. 44 EINHEIT 466–468.
Helwig, Gisela (1968): Verstärkte politische Indoktrination. 1 DEUTSCHLAND ARCHIV 212.
Helwig, Gisela (1983): Familienerziehung und Jugendhilfe in der DDR. 16 DEUTSCHLAND ARCHIV 279–283.

Heng, Liang & Judith Shapiro (1983): SON OF THE REVOLUTION. Vintage Books.

Heng, Liang & Judith Shapiro (1986): AFTER THE NIGHTMARE. Knopf.

Henke, Klaus-Dietmar & Hans Woller (1991): Einleitung. Klaus-Dietmar, Henke & Hans Woller, eds.: POLITISCHE SÄUBERUNG IN EUROPA: DIE ABRECHNUNG MIT FASCHISMUS UND KOLLABORATION NACH DEM ZWEITEN WELTKRIEG. Deutscher Taschenbuch Verlag.

Henke, Klaus-Dietmar et al. (1996): ANATOMIE DER STAATSSICHERHEIT: GESCHICHTE, STRUKTUR UND METHODEN. Der Bundesbeauftragte für die Unterlagen des Staatssicherheitsdienstes der ehemaligen DDR.

Henkys, Reinhard (1989): Die Evangelische Kirche in der DDR. Werner Weidenfeld & Hartmut Zimmermann, eds.: DEUTSCHLAND-HANDBUCH. Carl Hanser Verlag.

Henrich, Rolf (1989): DER VORMUNDSCHAFTLICHE STAAT: VOM VERSAGEN DES REAL EXISTIERENDEN SOZIALISMUS. Rowohlt.

Henrich, Rolf (1990): DER VORMUNDSCHAFTLICHE STAAT. Kiepenheuer Verlag.

Hering, Sabine & Hans-Georg Luetzenkirchen (1995): ANDERS WERDEN. Overall Verlag.

Herlemann, Horst (1984): Zur Frage politischer Partizipation in der Sowjetunion. 34 OSTEUROPA 318–328.

Herles, Wolfgang (1990): NATIONALRAUSCH. Kindler Verlag.

Herms, Michael & Gert Noack (1997): DER "SCHLESIERAUSSCHUSS" DER VVN IM VISIER DER SED FÜHRUNG. Gesellschaftswissenschaftliches Forum.

Herold, Ulrich (1984): WAS HABEN WIR VON MARTIN LUTHER? Mitteldeutscher Verlag.

Herrnstadt, Rudolf (1949): Über "die Russen" und über uns. Landesvorstand Sachsen der SED: DIE RUSSEN UND WIR. Landesvorstand.

Herrnstadt, Rudolf (1990): DAS HERRNSTADT-DOKUMENT: DAS POLITBÜRO DER SED UND DIE GESCHICHTE DES 17. JUNI 1953. Rowohlt Verlag.

Hertle, Hans-Hermann (1999): DER FALL DER MAUER. Westdeutscher Verlag.

Hertle, Hans-Hermann & Gerd-Ruediger Stephan, eds. (1997): DAS ENDE DER SED. Ch. Links Verlag.

Herzberg, Guntolf (2000): ABHÄNGIGKEIT UND VERSTRICKUNG: STUDIEN ZUR DDR-PHILOSOPHIE. Ch. Links Verlag.

Herzberg, Guntolf & Kurt Seifert (2002): RUDOLF BAHRO: GLAUBE AN DAS VERÄNDERBARE. Ch. Links Verlag.

Herzstein, Robert E. (1989): ROOSEVELT AND HITLER: PRELUDE TO WAR. Paragon House.

Hesse, Kurt R. (1988): WESTMEDIEN IN DER DDR. Verlag Wissenschaft und Politik.

Heuckendorf, Hans-Juergen (1981): Mit Herz und Verstand die künftigen Aufgaben meistern. 28 DER SCHÖFFE 185–190.

Heuer, Uwe-Jens (1965): DEMOKRATIE UND RECHT IM NEUEN ÖKONOMISCHEN SYSTEM DER PLANUNG UND LEITUNG DER VOLKSWIRTSCHAFT. Staatsverlag.

Heuer, Uwe-Jens (1984): Triebkräfte und Wirtschaftsrecht im Sozialismus. 33 STAAT UND RECHT 803–810.
Heuer, Uwe-Jens (1989): MARXISMUS UND DEMOKRATIE. Nomos Verlag.
Hexelschneider, Erhard & Erhard John (1984): KULTUR ALS EINIGENDES BAND? Dietz Verlag.
Heyen, Rolf (1972): JUGEND IN DER DDR. Neue Darmstädter Verlagsanstalt.
Heym, Stefan (1977): FIVE DAYS IN JUNE. Hodder and Stoughton.
Heym, Stefan (1990): STALIN VERLÄSST DEN RAUM. Reclam Verlag.
Heyme, Torsten (1991): ICH KAM MIR VOR WIE'N TIER: KNAST IN DER DDR. BasisDruck.
Hieblinger, Inge (1984): The Advancement of Women in the GDR. Arthur W. McCardle & A. Bruce Boneau, eds.: EAST GERMANY: A NEW NATION UNDER SOCIALISM? University Press of America.
Hildebrand, Gerold & Tom Sello, eds. (1995): GEGEN DIE VERDRÄNGUNG IM EIGENEN KOPF. Matthias-Domaschk-Archiv.
Hildebrandt, Alexandra (2001): DIE MAUER: ZAHLEN, DATEN. Verlag Haus am Checkpoint Charlie.
Hilger, Andreas et al., eds. (2001): DIKTATURDURCHSETZUNG. Hannah-Arendt-Institut.
Hiller, Horst (1986): STURZ IN DIE FREIHEIT: VON DEUTSCHLAND NACH DEUTSCHLAND. Universitas Verlag.
Hillgruber, Andreas (1983): DER ZWEITE WELTKRIEG, 1939–1945. 3d ed. Kohlhammer.
Hirch, Waldemar, ed. (2001): ZERSETZUNG EINER RELIGIONSGEMEINSCHAFT. Edition Corona.
Hiscocks, Richard (1957): DEMOCRACY IN WESTERN GERMANY. Oxford University Press.
Hitchens, D.M.W.N. et al. (1993): EAST GERMAN PRODUCTIVITY AND THE TRANSITION TO THE MARKET ECONOMY. Avebury.
Hochhuth, Rolf (1993): WESSIS IN WEIMAR. Verlag Volk & Welt.
Hoellen, Martin (1989): Die Katholische Kirche in der DDR. Werner Weidenfeld & Hartmut Zimmermann, eds.: DEUTSCHLAND-HANDBUCH. Carl Hanser Verlag.
Hoernigk, Therese & Alexander Stephan, eds. (2002): JEANS, ROCK UND VIETNAM: AMERIKANISCHE KULTUR IN DER DDR. Brecht Haus.
Hoerz, Helga (1960): Probleme bei der Erziehung der Jugendlichen zum sozialistischen Staatsbewusstsein. Institut für Philosophie der Humboldt-Universität Berlin: DER STAAT SIND WIR: BEITRÄGE ZU PROBLEMEN DER ENTWICKLUNG DES SOZIALISTISCHEN STAATSBEWUSSTSEINS IN DER DDR. Dietz Verlag.
Hoffmann, Dierk (2002): AUFBAU UND KRISE DER PLANWIRTSCHAFT. Oldenbourg Verlag.
Hoffmann, Dierk (2003): DIE DDR UNTER ULBRICHT: GEWALTSAME NEUORDNUNG UND GESCHEITERTE MODERNISIERUNG. Pendo Verlag.
Hoffmann, Stephen P. (1986): The GDR, Luther, and the German Question. 48 REVIEW OF POLITICS 246–263.
Hollander, Gayle D. (1972): SOVIET POLITICAL INDOCTRINATION: DE-

VELOPMENTS IN MASS MEDIA AND PROPAGANDA SINCE STALIN. Praeger.

Hollander, Paul (1987): Enduring Misconceptions about the Soviet Union. Sidney Hook et al., eds.: SOVIET HYPOCRISY AND WESTERN GULLIBILITY. Ethics and Public Policy Center.

Hollander, Paul (1992): DECLINE AND DISCONTENT: COMMUNISM AND THE WEST TODAY. Transaction Publishers.

Hollitzer, Tobias, ed. (1996): EINBLICK IN DAS HERRSCHAFTSWISSEN EINER DIKTATUR: CHANCE ODER FLUCH. Westdeutscher Verlag.

Holzweissig, Gunter (1997): ZENSUR OHNE ZENSOR: DIE SED-INFORMATIONSDIKTATUR. Bouvier Verlag.

Honecker, Erich (1974): REPORT OF THE POLITBÜRO TO THE CENTRAL COMMITTEE OF THE SED. Dietz Verlag.

Honecker, Erich (1978): REDEN UND AUFSÄTZE. Vol. 5. Dietz Verlag.

Honecker, Erich (1979): THE GERMAN DEMOCRATIC REPUBLIC: PILLAR OF PEACE AND SOCIALISM. International Publishers.

Honecker, Erich (1981): AUS MEINEM LEBEN. Dietz Verlag.

Honecker, Erich (1983): KARL MARX AND OUR TIME: THE STRUGGLE FOR PEACE AND SOCIAL PROGRESS. Zeit im Bild.

Honecker, Erich (1984): UNSERE REPUBLIK: STAAT DES FRIEDENS UND DES SOZIALISMUS. 84:9 EINHEIT 771–778.

Honecker, Erich (1987): REVOLUTIONÄRE THEORIE UND GESCHICHTLICHE ERFAHRUNGEN IN DER POLITIK DER SED. Dietz Verlag.

Honecker, Erich (1989): FÜR EINE WELTWEITE KOALITION DER VERNUNFT UND DES REALISMUS. Dietz Verlag.

Hook, Sidney (1934): The Fallacy of the Theory of Social Fascism. 8 MODERN MONTHLY 342–352.

Hook, Sidney (1955): MARX AND THE MARXISTS: THE AMBIGUOUS LEGACY. Van Nostrand.

Hook, Sidney (1962): POLITICAL POWER AND PERSONAL FREEDOM. Collier Books.

Hornbostel, Stefan, ed. (1999): SOZIALISTISCHE ELITEN. Leske & Budrich Verlag.

Hough, Jerry F. (1988): OPENING UP THE SOVIET ECONOMY. Brookings Institution.

Hoyles, John (1991): THE LITERARY UNDERGROUND: WRITERS AND THE TOTALITARIAN EXPERIENCE, 1900–1950. St. Martin's Press.

Hubatsch, Walther, ed. (1967): THE GERMAN QUESTION. Herder Book Center.

Huebner, Peter (1999): Einleitung: Antielitäre Eliten? Peter Huebner, ed.: ELITEN IM SOZIALIMUS. Böhlau Verlag.

Huebner, Peter & Klaus Tenfelde, eds. (1999): ARBEITER IN DER SBZ-DDR. Klartext Verlag.

Huebsch, Reinhard (2002): Eine Zusammenarbeit der beiden Parteien kann nicht in Frage kommen. Reinard Huebsch, ed.: HÖRT DIE SIGNALE: DIE DEUTSCHLANDPOLITIK VON KPD/SED UND SPD 1945–1970. Akademie Verlag.

Huemmler, Heinz (1983): Die Bündnispolitik der SED im Zerrspiegel bürgerlicher Darstellungen. Peter Bachmann et al., eds.: GESCHICHTE, IDEOLOGIE,

POLITIK: AUSEINANDERSETZUNGEN MIT BÜRGERLICHEN GESCHICHTSAUFFASSUNGEN IN DER BDR. Dietz Verlag.

Huemmler, Heinz (1989): BÜNDNISPOLITIK IN DEN FARBEN DER DDR. Dietz Verlag.

Huertgen, Renate & Thomas Reichel, eds. (2001): DER SCHEIN DER STABILITÄT. Metropol Verlag.

Hummel, Lothar & Hans Schieck (1985): Plan und Initiative. 40 EINHEIT 1093–1098.

Hutzler-Spichtinger, Margot & Klaus Schoenberger (1994): UNÜBERHÖRBARE WORTMELDUNGEN DER BÜRGER. Leipziger Universitätsverlag.

Iggers, Georg G. et al., eds. (1998): DIE DDR-GESCHICHTSWISSENSCHAFT ALS FORSCHUNGSPROBLEM. Oldenbourg Verlag.

Inkeles, Alex (1950): PUBLIC OPINION IN SOVIET RUSSIA: A STUDY IN MASS PERSUASION. Harvard University Press.

Inkeles, Alex (1954): The Totalitarian Mystique: Some Impressions of the Dynamics of Totalitarian Society. Carl J. Friedrich, ed.: TOTALITARIANISM. Harvard University Press.

Inkeles, Alex & Kent Geiger (1952): Critical Letters to the Editors of the Soviet Press: Areas and Modes of Complaint. 17 AMERICAN SOCIOLOGICAL REVIEW 694–703.

Inkeles, Alex & Kent Geiger (1953): Critical Letters to the Editors of the Soviet Press: Social Characteristics and Interrelations of the Critic and the Criticized. 18 AMERICAN SOCIOLOGICAL REVIEW 12–22.

Inkeles, Alex & Raymond A. Bauer (1959): THE SOVIET CITIZEN. Harvard University Press.

Institut für Theorie des Staates und des Rechts der Akademie der Wissenschaften der DDR (1986): ENTWICKLUNGSGESETZMÄSSIGKEITEN DES SOZIALISTISCHEN STAATES. Staatsverlag.

Internationale Erich-Fromm-Gesellschaft (1995): DIE CHARAKTERMAUER. Vandenhoeck & Ruprecht.

Investigating Committee of Free Jurists (undated): EX-NAZIS IN THE SERVICE OF THE "GERMAN DEMOCRATIC REPUBLIC."

Jacobsen, Hanns-D. & Heinrich Machowski (1988): Die Wirtschaftsbeziehungen zwischen beiden deutschen Staaten: Sonderstatus und Bedeutung. 88 EUROPÄISCHE RUNDSCHAU 31–43.

Jaeger, Andrea (1995): SCHRIFTSTELLER AUS DER DDR. Peter Lang Verlag.

Jahnke, Karl Heinz (1993): ICH BIN NIE EIN PARTEIFEIND GEWESEN: DER TRAGISCHE WEG DER KOMMUNISTEN FRITZ UND LYDIA SPERLING. Pahl Rugenstein Verlag.

Janka, Walter (1994): DIE UNTERWERFUNG. Carl Hanser Verlag.

Janos, Andrew C. (1976): Systemic Models and the Theory of Change in the Comparative Study of Communist Politics. Andrew C. Janos, ed.: AUTHORITARIAN POLITICS IN COMMUNIST EUROPE. Institute of International Studies, University of California, Berkeley.

Janson, Carl-Heinz (1991): TOTENGRÄBER DER DDR. Econ Verlag.

Jarausch, Konrad H. (1999b): Implosion oder Selbstbefreiung? Konrad H. Jarausch & Martin Sabrow, eds.: WEG IN DEN UNTERGANG. Vandenhoeck & Ruprecht Verlag.

Jarausch, Konrad H., ed. (1999a): DICTATORSHIP AS EXPERIENCE. Berghahn Books.

Jaubert, Alain (1989): MAKING PEOPLE DISAPPEAR. Pergamon-Brassey.

Jeese, Eckhard, ed. (1985): BUNDESREPUBLIK DEUTSCHLAND AND DEUTSCHE DEMOKRATISCHE REPUBLIK. Colloquium Verlag.

Jeffries, Ian & Manfred Melzer (1987): The New Economic System of Planning and Management 1963–70 and Recentralization in the 1970s. Ian Jeffries & Manfred Melzer, eds.: THE EAST GERMAN ECONOMY. Croom Helm.

Jeschonnek, Guenter (1988): Ausreise: das Dilemma des ersten deutschen Arbeiter-und-Bauern-Staats? Ferdinand Kroh, ed.: FREIHEIT IST IMMER FREIHEIT. Ullstein Verlag.

Jessen, Ralph (1999): AKADEMISCHE ELITE UND KOMMUNISTISCHE DIKTATUR. Vandenhoeck & Ruprecht Verlag.

Joas, Hans & Martin Kohli, eds. (1993): DER ZUSAMMENBRUCH DER DDR. Suhrkamp Verlag.

Jochum, Dietmar (1996a): DIE BEWEISAUFNAHME IM POLITBÜRO-PROZESS. Magnus Verlag.

Jochum, Dietmar (1996b): DAS POLITBÜRO AUF DER ANKLAGEBANK. Magnus Verlag.

Joensson, Christer (1985): SOVIET POLITICAL LANGUAGE. Paper delivered at the World Congress of the International Political Science Association, Paris, France.

Johnson, Priscilla (1965): KHRUSHCHEV AND THE ARTS: THE POLITICS OF SOVIET CULTURE, 1962–1964. MIT Press.

Joost, Angela (2000): ARBEIT, LIEBE, LEBEN. Ulrike Helmer Verlag.

Jordan, Bill (1985): THE STATE: AUTHORITY AND AUTONOMY. Basil Blackwell.

Joseph, Detlef (2002): NAZIS IN DER DDR. Edition Ost.

Juergs, Michael (1997): DIE TREUHÄNDER: WIE HELDEN UND HALUNKEN DIE DDR VERKAUFTEN. List Verlag.

Kadell, Franz (1991): DIE KATYN LÜGE: GESCHICHTE EINER MANIPULATION. Herbig Verlag.

Kaedtler, Juergen et al. (1997): BETRIEBSRÄTE IN OSTDEUTSCHLAND. Westdeutscher Verlag.

Kaff, Brigitte, ed. (1995): GEFÄHRLICHE POLITISCHE GEGNER. Droste Verlag.

Kaiser, Paul & Claudia Petzold (1997): BOHEME UND DIKTATUR IN DER DDR. Fannei & Walz Verlag.

Kallinich, Joachim & Sylvia de Pasquale, eds. (2002): EIN OFFENES GEHEIMNIS: POST- UND TELEFON-KONTROLLE IN DER DDR. Edition Braus.

Kaminsky, Annette (2001): WOHLSTAND, SCHÖNHEIT, GLÜCK: KLEINE KOSUMGESCHICHTE DER DDR. C. H. Beck Verlag.

Kaminsky, Annette (2002): Ungleichheit in der SBZ/DDR am Beispiel des Konsums. Lothar Mertens, ed.: SOZIALE UNGLEICHHEIT IN DER DDR. Duncker & Humblot.

Kappelt, Olaf (1981): BRAUNBUCH DDR: NAZIS IN DER DDR. Reichmann.

Kappelt, Olaf (1997): DIE ENTNAZIFIZIERUNG IN DER SBZ SOWIE DIE

ROLLE UND DER EINFLUSS EHEMALIGER NATIONALSOZIALISTEN IN DER DDR ALS EIN SOZIOLOGISCHES PHÄNOMEN. Verlag Dr. Kovac.

Karlsch, Rainer & Jochen Laufer, eds. (2002): SOWJETISCHE DEMONTAGEN IN DEUTSCHLAND 1944–1949. Duncker & Humblot.

Katzur, Klaus (2001): Schwimmen im Zeichen von Hammer und Privilegien. Friedrich Thiessen, ed.: ZWISCHEN PLAN UND PLEITE. Böhlau Verlag.

Kautsky, Karl (1964): THE DICTATORSHIP OF THE PROLETARIAT. University of Michigan Press.

Kawohl, Birgit (2000): BESSER ALS HIER IST ES ÜBERALL. Tectum Verlag.

Keck, Alfred (1991): DEUTSCHLAND IM WIEDERERSTEHEN. Deutsche Verlagsgesellschaft.

Keller, Dietmar & Juergen Reents, eds. (2000): NEUE GESPRÄCHE ÜBER GOTT UND DIE WELT. Verlag Schwarzkopf & Schwarzkopf.

Kennan, George F. (1960): SOVIET FOREIGN POLICY, 1917–1941. D. Van Nostrand.

Kessler, Heinz (1996): ZUR SACHE UND ZUR PERSON. Edition Ost.

Kessler, Horst-Guenter & Juergen Miermeister (1983): VOM GROSSEN KNAST INS PARADIES. Rowohlt Verlag.

Kiep, Walther Leisler (1974): A NEW CHALLENGE FOR WESTERN EUROPE: A VIEW FROM BONN. Mason & Lipscomb.

Kieslich, Lothar (1998): KOMMUNISTEN GEGEN KOMMUNISTEN. Kletsmeier Verlag.

Kintzel, Helmut et al. (1988): DEMOKRATIE IM ALLTAG. Dietz Verlag.

Kirkpatrick, Jeanne J. (1983): DICTATORSHIPS AND DOUBLE STANDARDS. Simon & Schuster.

Kitzinger, Uwe W. (1960): GERMAN ELECTORAL POLITICS. Clarendon Press.

Klein, Fritz (2000): DRINNEN UND DRAUSSEN: EIN HISTORIKER IN DER DDR. Fischer Verlag.

Klein, Helmut, ed. (1985): HUMBOLDT-UNIVERSITÄT ZU BERLIN: ÜBERBLICK 1818–1985. VEB Deutscher Verlag der Wissenschaften.

Klein, Margrete S. (1980): THE CHALLENGE OF COMMUNIST EDUCATION: A LOOK AT THE GERMAN DEMOCRATIC REPUBLIC. Columbia University Press.

Klein, Thomas (2002): FÜR DIE EINHEIT UND REINHEIT DER PARTEI. Böhlau Verlag.

Klein, Thomas et al. (1996): VISIONEN: REPRESSION UND OPPOSITION IN DER SED (1949–1989). Frankfurter Oder Editionen.

Klenner, Hermann (1967): CIVIL RIGHTS IN THE GERMAN DEMOCRATIC REPUBLIC. Committee for the Protection of Human Rights.

Klessmann, Christoph & Georg Wagner, eds. (1993): DAS GESPALTENE LAND. C. H. Beck Verlag.

Klingst, Peter (2001): Als Hotelier im Dienste des Sozialismus. Friedrich Thiessen, ed.: ZWISCHEN PLAN UND PLEITE. Böhlau Verlag.

Kloetzer, Sylvia & Siegfried Lokatis (1999): Criticism and Censorship: Negotiating Cabaret Performance and Book Production. Konrad H. Jarausch, ed.: DICTATORSHIP AS EXPERIENCE. Berghahn Books.

Kloth, Hans Michael (2000): VOM "ZETTELFALTEN" ZUM FREIEN WÄHLEN. Ch. Links Verlag.

Kluge, Ulrich et al., eds. (2001): ZWISCHEN BODENREFORM UND KOLLEKTIVIERUNG. Franz Steiner Verlag.

Knabe, Hubertus (2001): DER DISKRETE CHARME DER DDR: STASI UND WESTMEDIEN. Propyläen Verlag.

Knecht, Willi Ph. (1978): DAS MEDAILLENKOLLEKTIV. Verlag Gebr. Holzapfel.

Knuetter, Hans-Helmuth (1994): DIE FASCHISMUS-KEULE: DAS LETZTE AUFGEBOT DER DEUTSCHEN LINKEN. 2d ed.

Koch, H. W. (1972): HITLER YOUTH: THE DUPED GENERATION. Ballantine Books.

Koch, Hans (1988): KULTURFORTSCHRITT IM SOZIALISMUS. Dietz Verlag.

Koch, Klaus-Uwe (1989): Warum es keine "offene deutsche Frage" gibt. 44 EINHEIT 271–275.

Koch, Michael (2000): DIE EINFÜHRUNG DES WEHRUNTERRICHTES IN DER DDR. Verlagshaus Frisch.

Koch, Uwe & Stephan Eschler (1994): ZÄHNE HOCH KOPF ZUSAMMENBEISSEN: DOKUMENTE ZUR WEHRDIENSTVERWEIGERUNG IN DER DDR 1962–1990. Scheunen-Verlag.

Kocka, Juergen & Martin Sabrow, eds. (1994): DIE DDR ALS GESCHICHTE. Akademie Verlag.

Koedderitzsch, Peter & Leo A. Mueller (1990): RECTSEXTREMISMUS IN DER DDR. Lamuv Verlag.

Koehler, John O. (1999): STASI: THE UNTOLD STORY OF THE EAST GERMAN SECRET POLICE. Westview Press.

Koestler, Arthur et al. (1950): THE GOD THAT FAILED. Hamish Hamilton.

Kolakowski, Leszek (1969): MARXISM AND BEYOND. Pall Mall Press.

Kolakowski, Leszek (1981): MAIN CURRENTS OF MARXISM. Oxford University Press.

Kolloch, Klaus (2001): Humboldt oder Marx. Friedrich Thiessen, ed.: ZWISCHEN PLAN UND PLEITE. Böhlau Verlag.

Konrad, George & Ivan Szelenyi (1979): THE INTELLECTUALS ON THE ROAD TO CLASS POWER. Harcourt Brace Jovanovich.

Koop, Volker (1996): DEN GEGNER VERNICHTEN: DIE GRENZSICHERUNG DER DDR. Bouvier Verlag.

Koop, Volker (1997): ARMEE ODER FREIZEITCLUB: DIE KAMPFGRUPPEN DER ARBEITERKLASSE IN DER DDR. Bouvier Verlag.

Kopielski, Bernd et al. (1990): FEINDBILD ADE? Brandenburgisches Verlagshaus.

Kopstein, Jeffrey (1997): THE POLITICS OF ECONOMIC DECLINE IN EAST GERMANY, 1945–1989. University of North Carolina Press.

Koschyk, Hartmut & Konrad Weiss, eds. (1996): VON ERBLASTEN UND SEILSCHAFTEN. Olzog Verlag.

Kosing, Heinrich (1988): SOZIALISMUS UND UMWELT. Dietz Verlag.

Koziolek, Helmut & Otto Reinhold (1988): Gesellschaftspolitik und politische Ökonomie. 43 EINHEIT 715–722.

Krenz, Egon (1990): WENN MAUERN FALLEN. Paul Neff Verlag.

Krenz, Egon (1999): HERBST '89. Verlag Neues Leben.

Krenz, Egon (2000): BRIEFE UND ZEUGNISSE. Verlag Neues Leben.

Krieg, Harald (1993): ENTSCHEIDUNG GEGEN DEUTSCHLAND 1945–1950. Klemmerberg Verlag.

Krisch, Henry (1974): GERMAN POLITICS UNDER SOVIET OCCUPATION. Columbia University Press.

Krisch, Henry (1976): Politics in the German Democratic Republic (review). 9 STUDIES IN COMPARATIVE COMMUNISM 389–419.

Krisch, Henry (1985): THE GERMAN DEMOCRATIC REPUBLIC: THE SEARCH FOR IDENTITY. Westview Press.

Krisch, Henry (1989): The SED after Two Congresses: Party Policy in the Gorbachev Area. David Childs et al., eds.: EAST GERMANY IN COMPARATIVE PERSPECTIVE. Routledge.

Kroemke, Claus (1998): Deutsch-deutsche Wirtschaftskooperation, ihre politischen Rahmenbedingungen und Realitäten—Gespräche auf hoher Ebene. Juergen Hofmann & Detlef Nakath, eds.: KONFLIKT, KONFRONTATION, KOOPERATION. Brandenburger Verein für politische Bildung.

Kroh, Ferdinand, ed. (1988): FREIHEIT IST IMMER FREIHEIT. Ullstein Verlag.

Krolikowski, Werner (1988): JE STÄRKER DER SOZIALISMUS, DESTO SICHERER DER FRIEDEN. Dietz Verlag.

Krueger-Potratz, Marianne (1991): ANDERSSEIN GAB ES NICHT: AUSLÄNDER UND MINDERHEITEN IN DER DDR. Waxmann Verlag.

Kuczynski, Juergen (1994): EIN LEBEN IN DER WISSENSCHAFT DER DDR. Verlag Westfälisches Dampfboot.

Kuczynski, Rita (1999): Von der Schwierigkeit, in Deutschland eine Deutsche zu sein. Stefan Moses, ed.: ENDE MIT WENDE. Hatje Cantz Verlag.

Kuechler, Falk (1997): DIE WIRTSCHAFT DER DDR. Fides Verlag.

Kuehnhardt, Ludger et al., eds. (1994): DIE DOPPELTE DEUTSCHE DIKTATURERFAHRUNG. Peter Lang.

Kuehnrich, Heinz (1983): DIE KPD IM KAMPF GEGEN DIE FASCHISTISCHE DIKTATUR: 1933 BIS 1945. Dietz Verlag.

Kuhnert, Jan (1980): Wirtschaftswachstum und Lebensweise. DIE DDR IM ENTSPANNUNGSPROZESS. Edition Deutschland Archiv.

Kuhrig, Herta (1985): Familie und Familienglück. 40 EINHEIT 1099–1105.

Kuhrt, Eberhard, ed. (1996a): DIE SED-HERRSCHAFT UND IHR ZUSAMMENBRUCH. Leske & Budrich.

Kuhrt, Eberhard, ed. (1996b): DIE WIRTSCHAFTLICHE UND ÖKOLOGISCHE SITUATION DER DDR IN DEN 80ER JAHREN. Leske & Budrich.

Kuhrt, Eberhard, ed. (1999): DIE ENDZEIT DER DDR-WIRTSCHAFT: ANALYSEN ZUR WIRTSCHAFTS-, SOZIAL- UND UMWELTPOLITIK. Leske & Budrich.

Kunz, Frithjof & Joachim Michas (1975): SOZIALISTISCHE ARBEITSDISZIPLIN. Staatsverlag.

Kupferberg, Feiwel (2002): THE RISE AND FALL OF THE GERMAN DEMOCRATIC REPUBLIC. Transaction Publishers.

Kuppe, Johannes (1985a): Die Geschichtsschreibung der SED im Umbruch. 18 DEUTSCHLAND ARCHIV 278–294.

Kuppe, Johannes (1985b): Machtausbruch und Herrschaftspraxis. Eckhard Jesse, ed.: BUNDESREPUBLIK DEUTSCHLAND UND DEUTSCHE DEMOKRATISCHE REPUBLIC. 4th ed. Colloquium Verlag.

Kuppe, Johannes (1987): Die SED im Sowjetsystem und im Weltkommunismus. Ilse

Spittmann, ed.: DIE SED IN GESCHICHTE UND GEGENWART. Edition Deutschland Archiv.

Kuppe, Johannes (1990): Der Staat der SED in der Auflösung: Die Folgen. Ilse Spittmann & Gisela Helwig, eds.: DIE DDR AUF DEM WEG ZUR DEUTSCHEN EINHEIT: PROBLEME, PERSPEKTIVEN, OFFENE FRAGEN. Edition Deutschland Archiv.

Kuran, Timur (1995): PRIVATE TRUTHS, PUBLIC LIES. Harvard University Press.

Kurlantzick, Joshua (2004): Purple Haze. THE NEW REPUBLIC, August 30, 10–11.

Kusch, Guenter et al. (1991): SCHLUSSBILANZ—DDR. Duncker & Humblot Verlag.

Laatz, Horst H. (1983): Standortbestimmung: Brandenburg via Brandenburg. Gerhard Finn & Liselotte Julius, eds.: VON DEUTSCHLAND NACH DEUTSCHLAND. Verlag für Wirtschaft und Politik.

Lammich, Siegfried (1980): Das politische Strafrecht in der DDR und den anderen sozialistischen Ländern. 13 DEUTSCHLAND ARCHIV 843–854.

Lammich, Siegfried (1987): Grundzüge des Umweltschutzrechts in der DDR unter besonderer Berücksichtigung der rechtlichen Sanktionen. 31 RECHT IN OST UND WEST 15–23.

Land, Rainer & Ralf Possekel (1994): NAMENLOSE STIMMEN WAREN UNS VORAUS. POLITISCHE DISKURSE VON INTELLECTUELLEN AUS DER DDR. Winkler Verlag.

Landgrebe, Christiane (1999): DER TAG AN DEM DIE MAUER FIEL. Ullstein Verlag.

Lane, David (1976): THE SOCIALIST INDUSTRIAL STATE. Westview Press.

Langenhan, Dagmar & Sabine Ross (1999): The Socialist Glass Ceiling: Limits to Female Careers. Konrad H. Jarausch, ed.: DICTATORSHIP AS EXPERIENCE. Berghahn Books.

Langguth, Gerd (1987): DIE BERLIN-POLITIK DER DDR. Verlag Ernst Knoth.

Lapp, Peter J. (1988): DDR-BLOCKPARTEIEN HEUTE: DIE "BEFREUNDETEN" PARTEIEN DER SED. Verlag Wissenschaft und Politik.

Lasky, Melvin J. (1992): VOICES IN A REVOLUTION: THE COLLAPSE OF EAST GERMAN COMMUNISM. Transaction Publishers.

Latotzky, Alexander (2002): KINDHEIT HINTER STACHELDRAHT. Forum Verlag.

Laube, Adolf (1982): Martin Luther. 82:2 PRISMA 104.

Lauterbach, Albert (1954): Totalitarian Appeal and Economic Reform. Carl J. Friedrich, ed.: TOTALITARIANISM. Harvard University Press.

Lebahn, Axel (1988). Political and Economic Effects of Perestroika on the Soviet Union and Its Relations to Eastern Europe and the West. 39 AUSSENPOLITIK 107–124.

Lee, Andrea (1984): RUSSIAN JOURNAL. Random House.

Lehmann, Guenter & Hans-Joachim Schulz (1976): Zur Rolle der Arbeitskollektive bei der weiteren Festigung von Gesetzlichkeit, Ordnung, Sicherheit und Disziplin. 25 STAAT UND RECHT 154–162.

Lehmann, Horst & Heidrun Pohl (1986): Eingaben der Bürger und weitere Vervollkommnung der sozialistischen Demokratie. 35 STAAT UND RECHT 11–19.

Leidecker, Gudrun (1991): ICH WEISS NICHT OB ICH FROH SEIN SOLL. Metzlersche Verlagsbuchhandlung.

Leites, Nathan & Elsa Bernaut (1954): RITUAL OF LIQUIDATION: THE CASE OF THE MOSCOW TRIALS. Free Press.

Lemke, Christiane (1980): PERSÖNLICHKEIT UND GESELLSCHAFT: ZUR THEORIE DER PERSÖNLICHKEIT IN DER DDR. Westdeutscher Verlag.

Lemke, Christiane (1991): DIE URSACHEN DES UMBRUCHS 1989. Westdeutscher Verlag.

Lemmer, Ernst (1968): MANCHES WAR DOCH ANDERS: ERINNERUNGEN EINES DEUTSCHEN DEMOKRATEN. Verlag Heinrich Scheffler.

Lendvai, Paul (1981): THE BUREAUCRACY OF TRUTH: HOW COMMUNIST GOVERNMENTS MANAGE THE NEWS. Burnett Books.

Lengsfeld, Vera (1997): Der Ehemann als Stasi-Spitzel. Juergen Aretz & Wolfgang Stock, eds.: DIE VERGESSENEN OPFER DER DDR. Bastei Verlag.

Lenin, Vladimir I. (1960): COLLECTED WORKS. Foreign Languages Publishing House.

Leo, Annette & Peter Reif-Spirek, eds. (1999): HELDEN, TÄTER UND VERRÄTER: STUDIEN ZUM DDR-ANTIFASCHISMUS. Metropol Verlag.

Leo, Annette & Peter Reif-Spirek, eds. (2001): VIELSTIMMIGES SCHWEIGEN: NEUE STUDIEN ZUM DDR-ANTIFASCHISMUS. Metropol Verlag.

Leonhard, Wolfgang (1981): DIE REVOLUTION ENTLÄSST IHRE KINDER. Kiepenheuer & Witsch.

Leonhard, Wolfgang (1990): DAS KURZE LEBEN DER DDR. Deutsche Verlags-Anstalt.

Leonhard, Wolfgang (1992): SPURENSUCHE. Kiepenheuer & Witsch.

Leptin, Gert (1975): The German Democratic Republic. Hans-Hermann Hoehmann et al., eds.: THE NEW ECONOMIC SYSTEM OF EASTERN EUROPE. University of California Press.

Leske, Monika et al. (1982): WARUM ES SICH LOHNT UM BEGRIFFE ZU STREITEN. Dietz Verlag.

Lewis, Brenda Ralph (2000): HITLER YOUTH. MBI Publishing Co.

Lewis, Jonathan & Phillip Whitehead (1990): STALIN: A TIME FOR JUDGEMENT. Pantheon.

Lieberman, Evsei (1962): PRAVDA, September 9.

Lieberman, Evsei (1973): ÖKONOMISCHE METHODEN ZUR EFFIZIENZSTEIGERUNG DER GESELLSCHAFTLICH EN PRODUKTION. Staatsverlag.

Liebernickel, Martin (2000): ERPRESSUNG AUSREISEWILLIGER DDR-BÜRGER. Nomos Verlag.

Linklater, Beth V. (1998): UND IMMER ZÜGELLOSER WIRD DIE LUST. CONSTRUCTIONS OF SEXUALITY IN EAST GERMAN LITERATURES. Peter Lang Verlag.

Links, Christoph & Hannes Bahrmann (1990): WIR SIND DAS VOLK. Aufbau Verlag.

Loesdau, Alfred & Gerhard Lozek (1984): Die Totalitarismus-Doktrin also Grundelement antikommunistischer Geschichtsklitterung. 39 EINHEIT 357.

Loeser, Franz (1984): DIE UNGLAUBWÜRDIGE GESELLSCHAFT. Bund-Verlag.

Loew, Konrad, ed. (1993): URSACHEN UND VERLAUF DER DEUTSCHEN REVOLUTION 1989. Duncker & Humblot Verlag.
Lorenz, Thomas (1998): DIE RECHTSANWALTSCHAFT IN DER DDR. Berlin Verlag Spitz.
Loth, Wilfried (1994): STALINS UNGELIEBTES KIND: WARUM MOSKAU DIE DDR NICHT WOLLTE. Rowohlt Verlag.
Lucchesi, Joachim, ed. (1993): DAS VERHÖR IN DER OPER. BasisDruck.
Luchsinger, Fred (1951): Justice in East Germany. 1:4 SWISS REVIEW OF WORLD AFFAIRS 11–13 (July).
Luchterhandt, Otto (1985): DER VERSTAATLICHTE MENSCH. Carl Heymanns Verlag.
Ludwig, Andreas, ed. (1999): FORTSCHRITT, NORM UND EIGENSINN: ERKUNDUNGEN IM ALLTAG DER DDR. Ch. Links Verlag.
Ludz, Peter C. (1966): East Germany: The Old and the New. 15:4 EAST EUROPE 23–27 (April).
Ludz, Peter C. (1968): Politische Aspekte der kybernetischen Systemtheorie in der DDR. 1 DEUTSCHLAND ARCHIV 1–10.
Ludz, Peter C. (1977): DIE DDR ZWISCHEN OST UND WEST. C. H. Beck.
Ludz, Peter C., ed. (1974): BUNDESREPUBLIK DEUTSCHLAND-DDR: SYSTEMVERGLEICH 3. Bundesministerium für innerdeutsche Beziehungen.
Ludz, Peter C. (1980): MECHANISMEN DER HERRSCHAFTSSICHERUNG. Carl Hanser Verlag.
Luebbe, Peter (1980): DDR-Kader im westlichen Ausland. 13 DEUTSCHLAND ARCHIV 1069–1075.
Luft, Christa (1991): ZWISCHEN WENDE UND ENDE: EINDRÜCKE, ERLEBNISSE, ERFAHRUNGEN EINES MIDGLIEDS DER MODROW-REGIERUNG. Aufbau Taschenbuch Verlag.
Luft, Christa (1999): ZWISCHEN WENDE UND ENDE. Aufbau Verlag.
Maaz, Hans-Joachim (1995): BEHIND THE WALL: THE INNER LIFE OF COMMUNIST GERMANY. W. W. Norton.
MacGregor, Douglas A. (1989): THE SOVIET–EAST GERMAN MILITARY ALLIANCE. Cambridge University Press.
Machalz-Urban, Doris (1985): Die Vervollkommnung der sozialistischen Demokratie unter Führung der SED. Rat für staats- und rechtswissenschaftliche Forschung an der Akademie der Wissenschaften der DDR: VERVOLLKOMMNUNG DER SOZIALISTISCHEN DEMOKRATIE: TRIEBKRAFT DER SOZIALISTISCHEN GESELLSCHAFT. Staatsverlag.
Machtan, Lothar (2001): THE HIDDEN HITLER. Basic Books.
Macket, Gerhard (2000): REISEN NACH VERLORENLAND. GNN Verlag.
Mackiewicz, Joseph (1951): THE KATYN WOOD MURDERS. Hollis & Cater.
Macrakis, Kristie & Dieter Hoffmann, eds. (1999): SCIENCE UNDER SOCIALISM. Harvard University Press.
Maehlert, Ulrich (1994): Die gesamte junge Generation für den Sozialismus begeistern. Juergen Weber, ed.: DER SED-STAAT. Olzog Verlag.
Maehlert, Ulrich (1995): DIE FREIE DEUTSCHE JUGEND 1945–1949. Schöningh Verlag.
Maetzing, Heike C. (1999): GESCHICHTE IM ZEICHEN DES HISTORISCHEN MATERIALISMUS. Verlag Hahnsche Buchhandlung.

Mahnke, Hans H. (1969): Berlin: fünfte Besatzungszone oder Teil des sowjetischen Besatzungsgebiet? 2 DEUTSCHLAND ARCHIV 473–482.

Mahnke, Hans H. (1972): Der Zugang nach Berlin: Die Historische Entwicklung. 5 DEUTSCHLAND ARCHIV 140–148, 364–387.

Mahnke, Hans H. (1979): Das Hauptstadtproblem. Hans-Adolf Jacobsen et al., eds.: DREI JAHRZEHNTE AUSSENPOLITIK DER DDR. R. Oldenbourg Verlag.

Maier, Charles S. (1997): DISSOLUTION: THE CRISIS OF COMMUNISM AND THE END OF EAST GERMANY. Princeton University Press.

Malcolm, Neil (1984): SOVIET POLITICAL SCIENTISTS AND AMERICAN POLITICS. Macmillan.

Mallinckrodt, Anita D. (1972): WER MACHT DIE AUSSENPOLITIK DER DDR? Droste Verlag.

Malzahn, Manfred (1991): GERMANY 1945–1949: A SOURCEBOOK. Routledge.

Mampel, Siegfried (1974): DDR-Verfassung Fortgeschrieben. 7 DEUTSCHLAND ARCHIV 1152–1157.

Mampel, Siegfried (1982): DIE SOZIALISTISCHE VERFASSUNG DER DEUTSCHEN DEMOKRATISCHEN REPUBLIK. 2d ed. Metzner Verlag.

Mann, Golo (1961): DEUTSCHE GESCHICHTE: 1919–1945. Fischer Verlag.

Mansilla, H.C.F. (1984): Moraltheorien und Verhaltenssteuerung im sozialistischen System. 34 OSTEUROPA 309–317.

Manz, Guenter et al., eds. (2001): SOZIALPOLITIK IN DER DDR: ZIELE UND WIRKLICHKEIT. Trafo Verlag.

Marbach, Renate (1986): Trying to Come to Terms with Soviet Hanky-Panky. THE GERMAN TRIBUNE, June 15, 5.

Marcuse, Peter (1991): MISSING MARX. Monthly Review Press.

Marx, Karl (1933): DAS KAPITAL. Verlag für Literature und Politik.

Marx, Karl (1978): Contributions to the Critique of Hegel's Philosophy of Right. Robert C. Tucker, ed.: THE MARX-ENGELS READER. 2d ed. Norton.

Marx, Karl & Friedrich Engels (1953): DIE HEILIGE FAMILIE UND ANDERE PHILOSOPHISCHE FRÜHSCHRIFTEN. Dietz Verlag.

Marx, Karl & Friedrich Engels (1976): COLLECTED WORKS. Vol. 5. Lawrence & Wishart.

Mason, David S. & Daniel N. Nelson (1987): APATHY IN A COMMUNIST STATE: THE POLITICAL BEHAVIOR OF FUTILITY. Paper delivered at the Annual Meeting of the American International Political Science Association, Chicago.

Matern, Hermann (1959): The Multi-Party System in the GDR. 2:4 WORLD MARXIST REVIEW 26–33 (April).

Mathiopoulos, Margarita (1994): RENDEZVOUS MIT DER DDR. Econ Verlag.

Matschke, Werner (1988): DIE INDUSTRIELLE ENTWICKLUNG IN DER SOWJETISCHEN BESATZUNGSZONE DEUTSCHLANDS VON 1945 BIS 1948. Berlin Verlag A. Spitz.

Matthews, Marvyn (1978): PRIVILEGE IN THE SOVIET UNION: A STUDY OF ELITE LIFE-STYLES UNDER COMMUNISM. Allen & Unwin.

Mayer, Hans (1991): DER TURM VON BABEL: ERINNERUNGEN AN EINE DEUTSCHE DEMOKRATISCHE REPUBLIK. Suhrkamp Verlag.

Mayer, Herbert (1998): "Gewachsenes Vertrauen" zwischen SED und SPD. Juergen

Hofmann & Detlef Nakath, eds.: KONFLIKT, KONFRONTATION, KOOPERATION. Brandenburger Verein für politische Bildung.
Mayer, Wolfgang (2002): FLUCHT UND AUSREISE. Anita Tykve Verlag.
McAdams, A. James (1989): The GDR at Forty: The Perils of Success. 17 GERMAN POLITICS AND SOCIETY 14–26 (Summer).
McCardle, Arthur W. & A. Bruce Boenau, eds. (1984): EAST GERMANY: A NEW GERMAN NATION UNDER SOCIALISM? University Press of America.
McCauley, Martin (1979): MARXISM-LENINISM IN THE GERMAN DEMOCRATIC REPUBLIC: THE SOCIALIST UNITY PARTY (SED). Macmillan.
McCauley, Martin (1983): THE GERMAN DEMOCRATIC REPUBLIC SINCE 1945. St. Martin's Press.
McCauley, Martin (1985): The German Democratic Republic and the Soviet Union. David Childs, ed.: HONECKER'S GERMANY. Allen & Unwin.
McElvoy, Anne (1992): THE SADDLED COW: EAST GERMANY'S LIFE AND LEGACY. Faber & Faber.
McFalls, Laurence H. (1995): COMMUNISM'S COLLAPSE, DEMOCRACY'S DEMISE? New York University Press.
McKenna, David (1988): EAST GERMANY. Chelsea House Publishers.
McLellan, David S. (1966): THE COLD WAR IN TRANSITION. Macmillan.
Meckel, Ursula (1993): Jugend vor, während und nach dem Umbruch in der DDR. Werner Weidenfeld, ed.: DEUTSCHLAND: EINE NATION—DOPPELTE GESCHICHTE. Verlag Wissenschaft und Politik.
Medvedev, Roy A. (1977): ON SOCIALIST DEMOCRACY. Norton.
Medvedev, Roy A. (1989): LET HISTORY JUDGE. Rev. ed. Columbia University Press.
Mehls, Eckart (1998): UNZUMUTBAR: EIN LEBEN IN DER DDR. GNN Verlag.
Meier, Andreas (1998): JUGENDWEIHE—JUGENDFEIER. Deutscher Taschenbuch Verlag.
Mellor, Roy E. H. (1978): THE TWO GERMANIES: A MODERN GEOGRAPHY. Barnes & Noble.
Melville, Andrei (1990): A Personal Introduction. Andrei Melville & Gail W. Lapidus, eds.: THE GLASNOST PAPERS: VOICES ON REFORM FROM MOSCOW. Westview Press.
Melzer, Manfred (1987): The Pricing System of the GDR: Principles and Problems. Ian Jeffries & Manfred Melzer, eds.: THE EAST GERMAN ECONOMY. Croom Helm.
Menge, Marlies (1990): OHNE UNS LÄUFT NICHTS MEHR: DIE REVOLUTION IN DER DDR. Deutsche Verlags-Anstalt.
Merkel, Ina (1999): UTOPIE UND BEDÜRFNIS: DIE GESCHICHTE DER KONSUMKULTUR IN DER DDR. Böhlau Verlag.
Merkel, Ina, ed. (1998): WIR SIND DOCH NICHT DIE MECKER-ECKE DER NATION. Böhlau Verlag.
Merkl, Peter H. (1965): GERMANY: YESTERDAY AND TOMORROW. Oxford University Press.
Merkl, Peter H. (1993): GERMAN UNIFICATION IN THE EUROPEAN CONTEXT. Pennsylvania State University Press.
Merseburger, Peter (1988): GRENZGÄNGER: INNENANSICHTEN DER ANDEREN DEUTSCHEN REPUBLIK. Bertelsmann.

Mertens, Lothar (2002a): Ungelöstes gesellschaftliches Problem: Ehescheidungen in der DDR. Lothar Mertens, ed.: SOZIALE UNGLEICHHEIT IN DER DDR. Duncker & Humblot.

Mertens, Lothar (2002b): Was die Partei wusste, aber nicht sagte. Lothar Mertens, ed.: SOZIALE UNGLEICHHEIT IN DER DDR. Duncker & Humblot.

Meuschel, Sigrid (1992): LEGITIMATION UND PARTEIHERRSCHAFT: ZUM PARADOX VON STABILITÄT UND REVOLUTION IN THE DDR, 1945–1989. Suhrkamp.

Meyer, Alfred G. (1955): THE SOVIET POLITICAL SYSTEM: AN INTERPRETATION. Random House.

Meyer, Alfred G. (1965): THE SOVIET POLITICAL SYSTEM. Random House.

Meyer, Alfred G. (1967): Authority in Communist Political Systems. Lewis J. Edinger, ed.: POLITICAL LEADERSHIP IN INDUSTRIALIZED SOCIETIES. Wiley.

Meyer, Alfred G. (1969): The Comparative Study of Communist Political Systems. Frederic J. Fleron Jr., ed.: COMMUNIST STUDIES AND THE SOCIAL SCIENCES: ESSAYS ON METHODOLOGY AND EMPIRICAL THEORY. Rand McNally.

Meyer, Alfred G. (1970): MARXISM: THE UNITY OF THEORY AND PRACTICE. Harvard University Press.

Meyer, Fritjof (1968): Wird der Volksstaat absterben? 18 OSTEUROPA 384–387.

Miller, Barbara (1999): NARRATIVES OF GUILT AND COMPLIANCE IN UNIFIED GERMANY: STASI INFORMERS AND THEIR IMPACT ON SOCIETY. Routledge.

Milosz, Czeslaw (1960): Introduction. Abram Tertz, ed.: ON SOCIALIST REALISM. Pantheon Books.

Minnerup, Guenter (1982): DDR: VOR UND HINTER DER MAUER. isp-Verlag.

Mises, Ludwig von (1932): DIE GEMEINWIRTSCHAFT: UNTERSUCHUNGEN ÜBER DEN SOZIALISMUS. 2d ed. Fischer Verlag.

Mises, Ludwig von (1937): SOCIALISM: AN ECONOMIC AND SOCIOLOGICAL ANALYSIS. Macmillan.

Mises, Ludwig von (1944): OMNIPOTENT GOVERNMENT: THE RISE OF THE TOTAL STATE AND TOTAL WAR. Yale University Press.

Mises, Ludwig von (1947): PLANNED CHAOS. Foundation for Economic Education.

Misselwitz, Hans-J. (1993): DDR: Geschlossene Gesellschaft und offenes Erbe. Werner Weidenfeld, ed.: DEUTSCHLAND: EINE NATION—DOPPELTE GESCHICHTE. Verlag Wissenschaft und Politik.

Mittenzwei, Werner (2001): DIE INTELLEKTUELLEN. Faber & Faber Verlag.

Mitter, Armin & Stefan Wolle (1993): UNTERGANG AUF RATEN: UNBEKANNTE KAPITEL DER DDR-GESCHICHTE. C. Bertelsmann.

Moeller, Robert G. (1995): DRIVEN INTO "CONTEMPORARY HISTORY": THE EXPULSION FROM THE EAST IN THE PUBLIC MEMORY OF THE FEDERAL REPUBLIK OF GERMANY. Center for German and European Studies, University of California at Berkeley.

Moeller, Wulf-Hinrich (1988): DIE BUNDESREPUBLIK AUS DDR-PERSPEKTIVE. Peter Lang Verlag.

Moreau, Patrick & Juergen Lang (1994): WAS WILL THE PDS? Ullstein Verlag.

Mosher, Steven W. (1993): A MOTHER'S ORDEAL: ONE WOMAN'S FIGHT AGAINST CHINA'S ONE-CHILD POLICY. Harcourt.

Motschmann, Jens (1993): Evangelische Kirche und Wiedervereinigung. Konrad Loew, ed.: URSACHEN UND VERLAUF DER DEUTSCHEN REVOLUTION 1989. Duncker & Humblot Verlag.

Mueckenberger, Erich (1983): Fest mit den Massen verbunden und ihnen voran. 83:6 EINHEIT 815–820.

Mueckenberger, Erich (1985): Freundschaft mit de Sowjetunion: Herzenssache und Staatsdoktrin in unserem Lande. 85:4 EINHEIT 326–332.

Muehlberg, Dietrich (2000): Leben in der DDR: warum untersuchen und wie darstellen. Evemarie Badstuebner, ed.: BEFREMDLICH ANDERS: LEBEN IN DER DDR. Karl Dietz Verlag.

Muehlberg, Felix (2000): Eingaben als Instrument informeller Konfliktbewältigung. Evemarie Badstuebner, ed.: BERFREMDLICH ANDERS: LEBEN IN DER DDR. Karl Dietz Verlag.

Muehlen, Patrik von zur (2000): AUFBRUCH UND UMBRUCH IN DER DDR. Verlag J.H.W. Dietz.

Mueller, Bodo (2001): FASZINATION FREIHEIT: DIE SPEKTAKULÄRSTEN FLUCHTGESCHICHTEN. Ch. Links Verlag.

Mueller, Ernst F. & Peter Greiner (1969): MAUERBAU UND "NEUES DEUTSCHLAND." Bertelsmann.

Mueller, Hanno, ed. (1991): RECHT ODER RACHE: BUCHENWALD 1945–1950. Dipa-Verlag.

Mueller, Marianne & Erwin Mueller (1953): STÜRMT DIE FESTUNG WISSENSCHAFT: DIE SOWJETISIERUNG DER MITTELDEUTSCHEN UNIVERSITÄTEN SEIT 1945. Colloquium Verlag.

Mueller, Silvia & Bernd Florath, eds. (1996): DIE ENTLASSUNG: ROBERT HAVEMAN UND DIE AKADEMIE DER WISSENSCHAFTEN. Robert-Havemann-Gesellschaft.

Mueller-Enbergs, Helmut (1991): DER FALL RUDOLF HERRNSTADT. Ch. Links Verlag.

Mueller-Enbergs, Helmut et al. (1993): DAS FANAL: DAS OFFER DES PFARRERS BRÜSEWITZ UND DIE EVANGELISCHE KIRCHE. Ullstein.

Mueller-Enbergs, Helmut et al. (2000): WER WAR WER IN DER DDR? Ch. Links Verlag.

Mueller-Rieger, Monika, ed. (1997): WENN MUTTI FRÜH ZUR ARBEIT GEHT. Argon.

Mueller-Roemer, Dietrich (1974): DIE NEUE VERFASSUNG DER DDR. Verlag für Wirtschaft und Politik.

Muhlen, Norbert (1951): The New Nazis of Germany: The Totalitarians of the Eastern Zone. 11:1 COMMENTARY 1–10.

Mummert, Hartmut (1999): DIE ARBEITER-UND-BAUERN-INSPEKTION IN DER DDR ZWISCHEN ANSPRUCH UND WIRHLICHKEIT. Gesellschaftswissenschaftliches Forum.

Naimark, Norman M. (1995): THE RUSSIANS IN GERMANY: A HISTORY OF THE SOVIET ZONE OF OCCUPATION, 1945–1949. Harvard University Press.

Nastola, Edgar (1999): INDIVIDUELLE FREIHEIT UND STAATLICHE REGLEMENTIERUNGEN. Tectum Verlag.

Natter, Erik (1994): DIE INNEREN URSACHEN DES UMBRUCHS IN DER DDR. Forschungsgruppe Deutschland.

Nawrocki, Joachim (1967): DAS GEPLANTE WUNDER: LEBEN UND WIRTSCHAFTEN IM ANDEREN DEUTSCHLAND. C. Wegner.

Nawrocki, Joachim (1986): DIE BEZIEHUNGEN ZWISCHEN DEN BEIDEN STAATEN IN DEUTSCHLAND. Verlag Gebr. Holzapfel.

Nehring, Sighart (1974): Zu den Wirtschaftsbeziehungen zwischen der Bundesrepublik Deutschland und der DDR. Herbert Giersch, ed.: DIE WELTWIRTSCHAFT 2.

Nelson, Daniel N., ed. (1980): LOCAL POLITICS IN COMMUNIST COUNTRIES. University Press of Kentucky.

Nettl, J. P. (1951): THE EASTERN ZONE AND SOVIET POLICY IN GERMANY: 1945–50. Oxford University Press.

Neubert, Ehrhart (1990): EINE PROTESTANTISCHE REVOLUTION. Edition Kontext.

Neubert, Ehrhart & Bernd Eisenfeld, eds. (2001): MACHT, OHNMACHT, GEGENMACHT. Edition Temmen.

Neubert, Harald (2002): DIE HYPOTHEK DES KOMMUNISTISCHEN ERBES. VSA-Verlag.

Neugebauer, Gero (1978): PARTEI UND STAATSAPPARAT IN DER DDR. Westdeutscher Verlag.

NEUES DEUTSCHLAND, April 9, 1968, p. 1.

NEUES DEUTSCHLAND, May 8, 1989, p. 3.

NEUES DEUTSCHLAND, May 10, 1989, pp. 3–4.

Neuhaeuser-Wespy, Ulrich (1996): DIE SED UND DIE HISTORIE. Bouvier Verlag.

Nick, Harry (1994): WARUM DIE DDR WIRTSCHAFTLICH GESCHEITERT IST. Gesellschaftwissenschaftliches Forum.

Niemann, Heinz (1993): MEINUNGSFORSCHUNG IN DER DDR: DIE GEHEIMEN BERICHTE DES INSTITUTS FÜR MEINUNGSFORSCHUNG AN DAS POLITBÜRO DER SED. Bund-Verlag.

Nisbet, Robert (1988): THE PRESENT AGE: PROGRESS AND ANARCHY IN MODERN AMERICA. Harper & Row.

Nolywaika, Joachim (1994): DIE SIEGER IM SCHATTEN IHRER SCHULD. Deutsche Verlagsgesellschaft.

Nolywaika, Joachim (1998): DEUTSCHLAND ALS OFFER DER GESCHICHTE. Deutsche Verlagsgesellschaft Rosenheim.

Nooke, Maria (1999): DER VERRATENE TUNNEL. Edition Temmen.

Note (1979): Im Spiegel der Statistik. 26 DER SCHÖFFE 201.

Nothnagle, Alan L. (1999): BUILDING THE EAST GERMAN MYTH. University of Michigan Press.

Nove, Alec (1989): STALINISM AND AFTER: THE ROAD TO GORBACHEV. 3d ed. Unwin Hyman.

Novosti Press Agency (1976): USSR: A SOCIETY OF UNLIMITED OPPORTUNITIES. Novosti.

Novosti Press Agency (1977): THE RIGHTS AND FREEDOMS OF SOVIET CITIZENS. Novosti.

Novosti Press Agency (1978): USSR: 100 QUESTIONS AND ANSWERS. 2 parts. Novosti.

Obst, Werner (1983): REIZ DER IDEE, PLEITE DER PRAXIS: EIN DEUTSCH-DEUTSCHER WIRTSCHAFTSVERGLEICH. Edition Interfrom.

Oehme, Ralph & K-H. Schmidt-Lauzemis (1993): ICH WAR KEIN HELD: LEBEN IN DER DDR. Morgenbuch Verlag.

Oelssner, Fred (1955): Laying the Foundations of Socialism in the German Democratic Republic. 10 INTERNATIONAL AFFAIRS (MOSCOW EDITION) 17–29.

Oelssner, Fred (1957): Staat und Ökonomie in der Übergangsperiode. 5 WIRTSCHAFTSWISSENSCHAFT 321–331.

Oertel, Joachim (1988): DIE DDR-MAFIA: GANGSTER, MAOISTEN, UND NEONAZIS IM SED-STAAT. Anita Tykve Verlag.

Oesterreich, Tina (1988): ICH WAR RF. Verlag Haus am Checkpoint Charlie.

Offner, Hannelore & Klaus Schroeder (2000): EINGEGRENZT—AUSGEGRENZT: BILDENDE KUNST UND PARTEIHERRSCHAFT IN DER DDR 1961–1989. Akademie Verlag.

O'Hara, Michael (1982): WORKERS' OPPOSITION IN COMMUNIST POLITIES: WHY POLAND? WHY NOT EAST GERMANY? Paper delivered at the Annual Meeting of the Western Political Science Association, San Diego, CA.

Opgenoorth, Ernst (1984): VOLKSDEMOKRATIE IM KINO. Verlag Wissenschaft und Politik.

Opitz, Heinrich (1988): Revolutionäre Ideale unserer Gesellschaft. 43 EINHEIT 1106–1111.

Oppermann, Lothar (1989): Unsere Schule: historische Errungenschaft und gesellschaftliche Entwicklungspotenz. 44 EINHEIT 258–263.

Ostermann, Christian F. (2001): UPRISING IN EAST GERMANY 1953. Central European University Press.

Otto, Bertram (1961): HITLER MARSCHIERT IN DER SOWJET-ZONE. Berto Verlag.

Otto, Stefan (1983): Deutschland: Von zwei Seiten betrachtet. Gerhard Finn & Liselotte Julius, eds.: VON DEUTSCHLAND NACH DEUTSCHLAND. Verlag für Wirtschaft und Politik.

Overy, Ricard J. (1997): The Economy of the German "New Order." Ricard J. Overy et al., eds.: THE "NEUORDNUNG" EUROPAS: NS-WIRTSCHAFTSPOLITIK IN DEN BESETZTEN GEBIETEN. Metropol Verlag.

Page, John (1985): Education under the Honeckers. David Childs, ed.: HONECKER'S GERMANY. Allen & Unwin.

Panorama-DDR (1976): INTRODUCING THE GDR. Panorama DDR.

Panorama-DDR (1977): WHAT IS LIFE LIKE IN THE GDR? Panorama Verlag.

Panorama-DDR (1981): THE GDR's ECONOMY IN THE '80s. Panorama Verlag.

Panorama-DDR (1987): GDR '87: FACTS AND FIGURES. Panorama DDR.

Paraskewopoulos, Spiridon (1985): KONJUNKTURKRISEN IM SOZIALIMUS. Gustav Fischer Verlag.

Pasternack, Peer (1999): HOCHSCHULE & WISSENSCHAFT IN SBZ/DDR/OSTDEUTSCHLAND 1945–1995. Deutscher Studien Verlag.

Patzelt, Werner J. & Roland Schirmer, eds. (2002): DIE VOLKSKAMMER DER DDR. Westdeutscher Verlag.

Pätzold, Rainer (1991): WENN DIKTATOREN FALLEN. Haag & Herchen.

Perlmutter, Amos (1981): MODERN AUTHORITARIANISM: A COMPARATIVE INSTITUTIONAL ANALYSIS. Yale University Press.

Pernkopf, Johannes (1982): DER 17. JUNI 1953 IN DER LITERATUR DER BEIDEN DEUTSCHEN STAATEN. Akademischer Verlag Hans-Dieter Heinz.

Peterson, Edward N. (1999): RUSSIAN COMMANDS AND GERMAN RESISTANCE: THE SOVIET OCCUPATION 1945–1949. Peter Lang.

Petschull, Juergen (1981): WITH THE WIND TO THE WEST: THE GREAT BALLOON ESCAPE. Hodder & Stoughton.

Petzold, Hendrik (2001): EIN KESSEL BUNTES UND MEHR: HINTER DIE KULISSEN VON DDR-UNTERHALTUNGSSENDUNGEN GESCHAUT. Mitteldeutscher Verlag.

Peukert, Detlev J. K. (1994): Working-Class Resistance: Problems and Options. David C. Large, ed.: CONTENDING WITH HITLER: VARIETIES OF GERMAN RESISTANCE IN THE THIRD REICH. Cambridge University Press.

Pfaff, Dieter (1968): DIE ENTWICKLUNG DER SOWJETISCHEN RECHTSLEHRE. Verlag für Wirtschaft und Politik.

Philipsen, Dirk (1993): WE WERE THE PEOPLE. Duke University Press.

Phillips, Ann L. (1986): SOVIET POLICY TOWARD EAST GERMANY RECONSIDERED: THE POSTWAR DECADE. Greenwood Press.

Picaper, Jean-Paul (1982): DDR: BILD IM WANDEL. Colloquium Verlag.

Pieck, Wilhelm (1947): DER NEUE WEG ZUM GEMEINSAMEN KAMPF FÜR DEN STURZ DER HITLERDIKTATUR (Lecture, October 1935). Verlag Neuer Weg.

Pirker, Theo et al. (1995): DER PLAN ALS BEFEHL UND FIKTION. Westdeutscher Verlag.

Plato, Alexander von & Wolfgang Meinicke (1991): ALTE HEIMAT—NEUE ZEIT. Verlags-Anstalt Union.

Pleil, Ingolf (2001): MIELKE, MACHT UND MEISTERSCHAFT. Ch. Links Verlag.

Pleitgen, Fritz, ed. (2001): DIE AUSBÜRGERUNG: ANFANG VOM ENDE DER DDR. Ullstein Verlag.

Plischke, Elmer (1961): CONTEMPORARY GOVERNMENT OF GERMANY. Houghton Mifflin.

Plock, Ernest D. (1993): EAST GERMAN–WEST GERMAN RELATIONS AND THE FALL OF THE GDR. Westview Press.

Podewin, Norbert (1996): DER BITTE DES GENOSSEN WALTER ULBRICHT ZU ENTSPRECHEN. Gesellschaftswissenschaftliches Forum.

Podewin, Norbert (1999): WALTER ULBRICHTS SPÄTE REFORMEN UND IHRE GEGNER. Gesellschaftswissenschaftliches Forum.

Poeschel, Kurt & Joachim Tripoczky (1966): PROBLEME DER KADERARBEIT IN DER SOZIALISTISCHEN INDUSTRIE. Staatsverlag.

Pohl, Klaus (1999): DAS DEUTSCHLANDGEFÜHL. Rowohlt Verlag.

Pollack, Detlef (2000): POLITISCHER PROTEST: POLITISCH ALTERNATIVE GRUPPEN IN DER DDR. Leske + Budrich.

Pollack, Detlef & Dieter Rink, eds. (1997): ZWISCHEN VERWEIGERUNG UND OPPOSITION. Campus Verlag.

Pollock, James K. et al. (1955): GERMAN DEMOCRACY AT WORK. University of Michigan Press.

Pond, Elizabeth (1993): BEYOND THE WALL: GERMANY'S ROAD TO UNIFICATION. Brookings Institution.

Poppe, Eberhard (1980): GRUNDRECHTE DES BÜRGERS IN DER SOZIALISTISCHEN GESELLSCHAFT. Staatsverlag.

Poppe, Eberhard (1984): POLITISCHE UND PERSÖNLICHE GRUNDRECHTE IN DEN KÄMPFEN UNSERER ZEIT. Staatsverlag.

Poppe, Eberhard (1985): Menschenrechte: gesicherte soziale Tatbestände in unserem Land. 85:2 EINHEIT 156–162.

Pordzik, Wolfgang et al. (1993): GERMAN DEMOCRACY ON GUARD: CONFRONTING POLITICAL EXTREMISM, NEO-NAZISM AND XENOPHOBIA. Konrad-Adenauer-Stiftung.

Possner, Wilfried (1995): IMMER BEREIT! PARTEIAUFTRAG: KÄMPFEN, SPIELEN, FRÖHLICH SEIN. Edition Ost.

Possony, Stefan T. (1963): Berlin: Focus of World Strategy. David S. Collier & Kurt Glaser, eds.: BERLIN AND THE FUTURE OF EASTERN EUROPE. Henry Regnery.

Pounds, Norman J. G. (1962): DIVIDED GERMANY AND BERLIN. Van Nostrand.

Poutrus, Patrice G. (2002): DIE ERFINDUNG DES GOLDBROILERS: ÜBER DEN ZUSAMMENHANG ZWISCHEN HERRSCHAFTSSICHERUNG UND KONSUMENTWICKLUNG IN DER DDR. Böhlau Verlag.

Prauss, Herbert (1960): DOCH WAR ES NICHT DIE WAHRHEIT. Morus.

PRAVDA, September 9, 1962.

Pravda, Alex & Blair A. Ruble, eds. (1986): TRADE UNIONS IN COMMUNIST STATES. Allen & Unwin.

Pritchard, Gareth (2000): THE MAKING OF THE GDR 1945–53: FROM ANTIFASCISM TO STALINISM. Manchester University Press.

Prokop, Siegfried (1986): ÜBERGANG ZUM SOZIALISMUS IN DER DDR. Dietz Verlag.

Prokop, Siegfried (1994): Einig Vaterland? Von der DDR zur "distinct society." Horsta Krum & Siegfried Prokop, eds.: DIE LETZTEN JAHRE DER DDR. Gesellschaftswissenschaftliches Forum.

Prokop, Siegfried (2003): INTELLEKTUELLE IM KRISENJAHR 1953. Schkeuditzer Buchverlag.

Przybylski, Peter (1991): TATORT POLITBÜRO: DIE AKTE HONECKER. Rowohlt Verlag.

Pucher, Paul (1984): DES DEUTSCHEN VATERLAND: WENDIGKEIT STATT WENDE. Universitas.

Raabe, Thomas (1995): SED-STAAT UND KATHOLISCHE KIRCHE. Schöningh Verlag.

Raendchen, Oliver (2000): VIETNAMESEN IN DER DDR. Seacom Edition.

Rakowska-Harmstone, Teresa (1979): Aspect of Political Change. Teresa Rakowska-Harmstone, ed.: PERSPECTIVES FOR CHANGE IN COMMUNIST SOCIETIES. Westview Press.

Raue, Guenter (1986): GESCHICHTE DES JOURNALISMUS IN DER DDR 1945–1961. VEB Bibliographisches Institut Leipzig.

Rausch, Heinz (1974): Einleitung. Heinz Rausch & Theo Stammen, eds.: DDR; DAS POLITISCHE, WIRTSCHAFTLICHE UND SOZIALE SYSTEM. C. H. Beck.

Rausch, Heinz (1985): Herrschaftsstrukturen. Eckhard Jeese, ed.: BUNDESREPUBLIK DEUTSCHLAND AND DEUTSCHE DEMOKRATISCHE REPUBLIK. Colloquium Verlag.
Rauschek, Kurt (1984): ARBEITERKLASSE UND KÜNSTLER IM BÜDNIS. Dietz Verlag.
Rayfield, Donald (2004): STALIN UND SEINE HENKER. Blessing Verlag.
Read, Anthony & David Fisher (1988): THE DEADLY EMBRACE: HITLER, STALIN, AND THE NAZI-SOVIET PACT 1939–1941. Norton.
Rehlinger, Ludwig A. (1991): FREIKAUF: DIE GESCHÄFTE DER DDR MIT POLITISCH VERFOLGTEN 1963–1989. Ullstein Verlag.
Reich, Guenter (1996): VIER JAHRZEHNTE DDR: VERLORENE JAHRE? Frieling Verlag.
Reichelt, Hans (1997): BLOCKFLÖTE ODER WAS? ZUR GESCHICHTE DER DEMOKRATISCHEN BAUERNPARTEI DEUTSCHLANDS (DBD) 1948–1990. Edition Ost.
Reichert, Mike (1999): KERNENERGIEWIRTSCHAFT IN DER DDR. Scripta Mercaturae Verlag.
Reif-Spirek, Peter & Bodo Ritscher, eds. (1999): SPEZIALLAGER IN DER SBZ. Ch. Links Verlag.
Rein, Gerhard (1990): DIE PROTESTANTISCHE REVOLUTION 1987–1990. Wichern Verlag.
Reinhardt, Kurt F. (1989): GERMANY: 2000 YEARS. Rev. ed., vol. 2. Continuum Verlag.
Reinhold, Otto (1984): Die Krise der 80er Jahre in der Welt des Kapitals. 39 EINHEIT 250–256.
Reinhold, Otto (1985a): Unsere Ökonomie in der Gesellschaftskonzeption des entwickelten Sozialismus. 40 EINHEIT 7–13.
Reinhold, Otto (1985b): Sozialistische Planwirtschaft: Grundlage für die Politik der Hauptaufgabe. 40 EINHEIT 969–976.
Reinwarth, Hans & Joachim Schlegel (1966): Vervollkommnung des Arbeitsstils der Gerichte. 20 NEUE JUSTIZ 68–71.
REISEBUCH DDR (1986). VEB Tourist Verlag.
Reissig, Rolf (2002): DIALOG DURCH DIE MAUER: DIE UMSTRITTENE ANNÄHERUNG VON SPD UND SED. Campus Verlag.
Reissig, Rolf & Gert-Joachim Glaessner, eds. (1991): DAS ENDE EINES EXPERIMENTES. Dietz Verlag.
Reuth, Ralf & Andreas Boente (1993): KOMPLOTT: WIE ES WIRKLICH ZUR DEUTSCHEN EINHEIT KAM. Piper Verlag.
Revel, Jean-Francois (1977): THE TOTALITARIAN TEMPTATION. Doubleday.
Richert, Ernst (1958): DIE ROLLE DER VOLKSVERTRETUNGEN. Westdeutscher Verlag.
Richert, Ernst (1961): DIE SOWJETZONE IN DER PHASE DER KOEXISTENZPOLITIK. Landeszentrale.
Richert, Ernst (1963): MACHT OHNE MANDAT: DER STAATSAPPARAT IN DER SOWJETISCHEN BESATZUNGSZONE DEUTSCHLANDS. Westdeutscher Verlag.
Richert, Ernst (1966): DAS ZWEITE DEUTSCHLAND: EIN STAAT, DER NICHT SEIN DARF. Fischer Verlag.

Richert, Ernst (1967): SOZIALISTISCHE UNIVERSITÄT: DIE HOCHSCHULPOLITIK DER SED. Colloquium Verlag.

Richert, Ernst (1968): Bürger und Staat im Grundgesetz und in der DDR-Verfassung. 1 DEUTSCHLAND ARCHIV 593–600.

Richter, Edelbert (1998): AUS OSTDEUTSCHER SICHT. Böhlau Verlag.

Richter, Klemens (1980): Die DDR: Eine Ordensgesellschaft? 13 DEUTSCHLAND ARCHIV 1099–1101.

Richter, Michael (1990): DIE OST-CDU 1948–1952: ZWISCHEN WIDERSTAND UND GLEICHSCHALTUNG. Droste Verlag.

Richter, Michael (1995a): DIE REVOLUTION IN DEUTSCHLAND 1989/90. Hannah-Arendt-Institut.

Richter, Michael (1995b): Vom Widerstand der christlichen Demokraten in der DDR. Brigitte Kaff, ed.: GEFÄHRLICHE POLITISCHE GEGNER. Droste Verlag.

Riedel, Heide (1994): MIT UNS ZIEHT DIE NEUE ZEIT: 40 JAHRE DDR-MEDIEN. VISTAS Verlag.

Riedel, Ulrich (1973): DER EINFLUSS DES SOWJETRECHTS UND DER WEIMARER VERFASSUNG AUF DIE VERFASSUNG DER DEUTSCHEN DEMOKRATISCHEN REPUBLIK VOM 7.10.1949. Dissertation: Göttingen.

Riemann, Tord & Ernst-Otto Schwabe (1976): FREEDOM, DEMOCRACY, HUMAN RIGHTS: FOR WHOM AND FOR WHAT? Panorama.

Ritscher, Bodo et al. (1996): DIE SOWJETISCHEN SPEZIALLAGER IN DEUTSCHLAND. Wallstein Verlag.

Ritter, Gertraude (1973): Beschwerdeaussch üsse: Instrumente der örtlichen Volksvertretungen zur Wahrung der sozialistischen Gesetzlichkeit. 22 STAAT UND RECHT 380–392.

Ritter, Traudel (1971): About the Decree on Petitions Procedure in the GDR. 71:2 LAW AND LEGISLATION IN THE GDR 7–23.

Robbins, Lionel Charles (1937): ECONOMIC PLANNING AND INTERNATIONAL ORDER. Macmillan.

Robbins, Lionel Charles (1939): THE ECONOMIC BASIS OF CLASS CONFLICT AND OTHER ESSAYS IN POLITICAL ECONOMY. Macmillan.

Roberts, Henry L. (1956): RUSSIA AND AMERICA: DANGERS AND PROSPECTS. Mentor.

Rodden, John (2002): REPAINTING THE LITTLE RED SCHOOLHOUSE. Oxford University Press.

Roeder, Karl-Heinz & Wolfgang Weichelt (1981): Über das antisozialistische Pluralismus-Konzept. 81:7 EINHEIT 700–706.

Roepke, Wilhelm (1942): DIE GESELLSCHAFTSKRISIS DER GEGENWART. 4th ed. E. Rentsch.

Roepke, Wilhelm (1943): DIE LEHRE VON DER WIRTSCHAFT. E. Rentsch.

Roepke, Wilhelm (1947): DIE KRISE DES KOLLEKTIVISMUS. Kurt Desch.

Roesler, Joerg (1998): Fortschritte und Rückschritte in den Wirtschaftsbeziehungen zwischen beiden deutschen Staaten 1945–1989. Juergen Hofmann & Detlef Nakath, eds.: KONFLIKT, KONFRONTATION, KOOPERATION. Brandenburger Verein für politische Bildung.

Roessler, Ruth-Kristin (1994): DIE ENTNAZIFIZIERUNGSPOLITIK DER KPD/SED 1945–1948. Keip Verlag.

Rosenlöcher, Thomas (1997): OSTGEZETTER: BEITRÄGE ZUR SCHIMPF-KULTUR. Suhrkamp Verlag.
Rother, Ulrike (2001): KUNSTERZIEHUNG IN DER DDR. VDG Verlag.
Rottleuthner, Hubert, ed. (1999): DAS HAVEMANN-VERFAHREN. Nomos Verlag.
Rueddenklau, Wolfgang (1992): STÖRENFRIED: DDR-OPPOSITION 1986–1989, MIT TEXTEN AUS DEN "UMWELTBLÄTTERN." BasisDruck.
Rusinow, Dennison (1977): THE YUGOSLAV EXPERIMENT, 1948–1974. University of California Press.
Russell, Bertrand (1896): GERMAN SOCIAL DEMOCRACY: SIX LECTURES. Longmans, Green.
Rutland, Peter (1985): THE MYTH OF THE PLAN: LESSONS OF SOVIET PLANNING EXPERIENCE. Hutchinson.
Saechsische Landeszentrale für politische Bildung (1999): EINER VON BEIDEN MUSS SO BALD WIE MÖGLICH ENTFERNT WERDEN. Kiepenheuer Verlag.
Sager, Peter (1986): DIE VORENTHALTUNG DER MENSCHENRECHTE IN UNTERSUCHUNGSHAFT UND STRAFVOLLZUG DER DDR. Schweizerisches Ost-Institut.
Sahr, Siegfried (1987): Aufgaben der Gewerkschaften bei der weiteren Entwicklung der sozialistischen Demokratie. 41 NEUE JUSTIZ 86–89.
Sandford, Gregory W. (1983): FROM HITLER TO ULBRICHT: THE COMMUNIST RECONSTRUCTION OF EAST GERMANY: 1945–46. Princeton University Press.
Sarotte, M. E. (2001): DEALING WITH THE DEVIL: EAST GERMANY, DETENTE, AND OSTPOLITIK 1969–1973. University of North Carolina Press.
Satjukow, Silke & Rainer Gries, eds. (2002): SOZIALISTISCHE HELDEN. Ch. Links Verlag.
Sauer, Heiner & Hans-Otto Plumeyer (1993): DER SALZGITTER REPORT: ZENTRALE ERFASSUNGSSTELLE BERICHTET ÜBER VERBRECHEN IM SED-STAAT. Ullstein Verlag.
Sauermann, Ekkehard (1960): Staatsbürgerkunde-Unterricht und gesellschaftliches Leben. Institut für Philosophie der Humboldt-Universität Berlin: DER STAAT SIND WIR: BEITRÄGE ZU PROBLEMEN DER ENTWICKLUNG DES SOZIALISTISCHEN STAATSBEWUSSTSEINS IN DER DDR. Dietz Verlag.
Savada, Andrea M. (1994): NORTH KOREA: A COUNTRY STUDY. U.S. Department of the Army.
Scalapino, Robert A. (1992): THE LAST LENINISTS: THE UNCERTAIN FUTURE OF ASIA'S COMMUNIST STATES. Center for Strategic and International Studies.
Scalapino, Robert A. & Chong-Sik Lee (1972): COMMUNISM IN KOREA. 2 vols. University of California Press.
Scalapino, Robert A. & Dalchoong Kim, eds. (1988): ASIAN COMMUNISM: CONTINUITY AND TRANSITION. University of California, Center for Korean Studies.
Schabowski, Guenter (1991): DER ABSTURZ. Rowohlt Verlag.
Schabowski, Guenter (1994): ABSCHIED VON DER UTOPIE: DE DDR, DAS DEUTSCHE FIASKO DES MARXISMUS. Franz Steiner Verlag.
Schacht, Ulrich (1984): HOHENECKER PROTOKOLLE: AUSSAGEN ZUR

GESCHICHTE DER POLITISCHEN VERFOLGUNG VON FRAUEN IN DER DDR. Ammann Verlag.

Schalck-Golokowski, Alexander (2000): DEUTSCH-DEUTSCHE ERINNERUNGEN. Rowohlt Verlag.

Scharf, C. Bradley (1984): POLITICS AND CHANGE IN EAST GERMANY. Westview Press.

Scharschmidt, Gerhard (1989): Ökonomische Zusammenarbeit im gemeinsamen Haus Europa. 44 EINHEIT 264–270.

Schedlinski, Rainer (1991): DIE ARROGANZ DER OHNMACHT. Aufbau Verlag.

Scheel, Walter (1986): WEN SCHMERZT NOCH DEUTSCHLANDS TEILUNG? Rowohlt Verlag.

Schell, Manfred & Werner Kalinka (1991): STASI UND KEIN ENDE: DIE PERSONEN UND FAKTEN. Ullstein Verlag.

Schenk, Fritz (1962): IM VORZIMMER DER DIKTATUR: 12 JAHRE PANKOW. Kiepenheuer & Witsch.

Scherzer, Landolf (1997): MITLEID IST UMSONST, NEID MUSST DU DIR ERARBEITEN. Edition Ost.

Scherzer, Landolf (2002): DIE FREMDEN: UNERWÜNSCHTE BEGEGNUNGEN UND VERBOTENE PROTOKOLLE. Aufbau-Verlag.

Schiller, Dieter (2001): KURELLAS KULTURKOMMISSION. Gesellschaftswissenschaftlichs Forum.

Schimunek, Franz-Peter (2002): DIE UNHEILIGE NEUGIER: GLANZ UND ELEND SOZIALWISSENSCHAFTLICHER FORSCHUNG IN DER DDR. Peter Lang Verlag.

Schirdewan, Karl (1994): AUFSTAND GEGEN ULBRICHT. Aufbau Verlag.

Schirdewan, Karl (1998): EIN JAHRHUNDERT LEBEN. Edition Ost.

Schmidt, Gerd (1999): ICH WAR BUTLER BEIM POLITBÜRO. GNN Verlag.

Schmiedebach, Heinz-Peter & Karl-Heinz Spiess, eds. (2001): STUDENTISCHES AUFBEGEHREN IN DER FRÜHEN DDR. Franz Steiner Verlag.

Schmitt, Dieter (1993): DOKTRIN UND SPRACHE IN DER EHEMALIGEN DDR BIS 1989. Peter Lang Verlag.

Schneider, Eberhard (1978): THE GDR: THE HISTORY, POLITICS, ECONOMY, AND SOCIETY OF EAST GERMANY. C. Hurst.

Schneider, Gernot (1988): WIRTSCHAFTSWUNDER DDR: ANSPRUCH UND REALITÄT. Bund-Verlag.

Schneider, Matthias (1991a): UND PLÖTZLICH GING ALLES SO SCHNELL. Marianne Breuer Verlag.

Schneider, Michael (1990): DIE ABGETRIEBENE REVOLUTION: VON DER STAATSFIRMA IN DIE DM-KOLONIE. Elefanten Press.

Schneider, Michael C. (1998): BILDUNG FÜR NEUE ELITEN: ZUR GRÜNDUNG DER ARBEITER-UND-BAUERN-FAKULTÄTEN IN DER SBZ/DDR. Hannah-Arendt-Institut.

Schneider, Rolf (1991b): FRÜHLING IM HERBST: NOTIZEN VOM UNTERGANG DER DDR. Steidl Verlag.

Schneider, Rolf (1992): VOLK OHNE TRAUER: NOTIZEN NACH DEM UNTERGANG DER DDR. Steidl Verlag.

Schnoor, Rainer, ed. (1999): AMERIKANISTIK IN DER DDR. Trafo Verlag.

Schoenbaum, David & Elizabeth Pond (1996): THE GERMAN QUESTION AND OTHER GERMAN QUESTIONS. St. Martin's Press.

Schoeps, Hans-Joachim (1951): DIE EHRE PREUSSENS. F. Vorwerk Verlag.
Schoeps, Hans-Joachim (1967): PREUSSEN: BILDER UND ZEUGNISSE. Propylaen Verlag.
Scholz, Rupert (1988): DARAN HALTE ICH FEST. Verlag Bonn Aktuell.
Scholze, Jana (1999): Ausgezeichnete Höchstleistungen. Andreas Ludwig, ed.: FORTSCHRITT, NORM UND EIGENSINN: ERKUNDUNGEN IM ALLTAG DER DDR. Ch. Links Verlag.
Schramm, Christine (2001): Parteipolitik für den Mittelstand in der LDPD. Friedrich Thiessen, ed.: ZWISCHEN PLAN UND PLEITE. Böhlau Verlag.
Schreiter, Helfried, ed. (1990): DIE LETZTEN TAGE DER DDR: BÜRGER BERICHTEN VOM ENDE IHRER REPUBLIK. Edition Fischerinsel.
Schroeder, Klaus (2000): DER PREIS DER EINHEIT. Carl Hanser Verlag.
Schroeder, Richard (1990): DENKEN IM ZWIELICHT. J.C.B. Mohr Verlag.
Schueddekopf, Charles (1990): WIR SIND DAS VOLK. Rowohlt Verlag.
Schuerer, Gerhard (1968): New Methods of Socialist Planning and Economic Management. Willy Stoph et al., eds.: THE NEXT STEPS IN THE NATIONAL ECONOMY OF THE GDR ON THE ROAD TO THE COMPLETION OF SOCIALISM. Verlag Zeit im Bild.
Schuerer, Gerhard (1999): Planung und Lenkung der Volkswirtschaft in der DDR. Eberhard Kuhrt, ed.: DIE ENDZEIT DER DDR-WIRTSCHAFT. Leske & Budrich.
Schuessler, Gerhard (1979): The Development of the Political System of the Socialist Society. Wolfgang Weichelt & Karl-Heinz Roeder, eds.: POLITICAL SCIENCES IN THE GDR. National Committee for the Political Sciences in the GDR.
Schuessler, Gerhard (1980): Sozialistisches Rechtsbewusstsein und demokratischer Zentralismus. 27 DER SCHÖFFE 269–273.
Schuessler, Gerhard (1981a): Die Rolle des sozialistischen Staates und seines Rechtes bei der weiteren Gestaltung der entwickelten sozialistischen Gesellschaft. 35 NEUE JUSTIZ 50–53.
Schuessler, Gerhard (1981b): Die Beschlüsse des X. Parteitages der SED: Richtschnur der staats- und rechtswissenschaftlichen Forschung. 35 NEUE JUSTIZ 434–437.
Schuessler, Gerhard & Wolfgang Weichelt, eds. (1977): SOZIALISMUS UND DEMOKRATIE: DIE DEMOKRATIE IN THEORIE UND PRAXIS SOZIALISTISCHER LÄNDER. Staatsverlag.
Schuetzsack, Axel (1990): EXODUS IN DIE EINHEIT: DIE MASSENFLUCHT AUS DER DDR 1989. Verlag Ernst Knoth.
Schultz, Joachim (1956): DER FUNKTIONÄR IN DER EINHEITSPARTEI: KADERPOLITIK UND BÜROKRATISIERUNG IN DER SED. Ring-Verlag.
Schulz, Eberhard & Peter Danylow (1985): BEWEGUNG IN DER DEUTSCHEN FRAGE? Deutsche Gesellschaft für Auswärtige Politik.
Schulz, Eberhard et al., eds. (1982): GDR FOREIGN POLICY. M. E. Sharpe.
Schulz, Werner (1968): Bemerkungen zur neuen Verfassung der DDR. 9:2 JAHRBUCH FÜR OSTRECHT 7–16, 57–80.
Schulze, Gerhard (1978): GESELLSCHAFT, STAAT, BÜRGER. 2d ed. Staatsverlag.
Schulze, Gerhard (1980): Vom humanistischen Wesen sozialistischer Demokratie. 80 EINHEIT 765–770.
Schulze, Gerhard (1985): Sozialistische Demokratie und Entwicklung der Persön-

lichkeit. Rat für staats- und rechtswissenschaftliche Forschung an der Akademie der Wissenschaften der DDR: VERVOLLKOMMNUNG DER SOZIALISTISCHEN DEMOKRATIE: TRIEBKRAFT DER SOZIALISTISCHEN GESELLSCHAFT. Staatsverlag.

Schumpeter, Joseph A. (1950): CAPITALISM, SOCIALISM, AND DEMOCRACY. Harper.

Schuster, Ulrike (1999): MUT ZUM EIGENEN DENKEN? DDR-STUDENTEN UND FREIE DEUTSCHE JUGEND 1961–1965. Metropol Verlag.

Schwan, Heribert (1997): ERICH MIELKE: DER MANN, DER DIE STASI WAR. Droemer Knaur.

Schwarz, Sabine & Peter Schwarz (1997): Schwerter zu Pflugscharen. Juergen Aretz & Wolfgang Stock, eds.: DIE VERGESSENEN OFFER DER DDR. Bastei Verlag.

Schwarze, Hanns W. (1969): DIE DDR IST KEINE ZONE MEHR. Kiepenheuer & Witsch.

Schwarze, Hanns W. (1973): THE GDR TODAY: LIFE IN THE "OTHER" GERMANY. Wolff.

Schwarzer, Oskar (1999): SOZIALISTISCHE ZENTRALPLANWIRTSCHAFT IN DER DDR. Franz Steiner Verlag.

Schweigler, Gebhard L. (1975): NATIONAL CONSCIOUSNESS IN DIVIDED GERMANY. Sage.

Schweitzer, Carl-C. et al., eds. (1984): POLITICS AND GOVERNMENT IN THE FEDERAL REPUBLIC OF GERMANY: BASIC DOCUMENTS. Berg Publishers.

Segert, Astrid & Irene Zierke (2000): SOZIALSTRUKTUR UND MILIEUERFAHRUNGEN. Westdeutscher Verlag.

Seide, Gernot (1984): Religiöse Renaissance in der Sowjetunion: Mythos oder Wirklichkeit? 34 OSTEUROA 910–920.

Seidel, Dietmar (1981): Verantwortung und ihre rechtliche Relevanz. 35 NEUE JUSTIZ 112.

Seiffert, Wolfgang (1983): KANN DER OSTBLOCK ÜBERLEBEN: DER COMECON UND DIE KRISE DES SOZIALISTISCHEN WIRTSCHAFTSSYSTEMS. Gustav Lübbe Verlag.

Seiffert, Wolfgang & Norbert Treutwein (1991): DIE SCHALCK-PAPIERE. Zsolnay Verlag.

Selucky, Radoslav (1972): ECONOMIC REFORMS IN EASTERN EUROPE. Praeger.

Seppelt, Hans-Joachim & Holger Schueck, eds. (1999): ANKLAGE: KINDERDOPING. DAS ERBE DES DDR-SPORTS. Tenea Verlag.

Sharnoff, Philip (1983): PRINCIPLES OF SCIENTIFIC SOCIALISM: A PRIMER ON MARXISM-LENINISM. Ramparts Press.

Shevchenko, Arkady N. (1985): BREAKING WITH MOSCOW. Ballantine.

Shinn, Rinn-Sup et al. (1969): AREA HANDBOOK FOR NORTH KOREA. U.S. Government Printing Office.

Shlaes, Amity (1991): GERMANY: THE EMPIRE WITHIN. Farrar, Straus & Giroux.

Shlapentokh, Vladimir (1986): SOVIET PUBLIC OPINION AND IDEOLOGY. Praeger.

Shlapentokh, Vladimir (1988): SOVIET IDEOLOGIES IN THE PERIOD OF GLASNOST. Praeger.

Shub, David (1958): LENIN. Limes Verlag.

Sichel, Kenneth L. (1974): Your Illness Consists of Your Dissenting Opinions. 6 MICHIGAN STATE POLITICAL REVIEW 1–44.

Sichelschmidt, Gustav (1992): DER EWIGE DEUTSCHENHASS: HINTERMÄNNER UND NUTZNIESSER DES ANTIGERMANISMUS. Arndt Verlag.

Sichrovsky, Peter (1999): DER ANTIFA-KOMPLEX. Universitas Verlag.

Siebenmorgen, Peter (1993): STAATSSICHERHEIT DER DDR: DER WESTEN IM FADENKREUZ DER STASI. Bouvier Verlag.

Siebs, Benno-Eide (1999): DIE AUSSENPOLITIK DER DDR 1976–1989. Ferdinand Schöningh Verlag.

Siegert, Peter-Paul (1970): Weitere Vervollkommnung des Zusammenwirkens der Gerichte mit den Konfliktkommissionen. 24 NEUE JUSTIZ 257–260.

Siemon-Netto, Uwe (1995): THE FABRICATED LUTHER. Concordia Publshing House.

Siewert, Heinz (1988): über die demokratische Mitwirkung der Gewerkschaften bei der Verwirklichung des sozialistischen Arbeitsrechts. 43 EINHEIT 854–856.

Singer, Karl (2001): Das Bankensystem der DDR. Friedrich Thiessen, ed.: ZWISCHEN PLAN UND PLEITE. Böhlau Verlag.

Skilling, H. Gordon (1979): PLURALISM IN CZECHOSLOVAK POLITICAL CULTURE: CONTINUITY AND CHANGE IN AN INTERNATIONAL SETTING. Paper delivered at the World Congress of the International Political Science Association, Moscow.

Skribanowitz, Gert (1991): "FEINDLICH EINGESTELLT": VOM PRAGER FRÜHLING INS DEUTSCHE ZUCHTHAUS. Anita Tykve Verlag.

Sleeper, Raymond S., ed. (1987): MESMERIZED BY THE BEAR: THE SOVIET STRATEGY OF DECEPTION. Dodd, Mead.

Slider, Darrell (1986): Worker Participation in Socialist Systems: The Soviet Case. 18 COMPARATIVE POLITICS 401–418.

Smith, Arthur L., Jr. (2002): KIDNAP CITY: COLD WAR BERLIN. Greenwood Press.

Smith, Jean Edward (1967): The Red Prussians of the GDR. 82 POLITICAL SCIENCE QUARTERLY 368–385.

Smith, Jean Edward (1969): GERMANY BEYOND THE WALL. Little, Brown.

Smyser, W. R. (1992): THE ECONOMY OF UNITED GERMANY. St. Martin's Press.

Solga, Heike (1995): AUF DEM WEG IN EINE KLASSENLOSE GESELLSCHAFT? Akademie Verlag.

Sommer, Stefan (2002): DAS GROSSE LEXIKON DES DDR-ALLTAGS. Schwarzkopf & Schwarzkopf.

Sontheimer, Kurt & Wilhelm Bleek (1975): THE GOVERNMENT AND POLITICS OF EAST GERMANY. Hutchinson.

Sozialistische Einheitspartei Deutschlands (1983): THESES PROPOSED BY THE CENTRAL COMMITTEE OF THE SED FOR THE KARL MARX YEAR 1983. Verlag Zeit im Bild; also in: 83:1–2 LAW AND LEGISLATION 39–53 (1983).

Spanger, Hans-Joachim (1982): DIE SED UND DER SOZIALDEMOKRATISMUS: IDEOLOGISCHE ABGRENZUNG IN DER DDR. Verlag Wissenschaft und Politik.

Spechler, Dina R. (1982): PERMITTED DISSENT IN THE USSR. Praeger.

Spencer, Robert (1984): The Origins of the Federal Republic of Germany: 1944–1949. Carl-C. Schweitzer et al., eds.: POLITICS AND GOVERNMENT IN THE FEDERAL REPUBLIC OF GERMANY: BASIC DOCUMENTS. Berg Publishers.

Sperlich, Peter W. (1971): CONFLICT AND HARMONY IN HUMAN AFFAIRS: A STUDY OF CROSS-PRESSURES AND POLITICAL BEHAVIOR. Rand McNally.

Sperlich, Peter W. (1982): THE THEORY AND PRACTICE OF LAY ADJUDICATION: EAST GERMAN COMMISSIONERS AND UNITED STATES JURORS. Paper delivered at the World Congress of the International Political Science Association, Rio de Janeiro.

Sperlich, Peter W. (1985): THE INCENTIVE STRUCTURE OF LAY ADJUDICATORS IN TWO LEGAL CULTURES. Paper delivered at the World Congress of the International Political Science Association, Paris, France.

Sperlich, Peter W. (2002): ROTTEN FOUNDATIONS: THE CONCEPTUAL BASIS OF THE MARXIST-LENINIST REGIMES OF EAST GERMANY AND OTHER COUNTRIES OF THE SOVIET BLOC. Praeger.

Sperlich, Peter W. (forthcoming): POPULAR JUSTICE IN A MARXIST-LENINIST SOCIETY: THE EAST GERMAN SOCIAL COURTS AND OTHER ASPECTS OF GDR LAW. Praeger.

Spittmann, Ilse (1981): Die Mauer ist eine hässliche Sache. 14 DEUTSCHLAND ARCHIV 785–789.

Spittmann, Ilse (1990): DIE DDR UNTER HONECKER. Edition Deutschland Archiv.

Spittmann, Ilse, ed. (1987): DIE SED IN GESCHICHTE UND GEGENWART. Edition Deutschland Archiv.

Spittmann, Ilse & Karl W. Fricke (1988): Dokumentation. Ilse Spittmann & Karl W. Fricke, eds.: 17. JUNI 1953: ARBEITERAUFSTAND IN DER DDR. 2d ed. Edition Deutschland Archiv.

Staadt, Jochen (1995): AUF HÖCHSTER STUFE: GESPRÄCHE MIT ERICH HONECKER. Transit Verlag.

Stackhouse, Max L. (1984): CREEDS, SOCIETY, AND HUMAN RIGHTS: A STUDY IN THREE CULTURES. William B. Eerdmans.

Stadtmueller, Georg (1963): GESCHICHTLICHE OSTKUNDE. Vol. 2. 2d ed. Bogen-Verlag.

Stadtmueller, Georg (1981): SOZIALISMEN: NATIONAL-SOZIALISMUS, FASCHISMUS. Hans-Seidel-Stiftung.

Stahnke, Arthur A. (1986): Progress and the GDR Economy. Margy Gerber, ed.: STUDIES IN GDR CULTURE AND SOCIETY 6. University Press of America.

Stalin, Joseph (1939): FOUNDATIONS OF LENINISM. International Publishers.

Stalin, Joseph (1947): PROBLEMS OF LENINISM. Foreign Languages Publishing House.

Stammen, Theo (1974): Von der SBZ zur DDR. Heinz Rausch & Theo Stammen,

eds.: DDR; DAS POLITISCHE, WIRTSCHAFTLICHE UND SOZIALE SYSTEM. C. H. Beck.
Staritz, Dietrich (1986): Untertänigkeit: Heritage and Tradition. Margy Gerber, ed.: STUDIES IN GDR CULTURE AND SOCIETY 6. University Press of America.
Staritz, Dietrich (1994): WAS WAR: HISTORISCHE STUDIEN ZUR GESCHICHTE UND POLITIK DER DDR. Metropol Verlag.
Statistisches Bundesamt (1990): DDR 1990: ZAHLEN UND FAKTEN. Metzler Verlag.
STATISTISCHES JAHRBUCH DER DDR, 1955.
STATISTISCHES JAHRBUCH DER DDR, 1987.
Steele, Jonathan (1977): INSIDE EAST GERMANY: THE STATE THAT CAME IN FROM THE COLD. Urizen Books.
Steiner, Andre (1999): DIE DDR-WIRTSCHAFTSREFORM DER SECHZIGER JAHRE. Akademie Verlag.
Steininger, Herbert (1988): Inhalt und Wert unsere Freiheit. 88:3 EINHEIT 202.
Stephan, Gerd-Ruediger, ed. (1994): VORWÄRTS IMMER, RÜCKWÄRTS NIMMER! Dietz Verlag.
Stern, Carola (1965): ULBRICHT: A POLITICAL BIOGRAPHY. Praeger.
Stern, Fritz (1987): DREAMS AND DELUSIONS: THE DRAMA OF GERMAN HISTORY. Knopf.
Stern, Herbert J. (1988): JUDGMENT IN BERLIN. Signet Books.
Stief, Albert (1988): Die ABI: wichtiges Feld sozialistischer Demokratie. 43 EINHEIT 363–366.
Stiehler, Gottfried (1984a): Kollektivität und Individualität. 84:8 EINHEIT 692–697.
Stiehler, Gottfried (1984b): WORAUF UNSERE FREIHEIT BERUHT. Dietz Verlag.
Stillman, Edmund, ed. (1959): BITTER HARVEST: THE INTELLECTUAL REVOLT BEHIND THE IRON CURTAIN. Praeger.
Stoecker, Helmuth (2000): SOCIALISM WITH DEFICITS: AN ACADEMIC LIFE IN THE GERMAN DEMOCRATIC REPUBLIC. LIT Publishers.
Stojanovic, Svetozar (1981): IN SEARCH OF DEMOCRACY IN SOCIALISM: HISTORY AND PARTY CONSCIOUSNESS. Prometheus Books.
Stoph, Willi et al. (1968): THE NEXT STEPS IN THE NATIONAL ECONOMY OF THE GDR ON THE ROAD TO THE COMPLETION OF SOCIALISM. Verlag Zeit im Bild.
Strauss, Wolfgang (1982): AUFSTAND FÜR DEUTSCHLAND: DER 17. JUNI 1953. Druffel-Verlag.
Streit, Josef (1962): Der Staat schützt die Rechte der Bürger. 16 NEUE JUSTIZ 758–759.
Struetzel, Dieter & Lali Petzold, eds. (1985): EINHEITLICHKEIT UND DIFFERENZIERUNG IN DER SOZIALISTISCHEN KULTURENTWICKLUNG. Friedrich-Schiller-Universität Jena.
Stuber, Petra (1998): SPIELRÄUME UND GRENZEN: STUDIEN ZUM DDR-THEATER. Ch. Links Verlag.
Stuermer, Michael (1986): DISSONANZEN DES FORTSCHRITTS: ESSAYS ÜBER GESCHICHTE UND POLITIK IN DEUTSCHLAND. Piper Verlag.

Sturzbecher, Dietmar, ed. (1997): JUGEND UND GEWALT IN OSTDEUTSCHLAND. Verlag für Angewandte Psychologie.

Suckut, Siegfried (1982): DIE BETRIEBSRÄTEBEWEGUNG IN DER SOWJETISCH BESETZTEN ZONE DEUTSCHLANDS (1945–1948). Haag & Herchen Verlag.

Sudholt, Gert (1998): UNGESUEHNT! ANGLO-AMERIKANISCHE KRIEGSVERBRECHEN 1939–45. Druffel-Verlag.

Suess, Sonja (1998): POLITISCH MISSBRAUCHT: PSYCHIATRIE UND STAATSSICHERHEIT IN DER DDR. Ch. Links Verlag.

Sutterlin, James S. & David Klein (1989): BERLIN: FROM SYMBOL OF CONFRONTATION TO KEYSTONE OF STABILITY. Praeger.

Symposium (1982): Jugend in der DDR. 15 DEUTSCHLAND ARCHIV 1106–1116.

Szabo, Stephen F. (1992): THE DIPLOMACY OF GERMAN UNIFICATION. St. Martin's Press.

Szajkowski, Bogdan, ed. (1981): 2 MARXIST GOVERNMENTS. Macmillan.

Szawlowski, Richard (1982): The Supreme Control Organs in East Germany. 8 REVIEW OF SOCIALIST LAW 209–235.

Taylor, Jay (1993): THE RISE AND FALL OF TOTALITARIANISM IN THE TWENTIETH CENTURY. Paragon House.

Tenfelde, Klaus (1998): Einige Ergebnisse. Peter Huebner & Klaus Tenfelde, eds.: ARBEITER IN DER SBZ-DDR. Institut zur Erforschung der europäischen Arbeiterbewegung.

Teresiak, Manfred (1994): Liquidierung des Sozialdemokratismus. Eberhard Fromm & Hans-Juergen Mende, eds.: VOM BEITRITT ZUR VEREINIGUNG: SCHWIERIGKEITEN BEIM UMGANG MIT DEUTSCH-DEUTSCHER GESCHICHTE. Edition Luisenstadt.

Tertz, Abram (1960): ON SOCIALIST REALISM. Pantheon Books.

Terwey, Michael (1997): Weltanschauungen junger Menschen in Ost und West. Evelyn Brislinger et al., eds.: JUGEND IM OSTEN. Zentralarchiv für empirsche Sozialforschung.

Tesch, Joachim (2002): DER WOHNUNGSBAU IN DER DDR 1971–1990. Gesellschaftswissenschaftliches Forum.

Thalheim, Karl C. (1988): DIE WIRTSCHAFTLICHE ENTWICKLUNG DER BEIDEN STAATEN IN DEUTSCHLAND. 3d ed. Landeszentrale für politische Bildungsarbeit.

Ther, Philipp (1998): DEUTSCHE UND POLNISCHE VERTRIEBENE. Vandenhoeck & Ruprecht Verlag.

Thielbeer, Siegfried (1985): Ist die DDR ein totalitärer Staat? Eckhard Jesse, ed.: BUNDESREPUBLIK DEUTSCHLAND UND DEUTSCHE DEMOKRATISCHE REPUBLIK. Colloquium Verlag.

Thiessen, Friedrich, ed. (2001): ZWISCHEN PLAN UND PLEITE. Böhlau Verlag.

Thilenius, Richard (1957): DIE TEILUNG DEUTSCHLANDS: EINE ZEITGESCHICHTLICHE ANALYSE. Rowohlt Verlag.

Thomas, Siegfried (1966): ENTSCHEIDUNG IN BERLIN. 2d ed. Akademie-Verlag.

Timmermann, Heiner (1985): Die Entstehungsgeschichte. Eckhard Jesse, ed.: BUNDESREPUBLIK DEUTSCHLAND UND DEUTSCHE DEMOKRATISCHE REPUBLIK. 4th ed. Colloquium Verlag.

Tisch, Harry (1989): Demokratie vor und hinter dem Werktor. 44 EINHEIT 203–209.
Topitsch, Ernst (1985): STALINS KRIEG; DIE SOWJETISCHE LANGZEIT-STRATEGIE GEGEN DEN WESTEN ALS RATIONALE MACHT-POLITIK. Olzog Verlag.
Torpey, John C. (1995): INTELLECTUALS, SOCIALISM, AND DISSENT: THE EAST GERMAN OPPOSITION AND ITS LEGACY. University of Minnesota Press.
Trumpold, Harry (2001): Internationale Anerkennung. Friedrich Thiessen, ed.: ZWISCHEN PLAN UND PLEITE. Böhlau Verlag.
Turner, Henry A., Jr. (1987): THE TWO GERMANIES SINCE 1945. Yale University Press.
Ulbricht, Walter (1947): BRENNENDE FRAGEN DES NEUAUFBAUS DEUTSCHLANDS. Dietz Verlag.
Ulbricht, Walter (1961): DIE ENTWICKLUNG DES DEUTSCHEN VOLKS-DEMOKRATISCHEN STAATES. Dietz Verlag.
Ulbricht, Walter (1966): DAS PROGRAMM DES SOZIALISMUS. Dietz Verlag.
Uledow, A. K. (1964): DIE ÖFFENTLICHE MEINUNG: EINE STUDIE ZUM GEISTIGEN LEBEN DER SOZIALISTISCHEN GESELLSCHAFT. VEB Deutscher Verlag der Wissenschaften.
Ulrich, Peter (1984): ERFAHRUNGEN UND GEDANKEN EINES DDR-BÜRGERS. Colloquium Verlag.
Unger, Aryeh L. (1974): THE TOTALITARIAN PARTY: PARTY AND PEOPLE IN NAZI GERMANY AND SOVIET RUSSIA. Cambridge University Press.
Ungerleider, Steven (2001): FAUST'S GOLD: INSIDE THE EAST GERMAN DOPING MACHINE. St. Martin's Press.
Uniewski, Herbert & Rudolf Lambrecht (1994): Geheimer Sumpf. 24 STERN 124 (June 9).
United States Congress, House Select Committee on the Katyn Forest Massacre (1952): THE KATYN FOREST MASSACRE. U.S. Government Printing Office.
Untersuchungskommission (1991): UND DIESE VERDAMMTE OHNMACHT. BasisDruck.
Unverhau, Dagmar, ed. (2003): KARTENFÄLSCHUNG ALS FOLGE ÜBER-GROSSER GEHEIMHALTUNG. LIT Verlag.
Urban, Karl (1981): Effektive Zusammenarbeit erhöht den Nutzen. 28 DER SCHÖFFE 145.
Uschner, Manfred (1993): DIE ZWEITE ETAGE: FUNKTIONSWEISE EINES MACHTAPPARATES. Dietz Verlag.
Uschner, Manfred (1995): DIE ROTEN SOCKEN. Dietz Verlag.
Vahlefeld, Hans W. (2002): DEUTSCHLANDS TOTALITÄRE TRADITION: NATIONALSOZIALISMUS UND SED-SOZIALISMUS ALS POLITISCHE RELIGIONEN. Klett-Cotta Verlag.
Vaillancourt, Pauline M. (1986): WHEN MARXISTS DO RESEARCH. Greenwood Press.
Van den Bercken (1987): Holy Russia and the Soviet Fatherland. 15 RELIGION IN COMMUNIST LANDS 264.
VEB Bibliographisches Institut (1984): HANDBUCH: DEUTSCHE DEMO-KRATISCHE REPUBLIK. VEB Biblographisches Institut.
Veen, Hans-Joachim (1993): NATIONAL IDENTITY AND POLITICAL PRI-

ORITIES IN EASTERN AND WESTERN GERMANY. Konrad-Adenauer-Stiftung.

Venohr, Wolfgang (1989): DIE ROTEN PREUSSEN. Straube Verlag.

VERFASSUNG DER DEUTSCHEN DEMOKRATISCHEN REPUBLIK: 1949.

VERFASSUNG DER DEUTSCHEN DEMOKRATISCHEN REPUBLIK: 1968.

VERFASSUNG DER DEUTSCHEN DEMOKRATISCHEN REPUBLIK: 1974.

Verkade, E. M. (1991): RESTRUCTURING THE EAST GERMAN ECONOMY: SOME MODEL RESULTS. Central Planbureau, s'Gravenhage.

Vietzke, Siegfried (1989): Antifaschismus prägt unseren Weg, unsere Macht. 44 EINHEIT 935–940.

Villain, Jean (1990): DIE REVOLUTION VERSTÖSST IHRE VÄTER. Zytglogge Verlag.

Vogt, Timothy R. (2000): DENAZIFICATION IN SOVIET-OCCUPIED GERMANY, BRANDENBURG 1945–1948. Harvard University Press.

Voigt, Dieter (1975): SOZIOLOGIE IN DER DDR. Verlag Wissenschaft und Politik.

Voigt, Dieter & Lothar Mertens (1995): DDR-WISSENSCHAFT IM ZWIESPALT ZWISCHEN FORSCHUNG UND STAATSSICHERHEIT. Duncker & Humblot Verlag.

Voigt, Dieter et al. (1987): SOZIALSTRUKTUR DER DDR. Wissenschaftliche Buchgesellschaft.

Volkov, Leonid (1979): STANDARDS OF POLITICAL BEHAVIOR AND PERFECTION OF THE MANAGEMENT AND ADMINISTRATION OF DEVELOPED SOCIALIST SOCIETY. Paper delivered at the World Congress of the International Political Science Association, Moscow.

Volkov, Solomon (1980): TESTIMONY: THE MEMOIRS OF DMITRI SHOSTAKOVICH. Harper & Row.

Vollnhals, Clemens (1996): DIE KIRCHENPOLITIK VON SED UND STAATSSICHERHEIT. Ch. Links Verlag.

Vollnhals, Clemens (1998): DER FALL HAVEMANN. Ch. Links Verlag.

Vollnhals, Clemens & Juergen Weber, eds. (2002): DER SCHEIN DER NORMALITÄT. Olzog Verlag.

Volze, Armin (1999): Zur Devisenverschuldung der DDR. Eberhard Kuhrt, ed.: DIE ENDZEIT DER DDR-WIRTSCHAFT: ANALYSEN ZUR WIRTSCHAFTS-, SOZIAL- UND UMWELTPOLITIK. Leske & Budrich.

Vyshinsky, Andrei Y. (1948): THE LAW OF THE SOVIET STATE. Macmillan.

Wachtler, Johann (1983): ZWISCHEN REVOLUTIONSERWARTUNG UND UNTERGANG: DIE VORBEREITUNG DER KPD AUF DIE ILLEGALITÄT IN DEN JAHREN 1929–1933. Peter Lang Verlag.

Wagner, Matthias (1998): AB MORGEN BIST DU DIREKTOR: DAS SYSTEM DER NOMENKLATURKADER IN DER DDR. Edition Ost.

Wagner, Wolfgang (1959): THE PARTITIONING OF EUROPE. Deutsche Verlags-Anstalt.

Walker, Richard L. (1960): Chairman Mao and the Cult of Personality. 14:6 ENCOUNTER 31–43 (June).

Walter, Michael (1997): FREIE DEUTSCHE JUGEND: IHRE FUNKTIONEN IM POLITISCHEN SYSTEM DER DDR. Arnold Bergstraesser Institut.

Wassmund, Hans (1981): German Democratic Republic. Bogdan Szajkowski, ed.: MARXIST GOVERNMENTS. Vol. 2. Macmillan.

Wassmund, Klaus (1991): RIGHT-WING EXTREMISM AND NEONAZISM IN THE FORMER GDR. Paper delivered at the World Congress of the International Political Science Association, Buenos Aires.

Waterkamp, Dietmar (1983): Das Bildungswesen der DDR. Hans-Georg Wehling, ed.: DDR. Verlag W. Kohlhammer.

Weber, Adolf (1929): ENDE DES KAPITALISMUS? DIE NOTWENDIGKEIT FREIER ERWERBSWIRTSCHAFT. 2d ed. Hueber.

Weber, Adolf (1930): IN DEFENCE OF CAPITALISM. Allen.

Weber, Adolf (1944): DER MISSERFOLG DES BOLSCHEWISTISCHEN WIRTSCHAFTSSYSTEMS. Duncker & Humblot.

Weber, Adolf (1949): MARKTWIRTSCHAFT UND SOWJETWIRTSCHAFT: EIN VERGLEICH. R. Pflaum.

Weber, Adolf (1950): DOGMA UND WIRKLICHKEITSSINN IN DER SOWJETWIRTSCHAFT. Verlag der Bayerischen Akademie der Wissenschaften.

Weber, Gisela (1997): VON NORMAL BIS VERRÜCKT: RÜCKSCHAU EINER DDR-LEHRERIN. GNN Verlag.

Weber, Hermann (1964): ULBRICHT FÄLSCHT GESCHICHTE. Neuer Deutscher Verlag.

Weber, Hermann (1974): DIE SED NACH ULBRICHT. Fackelträger Verlag.

Weber, Hermann (1982a): DDR: GRUNDRISS DER GESCHICHTE, 1945–1981. Fackelträger Verlag.

Weber, Hermann (1982b): HAUPTFEIND SOZIALDEMOKRATIE: STRATEGIE UND TAKTIK DER KPD, 1929–1933. Droste Verlag.

Weber, Hermann (1985a): GESCHICHTE DER DDR. DTV.

Weber, Hermann (1985b): Der "sozialistische" deutsche Staat? Eckhard Jeese, ed.: BUNDESREPUBLIK DEUTSCHLAND AND DEUTSCHE DEMOKRATISCHE REPUBLIK. Colloquium Verlag.

Weber, Hermann (1988): DIE DDR 1945–1986. R. Oldenbourg Verlag.

Weber, Hermann (1991): DDR: GRUNDRISS DER GESCHICHTE: 1945–1990. Fackelträger Verlag.

Weber, Hermann & Fred Oldenburg (1971): 25 JAHRE SED: CHRONIK EINER PARTEI. Verlag für Wirtschaft und Politik.

Weber, Juergen (1994): Die DDR: Eine totalitäre Diktatur von Anfang an. Juergen Weber, ed.: DER SED-STAAT. Olzog Verlag.

Weber, Wolfgang (1993): DDR: 40 JAHRE STALINISMUS. Arbeiterpresse Verlag.

Wechsberg, Joseph (1964): JOURNEY THROUGH THE LAND OF ELOQUENT SILENCE: EAST GERMANY REVISITED. Little, Brown.

Wedel, Mathias (1996): ERICH WÄHRT AM LÄNGSTEN. Edition TIAMAT.

Weichelt, Wolfgang (1964): The Right to Vote and the Electoral System of the German Democratic Republic. 64:2 LAW AND LEGISLATION IN THE GDR 5–16.

Weichelt, Wolfgang (1981): Der X. Parteitag der SED und die weitere Festigung des sozialistischen Staates. 35 NEUE JUSTIZ 338–342.

Weichelt, Wolfgang (1982a): Die schöpferische Anwendung der Erfahrungen des Sowjetstaates: Garantie für den Sieg der Sache des werktätigen Volkes. 31 STAAT UND RECHT 963–971.

Weichelt, Wolfgang (1982b): POLITISCHE MACHT UND DEMOKRATIE IM SOZIALISMUS. Akademie-Verlag.

Weichelt, Wolfgang (1984): VERFASSUNG DES VOLKES—IM VOLKE LEBENDIG. Staatsverlag.

Weidenfeld, Werner, ed. (1993): DEUTSCHLAND: EINE NATION—DOPPELTE GESCHICHTE. Verlag Wissenschaft und Politik.

Weinert, Rainer (1993): Massenorganisationen in mono-organisationalen Gesellschaften: Über den strukturellen Restaurationszwang des Freien Deutschen Gewerkschaftsbundes im Zuge des Zusammenbruchs der DDR. Hans Joas & Martin Kohli, eds.: DER ZUSAMMENBRUCH DER DDR. Suhrkamp.

Weinke, Annette (2002): DIE VERFOLGUNG VON NS-TÄTERN IM GETEILTEN DEUTSCHLAND. Schöningh Verlag.

Weiss, Helmut (1998): VERBRAUCHERPREISE IN DER DDR: WIE STABIL WAREN SIE? GNN Verlag.

Weitz, Eric D. (1997): CREATING GERMAN COMMUNISM, 1890–1990. Princeton University Press.

Welsch, Wolfgang (1999): WIDERSTAND UND MfS IM SED-STAAT: FOLGEN UND KONSEQUENZEN. J. Schmidt-Pohl Verlag.

Welsh, Helga A. (1989): REVOLUTIONÄRER WANDEL AUF BEFEHL? ENTNAZIFIZIERUNGS- UND PERSONALPOLITIK IN THÜRINGEN UND SACHSEN (1945–1948). R. Oldenbourg Verlag.

Welsh, Helga A. (1991): Antifaschistisch-demokratische Umwälzung und die politische Säuberung in der sowjetischen Besatzungszone Deutschlands. Klaus-Dietmar Henke & Hans Woller, eds.: POLITISCHE SÄUBERUNG IN EUROPA: DIE ABRECHNUNG MIT FASCHISMUS UND KOLLABORATION NACH DEM ZWEITEN WELTKRIEG. Deutscher Taschenbuch Verlag.

Welsh, William A., ed. (1981): SURVEY RESEARCH AND PUBLIC OPINION IN EASTERN EUROPE AND THE SOVIET UNION. Pergamon Press.

Wenzel, Siegfried (1998a): PLAN UND WIRKLICHKEIT. Scripta Mercaturae Verlag.

Wenzel, Siegfried (1998b): WAR DIE DDR 1989 WIRTSCHAFTLICH AM ENDE? Hefte zur DDR-Geschichte.

Werkentin, Falco (1997): POLITISCHE STRAFJUSTIZ IN DER ÄRA ULBRICHT. Ch. Links Verlag.

Wettig, Gerhard (2002): Das Bemühen der sowjetischen Führung und der SED um Sozialdemokraten und bürgerliche Oppositionskreise in Westdeutschland (1946–1953). Reinard Huebsch, ed.: HÖRT DIE SIGNALE: DIE DEUTSCHLANDPOLITIK VON KPD/SED UND SPD 1945–1970. Akademie Verlag.

Weymar, Thomas (1985): IM TRABI ZUR SONNE, ZUR FREIHEIT. Verlag für Wirtschaft und Politik.

Wichner, Ernest & Herbert Wiesner, eds. (1993): LITERATURENTWICKLUNGSPROZESSE: DIE ZENSUR DER LITERATUR IN DER DDR. Suhrkamp Verlag.

Wicke, Peter (1988): Rock Music and Everyday Culture in the GDR. Margy Gerber, ed.: STUDIES IN GDR CULTURE AND SOCIETY 8. University Press of America.

Wierling, Dorothee (2002): GEBOREN IM JAHRE EINS. Ch. Links Verlag.

Wieschiolek, Heike (1999): ICH DACHTE IMMER, VON DEN WESSIS LERNEN HEISST SIEGEN LERNEN. Campus Verlag.

Wiesenthal, Simon (1968): FIRST FOR HITLER, NOW FOR ULBRICHT. Deutschland-Berichte.

Wightman, Margaret (1971): THE FACES OF GERMANY. George G. Harrap.

Wildavsky, Aaron (1979): SPEAKING TRUTH TO POWER: THE ART AND CRAFT OF POLICY ANALYSIS. Little, Brown.

Wildavsky, Aaron (1983): The Soviet System. Aaron Wildavsky, ed.: BEYOND CONTAINMENT: ALTERNATIVE AMERICAN POLICIES TOWARD THE SOVIET UNION. ICS Press.

Wildavsky, Aaron (1986): Choosing Preferences by Constructing Institutions: A Cultural Theory of Preference Formation. Manuscript. Department of Political Science, University of California, Berkeley.

Wilensky, Harold L. (1967): ORGANIZATIONAL INTELLIGENCE. Basic Books.

Wiles, Peter (1988): THE SOVIET ECONOMY ON THE BRINK OF REFORM. Unwin Hyman.

Wilhelmi, Juttta (1983): JUGEND IN DER DDR. Verlag Gebr. Holzapfel.

Wilhelmy, Frank (1995): DER ZERFALL DER SED-HERRSCHAFT. LIT Verlag.

Wilhelmy, Frank (1996): DER RÄTZELHAFTE MODUS DES DDR-ZUSAMMENBRUCHS. Gesellschaftswissenschaftliches Forum.

Wille, Manfred, ed. (1993a): SIE HATTEN ALLES VERLOREN. Harrassowitz Verlag.

Wille, Manfred, ed. (1993b): DIE SUDENTENDEUTSCHEN IN DER SOWJETISCHEN BESATZUNGSZONE DEUTSCHLANDS. Magdeburger Verlag.

Wille, Manfred, ed. (1996): DIE VERTRIEBENEN IN DER SBZ/DDR: DOKUMENTE. Vol. 1. Harrassowitz Verlag.

Wille, Manfred, ed. (1999): DIE VERTRIEBENEN IN DER SBZ/DDR: MASSENTRANSFER, WOHNEN, ARBEIT 1946–1949. Vol. 2. Harrassowitz Verlag.

Wimmer, Walter (1984): Geschichtliche Wurzeln des Werdens und Wachsens unserer Republik. 84:2 EINHEIT 105–110.

Wimmer, Walter (1985): Gemeinsam gegen den Faschismus für Frieden, Freiheit und Fortschritt. 85:10 EINHEIT 926–931.

Winckler, Lutz (1992): Mein Deutschland findet sich in keinem Atlas. G. Meyer et al., eds.: LEBENSWEISE UND GESELLSCHAFTLICHER UMBRUCH IN OSTDEUTSCHLAND. Verlag Palm & Enke.

Windolf, Paul et al. (1999): WARUM BLÜHT DER OSTEN NICHT? Edition Sigma.

Winkelmann, Egon (1992): MOSKAU, DAS WAR'S. Edition Ost.

Winkler, Arno (1969): Zum Wesen der bürgerlichen Konzeption vom "politischen Pluralismus." 18 STAAT UND RECHT 1084–1099.

Witt, Inge (2001): Im Zentrum der Macht: Verkaufsstellenleiterin im Konsum. Friedrich Thiessen, ed.: ZWISCHEN PLAN UND PLEITE. Böhlau Verlag.

Wolfe, Bertram D. (1954): Totalitarianism and History. Carl J. Friedrich, ed.: TOTALITARIANISM. Harvard University Press.

Wolfe, Bertram D. (1961): COMMUNIST TOTALITARIANISM: KEYS TO THE SOVIET SYSTEM. Rev. ed. Beacon Press.

Wolfe, James H. (1971): Minor Parties in the GDR. 4 EAST EUROPEAN QUARTERLY 457–478.

Wolfe, Nancy Travis (1992): POLICING A SOCIALIST SOCIETY: THE GERMAN DEMOCRATIC REPUBLIC. Greenwood Press.

Wolle, Stefan (1998): DIE HEILE WELT DER DIKTATUR. Ch. Links Verlag.

Woods, Roger (1985): The Significance of East German Intellectuals in Opposition. David Childs, ed.: HONECKER'S GERMANY. Allen & Unwin.

Woywod, Georg & Eckhard Heumeyer (1987): MENSCHENRECHTE IN DER DDR UND OST-BERLIN. Internationale Gesellschaft für Menschenrechte.

Wroblewsky, Clement (1990a): DA WACHSTE EINES MORGENS UFF UND HAST 'NEN BUNDESKANZLER: WIE DDR-BÜRGER ÜBER IHRE ZUKUNFT DENKEN. Rasch & Röhring.

Wroblewsky, Clement (1990b): WO WIR SIND IST VORN: DER POLITISCHE WITZ IN DER DDR. 2d ed. Rasch & Röhring.

Yakovlev, Yegor (1982): GLIMPSES OF LENIN. Novosti Press Agency.

Zadek, Alice & Gerhard Zadek (1998): IHR SEID WOHL MESCHUGGE. Dietz Verlag.

Zank, Wolfgang (1987): WIRTSCHAFT UND ARBEIT IN OSTDEUTSCHLAND: 1945–1949. Oldenbourg Verlag.

Zelikow, Philip & Condoleezza Rice (1995): GERMANY UNIFIED AND EUROPE TRANSFORMED. Harvard University Press.

Zeller, Bernd (2000): 101 GRÜNDE KEIN OSSI ZU SEIN. Rake Verlag.

Zeng, Matthias (2000): ASOZIALE IN DER DDR. LIT Verlag.

Ziemke, Earl F. (1968): THE BATTLE FOR BERLIN. Ballantine Books.

Zimmering, Raina (2000): MYTHEN IN DER POLITIK DER DDR. Leske & Budrich.

Zimmermann, Hartmut (1979): Die DDR in den 70er Jahren. Guenter Erbe, et al., eds.: POLITIK, WIRTSCHAFT UND GESELLSCHAFT IN DER DDR. Westdeutscher Verlag.

Zimmermann, Hartmut, ed. (1985): DDR HANDBUCH. 2 vols. Verlag Wissenschaft und Politik.

Zimmermann, Monika, ed. (1994): WAS MACHT EIGENTLICH? 100 DDR-PROMINENTE HEUTE. Ch. Links Verlag.

Zipser, Richard (1995): FRAGEBOGEN: ZENSUR. Reclam Verlag.

Zitelmann, Rainer (1993): Wiedervereinigung und deutscher Selbsthass. Werner Weidenfeld, ed.: DEUTSCHLAND: EINE NATION—DOPPELTE GESCHICHTE. Verlag Wissenschaft und Politik.

Zschiedrich, Angelika (1981): Sozialistischer Staat und Grundrechte der Bürger. 35 NEUE JUSTIZ 293–296.

Zschiedrich, Angelika (1985): Sozialistische Demokratie und verantwortungsbewusste Wahrnehmung der Grundrechte und Grundpflichten. Rat für staats- und rechtswissenschaftliche Forschung an der Akademie der Wissenschaften der DDR: VERVOLLKOMMNUNG DER SOZIALISTISCHEN DEMOKRATIE: TRIEBKRAFT DER SOZIALISTSICHEN GESELLSCHAFT. Staatsverlag.

Zuckermann, Moshe (2002): ZWISCHEN POLITIK UND KULTUR: JUDEN IN DER DDR. Wallstein Verlag.

Index

About the Author

PETER W. SPERLICH is Professor Emeritus, Department of Political Science, University of California, Berkeley. He is the author of *Rotten Foundations: The Conceptual Basis of the Marxist-Leninist Regimes of East Germany and Other Countries of the Soviet Bloc.*